Critical Criminology

This book is dedicated to the memory of Ian Taylor 1944–2001.

Critical Criminology
Issues, debates, challenges

Edited by Kerry Carrington and Russell Hogg

WILLAN
PUBLISHING

Published by

Willan Publishing
Culmcott House
Mill Street, Uffculme
Cullompton, Devon
EX15 3AT, UK
Tel: +44(0)1884 840337
Fax: +44(0)1884 840251
e-mail: info@willanpublishing.co.uk
Website: www.willanpublishing.co.uk

Published simultaneously in the USA and Canada by

Willan Publishing
c/o ISBS, 5824 N.E. Hassalo St
Portland, Oregon 97213-3644, USA
Tel: +001(0)503 287 3093
Fax: +001(0)503 280 8832
Website: www.isbs.com

First published 2002

ISBN 1-903240-69-7 (cased)
ISBN 1-903240-68-9 (paper)

British Library Cataloguing-in-Publication Data

A catalogue record for this book is available from the British Library.

Printed by T J International Ltd, Trecerus Industrial Estate, Padstow, Cornwall
Typeset by PDQ Typesetting, Newcastle-under-Lyme, Staffordshire

Contents

Preface

by Elliott Currie

When I first sat down to review this manuscript, what struck me most immediately was not the articles but the contributors' biographies. Between books and other writings, teaching, public service, and social activism, the diverse group of international scholars who have made this volume possible have, quite simply, done a lot. Individually and collectively, theirs is a record of strong accomplishment and accumulated usefulness. By the same token, those biographies stand as a record of how far 'critical criminology' has come in the roughly three decades since its beginnings.

A thorough reading of the chapters of this book reinforces the impression of a movement in criminology that has, in a very real sense, come of age. This book doesn't simply offer a description of some of the main currents and issues in critical criminology at the start of the new millennium – though it does do that, and does it well. It also represents the mature self-reflection of some of the most talented scholars in the field – scholars who are not shy about acknowledging the strengths and successes of progressive criminology, but also not afraid to question its trajectory and to confront its failures. There is no party line here; the contributors don't all speak with the same voice, but what links their diverse perspectives is a willingness to apply a critical lens not only to the work of their more conventional counterparts in the discipline but their own as well.

That sense of a movement mature enough to challenge itself is also apparent in the reach of some of the articles into largely uncharted areas that criminologists, critical and otherwise, have generally neglected in the past – including, among others, Russell Hogg's wide-ranging explorations into the impact of globalisation on a variety of criminological concerns, and Tony Jefferson's probing and thoughtful attempt to bring psychology 'back in' to a progressive criminology. These pieces, and others, break new ground and take us several steps down roads that criminology has, up to now, been hesitant to travel. And, again, they reveal a kind of criminological imagination that is able and willing to break free of old constraints and look at the problems of crime and punishment with fresh eyes.

That kind of criminological imagination has always been a great strength of the movement we loosely call critical criminology, but it has arguably never been as necessary as it is today, as we confront the new intellectual and political challenges that are raised by an increasingly volatile and interconnected planet: the challenge of creating justice systems permeated by respect for human rights in a world where those rights are threatened at every turn by the proliferation of autocratic and/ or failed regimes and of predatory and punitive ideologies; the challenge of creating and maintaining safe, vibrant and respectful communities in the face of global economic forces that threaten to erode communal stability and widen the inequality that is so often at the root of criminality; the challenge – noted by several contributors – of effectively confronting new forms of global violence while simultaneously promoting democracy and accountability in our institutions of criminal justice; and more. Handling those challenges is not, of course, something that criminologists, critical or otherwise, can take on by themselves. But in the broader movement for a just and secure world in the twenty-first century, progressive criminology should have an important and necessary place.

We may sometimes underestimate the role that the critical criminological imagination has *already* played in that respect. But in fact another sign of progressive criminology's coming of age is that it has inspired, or at the very least influenced, many of the organisations whose work has done the most to enhance justice around the world in the past twenty years – both in the negative sense of having held the line against some of the worst excesses of the increasingly punitive thrust of crime policy in many countries and, more positively, in significantly affecting public opinion on issues ranging from sentencing policy to the treatment of juvenile offenders, from health services in prisons to the response to domestic violence. Organisations like the Sentencing Project, the Justice Policy Institute, and the Eisenhower Foundation in the United States; NACRO and Penal Reform International in England; and their counterparts in Australia and elsewhere have tenaciously – and often successfully – fought to put a progressive view of crime and punishment on the political agenda and to keep it there despite enormous pressures to bury it. There is much to be proud of in that record, and much work ahead. And that work will need the steady infusion of the kind of engaged critical thinking so evident in this book.

Finally, I'd like to say how pleased I am that this book is dedicated to the memory of Ian Taylor. As many of the articles in this collection make abundantly clear, Ian was indisputably one of the most important founding influences on critical criminology, and one of its strongest and sanest voices throughout his professional life. He was also a dear friend and one of the best intellectual companions I ever had. It is a great loss to all of us that Ian is not here to read these articles. But I am sure he would be pleased.

Elliott Currie
School of Criminology and Criminal Justice, Florida State University
Legal Studies Program, University of California, Berkeley

May, 2002

Acknowledgements

As with all knowledge production, the conditions of its possibility frequently depend on the invisible work, generosity, support and dedication of friends, relatives and colleagues. Our foremost appreciation is to Dr Moira Carmody, the Director of the Critical Social Science Research Group at the University of Western Sydney, who supported the original conference out of which this collection arose. The continuing support of Vivianne Mulder, the Group's Research Officer, is also warmly appreciated. Obviously we are very grateful to the contributors for their dedication, hard work and especially for keeping to a fairly tight timeline. And for some this was achieved under very difficult personal circumstances. Their diligence was more than equally matched by that of our publisher Brian Willan to whom we are indebted for his confidence in this project. We thank our daughters Amie and Rosa for their forbearance of parents obsessed with the intellectual and political projects of critical criminology, not just throughout the writing of this manuscript, but over their entire life spans. To our newly born third daughter, Georgia, we thank you for keeping to your due date as well as our contributors have kept to theirs.

Between the time of our organising the conference on which this collection is based and February 2001 when it was held we all received the sad news of Ian Taylor's death. Ian was an erstwhile colleague of some of the contributors and a friend to many. His contribution to the development of critical criminology was nothing short of monumental, and is only signposted by some of his book-length publications: from the co-edited National Deviancy Conference collection *Politics and Deviance*, 1973 (with Laurie Taylor); through the ground-breaking period of *The New Criminology*, 1973, and *Critical Criminology*, 1975 (with Jock Young and Paul Walton); to his more conjunctural responses to the politicisation of law and order by the new right, *Law and Order: Arguments for Socialism*, 1981 and *The Social Effects of Free Market Policies*, 1990; to his more recent work engaging the challenges of critical analysis at the end of the millennium which includes *A Tale of Two Cities*, 1996 (with Karen Evans and Penny Fraser) and *Crime in Context*, 1999. The last was fittingly awarded the Hindelang Prize at the American Society of Criminology Conference in San Francisco in 2000. Ian Taylor was an inspiration for many working in and around critical criminological scholarship over the last three decades in New Zealand, the United Kingdom, Australia, Europe and North America. In recognition and gratitude we dedicate this collection to his memory.

Kerry Carrington and Russell Hogg
May 2002

About the authors

The contributors to this volume are internationally distinguished scholars, many of whom have been publishing in the field of critical criminology for three decades. The contributors span several countries and continents: New Zealand, the United Kingdom, Australia and the United States. Between them they have authored or co-authored at least 48 books and edited another 19 in the fields of sociology, social policy, criminology, criminal law, criminal justice, psychology, research methods, youth homelessness, women's imprisonment, truancy, female delinquency, cultures of violence, history of imprisonment, youth studies, media studies, sexual violence, masculinity, police work, the state, political and social theory, and penal policy. More detailed biographies for each author appear below.

Judith Bessant is an Associate Professor at the Australian Catholic University, Melbourne, Australia, where she currently teaches sociology and criminology. She has co-authored five books: *Understanding Criminology* (in press) (with R. Hil and R. Watts); *Sociology Australia*, 1999 (with R. Watts); *Youth Studies: An Australian Perspective*, 1998 (with H. Sercombe and R. Watts); *Making Groups Work: Rethinking Practice*, 1997 (with J. Benjamin and R. Watts); and *The Growth of a Profession: Nursing in Victoria, 1930s–1980s*, 1991 (with B. Bessant). Judith has co-edited another five books, four of which she was the chief editor: *Violation of Trust: How Schools and Welfare Systems have Failed our Young People*, (in press); *Against the Odds: Young People and Work in Australia*, 1998; *Women's Encounters with Violence: Australian Experiences*, 1997; *Youth Crime and the Media: Media Representations of and Reactions to Young People in Relation to Law and Order*, 1997; and *Cultures of Crime and Violence: the Australian Experience*, 1995.

Judith Bessant is also widely published in referred international journals on such topics as social work, youth work, sociology and criminology.

David Brown is a Professor in the Law School at the University of New South Wales, Sydney, Australia, where he teaches criminal law and criminology. He has been active in criminal justice movements, issues and debates for nearly three decades and is a regular media commentator on these issues. He has published widely in the field with over 100 articles and chapters in books. He has co-authored or co-edited *The Prison Struggle*, 1981; *The Judgments of Lionel Murphy*, 1986; *Death in the Hands of the State*, 1988; *Criminal Laws* in three editions, 1990, 1996 and 2001; *Rethinking Law and Order*, 1998; and *Prisoners as Citizens*, 2001.

Pat Carlen is Visiting Professor at the University of Keele, Department of Criminology in England where she worked from 1976 and was Professor of Criminology from 1989 to 1996. She has published *Magistrates' Justice*, 1976; *Women's Imprisonment*, 1983; *Women, Crime and Poverty*, 1988; *Alternatives to Women's Imprisonment*, 1990; *Jigsaw – A Political Criminology of Youth Homelessness*, 1996; and *Sledgehammer: Women's Imprisonment at the Millennium*, 1998. She is co-author of *Official Discourse*, 1979 (with F. Burton); *Criminal Women*, 1985 (with J. Hicks, J. O'Dwyer, D. Christina and C. Tchaikovsky); and *Truancy: The Politics of Compulsory Schooling*, 1993 (with Gleeson and Wardhaugh). She is editor of *The Sociology of Law* 1976; *Radical Issues in Criminology*, 1980 (with M. Collison); *Gender, Crime and Justice*, 1988 (with A. Worrall); *Paying for Crime*, 1989 (with D. Cook); and *Crime Unlimited?*, 1998 (with R. Morgan). Her edited book, *Women and Punishment: The Struggle for Justice* is being published by Willan Publishers in 2002. In 1997 she received the Sellin-Glueck Prize – awarded annually by the American Society of Criminology for Outstanding International Contributions to Criminology.

Kerry Carrington is an Associate Professor in the College of Social and Health Sciences at the University of Western Sydney, Australia. She is author of *Who killed Leigh Leigh?*, 1998, and *Offending Girls: Sex, Youth and Justice*, 1993. She is co-editor of *Cultures of Crime and Violence: The Australian Experience*, 1995 (with J. Bessant and S. Cook) and *Travesty! Miscarriages of Justice*, 1991 (with R. Hogg, M. Dever, A. Lohrey, and J. Bargen). She has published widely in the fields of criminology, youth studies, feminism and sociology. Her research interests include the study of violence in rural Australia, sexual violence and sexual ethics, youth cultures and female delinquency, and feminist criminology. In 1991 she won the Jean Martin Award for the best PhD in the social sciences in

Australia and is currently on the editorial board of the *Journal of Sociology*. From 1990 to 1993 she was chair of Academics for Justice, and has been involved in specific struggles for justice for the wrongly convicted, as well as for victims (especially sexual assault victims) wronged by the justice system.

Russell Hogg teaches and researches criminology in the College of Social and Health Sciencies at the University of Western Sydney, Australia. He is co-author of *Rethinking Law and Order*, 1998 (with D. Brown) and *Death in the Hands of the State*, 1988 (with D. Brown and M. Hogan); co-editor of *Understanding Crime and Criminal Justice*, 1988 and *Travesty! Miscarriages of Justice*, 1991. He has published numerous book chapters and journal articles in the fields of criminal law, penality and criminology. His current research interests include the racialisation of crime, punishment and penality, violence and civilising processes, environmental criminology and crime and rurality. He has had a long history of involvement in struggles over specific instances of miscarriages of justice and was the secretary of Academics for Justice in the early 1990s. From 1997 to 2000 he was appointed to the NSW Premiers' Committee on Crime Prevention.

Tony Jefferson is a Professor of Criminology in the Department of Criminology, Keele University in the United Kingdom. He has researched and published widely on questions to do with youth subcultures, the media, policing, race and crime, masculinity, and (with Wendy Hollway) gender difference, anxiety and the fear of crime, and qualitative research methodology. His published works include: *Doing Qualitative Research Differently*, 2000 (with Wendy Hollway); *Masculinities, Social Relations and Crime*, 1996 (edited with Pat Carlen); *Research, Crime and Justice in Europe*, 1995 (edited with P. Robert, L. van Outrive and J. Shapland); *The Case Against Paramilitary Policing*, 1990; *Introducing Police-work*; 1988 (with M Brogden and S Walklate); *Interpreting Policework*, 1987 (with R Grimshaw); *Controlling the Constable*, 1984 (with R Grimshaw); *Policing the Crisis*, 1978 (with Stuart Hall et al.); and *Resistance through Rituals*, 1976 (edited with Stuart Hall). He is the British Editor for the international journal *Theoretical Criminology*.

Michael J. Lynch is Professor and Director of the PhD Program in the Department of Criminology at the University of South Florida, in the United States. He was previously Associate Professor in the School of Criminology and Criminal Justice, Florida State University. He earned his PhD from the School of Criminal Justice, State University of New York at Albany. He has edited or authored seven books and numerous book chapters and articles. His articles have appeared in *The Archives of Paediatric and Adolescent Medicine; Sociological Quarterly; The British Journal of Criminology; Justice Quarterly; Social Justice, Humanity and Society; Journal of Research in Crime and Delinquency; The Journal of Criminal Justice;* and *Crime, Law and Social Change,* among others. His research interests include radical criminology, environmental crime and justice, corporate crime, and racial bias in the criminal justice system.

John Pratt is a Reader in Criminology at Victoria University of Wellington in New Zealand. He has undertaken extensive research on the history and sociology of punishment. He has published over 60 journal articles, and his books are *Punishment in a Perfect Society,* 1993; *Governing the Dangerous,* 1998; and *Dangerous Offenders: Punishment and Social Order,* 2000 (with Mark Brown). His forthcoming book *Punishment and Civilization* is to be published by Sage. He is the current editor of *The Australian and New Zealand Journal of Criminology.*

Professors Julia and Herman Schwendinger have published articles and books on crimes against women, human rights, adolescent subcultures, delinquency and the historical development of sociology in the United States. Their latest book, entitled *Who Killed the School of Criminology? Round Up the Usual Suspects!,* deals with their experiences during the 1960s at the University of California in Berkeley. While based largely in the United States throughout their academic careers, they have been exchange scholars at universities in Berlin, St Petersburg, Moscow and Almaty (in central Asia). Their seminal writings have received the Distinguished Scholar Award from the Crime, Law and Deviance Section of the American Sociology Association, the Outstanding Scholar Award from the Society for the Study of Social Problems, the Tappan Award from the Western Society of Criminology, the Major Achievement Award from the Critical Criminology Division of the American Society of Criminology and an award for Special Recognition of their Scholarship and Research on Women and Crime from the Women's Division of the American Society of Criminology. Herman received the coveted State University of New York Excellence Award 'in recognition of sustained, outstanding performance and superior service to the State University and the State of New York [SUNY].' He was elected in 1982 to the New York Academy of Sciences. Julia was a co-founder of the first anti-rape crisis group in the world. She has been a Parole Commissioner and Director of the Women's Resource Center for San Francisco Jails as well as a private investigator for JBA Investigations in the San Francisco Bay Area. She has also served as a private consultant providing pre-sentencing reports on offenders for defence attorneys and judges. Upon retiring from SUNY, the Schwendingers moved to Florida where they spend time sailing on the Gulf of Mexico while still engaging in teaching, research and writing as Professors of Criminology at the Department of Criminology, University of South Florida, Tampa, in the United States.

Phil Scraton is the Professor and Director of the Centre for Studies in Crime and Social Justice at Edge Hill University College, in the United Kingdom. His main research interests include: the politics and regulation of sexuality; the rights of survivors and the bereaved in the aftermath of disasters; police powers and accountability; the politics of imprisonment; deaths in custody; children's rights; and critical analysis and its application. He is author of: *The State of the Police*, 1985; *Hillsborough: The Truth Mainstream*, 1999/2000; and editor of: *Law, Order and the Authoritarian State: Readings in Critical Criminology*, 1985; and *'Childhood' in 'Crisis'?*, 1997. He is co-author of the following books: *In the Arms of the Law*, 1987 (with Kathryn Chadwick); *Prisons Under Protest*, 1991 (with Joe Sim and Paula Skidmore); *No Last Rights: The Denial of Justice and the Promotion of Myth in the Aftermath of the Hillsborough Disaster*, 1995 (with Sheila Coleman and Ann Jemphrey); *Understanding Prisons*, forthcoming (with Kathryn Chadwick and Margaret Malloch); and *Disaster, Trauma, Aftermath*, forthcoming (with Howard Davis). He co-edited *Causes for Concern*, 1984 (with Paul Gordon); and *The State v The People : Lessons from the Coal Dispute*, 1985 (with Phil Thomas). He has written extensively on a range of human rights and social justice issues and campaigned tirelessly for justice for the victims of the Hillsborough disaster. He is currently editing an international collection of essays entitled *After September 11: An Anthology of Dissent*.

Jock Young has been a Professor of Sociology at Middlesex University and Head of the Centre for Criminology since 1986. He started as a lecturer at Middlesex in 1966 and has remained there ever since – a fact, as he puts it: 'which either shows great psychological stability or the opposite'. He was the first member of his family to go to University, starting off as a biochemist but quickly switching to Sociology at the London School of Economics where he took a BSc in 1965 and a MSc in 1966. Always fascinated by criminology and the sociology of deviance he was a founder member of The National Deviancy Symposium – a group of radical criminologists – in 1968, in which year he gave his first academic paper. He published his first book, *The Drugtakers* in 1971 and gained his PhD at LSE on the ethnography of drug use in the Notting Hill area of West London in 1972. In 1973 he published with Paul Walton and Ian Taylor *The New Criminology,* which is still in print, and in the same year *The Manufacture of News* with Stan Cohen. In subsequent years he wrote and edited books on abortion, the mass media, urban riots and on general sociology. More recent work has centred on the development together with his colleagues of a theoretical perspective on crime – left realist criminology. Of particular significance in this project was the Penguin book written with John Lea; *What is to be Done About Law and Order?* 1984, and a series of locally-based victimization surveys, in particular, *The Islington Crime Survey,* published in 1986 with Trevor Jones and Brian MacLean. The victimization research was extended to include white collar crime (with Frank Pearce) and under the direction of Jayne Mooney, the first large scale prevalence study of domestic violence in Britain. Jock is the course leader of the MA in Criminology at Middlesex which has strong European links with parallel programmes and two common study sessions per year rotating around the sister institutions in Hamburg, Ghent, Komotini and Barcelona. His most recent book is *The Exclusive Society: Social Exclusion, Crime and Difference in Late Modernity* published by Sage in 1999. He is at present working on a book entitled *Strange Days: The Journey into Late Modernity.*

Chapter 1

Critical criminologies: an introduction

Kerry Carrington and Russell Hogg

A quarter of a century ago Taylor, Walton and Young referred to the science of criminology as one of the most influential and state-dominated branches of the social sciences (Taylor, Walton and Young, 1975: 5). Criminology has always risked a certain intellectual disreputability for its promiscuous scavenging among more established and respectable disciplines from across the sciences (from biology, law and medicine to sociology) and for courting political favour and relevance with the powers that be. Intellectual rigour and detachment were sacrificed to immediate utility in an always urgent fight against an unmistakable enemy or threat. Theory, explanation, moral reflection could be readily cast aside as unnecessary diversions from the task at hand, and worse as equivocation about the wrongfulness of crime itself and as little more than affording excuses for criminals. In Britain, the United States and Australia at least, criminology for the better part of its history in the twentieth century was largely trapped in, and servant to, this broad political and cultural consensus (Garland, 1994; Cohen, 1998; Carson and O'Malley, 1989; Hall et al., 1978; Schwendinger and Schwendinger, 1975), albeit it frequently worked at the liberal edges of it, championing the cause of rehabilitative over deterrent approaches to punishment and challenging the efficacy and defensibility of capital punishment.

Of course alongside this more pragmatic tradition there existed a substantial body of European and North American sociological research and theory concerned with deviance, crime and social control which provided the platform for the emergence of radical and critical criminologies in the anglophone world in the 1960s and 1970s (i.e. Becker, 1963; Cicourel, 1968; Cohen, 1971; Matza, 1964). In addition, forums like the European Group for the Study of Deviance and Social Control, which first met in 1973 and is still convening, provided alternative gatherings for radical criminologists. This body of scholarship was overwhelmingly sociological (and later Marxist) in orientation, eschewed any association with the state authorities in charge of the apparatuses of social control, and its political allegiances lay firmly with the counterculture, the New Left and anti-institutional social movements such as the prisoner and anti-psychiatry movements (Mathiesen, 1974; Fitzgerald, 1977; Zdenkowski and Brown, 1982; Sedgewick, 1982), anti-racist and anti-colonial struggles (Fanon, 1963), civil rights and later (and more problematically) feminism (see Chapter 5). A central concern was the manner in which social scientific knowledge itself was entangled with, and deployed in the service of, power thus raising for criminologists and others several sets of questions.

If knowledge was so entangled with power then the existing structure and internal life of the social science disciplines carried no necessary, obvious or rationally given validity and should be laid open to critical scrutiny and possible radical reorganisation (Foucault, in Gordon, 1980). From this standpoint the eschewal of conventional disciplinary boundaries such as was to be found in emerging fields like cultural studies and even established and more pragmatically oriented ones like criminology gave rise to new, more radical intellectual possibilities, connected with the experimental mood of the times and opened up emancipatory opportunities for students confined within traditional and staid disciplines like English (in the case of the future practitioners of cultural studies) and law (in the case of many future criminologists). Thus a critical intellectual rationale could be sought (if in the eyes of many never quite achieved) for a project like criminology when transgressing rather than observing traditional disciplinary boundaries became a sign of radical intellectual respectability. And far from this necessitating the cosying up to established powers in the apparatus of social control, the new intellectual rationale was to be nurtured by its association with new, radical, oppositional political possibilities.

While there have been many differences in the theoretical and empirical focuses of critical criminologies, they have tended to share an opposition to the kind of criminology that takes so much of the status quo for granted. Increasingly, however, as David Brown points out in Chapter 4, the lines between administrative and critical criminology tend to be more blurred in practice than they are at the level of rhetoric. Nevertheless, rejection of the correctionalism of orthodox criminology, and the methods and epistemology of positivism, a questioning of the definition of crime and its measurement by official statistics, accompanied by a critical posture towards the agents, systems and institutions of social control (i.e. prisons, courts, police, judiciary), tend to characterise much of the work in the dynamic field of critical criminology. So too does a commitment to connecting these intellectual projects with the politics of social justice and change, although there are many quarrels about just how these connections operate (Young, 1988:160). Sociological explanations tend to be favoured over individualist theories of crime and deviance, and pretences to the criminologist as a neutral scientific expert also tend to be disavowed. The emphasis in critical approaches to criminology has been on analysing how the effects of social power and the inequalities of the social order underscore the commission of crime, the experience of victimisation and the politics of the criminalisation process, although there is no agreement about any of this. All this contrasts significantly with the assumption upon which much 'scientific' criminology has been based, that the social order is underscored by a consensus, that its policing is unproblematic and the legal definition of crime uncontested. The genealogy of this kind of sceptical thinking about criminology, as the various contributions to the first part of this book demonstrate, cannot simply be located with the publication of a single text such as *The New Criminology* (1973) or the influence of neo-Marxism, or the emergence of a single set of National Deviancy Conferences. Although all of these have been significant in this genealogy, as Stan Cohen (1998) reminds us, the impetus for critical criminology grew out of a much wider constellation of deconstructionist radical agendas, to challenge the status quo, modernist modes of social control, the claims of science and other disciplinary knowledges, the dominance of patriarchy and the underlying moral order of Anglophone culture. The various contributions to this book illustrate just how diverse those influences have been, and continue to be in shaping not only new directions but new challenges for future scholarship in critical criminology.

During the 1970s and 1980s critical criminology confidently staked out its ground around transformative projects in politics and intellectual work. Arguably this ground has been eroded in the harsher social, political and academic climate of the 1990s, leaving a question mark over the future directions that critical criminologies might or could take in the twenty-first century. This collection of essays debates the shortcomings and achievements of critical criminology, while exploring the possibilities for future critical criminological scholarship. The book's genesis arose out of a small conference on 26 February 2001 when a group of international scholars from several countries met at a forum at the University of Western Sydney. The papers they gave addressed specific issues that connected coherently into an overall analysis of the past, present and future of critical criminology. Earlier versions of most of the chapters in this book were presented as conference papers at that forum. Other chapters from continents, and on themes, not adequately represented at that conference were then solicited to complement these.

While multi-authored this edited collection coheres around a number of integrated themes. The first comprises a set of reflections on the crucial issues and debates in critical criminology over the last three decades authored mainly by key players in the praxis of critical criminology over the same time-frame: David Brown from Australia, Phil Scraton from the United Kingdom and Julia and Herman Schwendinger from the United States. These contributions are complemented by Kerry Carrington's chapter which analyses the vital role of feminism in the genealogy of critical approaches to criminology. Collectively, these four chapters locate the virtues and limitations of critical criminology in Australia, the USA and Britain in a historical and genealogical context. The second part of the book considers the possibility of re-envisioning the intellectual and political projects of critical criminology in the twenty-first century, given these challenges: the critiques of the 'rational' subject of western thought, the shortcomings of the universalising ideals of the 'new criminology', the rise of a 'govermentalised' criminology of risk, the impact of globalisation, the erosion of the sovereignty of nation states, the shifts in strategies of social control and criminal justice and an increasingly corporatised university sector ill-equipped or uninterested in supporting critical research. Beyond this the themes addressed by the contributors include the following:

- Is there a 'tradition' of critical criminology able to be sustained and worth sustaining under current conditions? If so, what are its defining elements?

- What has been the impact on the critical project of political, social and economic changes since the heyday of critical criminology in the 1960/70s?

- How have feminism, new social movements, 'neoliberalism' and 'third way' politics, impacted on the directions and possibilities for critical criminology?

- How should we assess the role, achievements and limitations of critical criminology in relation to changes in law and order politics and shifts in criminal justice and modes of social control?

- How has globalisation affected the boundaries and focus of critical criminology with its traditional focus on the criminal justice systems of nation states?

- What impact has the postmodern critique of enlightenment discourses had on what may appear to be the 'modernist' project of critical criminology?

- Critical criminology has been resolutely sociological in orientation. Do concerns within criminology (such as the role of sexism, racism and punitive sentiment in criminal justice policy) open up a role for psychosocial knowledges in the future of critical criminology?

The opening substantive chapter by Phil Scraton suggests that the application of critical analysis to the study of crime, 'deviance' and criminal justice within social democracies is crucial to understanding, interpreting and challenging the authoritarianism of state institutions committed to increasing police powers and expanding imprisonment. He argues that 'critical criminology' has provided the analytical means to theorise and explain 'crime', 'deviance' and 'social conflict' alongside the formalised processes of law-making, differential enforcement and punishment. His argument draws upon the important neo-Gramscian debates around ideology and hegemony and the Foucauldian analysis of the power–knowledge axis. Arguing that while much of what constitutes 'critical' analysis in criminology has been (wrongly) dismissed as reductionist or 'idealist', critical theorists have retained a commitment to advancing the critique of administrative criminology and criminal justice policy and practice through questioning the determination of power and the legitimation of knowledge. Focusing particularly on official discourses, including what is accepted and promoted as 'scientific' or 'evidence-based' knowledge, critical research demonstrates how structural inequalities are woven into the fabric of the 'advanced' democratic state and civil society. In endeavouring to broaden the scope of analysis to a consideration of harm rather than crime, social justice rather than criminal justice, treatment rather than punishment and discourses of rights rather than discipline and control, Scraton argues that critical criminology presents a form of intellectual resistance, turning cases into issues. As a challenge to powerful institutions and their collective regimes of truth, his piece shows how critical criminology can become associated with campaigns for social reform and political change mobilising a human rights discourse and agenda to provide a procedural alternative to the administration of law and criminal justice.

Chapter 3 which follows is a historically significant and similarly reflexive piece written by Julia and Herman Schwendinger with Michael Lynch. Thirty years ago the Schwendingers wrote a famous piece first published in *Issues in Criminology* (1970) and republished in *Critical Criminology* (1975) edited by Walton, Taylor and Young that challenged both legalistic and positivistic definitions of crime. In it they asked: 'Isn't it time to raise serious questions about the assumptions underlying the definition of the field of criminology, when a man who steals a paltry sum can be called a criminal while agents of the State, can, with impunity, legally reward men who destroy food so that price levels can be maintained whilst a sizable portion of the population suffers from malnutrition?' (Schwendinger and Schwendinger, 1975: 17). They argued that criminological work should not be confined to the analysis of crime sanctioned by the institutions of criminal justice (Schwendinger and Schwendinger, 1975: 113–18). They also rejected the claim that morality and value judgements have no role in the definition of crime (Schwendinger and Schwendinger, 1975: 132). They convinced a growing generation of budding critical criminologists around the globe that the definition of crime had to be broadened to include not just social harms, injuries and public wrongs but importantly also the violation of human rights. As racism, sexism, imperialist war and economic systems that create poverty and inequality violate human rights, these crimes, they argued, are vitally relevant to the domain of criminology as legitimate objects of study (Schwendinger and Schwendinger, 1975: 136). To defend human rights, rather than the status quo, they proposed that criminologists 'must be able to sufficiently identify the violations of these rights – by whom and against whom; how and why' (Schwendinger and Schwendinger, 1975: 134). The Berkeley School of Criminology where they worked set about doing just that and Julia and Herman Schwendinger became, along with their radical colleagues, the targets of vicious state-backed attacks on their academic freedom and livelihood.

The chapter, which Julia and Herman Schwendinger have generously written for this book with Michael Lynch, interrupting their retirement and recovery from serious illness, is in itself a testament to their indomitable spirits. It provides a detailed historical account of the rise and demise of the Berkeley School of Criminology at the University of California, arguably the most significant institutional site for the cultivation of critical criminology in the United States in late 1960s to the mid-1970s. At that time they wrote about the possibility of criminologists becoming the defenders of human rights, rather than the guardians of the social order. Their bold vision for a broader concept of crime to include social harm and the violation of human rights, challenging the narrow definitions of state defined criminality, opened the pathway for much contemporary criminological research, on corporate crime, state crime, government and police corruption, environmental crimes, war crimes, human rights abuses and so on. We appreciate the immense historical significance of this piece to the collection and hope you will too.

The business of being and living out a life as a critical criminologist entails moments of joy, seriousness, disappointment, frustration, challenge and change. Chapter 4 by David Brown reflects on three decades as a student and teacher of critical criminology, criminal justice and criminal law. While he notes the danger of engaging in reflection – the production of inconsequential, self-indulgent, sanitised accounts prey to the vagaries of memory – he hopes his reflections will assist in analysing the deeply problematic relationship between the intellectual and political projects of critical criminology. His chapter aims to demonstrate some of the problematic and undesirable features of critical criminology, alongside the immense value and enduring legacies of much work carried out in this tradition. His piece draws upon a rich history of thirty years of involvement in radical criminology and criminal justice politics in Australia manifest in the establishment of the *Alternative Criminology Journal*, involvement in the prisoners' movement and the establishment of criminology in Australian universities. The key theme to emerge from his argument is the contingent and context-specific nature of doing critical criminology, over and against forms of critical theory that presume a timeless universal validity. While suitably serious for the most part, the style of this chapter is witty, light-hearted and reflexive.

Feminists as scholars and activists have long been perturbed by the masculinist bias of both the discipline of criminology *and* the criminal justice system's treatment of women as victims and offenders. Arguably, these feminist critiques have had a profound and lasting impact on the direction that critical criminology took although frequently overlooked in genealogies of this tradition. It was after all left largely to feminists to point out that neo-Marxist versions of critical criminology in rushing to romanticise the delinquent as a working-class resister forgot about the victim, who in many instances was a vulnerable and female member of the working classes or oppressed racial minorities. Chapter 5 by Kerry Carrington, the last along the theme of reflection, reviews the genealogical significance of the impact of feminist incursions into criminological debates and its influence over the directions of critical criminology over the last three decades. However, in rushing to condemn criminology's masculinist bias, she argues that some essentialist versions of feminist criminology lost sight of their critical edge, slipped into residual biologisms about the innate criminality of men as men, underestimated the politics of criminal justice, and overlooked the way in which women were situated, not as a single unified grouping, but differently in relation to the operation of the criminal process. Her chapter concludes by outlining a number of future challenges to the intellectual and political projects of feminist research in criminology.

Most importantly she argues that feminist criminology has been integral and not just incidental to the intellectual and political projects of critical criminology.

The various contributions to the second part of the book seek in highly original ways to re-envision, redirect or renew the directions of critical criminology in the twenty-first century. This section is opened by Chapter 6 authored by Tony Jefferson, who like many of the contributors to this book has been working, writing and publishing broadly in the field of critical criminology for several decades. While the concept of crime has been questioned by much critical criminology, rarely has the notion of the subject received any critical attention at all. A riveting read that draws upon a vast depth and breadth of scholarship, Tony Jefferson's piece argues for a psychosocial criminology. He argues that the subject presumed by criminology, whether traditional or radical, is hopelessly inadequate. The subject presumed by a traditional Freudian approach is a 'disturbed'/abnormal individual; that presumed by Marxism, feminism or left realism is purely social, a product of social structure or, more recently, discourse; and that presumed by administrative criminology or rational choice theorists is purely rational/voluntaristic. Jefferson points out that one result of this collective failure is to enable traditional psychology, with its equally problematic notion of a purely cognitive, information-processing subject, to inhabit the space. What is needed, he argues, is a recognition of the importance of unconscious as well as conscious motivations – the psychic dimension of subjectivity – in combination with an understanding of the available culturally inscribed discursive meanings – the social dimension – and, crucially, a theory of identification, i.e. an understanding of how particular individuals come to invest in/identify with particular cultural meanings. The resulting subject he calls psychosocial. The chapter then looks at some areas where such a psychosocial subject is being introduced into criminology, and at others which would benefit particularly from such a notion. It ends by setting out a modest agenda for future work on this topic.

As the subtitle to Chapter 7 clearly indicates, John Pratt's piece has as its main referent Stan Cohen's (1985) *Visions of Social Control*. His purpose is not to offer some belated review of such an important contribution to the critical criminology canon, but to outline his visions of the new and emergent forms of social control taking root in increasingly punitive societies, such as the US, the UK, New Zealand and Australia, since the publication of Stan Cohen's important book some fifteen years ago now. Putting Stan Cohen's visions in appropriate light, what John Pratt suggests is that it is now also possible to discern 'visions of social control' which were not anticipated in this book that seem to depart from the 'master pattern' hitherto implicit in modern penal development. He argues that perhaps Cohen's book should now be seen as an emblem for a phase in modern penal development which has now passed – or is at least undergoing a process of significant reconfiguration. He leaves us with disturbing images of new and emergent forms of social control – that of increased state power in the form of new forms of western gulags on the one hand, with vigilantism on the other incubated by increased demands for public participation in punishment and 'restorative' justice. Somewhat ironically these visions have been made all the more possible by the withdrawal of the state in managing the social body through neo-liberal policies of governing at a distance – and at a time of increasing global instability and insecurity. John Pratt's chapter reminds us of the fragility and contingency of the forms of social control in the so called civilised world a theme further explored in the chapter which follows.

No one in the world could have been untouched by the terrorist attacks in the United States on 11 September 2001, killing several thousand people, most of them civilians going about their normal everyday activities. This incident illustrates more than ever the increasingly global nature of issues facing criminologists in the twenty-first century. As the World Trade Center imploded that dreadful day, so too has the faith vested in the false security of the boundaries of the nation state. Chapter 8 by Russell Hogg surveys new fields of analysis for criminology opened up by geopolitical and economic change in the post-Cold War world. Criminology is a creature of the nation state. Its characteristic forms and practices of rule – such as the principle of national sovereignty and the distinction between civil and military life – have set the taken-for-granted parameters to criminology's intellectual and political life. A range of contemporary developments are destabilis-ing these parameters, including globalisation, the increase in refugee movements, the growth of transnational crime and the expansion of a human rights culture. Many of these developments blur the boundaries between domestic and foreign policy, internal and external security, civil and military power, and crime and war. The events of 11 September were merely the latest and most shocking reminder of these global shifts and of a whole new terrain of criminological analysis.

Judith Bessant's contribution in Chapter 9 focuses on the very possibility of sustaining a critical criminology at a time characterised by pessimism, splintered solidarities and 'self-indulgent' postmodernists in denial about 'truth' and 'reality'. Given this she asks how can we begin talking about developing a contemporary progressive criminology and on what basis. Her chapter explores four interrelated questions: How should contemporary criminology be characterised? Do the various critical traditions in criminology offer any prospect for developing a radical, progressive or critical criminology? What role could 'postmodernist' social theory play in promoting a progressive project? More specifically is there any potential in post-foundational frameworks for carving out new spaces for critique; can they generate new solidarities, and can they be tied to progressive social action? This also means asking what is meant by progressive political theory and practice today in the twenty-first century. She argues that feminist and post-foundationalist frameworks can help carve out new spaces for critique and generate new modes of solidarity tied to progressive social action. Bessant suggests that any activity related to theorising, research, teaching and the knowledge-making process is political, which means the theoretical is linked to, and indeed is, political action. She shows how theory informs ways of seeing and doing and shapes policy, practice and political action. Above all, she argues that a political commitment to progressive social change also needs to be seen as part of scholarship and other academic practices.

Chapter 10 by Pat Carlen proposes a set of challenges to and achievements of critical criminology. As a project that falls between theory and politics critical criminology is – as Carlen suggests – primarily a strategy that has promoted and can continue to promote a strong and robust relationship between social justice and criminal justice. She argues that there is certainly a lot of criminology around that is not critical, and that the 'criminological environment' in Britain is being increasingly organised around assumptions which are not only 'anti-critical' but also anti-intellectual and anti-social. The enemies of critical criminology to which she refers are not people but texts, dominant or obscure epistemologies or ideologies, and all the disciplinary practices relating to the production of criminological knowledge – whether they be found in the academy or the courts or the prisons. Of course, all knowledge work, whether striving to be critical or not, is produced within ideological conditions that are inimical to the critical project. The point made by Pat Carlen is that the critical project should strive continuously both to cherish its inherent and inherently contradictory tendencies and *to work on them*, that is to act reflexively. Her insightful and beautifully crafted analysis over a vast range of fields of scholarship in politics, social theory, criminology, social policy, sociology and feminism is framed around the difficulties of working and writing both within and without those contradictions.

The final chapter is by Jock Young, a leading figure in critical criminology since 1968. The chapter, specially written for this volume, is at the cutting edge, pushing the boundaries of critique and intellectual analysis. He points out, quite rightly, just how much social order and disorder has been a concern of all major social theorists, from eighteenth and nineteenth century thinkers through to the post-modern social theorists of the twenty-first century, and consequently how important the intellectual work of critical criminology is to social theory more broadly. However he argues against notions of constructing criminology (in any of its variations critical, administrative or otherwise) as a discipline. Instead he locates the continued vibrancy of critical criminology into the new millennium as a dynamic field of intellectual and political endeavour with a focus on crime, criminological theory, criminal law and the sociology of deviance. Importantly his argument challenges the revisionist history of critical criminology as little more than a reactionary mid-wife that failed because diversionary measures and alternatives to imprisonment turned out to be disciplinary forms of penal-welfarism. This, as he stresses, is hardly the fault of critical criminology, but rather the outcome of a law and order politics driven by a conservative political agenda, that points to an even greater need for critical engagement. Rather than becoming obsolete in response to the neo-liberal policies of penal welfarism, he illustrates how the critical tradition in criminology has flourished 'in a world of broken narratives where economic and ontological insecurity abounds, where crime, far from being mundane and calculative, is transgressive and sensual, where punishment is frequently vituperative and vindictive and where society, rather than being a one-dimensional scenario of rational contractual atoms, is divisive, contested, contradictory and ironic' (Young this volume p. 258). His chapter culminates in an incisive analysis of inequality, identity, identity crisis and crime control in late modernity drawing upon arguments developed more fully in his most recent book *The Exclusive Society*.

The issues and themes examined by Jock Young in this final chapter echo many of those explored earlier by other contributors to this edited volume. Among them: the disjuncture between justice and social justice (all chapters); new visions of social control and punitiveness in late modernity (Pratt and Brown); the trans-national and increasingly global context of crime and crime control policy (Hogg); the flourishing of critical traditions in criminology among them radical, feminist, cultural, neo-marxist, Foucauldian and post-foundationalist criminologies (Scraton, Carrington, Brown and Bessant); the ironies and internal contradictions of critical criminology as an oxymoron (Carlen); the unfinished business of immanent critique, the necessity for constant renewal and the importance of reflexivity (Brown, Herman and Julia Schwendinger and Lynch); the limits of critique without a vision for a transformative politics of social change (Bessant, Scraton, Herman and Julia Schwendinger and

Lynch); and the deconstruction of conventional categories of criminality through a questioning of essentialisms and especially the othering of the 'criminal' as distinct from rather than overlapping with conventional psycho-social behaviours and practices (Jefferson and Carrington). There could hardly be a more fitting conclusion to this book than the one offered by Jock Young, which invites self critique and renovation, relishes irony, and challenges complacency while also celebrating the considerable achievements of critical traditions in criminology, but above all 'with a bit of fun'.

Bibliography

Becker, H. (1963) *Outsiders: Studies in the Sociology of Deviance*. New York: Free Press.

Carson, K., and O'Malley, P. (1989) 'The institutional foundations of contemporary Australian criminology', *Australian and New Zealand Journal of Sociology*, 25(3): 333–55.

Cicourel, A. (1968) *The Social Organisation of Juvenile Justice*. London: Heinemann.

Cohen, S. (1971) *Images of Deviance*. London: Penguin.

Cohen, S. (1985) *Visions of Social Control*. Cambridge: Polity Press.

Cohen, S. (1998) 'Intellectual scepticism and political commitment: the case of radical criminology', in P. Walton, J. Young. (eds) *The New Criminology Revisited*. London: Macmillan; New York: St. Martin's Press.

Fanon, F. (1963) *The Wretched of the Earth*. London: Penguin.

Fitzgerald, M. (1977) *Prisoners in Revolt*. New York: Penguin.

Garland, D. (1994) 'Of crimes and criminals: the development of criminology in Britain', in M. Maguire, R. Morgan, R. Reiner (eds), *Oxford Handbook of Criminology*, 2nd edn. Oxford: Oxford University Press.

Gordon, C. (ed.) (1980) *Michel Foucault, Power/Knowledge*. Sussex: Harvester Press.

Hall, S., Critcher, C., Jefferson, T., Clarke, H. and Roberts, B. (1978) *Policing the Crisis: Mugging, the State and Law and Order*. London: Macmillan.

Mathiesen, T. (1974) *The Politics of Abolition: Scandinavian Studies in Criminology*. London: Martin Robinson.

Matza, D. (1964) *Delinquency and Drift*. New York: John Wiley & Sons.

Schwendinger, H. Schwendinger, J. (1975) 'Defenders of order or guardians of human rights', in I. Taylor, P. Walton and J. Young. (eds), *Critical Criminology*. London: Routledge.

Sedgwick, P. (1982) *Psyco Politics*. London: Pluto Press.

Taylor, I., Walton, P. and Young, J. (eds) (1975) *Critical Criminology*. London: Routledge.

Young, J. (1988) 'Radical criminology in Britain', *British Journal of Criminology*, 28(2): 159–83.

Young, J. (1999) *The Exclusive Society: Social Exclusion, Crime and Difference in Late Modernity*. London: Sage.

Zdenkowski, G. and Brown, D. (1982) *The Prison Struggle*. Sydney: Penguin.

Part I
Issues and Debates in Critical Criminology

Chapter 2

Defining 'power' and challenging 'knowledge': critical analysis as resistance in the UK

Phil Scraton

Introduction

April 1989. Ninety-six people die at a football match in Sheffield, England. In the immediate aftermath hundreds of police statements go through a hidden process of review and alteration involving the force senior management and a major law firm. The investigating force, the public inquiry team, the coroner and the Home Office all knew.

Personal trouble or public issue?

August 1989. Over half of the 51 people killed in the sinking of the Marchioness pleasure boat on the Thames had their hands removed, their bodies returned in sealed coffins and no explanation offered to the bereaved.

Personal trouble or public issue?

February 1993. Two ten-year-old boys abduct and kill a two-year-old in Bootle, Merseyside. They are held in custody for nine months without counselling or appropriate psychological support, then tried for murder in an adult court, in the full glare of the media.

Personal trouble or public issue?

March 1996. In the immediate aftermath of the murder of 16 schoolchildren and their teacher at Dunblane Primary School, a bereaved mother is visited by a senior police officer who bullies and threatens her over her complaints concerning the police handling of the case.

Personal trouble or public issue?

April 1997. Robert Hamill, a young Catholic, is kicked and stamped on by a group of loyalists in the presence of Royal Ulster Constabulary officers who fail to intervene. Ten days later he dies from his injuries.

Personal trouble or public issue?

March 1999. Rosemary Nelson, a human rights lawyer handling republican cases in Belfast, is assassinated by a car bomb attached to the underside of her car. The object of many death threats, she was supposed to be under protective surveillance.

Personal trouble or public issue?

The defining critical sociological text of the post-war decade was C. Wright Mills' *The Sociological Imagination* (1959). Lucidly written and fiercely argued, it revealed a deep scepticism regarding the growth and consolidation of mainstream social science within the USA. Wright Mills (1959: 20) railed against the 'bureaucratic techniques which inhibit sociological inquiry by "methodological" pretensions', its persistent 'obscurantist conceptions' and, most significantly, its trivialising of 'publicly relevant issues' by a misconceived and overstated 'concern with minor problems'. In particular, state-sponsored academic social research had become confined by 'inhibitions, obscurities and trivialities'. The consequence was the decontextualisation of the lives, experiences and opportunities of people, their neighbourhoods, their communities and their associated tensions. Researching and teaching in the shadow of McCarthyism, sociology had sacrificed its reforming zeal; its 'tendencies towards fragmentary problems and scattered causation conservatively turned to the use of the corporation, army and the state'.

For Wright Mills the city, the neighbourhood and the street represented to social science little more than social laboratories. In this disconnected and ahistorical context social science reconstructed reality through its theories, its knowledge and its discourse. The experiences of people, their values and their opportunities were, at best, diminished and, at worst, marginalised. Government-funded, industry-led and foundation-endowed research denied social inquiry its critical potential. The 'big picture' had been lost, the independence and integrity of professional academics compromised by their close association, even affiliation, to the military-industrial complex. State welfarism, in its employment of trained 'social scientists', progressed interventionist policy and practice geared to classification and regulation rather than care and advocacy.

Wright Mills' primary concern, and major contribution to a radical discourse, was with historical and structural contextualisation, that no person was an island. The sociological imagination lay in analysing the dynamics between biography and history. He argued for a critical framework with the capacity to explore the relationship between *personal troubles*, the routine daily struggles of family, friendship, community and work, and *public issues*, 'the larger structure of social and historical life'. This is the basis of what has been more recently represented as agency and structure. Returning to the opening questions, glimpses of a decade's research into controversial cases: personal troubles or public issues? Of course, the common answer is 'both', each with complex dimensions and mediations, reflecting and advancing the dialectic between the 'personal' and the 'public'.

Context, Correspondence and Compromise

> To *appeal* to the powerful, on the basis of any knowledge we now have, is utopian in the foolish sense of that term. Our relations with them are more likely to be only such relations as they find useful, which is to say that we become technicians accepting their problems and aims, or ideologists promoting their prestige and authority.
>
> (Wright Mills, 1959: 193)

Seven years after *The Sociological Imagination* was published Howard Becker delivered his presidential address to the Annual Meeting of the Society for the Study of Social Problems. At the height of civil unrest in the Deep South, of the big chill of Cold War politics and of US incursions deep into Asia, he argued that contemporary sociologists studying 'problems that have relevance to the world we live in' found themselves 'caught in the crossfire': 'to have values or not to have values ' (Becker, 1967: 240). It constituted a 'painful dilemma' derived in the perpetuated myth of value neutrality. It was not possible, he argued, 'to do research uncontaminated by personal and political sympathies'. The appropriate question was not about 'whether we should take sides' – this was inevitable – 'but rather whose side are we on?'(Becker, 1967: 240).

Becker's instructive conclusion was that social research should 'get into the situation enough to have a perspective on it' and, in so doing, challenge institutional and professional discourses – for these constituted the 'view from above'. Although initially Becker did not progress this line of argument, such discourses could not be divorced from the structural relations and social arrangements legitimated within the state and the economy. Becker's proposition was to 'take sides as our personal and political commitments dictate' employing 'theoretical and technical resources' to mediate values and avoid distortions (Becker, 1967: 247). The prevalent 'hierarchy of credibility' had to be recognised 'for what it is'. Once exposed it should be challenged. In a later paper, Becker and Horowitz (1972) were unequivocal; most social scientists had undertaken research designed to further the interests of the powerful at the expense of the powerless.

In a scathing speech to the American Sociological Association, Martin Nicolaus (1972) extended Becker's attack on the politics of social science. Professionally organised and institutionally integrated sociology, the discipline with the greatest radical potential, had been 'grafted seam-lessly, with contractual cement, to the civil, economic and military sovereignty' of the advanced capitalist state. Social sciences in general amounted to a 'source of legitimation' for repressive policies and practices utilising a 'laboratory of refinements'. The academic associations and their members were 'house-servants of civil, military and economic sovereignty'. The academic project, its consistent and mainstream direction, was constituted as 'servile to the demands of US imperialism abroad and US welfare and criminal justice strategy in the policing of class, "race" and gender confrontations at home' (Sim, Scraton and Gordon, 1987: 3).

In his defining text, *The Coming Crisis of Western Sociology*, Alvin Gouldner, like Wright Mills a decade earlier, directed a fierce critique against the conservatism inherent within the dominant academic assumptions that constituted the structural-functionalist paradigm and the methodological grip of positivism. At the same time he was sceptical of the emergence of phenomenology and ethnomethodology and their focus on the micro-social aspects of interaction at the expense of historical and material context. Through research sponsorship and professional training, social scientists had become 'technician[s] of the welfare state and its zoo-keepers of deviance' (Gouldner, 1973: x). To be 'rational' and 'liberative' – to develop a radical or critical agenda – a 'larger theoretical construction', both reflexive and structurally contextualising, was essential, 'without patronising the concrete and smaller worlds, without using them simply as examples or points of departure' (Gouldner 1973: x).

Writing just six years after the publication of Howard Becker's presidential address, and central to the emerging critical debate in the UK, Taylor, Walton and Young (1973: 168–9) argued persuasively that social reaction theorists, particularly Becker, remained trapped theoretically 'within the confines of liberal ideologies'. The implicit acceptance of western states as pluralist, inclusive democracies resulted in the failure 'to lay bare the structural inequalities which underpin the processes through which laws are created and enforced'. For the 'new criminology' both 'deviancy and criminality' were 'shaped by society's larger structure of power and institutions'. Power, as Gouldner (1971: 297) illustrated, secured the opportunity 'to enforce one's moral claims' enabling the powerful to 'conventionalise their moral defaults' while legitimating the institutions and processes of 'normalised repression'.

For Davis (1975: 205) the integrated processes of 'institutionalization, defining, labelling and categorizing', at the core of Becker's work, 'provide the commonsense reality within which social control proceeds', the context being, 'an unequal society divided by class, ethnicity, sex and political and economic differences' embodying 'politically powerful groups' which drafted 'and enforce[d]...rules detrimental to the interests and needs of powerless groups'. Reflecting on Becker's challenge, Hall and Scraton (1981: 465) interpreted it as a 'clarion call to a more overt radical political commitment, with sociologists and criminologists taking up a clear, 'partisan' stance'. This commitment was to be 'directed against the hidden agenda of "control" behind the liberal front of welfare policies'. As Muncie more recently comments, Becker was significant in revealing the key role of social scientists in providing oppressive state institutions with a 'spurious legitimacy' (Muncie, 1999: 128). The ensuing achievement was the 'radical reconstitution of criminology as part of a more comprehensive sociology of the state and political economy, in which questions of political and social control took precedence over behavioural and correctional issues' (Muncie, 1999: 128).

None of this came as any surprise to critical political economists. Two highly influential texts, Baran and Sweezy's *Monopoly Capital* (1966) and Braverman's *Labour and Monopoly Capital* (1984), had reminded readers of the essential role and function of academic training and consultation. The history of the rise of the giant corporation, with its boomtown 'cradle to grave' political-economic *and* socio-cultural agendas, was one of being served and serviced – internally and externally – by academic social sciences. Further, contemporary welfare states, whatever their specific organisational form, had emerged and consolidated from within the material context of multinational capitalism, its structural contradictions and consequent social inequalities. From the outset social sciences, in sponsorship and in employment opportunities, were incorporated into the post-Keynesian relationship of monopoly capital and state welfarism. As so many social science foundation courses have problematised since, the dichotomy for critical work was how effective, structural change could be realised to resolve inherent social and material conflict within political-economic conditions constructed to guarantee continuity. Containing conflict, managing dissent and deterring crime thus became essential elements of the academic sponsorship deal.

Social science, whatever the particular discipline, could no longer maintain a convincing claim to value-freedom and political neutrality. Its academic research, its application and its correspondence to the demands of the advanced capitalist state were a part of, rather than apart from, their historical, material and political contexts. In particular, the 'emphases and methodologies of applied work' could only be interpreted and explained within 'the economic, political and social conflicts of the time' (Sim, Scraton and Gordon, 1987:5). This led to a conclusion consistent with C. Wright Mills: 'balancing the lived experiences of people and the immediate, social contexts of daily interaction with often less visible structural arrangements – the political, economic and ideological management of daily life – set the radical agenda for the development of critical analysis within criminology' (Sim, Scraton and Gordon, 1987: 5). Yet, as Cohen (1981: 229) reflects, 'within the institutions of British criminology and the official or quasi-official grant-giving bodies on which individual researchers were dependent, the question was simply not on the agenda'. Despite this, and the cosy relationship between government departments, grant-awarding bodies and established academic departments, the tension between administrative criminology (including its liberal, 'progressive' variants) and critical work remained (see also Carlen's chapter this volume). It was a tension around the theorisation of power, authority and legitimacy. It arose from the undeniable structural inequalities derived in and sustained by the 'determining contexts' of class, patriarchy, 'race' and age.

Interpreting Authoritarianism

State-monopolized physical violence underlies the techniques of power and mechanisms of consent: it is inscribed in the web of disciplinary and ideological devices; and even when not directly exercised, it shapes the materiality of the social body upon which domination is brought to bear.

(Poulantzas 1978: 81)

Throughout the 1970s state power within advanced democratic societies, particularly the relationship between coercion and consent, became the defining focus of critical analysis. Oppositional initiatives underpinned by alternative discourses emerged within western criminology. The Union of Radical Criminologists in the USA and the National Deviancy Conference in the UK (see Cohen, 1981) became influential, the latter contributing significantly to the founding of the European Group for the Study of Deviance and Social Control. The 'new' or 'radical' criminology was grounded in the 'diverse and unique world of everyday life, the claimed location of the interactionists, yet it adapted and contextualized new deviancy theory within the structural dynamics of power and social control' (Scraton and Chadwick, 1991: 165).

Criminology's 'radical break' emphasised the structural processes of economic marginalisation and criminalisation within the context of class divisions and conflict inherent within advanced capitalism. Taylor, Walton and Young (1973) were unequivocal in setting a radical agenda based on 'a state of freedom from material necessity – a release from the constraints of forced production, an abolition of the forced division of labour, and a set of social arrangements, therefore, in which there would be no politically, economically, and socially induced *need* to criminalize deviance' (Taylor, Walton and Young, 1973: 270). Their ink had hardly dried on the page when criticisms of economic reductionism flew from mainstream criminology while concerns over neglecting analyses of neo-colonialism and patriarchy as structures of criminalisation were voiced by critical reviewers. Yet the critical challenge to academic orthodoxies 'returned to prominence the significance of structural relations, the question of power and the processes which underpinned its legitimacy'. The emphasis was derived from 'the *contexts* of social action and reaction' and 'the often less visible structural arrangements – the political, economic and ideological management of social worlds...' (Scraton and Chadwick, 1991: 165). But how was the clearly evident rise in authoritarianism within liberal democracies to be explained?

In his exhaustive analysis of state power Poulantzas regarded the 'split between law and violence' (Poulantzas, 1978: 76) to be false. State power was manifested in its rules and laws constituting 'an initial field of injunctions, prohibitions and censorship law is the code of organized public violence' (Poulantzas, 1978: 77). Poulantzas was eager not to sacrifice the significance and persuasive influence of 'organized physical violence' or 'physical repression, in the strong sense of deadly, armed constraint of the body', to an exaggerated emphasis of 'ideological-symbolic *manipulation*, the organization of consent, and the internalization of repression (the "inner cop")' (Poulantzas, 1978: 78). The 'role of violence in grounding power', he argued, should not be diminished by searching for 'reasons for consent' which would reduce power 'to prohibition and symbolic or internalized oppression' (Poulantzas, 1978: 79).

Returning to Weber, Poulantzas reaffirmed that the capitalist state holds the monopoly in the legitimate use of physical violence. From discipline on the factory floor through to punishment in the prison, physical coercion – mind and body – is legitimated through regulations, codes and laws. He maintained that 'state monopolization of legitimate violence' constitutes the 'determining element of power, even when such violence is not exercised in a direct or open manner' (Poulantzas, 1978: 82). Yet there is another repressive dimension, 'something about which people seldom talk: namely *the mechanisms of fear*' (Poulantzas, 1978: 83). For Poulantzas western democracies were experiencing a transformation to a new state form, *authoritarian statism*, exemplified by 'intensified state control over every sphere of socio-economic life *combined with* radical decline of the institutions of political democracy and with draconian and multiform curtailment of so-called "formal" liberties, whose reality is being discovered now they are going overboard' (Poulantzas, 1978: 203-4). Alongside this intensification of state intervention 'an entire institutional structure' had been constructed 'serving to prevent a rise in popular struggles and the dangers which that holds for class hegemony' (Poulantzas, 1978: 210).

Throughout the early 1970s students, workers, political activists and campaigners in the UK certainly felt the draught of hardening, repressive state interventionism. Tougher policing and harsher penalties were directed towards trade unionists, student protestors, anti-Vietnam and anti-apartheid campaigners, claimants unions, black communities and so on. Most significant, yet persistently overlooked in most criminological writing, was the deployment of the British army on the streets of the North of Ireland. This military presence, now spanning four decades, supported civil policing derived almost exclusively from loyalist and unionist communities. Had Poulantzas required an exemplar representation of authoritarian statism, in both its overt and covert forms, he needed to look no further than the North of Ireland. Almost disregarding the 'Ireland question', however, Hall et al. (1978) mapped the 'crisis' being policed in British towns and cities throughout the late 1960s and into the 1970s. At its base it was 'a crisis of and for British capitalism', an advanced capitalist political economy attempting 'to stabilise itself in rapidly changing global and national conditions, on an extremely weak, post-imperial base' (Hall et al., 1978: 317).

World economic recession hardly provided an appropriate backcloth against which a vibrant free-market economy could be developed. The crisis, the authors argued, did not end there. There was a crisis in the 'relations of social forces' caused by economic instability, a 'crisis in the political class struggle and in the political apparatuses'. Alongside and connected to this was a 'crisis of the state' in securing 'the conditions for the continued expansion of capital' and 'in the economic management of capital' (Hall et al., 1978: 318–19). For the role of the state in terms of civil society was to construct both consent and legitimacy for its political-economic strategies. Yet there was a 'crisis in political legitimacy, in social authority, in hegemony and in the forms of class struggle and resistance' (Hall et al., 1978: 319). Hall et al. considered that the early to mid 1970s brought closure to the equilibrium and stability on which post-war capitalist state power had depended. The consequences, particularly regarding industrial conflict and public order, had to be managed politically through the 'extension' of the rule of law.

Consensus, in the liberal-democratic sense, was illusory and required political manipulation. Underacknowledged, yet vital to the forging of consent, was the 'law' – 'in winning over the silent majority to a definition of the crisis...making it more legitimate for "public opinion" to be recruited...in favour of a strong state'. This constituted the 'ebb and flow of authoritarian populism' defining and reproducing 'social discipline' (Hall et al., 1978: 304–5), the point being that the 'authoritarian' or 'strong' state could not progress within liberal democracies without winning the hearts and minds of an influential constituency. As Poulantzas proposed, sustaining social stability through a period of economic austerity and hardening political-legal intervention necessitated shrewd ideological management.

Such management, however, does not operate on a clean slate. People are not easily-led 'dupes'. Shrewd political and ideological management appeals to traditions, prejudices and fears within diverse communities. Hall et al. identified a 'pincer movement' which combined the 'popular moral pressure from below' and the 'thrust of restraint and control from above' (Hall et al., 1978: 278). A decade before Margaret Thatcher effectively deployed the phrase 'the enemy within' against those who opposed her second, draconian administration, Hall et al recorded the state's mobilisation of repressive forces against the 'enemy in any of [its] manifold disguises'. The gradual 'shift to control' involved 'the law, the police, administrative regulation, public censure, [a] qualitative *shift* in the balance and relations of force' amounting to 'a deep change' (Hall et al., 1978: 278).

A quarter of a century on from the 1974 defeat of Heath's Conservative government at the hands of a determined and well-organised trade union movement, it seems incredible that at the time those in power were gripped by extreme paranoia. Brendon Sewill, special assistant to the Chancellor of the Exchequer, recalled that 'many of those in positions of influence looked into the abyss and saw only a few days away the possibility of the country being plunged into a state of chaos not so very far removed from that which might prevail after a minor nuclear attack' (Sewill, 1975: 50). Such was 'the power that existed to hold the country to ransom...the fear of that abyss' that all 'subsequent policy' was significantly affected.

While the Labour government struggled with the economic inheritance left by the Conservatives, the broader political agenda was seized by the ascendant New Right. As noted elsewhere:

> the issue of the 'power of the unions' slotted in neatly alongside other essential strands: the dependency-creating welfare state and the pervasiveness of 'scrounging'; the 'decline' of education standards and performance due to comprehensive education; the escalation of street crime, crimes of violence and 'political terrorism'; the growth of 'permissiveness', the 'decline' of morality and the undermining of the family unit.
>
> (Scraton, 1987: 156).

Responding to the Thatcherite agenda, Stuart Hall wrote: '[w]e are now in the middle of a deep and decisive movement towards a more disciplinary, authoritarian kind of society' in which 'the drive for "more Law and Order" is no short-term affair'. In their manipulation of what Poulantzas termed 'mechanisms of fear', politicians and media commentators articulated a 'regression to a stone-age morality' (Hall, 1980: 3). The populist appeal triggered a 'blind spasm of control' as the '*only* remedy for a society...declared "ungovernable" is the imposition of order through a disciplinary use of the law by the state' (Hall, 1980: 3). The 'language of law and order', was 'sustained by moralisms' – 'where the great syntax of "good versus evil", of civilised and uncivilised standards, of the choice between anarchy and order' divided and classified social action (Hall, 1979: 19). Anticipating subsequent criticism, Hall argued that populism was not a 'rhetorical device or trick' but operated on 'genuine contradictions' which reflected a 'rational and material core' (Hall, 1979: 20).

It was the appeal to traditional values and morality that provided the 'law and order crusade' with its 'grasp on popular morality and common-sense conscience'. The consolidation and selective enforcement of repressive laws, the acceptance – however grudging – of the operational independence of the police, the widespread support for reactionary court decisions, harsh sentences and prison expansionism, were manifestations of the iron grip of New Right law and order ideology. This strong expression of deep-seated ideologies and opportunistic political strategies secured and reproduced a lasting constituency within popular consent.

Critics of the authoritarian populism 'thesis' argued that in its application to 'Thatcherism' it overdetermined the significance of ideology while underplaying political-economic conditions. Jessop et al. (1988) rejected the claim that Thatcherism had delivered hegemony, maintaining there had been no evidence of coherent popular consensus. They also considered that Hall and his co-authors had idealised the post-war achievements of social democracy. Further, the New Right had not gained legitimacy for its objectives. Finally, the thesis failed to explain and analyse the broader context of global economic restructuring.

In an uncompromising response to his critics Stuart Hall refuted the claim that authoritarian populism had been conceived to provide a comprehensive analysis of Thatcherism. It was 'preposterous' to suggest he had proposed that hegemony had been secured by Thatcherism. Acknowledging Gramsci, he stated that hegemony could neither be conceptualised nor achieved without positioning the economy as the 'decisive nucleus' around which civil society developed (Hall, 1985: 120). This, he concluded, was the shared politics of western advanced capitalist states. Authoritarianism, inherent within liberal democratic states, resolved the crisis politically through expanding and centralising powers within the 'permanent agencies of the state' particularly 'in relation to the maintenance of public order, the handling of emergencies and the gathering of intelligence' (Gamble, 1988: 183).

Despite publicly proclaiming that the state, especially the *welfare* state, had become *too* powerful and *too* interventionist in people's lives, the New Right harnessed and used state power to manage consent, systematise regulation, secure hegemony and crush opposition. Successive Thatcher administrations, buoyed by the 1982 'victory' in the South Atlantic, took on the most powerful and popular of unions, the National Union of Mineworkers, and defeated it not only by economic means but through directly hostile and aggressive policing and prosecutions. The hard-line state responses to uprisings in black communities in 1980, 1981 and 1985 were directed towards mining communities.

Managing 'Knowledge' and the Production of 'Truth'

Acts are not, they *become*. So it is with crime. Crime does not exist. Crime is created. First there are acts. Then follows a long process of giving meaning to these acts.

(Christie, 1998: 121)

Perhaps the most quoted paragraph in post-war criminology begins with Howard Becker's assertion that deviance does not create social control but is created by social control. Invariably it is a precursor to any discussion of the labelling perspective, emphasising the significance of social reaction in ascribing negative status to the breach of established conventions and social rules. And so *outsiders* are socially created, marginalised and shunned. Nils Christie, however, considers the ascription of crime through the institutional and classificatory processes of *state* control. There is no 'crime', there are only *acts*-in-the-making; 'crime' and 'criminals' are invested with meaning in the socio-cultural and political-economic context of definition, enforcement and application of the rule of law. As the previous sections demonstrate, these are dynamic processes which result in the historically specific and materially relevant construction of criminalisation. It is the structural creation, marginalisation and punishment of outsiders as *outlaws*.

Stuart Hall and his co-authors made a major contribution to the advancement of critical analysis by stressing the centrality of ideology in representing and reconstructing material reality. Criminalisation is not just a process restricted to 'the application of the criminal label to a particular social category', but also extends to 'political containment' mobilising 'considerable popular approval and legitimacy behind the state' (Hall and Scraton, 1981: 488–9). Thus it became a defining aspect of the political management of 'opposition' discussed earlier. Given the 'meaning' ascribed to certain acts and groups, it also became essential to the political management and differential policing of *identity*. This issue was prominent in Hall et al.'s *Policing the Crisis*, particularly their empirical analysis of the relationship between 'mugging', black youth and policing. It was an analysis derived from earlier work on negative identity (folk devils) and social reaction (moral panics).

When Jock Young (1971) and Stan Cohen (1972) first published their important studies on 'drug takers' and 'mods and rockers' respectively, they could not have envisaged the extent to which their conceptualisation of 'moral panics' would become part of popular discourse. Their mutual concern was to explain how certain acts or identifiable individuals or groups (folk devils) were represented as posing demonstrable threats to the established social and political order. Partly because of its loose use and ubiquity, but also due to academic critiques which framed the 'moral panic' as an ideological rather than material concept, its currency has been devalued. Yet 'folk devils' are tangible, both in their creation and in the social and *societal* reactions they induce. Within public discourse certain acts and behaviours are represented as underpinning social conventions and moral values regarded as 'sacred' or 'fundamental'

(Thompson, 1998: 8). So serious is the threat that the 'social order itself or an idealized conception of some part of it' becomes destabilised (Thompson, 1998: 8).

In the ensuing 'moral panic', what follows is an orchestrated, hostile and disproportionate reaction by the authorities incorporating surveillance, containment and regulation. Tangible and material, they involve concrete strategies, techniques and resources of response and reaction with social, political and economic consequences. Such authority gains legitimacy, as discussed earlier, from 'heightened emotion, fear, dread, anxiety, hostility and a strong sense of righteousness' (Goode and Ben-Yehuda, 1994: 31). More broadly, as Muncie argues, moral panics 'form part of a sensitizing and legitimizing process for solidifying moral boundaries, identifying "enemies within", strengthening the powers of state control and enabling law and order to be promoted without cognisance of the social divisions and conflicts which produce deviance and political dissent' (Muncie, 1996: 55). The 'public anxiety and uncertainty' generated by the moral panic finds resolution through scapegoating.

Far from this being reducible to ideology, the real societal impact is derived in power relations: 'the more power a group or social category has, the greater the likelihood it will be successful in influencing legislation... consistent with the views, sentiments and interests of its members...' (Goode and Ben-Yehuda, 1994: 82). Closely associated with the moral outrage surrounding a particular act or sequence of events is a widely and immediately disseminated rush to judgement invariably feeding highly publicised calls for increasingly regulatory interventions. It is a pattern which strengthens state control: 'tougher or renewed rules, more intense public hostility and condemnation, more laws, longer sentences, more police, more arrests and more prison cells... a crackdown on offenders' (Goode and Ben-Yehuda, 1994: 31).

In courting and retaining political popularity, and in driving forward an agenda based on securing social stability through the policing of what Spitzer (1975) previously called 'problem populations', the New Right both in the USA and in the UK attempted to use prison as a 'way out' of the 'violent crime problem' (Currie, 1998: 185). Despite the media-endorsed, quasi-academic constructs of 'Reaganism' and 'Thatcherism', however, the consolidation of authoritarianism throughout the 1980s and into the 1990s went beyond the personalities of leaders, however influential in their own right. The lasting socio-political change of this period was the harnessing of official discourse, including official 'truth', to popular discourse.

Introducing a 'propaganda model' to analyse the role and function of the mass media, Herman and Chomsky (1988: 298) conclude that the 'societal purpose of the mass media is to inculcate and defend the economic, social, and political agenda of privileged groups that dominate the domestic society and the state'. While seemingly overdeterministic and reductionist, their position accepts that 'spirited debate, criticism and dissent' is encouraged as part of a 'free press'. There are limits set, however, by a 'system of presuppositions and principles that constitute an élite consensus, a system so powerful as to be internalized largely without awareness'. This is what Williams refers to as the 'underlying structure of communicative relationships within a particular social order' (Williams, 1989:116). For Foucault this structure re-presents truth and orders knowledge, 'linked in a circular relation with systems of power which produce and sustain it, and to effects of power which it induces and which extend it' (Foucault, 1980: 133). What is constructed is a 'régime of truth'.

For Foucault, 'formal' truth cannot be understood outside the relations of power:

> Each society has its régime of truth, its 'general politics' of truth ... the types of disclosure which it accepts and makes function as true; the mechanisms and instances which enable one to distinguish true and false statements, the means by which each is sanctioned; the techniques and procedures accorded value in the acquisition of truth; the status of those who are charged with saying what counts as true.
>
> (Foucault, 1980: 131).

However diverse, the 'relations of power which permeate, characterise and constitute the social body', their influence and effectiveness, depend on the 'production, accumulation, circulation and functioning of a discourse' which itself is directly associated with the 'production of truth' (Foucault, 1980: 93).

The production of truth and the exercise of power are inextricably interwoven. Power, concludes Foucault, 'never ceases its interrogation, its inquisition, its registration of truth: it institutionalises, professionalises and rewards its pursuit...' (Foucault, 1980: 94). This includes the 'scientific' discourses of academic and state institutions alike, the production of formally sanctioned knowledge. As such, 'truth' and 'knowledge' are constrained by political and economic imperatives. Matters of 'state security' are subject to misinformation and disinformation 'in the public interest'. Yet, beyond the management of information and the manufacture of news is the self-serving and self-preserving 'spin' of governments, state institutions and corporations.

The relationship between power and knowledge, manifested in the construction of official discourse as truth, is 'dispersed through the body of society' and central to the processes of 'discipline, surveillance, individualization and normalization' (Sim, 1990: 9). In the methodologies, techniques and functioning of professional intervention, particularly regarding the 'logic and language of control', the awesome 'power to classify' generates established bodies of knowledge within the determining contexts of material power relations (Cohen, 1985: 196). While professionals appear to possess discretion, working with 'clients' in a relatively autonomous relationship, immediate institutional and broader structural imperatives regulate and institutionalise their interventions. Critical analysis within criminology and its application to the criminal justice process regards the relations of power as central to the determination and containment of personal action and social interaction. While accepting that all acts are ascribed meaning at the micro-level at which they occur, they can only be interpreted fully through analysis of their historical and material contexts. As Messerschmidt states, 'structural action' is 'what people do under specific structural constraints' (Messerschmidt, 1997: 6).

Such structural constraints are derived in and maintained through the determining contexts of production and distribution (class), reproduction, gender and sexuality (patriarchy), 'race' and 'ethnicity' (neo-colonialism) and childhood (age). Each of these determining contexts is evident at the cutting edge of subjugation, exploitation and violence. Poverty, wherever the breadline is drawn, blights the daily lives, health and welfare of the low-paid and unemployed. Women, despite 'equal opportunities' legislation, remain unequally paid and endure physical and sexual violence regardless of class, 'race', religion or age. Black, Asian and Traveller families are routinely subjected to racist abuse and violence, across a spectrum, to fire-bombings and murder. Children and young people, whether in 'families' or in 'care', are routinely physically chastised, degraded, harmed and exploited – frequently extending to physical and sexual abuse. Each instance of impoverishment, sexism, homophobia, racism or child-hate as an expression of *agency* has its particular circumstances and lived history. Yet none can be researched, analysed and fully comprehended without location in the determining contexts of *structure*.

Critical Analysis as Resistance

> ... succinctly, the point is to change the world, not only to study it.
>
> (Stanley, 1990: 15)

Even with the benefit of hindsight and multiple media and academic interpretations, it is difficult to assess accurately the euphoria that greeted the election of 'New Labour' in 1997. Undoubtedly, the public outpouring of enthusiasm for Tony Blair and his associates was as much about relief – an escape from the immediate past and the long shadow of Thatcherism – as it was about any obvious change in political direction. Certainly many people were pleased to see the back of Michael 'Prison Works' Howard as Home Secretary, wrongly assuming that his arrogant authoritarianism, including meddling in judicial matters beyond his political remit, would be replaced by a more liberal agenda. Yet, while a raft of education, health and welfare reforms as promised by the incoming government, supported by a 'realist' pragmatic and quasi-intellectual vision of public–private sector collaboration promoted as the 'Third Way', the law and order agenda did not waver from its inheritance. Given the emphases adopted by Labour leaders prior to the election their acceptance of the authoritarian mantle was unsurprising.

Following the killing of a two-year-old child by two ten-year-olds in 1993 Tony Blair, then Shadow Home Secretary, had warned of the 'descent into moral chaos'. There existed, he argued, a 'moral vacuum' that could be resolved only through 'being tough on crime and tough on the causes of crime' (*Guardian*, 20 February 1993). Three years later Blair was Labour leader, replaced as Shadow Home Secretary by Jack Straw. While Howard was extolling the virtues of military-style boot camps for young male offenders and secure accommodation (a euphemism for imprisonment) for 12- to 14-year-olds, Straw promoted further expansion of child custody and curfews for children aged ten and younger (*Sunday Times*, 18 August 1996). Well aware of the impending election, Straw attacked 'the excuse culture' within youth justice which 'excuses itself for its inefficiency and too often excuses young offenders...wrecking other people's lives' (*Guardian*, 21 November 1996). There was no acknowledgement of the many schemes and advances within youth justice that had succeeded in decarceration, diversion and decriminalisation (see Goldson, 1997).

Instead, Straw promised a 'root and branch' reform of youth justice. This echoed simultaneous recommendations made by the Audit Commission for preventive measures directed towards: 'inadequate parenting; aggressive and hyperactive behaviour in early childhood; truancy and exclusion from school; unstable living conditions; lack of training and employment; drug and alcohol abuse' (Audit Commission, 1996: 3). Also emphasised was the 'cycle of antisocial behaviour', a construct consistent with New Labour's 1996 consultation document on youth crime. There was no sign of innovative analysis or critical thought in these priorities. They reflected the classical traditional mix of individual and social pathologies.

Against this background, and within months of the 1997 election, the Labour government published consultation documents anticipating a Crime and Disorder Bill. Minimal consultation gave the illusion of inclusivity but the key themes and issues had been decided. The Bill raced through Parliament and within a year the Crime and Disorder Act was on the statute book. 'Disorder', a nebulous category closely aligned to 'antisocial behaviour', was juxtaposed with 'crime'. It constituted a new label inscribed within the law, to be ascribed through its discretionary enforcement. Presented as the linchpin of a more comprehensive package of law reform, the Act was intended to deliver a new morality supporting a more disciplined and more responsible society. It compelled non-criminal justice agencies – local authorities, education, youth and community work, welfare and health – to become directly involved in the establishment and implementation of locally based crime strategies informed by 'independent' crime audits.

At the core of this diverse and far-reaching legislation were a series of *civil* injunctions. These could be invoked by either the police or the local authority in consultation with the other. The breach of an injunction, however, constituted a criminal offence. Cases decided on the 'balance of probabilities' could be criminalised without the 'beyond reasonable doubt' test being applied. Injunctions included: antisocial behaviour orders, parenting orders, child curfews and child safety orders. Antisocial behaviour was defined as behaviour causing harassment to a community, disrupting the peaceful and quiet enjoyment of a neighbourhood or intimidation of others. The strategy, imported from New York, although prevalent among US cities, was zero tolerance. As demonstrated within the USA, it constitutes a strategy of 'lockdown' leading inexorably and inevitably to differential policing, discriminatory targeting, universal surveillance, criminalisation and an escalation in the prison population (see Christie, 1993; Currie, 1998; Parenti, 1999). In the UK early indications are consistent with the USA as more children, young people and adults are caught in the widening net.

The Act also abolished the presumption of *doli incapax* for children aged ten to 14, allowing the courts to draw inferences from an accused child's failure to give evidence or decision to remain silent. It reaffirmed the UK's commitment to secure custody for serious or repeat young offenders. In so doing it flew in the face of the UN Committee on the

Rights of the Child whose 1995 response to the UK's implementation of the UN Convention heavily criticised the procedures of prosecution, conviction and punishment of children and young people (see Scraton and Haydon, 2002). As Muncie concludes, the Act was 'an amalgam of "get tough" authoritarian measures with elements of paternalism, pragmatism, communitarianism, responsibilization and remoralization whose new depth and legal powers might be best described as "coercive corporatism"' (Muncie, 1999: 154).

The focus here on the expansion of regulation of children and young people, including extensive changes in the organisation and delivery of youth justice, well illustrates a deepening concern about the authoritarianism at the heart of the government's broader programme of 'moral renewal'. Taken together with the removal of the right to silence, proposals for mandatory drug testing of suspects as well as prisoners, challenges to the right to jury trial, the legal regulation of asylum seekers and the scope and force of the Terrorism Act 2000, the long march of authoritarianism has continued unabated. The political accountability of 'local' policing has been eroded to the extent that senior officers enjoy relative autonomy. Further, cross-border policing and many 'national' initiatives are developed and progressed outside the domain of formal politics. Sentences have hardened and tariffs have lengthened. There continues to be a dramatic increase in the incarceration of children and women. The prison population has spiralled beyond the most pessimistic estimates, increasing by more than a third during the first New Labour administration. Consequently, Victorian prisons due for demolition remain overcrowded, infested and insanitary while regimes are locked into the priorities of security, discipline and order.

'Getting tough' on crime and antisocial behaviour has become a necessary, albeit inflated, feature of major political party manifestos throughout advanced democratic societies. As the earlier discussion shows, the populist appeal of authoritarian rhetoric is its promotion and provocation of material policy outcomes. Hudson concludes that 'deserved retribution', 'protection from dangerous or persistent offenders' and 'strong action against kinds of offending that become suddenly prevalent' (Hudson, 1996: 55) are now established as priorities within western criminal justice processes. Christie considers that this 're-active framework' has unleashed a 'new situation' in which 'an unlimited reservoir of acts can be defined as crimes' bringing 'unlimited possibilities for warfare against all sorts of crimes' (Christie, 1993: 24). The policy and policing response reaffirms the individual, the identifiable group or community as criminal or deviant rather than 'attacking social exclusion – reducing poverty, creating opportunities for sustaining work, supporting besieged families and the marginalised young...making a real, rather than a theoretical commitment to reintegrating offenders into the community and protecting local communities from serious crime' (Currie, 1998: 195).

Within the UK generous funding has been made available through the Home Office to meet the costs of crime prevention strategies and their evaluation. This has led to a 'new generation' of academic work based around local as well as national government surveys, audits and evaluations. In-depth qualitative research is virtually absent from what amounts to a naive and partial approach to the assessment of policy or programme effectiveness. In this politically driven process legitimacy has been given to the pragmatism of a renewed form of positivism, ironically and erroneously masquerading under the guise of 'evidence-based' research.

Alongside this investment in crime prevention strategies and their 'empirical' evaluation has been a remarkable expansion of centres and institutes of criminal justice studies. While many applied social sciences courses are in decline, criminology undergraduate courses have burgeoned. As with the emphasis on commissioned research, from state institutions or private corporations, university teaching programmes are pulled towards vocational 'relevance' and professional 'training'. In both contexts, research (evaluation) and teaching (training), the availability of funding and the pull of market forces dictates and delimits the academic agenda compromising its freedom and independence.

Writing a quarter of a century after C. Wright Mills, Nils Christie (1993: 58) illustrates how pervasive and pernicious has been the 'invasion' of 'management ideology' and vocational 'correspondence' within universities. The demand for 'useful knowledge' is passed from 'managers within the state and business' to students and, given the pressure to attract increased numbers of students, to academics. Consequently 'university standards of critical thinking' are compromised and 'the moral power of the question-makers' is diminished. Just as social sciences in general served the post-war military-industrial complex, so administrative criminology today serves the punishment-industrial complex. Never has there been a more potentially lucrative period for, as Christie famously put it, 'crime control as industry'.

Inevitably these developments have strengthened 'mainstream' or administrative criminology, the foundations of which are rooted in focusing attention on the personal and social rather than the structural. Despite generating an impressive research-based literature, critical criminology remains under-represented in established academic and professional journals and curiously absent from the various 'handbooks' of criminology. Further, government departments and state institutions regularly refuse or inhibit access to academic researchers whose 'independence' they cannot monitor or regulate.

Despite this 'pessimism of the intellect', however, not all academics have forsaken the 'optimism of the will' (apologies to Gramsci and Rolland) to walk the corridors of government departments, to present under-researched papers at association conferences and to accept sponsorship tarnished by political imperatives. Within mainstream criminology and relevant state institutions there has been persistent pressure to disqualify or delegitimise critical analysis, using strategies of denial, neutralisation and incorporation. Yet critical research, teaching and publication have survived. It is not possible here to cover the full range of work which includes foci on policing, imprisonment, surveillance, reparation, secrecy, authoritarianism, accountability and so on. It is work which has advanced the relevance of contemporary class analysis and the significance of 'race' and racism and has integrated feminist critiques.

As Hudson states in her critical analysis of penal policy and punishment, 'legal theory and criminology' cannot provide adequate explanations of crime, social problems or the administration of criminal justice. Rather, it is necessary to construct a 'critical theory of the contemporary state' as the 'structural context in which criminal justice is enacted' where the 'rhetoric of law and order, crime and punishment has prevailed over treatment' (Hudson, 1993: 6–7). The 'defining tradition' of 'critical social science' underpinning Hudson's analysis is intellectual engagement 'on behalf of those on the downside of power relations'. Put another way, critical social research examines 'how social systems really work, how ideology or history conceals the processes which oppress and control people ... direct[ing] attention to the processes and institutes which legitimate knowledge' (Harvey, 1990: 6). Little wonder, as Hudson concludes, that 'mainstream', administrative criminology 'has the most dangerous relationship to power: the categories and classifications, the labels and diagnoses and the images of the criminal being both stigmatizing the pejorative' (Hudson, 2000: 177).

The potential of critical analysis for challenging and affecting change in the established politics and practices of criminal justice is well illustrated by Mathiesen's (1990) important critique of prisons and punishment. Concerned with the 'material underpinnings' of the ideological functions of imprisonment, he notes that society's bifurcation 'between the productive and the unproductive ... places prisoners in a [structurally] powerless position' (Mathiesen, 1990: 138). While the crimes and conventions of the powerful are neglected, those of the powerless become increasingly stigmatised. Thus prisons 'appear meaningful and legitimate'. He concludes: 'By relying on the prison, by building prisons, by building more prisons, by passing longer prison sentences' politicians and civil servants 'obtain a method of showing they act on crime that they are doing something about it, that something is presumably being done about law and order' (Mathiesen, 1990: 139). Mathiesen's version of prison expansionism was prophetic and, regarding the USA and the UK, remains directly relevant to all aspects of criminalisation and net widening.

Critical research, publication and teaching within criminology has a significant role in resisting the political and ideological imperatives of official discourse, state-sponsored evaluations of official policy initiatives and the correspondence of vocational training to the requirements of the crime control industry. Its critical agenda responds to Sivanandan's call to turn cases into issues. Returning to Wright Mills, such an agenda contextualises the experiential realities of personal troubles as public issues, analysing and exposing prevailing regimes of truth within official discourse. Further, it locates state interventionism within structural relations. In seeking out, representing and valuing the 'view from below', critical criminologists promote structural change within social democracies, undermining the 'complex discourse of denial' and procedural arrangements that provide a sophisticated 'legal defense' (Cohen, 1996: 517).

The range of critical work included in the concluding notes to this chapter acknowledges the breadth and depth of the academic contribution in developing and sustaining an alternative discourse. Politically, the significance of critical research is marked by its close association with people's movements or community campaigns. For it is the harm, suffering and exclusion endured by those struggling for social justice, formal acknowledgement and 'truth' that provides the least deniable evidence of the incursion of authoritarianism into everyday life. It is at this level of investigation and contextualisation that cases are transformed into issues, experiential moments of agency challenge the often disguised processes of structure and the doublespeak of manufactured official discourse becomes enmeshed in its own rhetoric and spin.

This chapter opened with a set of snapshots taken from a decade's critical research in which the personal and the political has been inseparable, and rightly so. Each case has been progressed by strong grassroots campaigns involving those directly affected working alongside human rights lawyers and critical researchers. From the testimonies presented, the experiences researched and the procedures observed, several features emerge which are consistent and demonstrate an officially sanctioned and sealed version of the 'truth' (see Scraton, 2000; North, 2000; Haydon and Scraton, 2000; Rolston, 2000; Davis and Scraton, 2002). These features include:

- the abuse of discretionary powers with impunity;

- the inadequacy of investigations through lack of disclosure; the pathologising of 'victims', survivors and campaigners;

- the silencing of alternative accounts through condemnation and vilification;

- the reconstruction of causation to give the appearance of self-inflicted harm;

- the manipulation and management of the media including purposeful misinformation;

- the institutional and governmental denial of responsibility combined with a longer-term refusal to acknowledge the full circumstances of controversial deaths.

In the introduction to his in-depth study of state killings in the North of Ireland, research based on extensive interviews with the bereaved, Rolston (2000: xv) reflects on 'how far the state degraded the ideal of human rights over three decades and how some people struggled to uphold the ideal in the most hostile of environments'. What cases such as the investigation into the murder of Stephen Lawrence and the circumstances of black deaths in custody demonstrate, however, is the broader relevance of Rolston's assessment to Britain. Similar concerns exist concerning the circumstances and investigative responses regarding the deaths of young people and women in custody (particularly at Cornton Vale, Scotland) and the Hillsborough, Lockerbie, *Marchioness* and Dunblane tragedies. Alongside these cases is growing concern about miscarriages of justice.

Rolston's concluding comment, therefore, resounds throughout the UK criminal justice systems: 'Through campaigning, their [the bereaved] private ills were transformed into public issues. Their individual experience became a spur to political action' (Rolston, 2000: 319). It is with this profound process of transformation that the critical criminologist should be concerned. In considering Chomsky's position on intellectual responsibility, Stan Cohen notes: 'Intellectuals who keep silent about what they know, who ignore the crimes that matter by moral standards, are even more morally culpable when society is free and open. They can speak freely, but choose not to' (Cohen, 2001: 286). For critical criminology silence can never be an option. Despite well-rehearsed and important critiques of human rights legislation, a positive rights discourse and agenda which recognises the determining contexts of social injustice and the realities and consequences of personal suffering can provide a starting-point; a processual and procedural alternative to the administration of the law and criminal justice. Those who endure institutionalised harm at the hands of advanced democratic states more readily now raise their voices to demand thorough investigations, effective inquiries, disclosure of information and the fair administration of justice. They are voices that will not be hushed. As Maya Angelou writes: 'You may write me down in history/With your bitter, twisted lies... But still, like dust, I'll rise' (Angelou 1986: 41–2).

Acknowledgements

An early version of this paper was presented to the European Group for the Study of Deviance and Social Control at Komitini, Greece. A more developed version was presented to the 'Whither Critical Criminology in the twenty-first Century?' Conference at the University of Western Sydney in February 2001. Many thanks to all who commented and gave encouragement following both sessions. Also my thanks to Kathryn Chadwick, whose contribution is implicit throughout, to Deena Haydon and to my co-workers in critical criminology at the Centre for Studies in Crime and Social Justice. Finally, much appreciation to Kerry Carrington and Russell Hogg, both patient and supportive editors.

Further Texts

It is difficult to prioritise contributory texts to the critical criminological debate. More broadly were the following: Ian Taylor, Paul Walton and Jock Young (eds), *Critical Criminology* (London: RKP, 1975); Carol Smart, *Women, Crime and Criminology* (London: RKP, 1976); Steven Box, *Power, Crime and Mystification* (London: Tavistock, 1983) and *Recession, Crime and Punishment* (London: Macmillan, 1987); Mike Brake and Chris Hale, *Public Order and Private Lives* (London: Routledge, 1992); Paddy Hillyard and Janie Percy-Smith, *The Coercive State* (London: Fontana, 1988). Feminist critiques of criminology have been crucial to the development of critical analysis. They are well reviewed in Loraine Gelsthorpe and Allison Morris (eds), *Feminist Perspectives in Criminology* (Buckingham: Open University Press, 1990) and Sandra Walklate, *Gender and Crime: An Introduction* (London: Prentice Hall, 1995). Pat Carlen's work has remained central (including *Women and Imprisonment*, London: RKP, 1983; *Women, Crime and Poverty*, Buckingham: Open University Press,

1988; *Alternatives to Women's Imprisonment*, Buckingham: Open University Press, 1990; *Gender, Crime and Justice*, Buckingham: Open University Press, 1987; with Anne Worrall (eds), *Sledgehammer: Women's Imprisonment at the Millenium*, London: Macmillan, 1998). Her *Criminal Women* (Oxford: Basil Blackwell, 1985), co-authored with women ex-prisoners and campaigners, was an excellent example of interventionist, experiential work. Also influential has been the extensive body of research on male violence against women, particularly Elizabeth Stanko, *Intimate Intrusions* (London: Unwin Hyman, 1985) and *Everyday Violence* (London: Virago, 1990); Liz Kelly, *Surviving Sexual Violence* (Cambridge: Polity Press, 1988).

More specific examples of critical research based on 'turning cases into issues' include: *on prisons* – P. Scraton J. Sim and P. Skidmore, *Prisons Under Protest* (Buckingham: Open University Press, 1990); Margaret Malloch, *Women, Drugs and Custody* (Winchester: Waterside Press, 2000); Diana Medlicott, *Surviving the Prison Place* (Aldershot: Ashgate, 2001); *on deaths in custody* – P. Scraton and K. Chadwick, *In the Arms of the Law* (London: Pluto, 1987); *on the North of Ireland* – Paddy Hillyard, *Suspect Community* (London: Pluto, 1993); *on the Irish communities in Britain* Brian Campbell et al. (eds), *Nor Meekly Serve My Time* (Belfast: Beyond the Pale, 1994); Laurence McKeown *Out of Time* (Belfast: Beyond the Pale, 2001); *on the police* – Penny Green, *The Enemy Without: Policing and Class Consciousness in the Miners' Strike* (Buckingham: Open University Press, 1990); Phil Scraton, *The State of the Police* (London: Pluto, 1985).

Finally, a range of important campaign organisations have retained close links with critical research and have continued to publish important case-based analyses (for example: the Institute of Race Relations, *Race and Class*; Statewatch, *Bulletin*; Inquest, *Briefing Papers* and *Case Reviews*).

Bibliography

Angelou, M. (1986) *And Still I Rise*. London: Virago.

Audit Commission, (1996) *Misspent Youth: Young People and Crime*. London: Audit Commission.

Baran, P. and Sweezy, P. (1966) *Monopoly Capital*. New York: Monthly Review Press.

Becker, H. (1967) 'Whose side are we on?, *Social Problems*, Winter.

Becker, H. S. and Horowitz, I. L. (1972) 'Radical politics and sociological research', *American Journal of Sociology,* 78(1).

Braverman, H. (1984) *Labour and Monopoly Capital*. New York: Monthly Review Press.

Christie, N. (1993) *Crime Control as Industry*. London: Routledge.

Christie, N. (1998) 'Between civility and the state', in V. Ruggiero, N. South and I. Taylor (eds), *The New European Criminology: Crime and Social Order in Europe*. London: Routledge.

Cohen, S. (1972) *Folk Devils and Moral Panics*. London: MacGibbon & Kee.

Cohen, S. (1981) 'Footprints in the sand: a further report on criminology and the study of deviance in Britain', in M. Fitzgerald, G. McLennan and J. Pawson (eds), *Crime and Society*. London: Routledge & Kegan Paul.

Cohen, S. (1985) *Visions of Social Control*. Cambridge: Polity Press.

Cohen, S. (1993) 'Human rights and crimes of the state: the culture of denial', *Australian and New Zealand Journal of Criminology*, 26(2): 97–115.

Cohen, S. (1996) 'Crime and politics: spot the difference', *British Journal of Sociology*, 47(1): 1–21.

Cohen, S. (2001) *States of Denial: Knowing About Atrocities and Suffering*. Cambridge: Polity Press.

Currie, E. (1998) *Crime and Punishment in America*. New York: Metropolitan Books.

Davis, H. and Scraton, P. (2002) *Disaster, Trauma, Aftermath*. London: Lawrence & Wishart.

Davis, N. J. (1975) *Social Constructions of Deviance: Perspectives and Issues in the Field* Dubuque, IA: W. C. Brown Co.

Foucault, M. (1980) *Power/Knowledge: Selected Interviews and Other Writings 1972–1977*, ed. C. Gordon. Brighton: Harvester Wheatsheaf.

Gamble, A. (1988) *The Free Market Economy and the Strong State*. London: Macmillan.

Gelsthorpe, L. and Morris, A. (eds) (1990) *Feminist Perspectives in Criminology*. Buckingham: Open University Press.

Goldson, B. (1997) 'Children in trouble: state responses to juvenile crime', in P. Scraton (ed.) *'Childhood' in 'Crisis'?*. London: UCL Press.

Goode, E. and Ben-Yehuda, N. (1994) *Moral Panics: The Social Construction of Deviance*. Cambridge, MA: Blackwell.

Gouldner, A. W. (1971) *The Coming Crisis in Western Sociology*. London: Heinemann.

Gouldner, A. W. (1973) 'Foreword', in I. Taylor, P. Walton and J. Young (eds), *The New Criminology*. London: Routledge & Kegan Paul.

Gramsci, A. (1971) *Selections from the Prison Notebooks*. London: Lawrence & Wishart.

Hall, S. (1979) 'The great moving right show', *Marxism Today*, January.

Hall, S. (1980) *Drifting into a Law and Order Society*. London: Cobden Trust.

Hall, S. (1985) 'Authoritarian populism: a reply to Jessop et al.', *New Left Review*, 151: 115–24.

Hall, S. and Scraton, P. (1981) 'Law, class and control', in M. Fitzgerald, G. McLennan and J. Pawson (eds), *Crime and Society*. London: Routledge & Kegan Paul.

Hall, S., Critcher, C., Jefferson, T., Clarke, J. and Roberts, B. (1978) *Policing the Crisis*. London: Macmillan

Harvey, L. (1990) *Critical Social Research*. London: Sage.

Haydon, D. and Scraton, P. (2000) ' "Condemn a little more: understand a little less": the political context and rights implications of the domestic and European rulings in the Venables-Thompson Case', *Journal of Law and Society*, 27(3): 416–48.

Herman, E. S. and Chomsky, N. (1988) *Manufacturing Consent: The Political Economy of Mass Media*. New York: Pantheon.

Hudson, B. A. (1993) *Penal Policy and Social Justice*. London: Macmillan.

Hudson, B. A. (1996) *Understanding Justice*. Buckingham: Open University Press.

Hudson, B. A. (2000) 'Critical reflection as research methodology', in V. Jupp, P. Davies and P. Francis (eds), *Doing Criminological Research*. London: Sage.

Jessop, B. et al. (1988) *Thatcherism*. Cambridge: Polity Press.

Mathiesen, T. (1990) *Prison Trial*. London: Sage.

Messerschmidt, J. (1997) *Crime as Structured Action*. Thousand Oaks, CA: Sage.

Muncie, J. (1996) 'The construction and reconstruction of crime', in J. Muncie and E. McLaughlin (eds), *The Problem of Crime*. London: Sage.

Muncie, J. (1999) 'Institutionalised intolerance: youth justice and the 1998 Crime and Disorder Act', *Critical Social Policy* 19(2): 147–75.

Nicolaus, M. (1972) 'The professional organisation of sociology: the view from below', in R. Blackburn (ed.), *Ideology in Social Science*. London: Fontana.

North, M. (2000) *Dunblane: Never Forget*. Edinburgh: Mainstream.

Parenti, C. (1999) *Lockdown America: Police and Prisons in the Age of Crisis*. London: Verso.

Poulantzas, N. (1978) *State, Power, Socialism*. London: Verso.

Rolston, B. (2000) *Unfinished Business: State Killings and the Quest for Truth*. Belfast: Beyond the Pale Publications.

Scraton, P. (1987) 'Unreasonable force: policing, punishment and marginalisation', in P. Scraton (ed.), *Law, Order and the Authoritarian State*. Buckingham: Open University Press.

Scraton, P. (ed.) (1997) *'Childhood' in 'Crisis'?* London: UCL Press.

Scraton, P. (2000) *Hillsborough: The Truth*. Edinburgh: Mainstream.

Scraton, P. and Chadwick, K. (1991) 'Challenging the new orthodoxies: the theoretical and political priorities of critical criminology', in K. Stenson and D. Cowell (eds), *The Politics of Crime Control*. London: Sage.

Scraton, P. and Haydon, D. (2002) 'Challenging the criminalisation of children and young people', in J. Muncie, G. Hughes and E. McLaughlin (eds), *Youth Justice: Critical Readings in History, Theory and Policy*. London: Sage.

Sewill, B. (1975) 'Two views', in R. Harris B. and Sewill (eds), *British Economic Policy 1970–1974*. London: Institute of Economic Affairs.

Sim, J. (1990) *Medical Power in Prisons*. Buckingham: Open University Press.

Sim, J., Scraton, P. and Gordon, P. (1987) 'Crime, the state and critical analysis: an introduction', in P. Scraton (ed.), *Law, Order and the Authoritarian State: Readings in Critical Criminology*. Buckingham: Open University Press.

Spitzer, S. (1975) 'Towards a Marxian theory of deviance', *Social Problems*, 22: 368–401.

Stanley, L. (ed.) (1990) *Feminist Praxis*. London: Routledge.

Taylor, I., Walton, P. and Young, J. (1973) *The New Criminology*. London: Routledge & Kegan Paul.

Thompson, K. (1998) *Moral Panics*. London: Routledge.

Williams, R. (1989) *What I Came to Say*. London: Hutchinson.

Wright Mills, C. (1959) *The Sociological Imagination*. New York: Oxford University Press.

Young, J. (1971) 'The role of police as amplifiers of deviance, negotiators of drug control as seen in Notting Hill', in S. Cohen (ed.), *Images of Deviance*. London: Penguin.

Chapter 3

Critical criminology in the United States: the Berkeley School and theoretical trajectories

Herman Schwendinger, Julia R. Schwendinger and Michael J. Lynch

Introduction: the Rise of the Berkeley School of Criminology

The 1960s produced a crisis of order and authority unknown in the United States since the Civil War (Chatfield, 1990). Almost 35 years have passed, yet the US government and mass media still blame this crisis on the 'usual suspects', the political dissidents sired by the 1960s, rather than the 'defenders of order' who fought long-overdue demands for equality by resorting to political repression, police brutality and war crimes to serve corporate interests and imperial aims.

When Cambodia and Laos were invaded in 1970, the opposition to the war by students and academics made Governor Ronald Reagan shut down all nine campuses of the University of California (UC) despite his vow to keep the system open 'at the point of bayonets' if necessary. At that time, the 'usual suspects' at UC Berkeley's School of Criminology included one associate professor, four assistant professors, a lecturer and more than 30 undergraduate and graduate students. These self-proclaimed radical criminologists were 'suspects' because they opposed the war, advocated prison reforms, supported civil rights movements and affirmative action, and collaborated with Black Panthers and other community groups to curb police brutality.

Conventional criminologists stereotype these radicals as 'extremists' and 'utopians' with ultra-left aims. But most radicals at the school never fitted these stereotypes. In fact, it is impossible to understand them accurately without realising that political movements pulled them together despite their diverse positions and professional interests. Feminists, social democrats, Maoists, anarchists, left-liberals, moderate liberals, Marxists and people with no distinct political perspective were found among the radicals. They certainly included people whose utopian socialist dreams at that time made life bearable but they also included others.

Although they organised themselves and supported anti-war protests, sponsored conferences, launched a journal and wrote articles, books and model legislation, and although one could find the same people drinking beer and dancing at The Starry Plough, their network was fluid and expanded or contracted depending upon what was happening outside the school. This network converged with political movements in the San Francisco Bay Area and, until the school itself was in peril, most of its activities were characterised by short-term – often reactive and spontaneous – responses to events outside the school.

Yet a single strand tied these diverse people together. Despite their long hair, pony tails, beards, hippie argot, cowboy hats, Mao hats, headbands, tie-dyed shirts, mini skirts and bongo drums – despite the revolutionary sloganeering, 'Power to the people!' and posturing – the students and academics who created the programme so despised by the university administration and its allies were *radical democrats* whose members shared the same political and social likes and dislikes. They believed their 'new criminology' would advance equality, justice and 'participatory democracy'. They really did believe in what America was supposed to be. The majority still does.

The UC Berkeley School of Criminology actually offered a politically balanced curriculum taught by conservative and moderate liberals as well as radical democrats. Out of about a dozen professors, for most of the period in question, only four were considered radicals and three of them did not have tenure. The curriculum as a whole emphasised traditional professional courses, but the radicals also initiated criminology courses rarely offered elsewhere. Barry Krisberg, Tony Platt and Paul Takagi, for example, reorganised the introductory course and provided radical as well as non-radical topics dealing with the causes, characteristics and control of crime.[1] They designed the course for students at large, attracting some 800 undergraduates eager to know what the field was about even though most were enrolled in other departments. Like other courses offered by radicals, these instructors emphasised economic, political and social relations that determined the historical development of crime and criminal justice. In addition, Herman Schwendinger taught theoretical courses on crime and delinquency and seminars on 'instruments of discovery' that veered away from the blind empiricism and sterile survey methods dominating the field.[2] Although they were a minority, the radical staff introduced standpoints inconceivable in schools of criminal justice and criminology elsewhere. As a result, Richard A. Myren, author of *Education in Criminal Justice*, in 1970 observed: 'Berkeley exhibits probably the widest range of attention to crime studies of any university in the United States today.'

Other members of the staff also contributed to a new beginning in learning. Elliot Currie (who has written the preface for this book) was originally a lecturer and eventually an acting assistant professor in the school who played an important role in this regard. Jim Brady and other graduate-student lecturers described grassroots restorative justice developments in other countries. Drew Humphries and other female graduate students who taught courses also contributed. Staff such as Aviva Menkes, Richard Korn, Lloyd Street and John Davis focused on racial and ethnic repression, crimes against women, civil liberties and reforms of the police and correctional institutions.

Contact with visiting professors such as Marie Bertrand, an outstanding feminist scholar from the University of Montreal, Richard Quinney, a pioneer in critical criminology, Alphonso Pinckney, a noted black sociologist from Hunter College, John Irwin, who broke away from structural functionalism in penal studies, and David Dubois, the son of W. E. B. Dubois and editor of the Black Panther party's newspaper, expanded the new learning.

Speakers from labour organisations such as the United Farm Workers were invited to relate how police harassment and brutality repressed the unionisation of migratory workers. Finally, the School was further enriched by campus-wide talks featuring lecturers such as Ralph Nader, who excoriated 'Crime in the Suites'.

The radical staff helped reorganise the School's curriculum. They encouraged a systematic approach to criminology, developed internships in grassroots organisations and criminal justice agencies and administered individual studies that catered to student interests. It was no secret that the curriculum had been influenced by these academic staff but, when the school was attacked, virtually every course with socially critical content was labelled as 'radical'.

Despite their small number, the school generated a vibrant intellectual climate. Fundamental political and economic questions were raised about America's class, gender and racial inequality. And interaction between radical students and staff brought about the critical mass that produced an Enlightenment-like explosion of rich theoretical ideas about the nature of crime and criminal justice.

Some of the students educated by the radicals helped edit *Issues in Criminology*, publishing articles and interviews that would not have appeared in major criminology journals. Interviews with pioneering scholars,[3] and some of the earliest challenges to mainstream ideas appeared there – including Gene Grabiner's attack on value-free science and state morality, Barry Krisberg's trenchant critique of a University of Pennsylvania programme for gang leaders, and the Schwendingers' ground-breaking article on the legal definition of crime. Critical historical studies included Melanie Fong and Larry D. Johnson's critique of the Eugenicist movement and institutionalised racism, Dorie Klein's exposé of sexism in theories of female criminality, Martin B. Miller's scrutiny of progressive-era prison reforms, John Pallas and Bob Barber's study of prison struggles, Tony Platt and Randi Pollock's assessment of public defenders, Joyce Clements' analysis of the rhetoric of repression, Elliot Currie's article on medieval witch hunts and Richard Quinney's approach to legal order.

Racism in criminal justice was further targeted by John Davis' study of the views of black men toward crime and law, Charles Reason's study of prisoners' rights, Larry D. Trujillo's analysis of the criminological scholarship on Chicanos, and Homer Yearwood's critique of police discrimination against blacks. In addition, in 1973, the editors of *Issues* also broke new ground by publishing an entire edition devoted to women with articles by Dorie Klein, Meda Chesney-Lind, Kurt Weis, Sandra S. Borges and Dale Hoffman-Bustamante.[4]

The radical staff, in addition, published articles in *The Journal of Marriage and the Family*, *Federal Probation*, *Social Problems*, *Issues in Criminology*, *Insurgent Sociologist*, *Crime and Social Justice* and so forth. Works by Platt and Schwendinger also appeared in anthologies such as *The Politics of Riot Commissions, 1917–1970*, and *Delinquency and Group Processes*.

Toward the end of the 1960s, a notable proportion of studies conducted by doctoral students began to depart from those traditionally conducted by students at the school. Graduate students, of course, continued to adopt technocratic paradigms for studying crime, crime control or managerial problems, for instance. But Lynn B. Cooper's (1976) dissertation scrutinised the expansion of the 'state repressive apparatus', spurred by the Law Enforcement Assistance Administration (LEAA). Richard C. Speiglman (1976) studied this expansion in California's prison hospital and his access to medical records exposed 'new prison walls' based on the massive and unjustified use of tranquillising drugs in treatment of MDOs, i.e., 'Mentally Disordered Offenders'.

Doctoral students also produced a penetrating series of historical police studies. Virginia Engquist Grabiner's (1976) research documented the repressive police tactics used against the militant members of the women's suffrage movement. Studies, by Joyce Clements (1975), Robert Mintz (1974) and Charles Keller (1974), investigated the economic and political factors behind the recurring employment of police forces to crush San Francisco maritime strikes, mine workers' unions and Native Americans. Discarding a 'great man theory' of policing, Michael Rustigan (1974) showed that Jeremy Bentham was not the sole catalyst for the creation of the early nineteenth century metropolitan police. Instead, the Benthamite movement in London successfully brought the first police force into being because London business interests backed it. Greg Mark (1975) scrutinised the American imperial policies expanding the opium trade in China. Vast fortunes were made as American ships (i.e., the 'China Clipper') transported tremendous quantities of opium from the near east to China. After British and American warships crushed China's attempt to block the trade, the 'foremost families' of the nation, the Cabot, Cushing, Forbes, Surges, Peabody and Delano families, poured their drug fortunes into railroads and industry. We know from Mark's study that opium trafficking backed the rise of the greatest industrial power in the world.

Significant information about the origins of criminal justice appeared in other dissertations. James Brady (1974) described the centuries-long evolution of restorative 'popular justice' in China while Gregg Barak (1974) probed the origins of the public defender system in the United States. Contrary to liberal explanations, the movement to establish a public defender system was not the outcome of progressive and humanitarian reform but rather part of a larger regulative movement occurring both inside and outside the criminal justice system.[4]

Some graduate students focused on feminist topics. Frances Coles (1974) examined the experiences of women lawyers while Julia Schwendinger's (1975) dissertation was devoted to the rape victim and her treatment by the justice system. Lynn Osborne (1973) and Drew Humphries (1973) dissected the politics of anti-homosexual and anti-abortion laws as well as the racial, gender and social class inequities in criminal justice agencies.

Race and crime was another topic. David Dodd (1972) examined the formation and disintegration of personal identity in urban Afro-America. George Napper (1971) researched the African American student movement and Llewellyn (Alex) Swan (1972) investigated the causes of race riots.

Tetsuya Fujimoto (1975) adopted ideas from political economy rather than social-control theory to explain low crime rates among Japanese immigrants who settled in California at the end of the nineteenth century. Unlike the crime rates among European immigrants who settled in northeastern cities, these low crime rates were determined by the widespread involvement of Japanese immigrants in family farming rather than in industrial labour markets and their surplus labour force.

Robert E. Meyers (1974) showed how funds for Los Angeles parks and recreation programmes were used to control the poor. During economically and politically volatile periods, the funds shifted dramatically from middle-class communities to working-class communities. But in 'normal times,' the LA government gave the lion's share of these funds to middle-class communities.

Examination of social class and delinquency produced Anthony Poveda's (1970) and Joseph Weis' (1974) studies of working-class and middle-class communities. Unlike simple-minded research encouraged by delinquent subculture and social control theories, their fieldwork focused on complex relations connecting social classes, adolescent subcultures and delinquency.

The variety of critical studies at the school was simply extraordinary. As a result of these and other studies – such as Ronald Glick's (1969) dissertation on New Left organisers in a southern community and Renee Kasinsky's (1972) study of men who escaped the draft by settling in Canada – the graduate students helped broaden the research conducted in critical criminology today.

Furthermore, the intellectual achievements at the school did not end with dissertations. A staff–student collective created an entirely new journal, *Crime and Social Justice*, devoted to radical criminology (Schwendinger and Schwendinger, 1999). The first edition featured articles on radical criminology, the political origins of American prisons, the prison movement in Scandinavia and a conference sponsored by European critical criminologists held in Florence, Italy.[6] It published 'The garrison state in a democratic society' and 'Rape myths in legal, theoretical and everyday practice' – articles addressing the unwarranted number of racially biased killings by police and the questionable view of rape in criminology. This extraordinary journal has continued to be edited by people originally associated with the school. Renamed *Social Justice: A Journal of Crime, Conflict and World Order*, the journal's twenty-fifth Anniversary Edition was published in the autumn of 1999.

The radicals published several books. Tony Platt and Lynn Cooper (1974) edited *Policing America*, and radicals at the school who formed the Staff of the Research Center on Criminal Justice (1975) produced *The Iron Fist and Velvet Glove*, dealing with topics rarely covered in criminology, such as the police–industrial complex and counterinsurgency. The Schwendingers' *Sociologists of the Chair* described the origins of corporate liberalism, the operating restrictions on academic freedom and the technocratic category, 'social control', which still dominates theoretical criminology.

The changes produced by the radicals went beyond the school. Julia Schwendinger, Tommie Hannigan, Suzie Dod and other women students joined with local Berkeley women to create the first anti-rape group in the United States, Bay Area Women Against Rape. These women forced Herrick Hospital authorities to remove the emergency room chief who treated victims like 'pieces of meat' and pressured the institution to adopt medical protocols treating rape victims as human beings.[7] They established support programmes and a telephone hotline for victims, issued community information bulletins and tacked 'street-sheets' with descriptions of rapists and their modus operandi to telephone poles. After pressuring the Berkeley DA's office and Police Department, they instituted a victim advocacy programme for court cases and created sensitivity training sessions for police officers handling rape victim cases. This vital organisation and its programmes are still active as we write.

Also, with the help of Cyril Robinson, Takagi and Schwendinger initiated discussions that led to the first radical criminology sessions at annual meetings of the American Society of Criminology. Some students and staff were servicing organisations and movements that were independent of the criminal justice agencies and, in some cases, in conflict with them. The school, therefore, was providing assistance to elements in civil society that truly symbolised and fostered democracy.

Takagi, who was at that time the first and only tenured Asian American social science professor at UCB, held the first Asian American Studies course in the United States. He helped municipal governments and police and probation departments introduce police training, cultural sensitivity training and research into the treatment of racial minorities. He was repeatedly asked by the community relations division in the Department of Justice to participate in training sessions, conferences, LEAA planning sessions and so forth as an expert on affirmative action and racial discrimination. On one occasion, the director of the division, in his introductory comments, reported that nine out of the ten black criminologists with doctorates in the United States had graduated from 'Paul Takagi's shop at Berkeley'.[8] Also, largely due to affirmative action initiated by the radicals, the School of Criminology graduated at least twenty women with doctorates before it was closed down.

About 80 per cent of the students in the doctoral programme obtained jobs in universities and research institutes. (Most are still employed today as professors, chairpersons and deans.) One of the foremost criminal justice research institutes in the United States, the Michael Hindelang Institute, is named after a student in the programme at that time. School graduates also became administrators in other public institutions and included the head of the Atlanta Police, Director of the Georgia Juvenile Justice System, Chief of Police for Charleston (North Carolina), a General in the United States Army, Chief of Detroit Police and Sheriff of San Francisco County. One of the most famous prison reformers of the last century, Tom Murton, was a graduate of the school. As Superintendent of the Arkansas Correctional System, he courageously instituted democratic reforms, exposed administrative corruption and the routine assassination of prisoners by trustees, allegedly committed at the behest of the guards. Robert Redford dramatised him and his work in the Hollywood film, *Brubaker*.

McCarthyism, US War Crimes, Anti-War Protests and the Assassination of the School

Although the school was assassinated a quarter of a century ago and the radicals were framed for the murder, the contract for the kill was actually put out by government officials, UC bureaucrats and staff whose commitment to 'friendly fascism' was bred by decades of McCarthyism and the Cold War.[9] The officials provided ordnance for the on-campus assassination team. Their arsenal of demagogic injunctions, covert surveillance, police repression and budget cuts rallied the team's supporters, neutralised its opposition and extorted cooperation and silence from the faculty at large. Ronald Reagan, who had been an informer for the House Un-American Activities Committee long before he became Governor of California in 1966, had promised to cut the budget when elected and clean up 'the mess in Berkeley'. To monitor the School of Criminology, he appointed his 'troubleshooter', Edwin Meese III, to its Advisory Council.[10] He also appointed people like Max Rafferty, the notoriously right-wing State Superintendent of Public Instruction, as UC Regents. The Regents, in turn, stepped up opposition to the campus anti-war and civil liberties movements.

The 24 Regents and their powerful associates owned and operated the State of California. None of the Regents except Max Rafferty were educators by profession. Even H. R. Haldeman, later of Watergate fame, was a Regent before he resigned to join the Nixon administration. The Regents also included people who served on the boards of directors or as CEOs of some of the largest corporations in the country.[11] They were plugged into transnational corporations with subsidiaries in Europe, the Caribbean, Latin America, Africa and Asia. Their names symbolised a who's who of the American industrial empire, with financial holdings and directorships in industry, agribusiness, mass media, financial institutions and defence and intelligence agencies.[12]

They held commanding positions in firms supported by military contracts such as the Lockheed Corporation, Stanford Research Institute, Brookings Institution, Institute for Defense Analysis, Communication Electronics Inc., Watkins-Johnson Co., Center for Strategic Studies, Asia Foundation and Hoover Institution on War, Revolution and Peace. Charles Hitch, President of UC and another member of the Regents, had previously been employed in military agencies and research institutes supported by the Pentagon before Robert McNamara appointed him Assistant Secretary of Defense. To support the US military–industrial complex, the University of California received more money than any other university system from Department of Defense agencies and foundations serving as CIA conduits.

The Regents helped ensure that Berkeley was celebrated as long as the academic staff didn't challenge the interests of their military–industrial empire. When these interests were critically spotlighted in the 1960s, however, they seized the power to veto tenure recommendations – a power traditionally given to UC chancellors.

This veto power affected the outcome of one of the most notorious academic freedom cases to occur on the Berkeley campus: the case of Tony Platt.[13] Despite favourable recommendations from two tenure review committees, the UCB Chancellor steadfastly refused to grant tenure to Platt, an assistant professor in the School of Criminology.

The school was evaluated in 1971 by 'The Wolfgang Committee' composed of nationally renowned criminologists, Martin Wolfgang, Donald Riddle, Richard Myren and James Short. This committee reported the school was 'healthier than ever before'. It found an overworked academic staff and recommended limiting the undergraduate pro- gramme. But it said the school was academically sound, the academic staff stable, student field placements in criminal justice agencies good, agency relationships existed and could be improved. Leslie Wilkins, who was Dean at this time, was considered an excellent choice. The students were firmly behind the school and the academic staff and student morale was high. Yet, even though this committee considered the school outstanding, the guardians of the military–industrial complex and corporate state abolished it in 1976.

The school was closed for several reasons. First, law enforcement officials were angered by any academic opposition to police brutality. The inescapable truth is that the police were primarily responsible for violence occurring at demonstrations throughout the San Francisco Bay Area.[14] Take, for example, police actions in October 1967 during 'Stop the Draft Week' demonstrations. On Monday, the first day, approximately 6,000 students had protested the war at an on-campus rally. On 'bloody

Tuesday', another 3,000 students – including criminology students – joined 1,000 demonstrators in an act of civil disobedience to shut down the Oakland Induction Center, which processed men drafted for the Vietnam War. Suddenly, some two hundred police officers in a rapidly advancing wedge formation kicked, clubbed and beat the unarmed and non-violent demonstrators who were blocking the Center. A policeman on the scene said the demonstrators 'weren't allowed enough time to get away'. Most of the crowd tried to back off as the wedge advanced but could not move fast enough without trampling each other. 'They handcuffed this guy,' one demonstrator reported. 'He started to move and they knocked him down. Then four policemen got on him and beat him unconscious.' A girl who talked back to police 'was molested in a most disgusting way by five policemen.' A physician called the scene a 'massacre' and, while going to the aid of an injured woman, was hit by a policeman. After asking for the policeman's badge number, he was struck in the jaw. Paul Gorman, a United Press International photographer, said he was standing on the sidewalk as the police moved forward; nevertheless, he was clubbed and kicked repeatedly in the head. The beating continued even though he pointed to his camera and repeatedly shouted that he was a press photographer (Buel and Stone, 1967).

Police commissions had denounced police violence and found it escalated rather than contained political protests. Consequently, it was no surprise to find that more than 10,000 demonstrators responded to 'bloody Tuesday' by defying the police. Up to and including Friday, students were showing up with helmets, gas masks and shields. They pushed automobiles into the streets leading to the induction centre and punctured tyres to block busloads of inductees. Police chased 'mobile units' of students that suddenly dispersed and reformed at prearranged locations to halt the centre's operation.

The Dean of the Criminology School, Joseph Lohman, who had been Sheriff of Cook County, when interviewed by a *Wall Street Journal* reporter said the police should have used non-violent alternatives, which had at times been used effectively in the 'free speech' movement sit-in in 1964.[15] Gordon Misner, an ex-police chief and a visiting professor at the school, also told the reporter that the tactics were ill advised. He suggested the demonstration could have been easily defused by temporarily moving the induction centre to the Oakland Army base.

These professional criticisms were mild compared to the response from four faculty members and a graduate student from the Criminology School.[16] A letter published in the *Daily Californian*, signed by these members, condemned the police brutality outright.[17] It called the police 'sadists' and demanded an end to police 'vengeance, brutality and terror'.

It said, the justification for police brutality 'is as old as dictatorship: "In order to enforce the law we must be free to violate it when our opponents violate it".' Speaking as teachers and citizens, the signers added: 'the right to engage in law violation to prevent crime is a contradiction – one cannot stop crime by committing it. If this is done, crime merely becomes the exclusive province of the police and a society of law and justice is destroyed from within, by its own protectors.'

Nevertheless, Charles R. Gain, Oakland's Chief of Police, defended his force's tactics even though they had previously dispersed the demonstrators effectively by resorting to non-violent mass arrest on Monday. Governor Reagan declared: 'The police action – swift and effective – was in the finest tradition of California's law enforcement agencies.' Don Fach, President of the California Peace Officers Research Association, denounced the critics from the School of Criminology. His 'open letter' was sent to Governor Reagan, the Board of Regents, the International Association of Chiefs of Police, California law enforcement agencies and Dean Lohman,[18] indignantly declaring that the police hadn't confused 'necessary force with brutality'. The criminology academics, he said, were 'unprofessional' because their public statements undermined police attempts to block 'government by mob rule'.[19]

The Director of the Federal Bureau of Investigation, J. Edgar Hoover, received the letter from Fach even though his agency was as guilty as the Oakland police of abrogating the democratic rights of citizens. The FBI had forged letters and sent undercover agents to provoke dissension among civil rights leaders, spreading rumours about Martin Luther King and others to discredit them. Fred Hampton, a Black Panther leader, was assassinated by the Chicago police department at the instigation of memos and agents from the FBI. In Oakland, the Black Panther Party had started community self-help programmes, a breakfast programme for children and educational forums and classes. But these reformist changes did not safeguard their headquarters from FBI-backed police raids that planted weapons, stole precinct lists and vandalised offices.[20]

Subsequently, in 1968 and 1969, police were used on nearly one hundred campuses, the National Guard on six. More than 4,000 demonstrators were arrested. At Texas Southern University and in Orangeburg, South Carolina, black students were shot and killed. The National Guard occupied the black ghetto of Wilmington, Delaware, for nine months. Over a thousand Black Panther Party members were arrested in a nationally coordinated round up. The two central events that year in Berkeley were the student strike led by the Third World Liberation Front (TWLF), spearheaded by Asian students and the Black Student Union, which demanded the establishment of a Third World

Studies department; the second event was the destruction of People's Park. Massive retaliatory violence against demonstrators was employed in both of these events.

But the Cambodian invasion provoked the greatest crisis in the history of the university. The Criminology Students Association (CSA) voted unanimously to back a general strike to which the criminology staff of the school overwhelmingly assented. Furthermore, despite Reagan's attempt to contain further disorder by closing down the public universities and colleges in California, thousands of students swarmed on campus to hold teach-ins, rallies and organising sessions devoted to ending the war. Their endless agitation amplified the popular outrage that forced Nixon, three months after the invasion, to withdraw US troops from Cambodia. The invasion had turned into a military and political catastrophe.[21]

A generation that did not live through this historical period may not fully understand the crimes committed by the US government during the war. In 1971, the publication of the 'Pentagon Papers', a historical study with 4,000 classified documents, written by officers who had served in Vietnam, revealed that the government had repeatedly lied to the public about the origin of the war.[22] For example, in 1957, the Viet Minh insurgents, France and its colonial South Vietnamese government, agreed to a ceasefire that would be followed by a democratic election. Realising that the Viet Minh would win the election, the US subverted the agreement.[23] It then engineered the overthrow of the South Vietnamese government and its replacement with a military dictatorship. It committed what the Nuremberg Tribunal had called a war crime, *the crime of aggression*, by invading Vietnam in support of the illegitimate dictatorship.

The Pentagon Papers demonstrated that the anti-war movement had been right all along. The crimes committed by US forces were astounding. Ignoring the distinction between civilians and combatants in the rules of war, American planes dropped countless antipersonnel bombs that each released several hundred pellets to kill or wound all living creatures within two-thirds of a square mile – even in the most densely populated parts of North Vietnam cities. In 1966, 25 provincial cities were bombed – six of which were completely razed. The city of Dong Hoi – covering an area of 3.2 square kilometres, and with 16,000 inhabitants – was bombed 396 times, including 160 night attacks. Of the 110 district centres, 72 were bombed, leaving 12 of them in ruins and 25 completely destroyed. Furthermore, such bombing, as indicated, was not restricted to the North. In the South, residential areas, schools, hospitals, clinics and churches were bombed. High explosive bombs, fragmentation bombs, napalm bombs and antipersonnel bombs pounded regions occupied by the Vietcong. United States forces dropped herbicides and so-called 'defoliants' that destroyed hundreds of thousands of farming acres.[24] On returning from a session with President Johnson and his advisers in 1967, John Naughton, an Assistant Secretary of Defense, admitted: 'We seem to be proceeding on the assumption that the way to eradicate the Vietcong is to destroy all the village structures, defoliate all the jungles, and then cover the entire surface of South Vietnam with asphalt.'[25]

The United States violated every law about the conduct of nations at war. During the '25 days of horror' inflicted in March 1968 in response to the Tet Offensive, United States bombers reduced Hue, a city occupied by the Vietcong, to rubble. Further atrocities – such as the My Lai massacre and the systematic torture and execution of political dissenters and prisoners of war – demonstrated how far US troops and their South Vietnamese allies were willing to go in violating the law. The 'carpet bombing', 'free fire zones' and 'search and destroy' missions employed by the United States were comparable to the genocidal warfare conducted by Europeans and their descendants against Native Americans in North America.

United States campaigns were also comparable to crimes committed by Nazi Germany in occupied nations. The NLF controlled most of the territory of South Vietnam. To wrest territorial control, the US forcibly depopulated NLF regions through so-called 'pacification campaigns'. After investigating the 'pacification' of Kien Hao in the Mekong Delta, for instance, Kevin Buckley, a Saigon bureau chief for Newsweek, disclosed: 'All the evidence I gathered pointed to a clear conclusion: a staggering number of non-combatant civilians – perhaps as many as 5,000 according to one official – were killed by US firepower to "pacify" Kien Hoa. The death total there made the My Lai massacre look trifling by comparison.'[26] After terrorising and killing people in these regions, the US forcibly relocated tens of thousands of men, women and children in detention camps near urban centres. Simultaneously, secret CIA operations such as the Phoenix Program assassinated over 20,000 suspected NLF guerrillas, many of them innocent civilians.

But the government's crimes were not confined to McNamara's 'dirty war' in Southeast Asia. Voices had also been raised against crimes committed in Africa and other parts of the world. The State Department and CIA had created monsters such as Idi Amin in Uganda and General Mobutu in Zaire while subverting, imprisoning or killing national-liberation leaders including Patrice Lumumba in the Congo, Kwame Nkrumah in Ghana and Nelson Mandela in South Africa. Intelligence agencies and United States military policies had propped up or installed homicidal regimes in Southern Rhodesia, Portuguese Angola, Mozambique, Guinea-Bissau and South Africa.

Some links between several members of the Berkeley academic staff and the harms committed by government agencies turned out to be extraordinary. While the United States secretly armed the Indonesian military, for instance, one staff member served as a consultant for a CIA-subsidised 'think tank', the Rand Corporation. He urged his contacts in the Indonesian military to assassinate President Sukarno because his policy of 'national conciliation' included the Indonesian Communist Party (PKI). The CIA helped destabilise the Indonesian economy as a result of an official State Department recommendation in 1962, which he helped write. When the destabilisation occurred, a special Military Training Advisory Group was set up in Jakarta to set the stage for the 1965 assassination and coup. Finally, Suharto, the dictator installed by the military, ruthlessly initiated what the CIA itself has called 'one of the worst mass murders in the twentieth century'. Almost a million Indonesians were massacred. During the slaughter, observers reported rivers running with blood, filled with corpses of men, women and children, killed because they were family or friends of people supporting the PKI.

Finally, the radicals were revolted by the hypocrisy, corruption and 'high crimes and misdemeanours' exhibited at top levels of government. President Nixon was guilty of impeachable offences – not because he had sex with an intern but because he sanctioned the illegal suppression of political opponents and requisitioned burglaries, illegal phone taps, money laundering and other criminal activities aimed at subverting political dissent and democratic elections. Vice President Spiro Agnew, who was eventually convicted of bribe-taking, repeatedly posed with Nixon as a champion of 'law and order'. As the Criminology School was being set up for the kill, the former UC Regent, H. R. Haldeman, and Attorney General John N. Mitchell were spilling the beans about their involvement in the unlawful Watergate conspiracy.[27]

How in the world could the most conscientious criminology students and academic staff, whose very subject was crime, remain silent in the face of these criminal developments? These people wrote, lectured and participated in one demonstration after another, especially as the war crimes came to light. On the other hand, many at the school were not radicalised by these events. Certainly, some students and academic staff objected to those who were because they themselves supported the war. Still others who were fearful or apolitical went no farther than signing a petition or complaining that the radicals interfered with their careers or education. Reminded years later about their responses, we recalled a story told about Ralph Waldo Emerson and his friend, Henry David Thoreau, who had been jailed for opposing the war against Mexico by refusing to pay taxes. On seeing Thoreau behind bars, Emerson exclaimed, 'Henry, what are you doing in there?' Thoreau replied, 'What are *you* doing out there?'

Moving On

The sources of radical criminology reached beyond Berkeley (Michalowski, 1996). Students at the school were avidly reading publications by scholars who were developing compatible perspectives especially toward law and the state. In the United States, Canada, Britain and Australia, William Chambliss, Richard Quinney, Ian Taylor, Paul Walton, Jock Young, Frank Pierce, Gill Boehringer, Michael Ignatieff, David Brown and others were enriching radical criminology. Scholars like Falco Werkentin, Dario Melosi, Thomas Mathiesen and Rosa Del Olmo from West Germany, Italy, Norway, Venezuela and other countries were espousing similar standpoints. During the immediate years following the school's demise, international and Australian journals (*Contemporary Crisis*, *The International Journal of the Sociology of Law* and *Alternative Criminology Journal*) appeared. Prisoners' movements, left-wing political parties and criminal justice reform groups, were also providing comparable works on popular justice, prison conditions, crimes by state officials and corporate heads, and criminogenic characteristics of capitalism.

But the sharp swing to the right in American politics manifested itself everywhere. In 1979, James Inciardi and a group of mainstream criminologists attacked the radicals in a special edition of *Criminology*, the official journal of the American Society of Criminology. This edition, devoted to radical criminology, was unprecedented. It was the first time any professional society had published a separate edition of its official journal aimed at discrediting an up-and-coming theoretical and policy perspective in its field.[28]

Yet, despite this unprofessional and mean-spirited assault, the body of knowledge identified as radical criminology kept growing. Subsequently, the editor of *Crime and Delinquency* and the *Insurgent Sociologist* countered *Criminology* by publishing special editions devoted to radical criminology (Garofalo, 1981). New anthologies and textbooks appeared. Finally, because 'radical criminology' was (and still is) identified with left-wing and Marxist writings, it has been replaced by the umbrella term 'critical criminology', which signifies wider resistance to established institutions and their technocratic standpoints. Today, the numbers of publications epitomising the populist, anarchist, feminist, left-liberal, Marxist, peacemaking, postmodern and cultural standpoints of critical criminologists have become so large, it is difficult to keep up with them.

Some books and anthologies published by critical criminologists deal, among others topics, with gender, race, class and crime, capitalism and crime, violence and inequality, the politics of injustice, the political economy of justice, state crimes, crimes against women, corporate crimes, subcultural crimes and hate crimes (Iadicola and Shupe, 1998; Henry and Lanier, 2001; Renzetti and Goodstein, 2001; Messerschmidt, 1997; Barak, Flavin and Leighton, 2001; Beckett and Sasson, 2000; Lynch and Michalowski, 2000; Schwartz and Milovanovic, 1996; Ferrell and Sancers, 1995; Friedrichs, 1996; Hamm, 1993; Daly, 1999; Arrigo, 1999, Barak, 1991; Greenberg, 1993, Ross, 1998.).[29] And, of course, notable articles not found in anthologies are published in periodicals, including Jim Petras' (2001) startling exposé of the billions laundered with impunity annually by major American banks.

Obviously, we cannot wrap up this chapter by covering everything. We certainly cannot with our limited space do justice to changes in criminal justice or political standpoints epitomised by left-realism and peacemaking criminology, for instance. We will instead devote the remainder of this chapter to clarifying epistemological differences between two largely incompatible theoretical trajectories. Our reasons for this seemingly arbitrary choice will be self-evident when we are done.

The Postmodern Challenge

At the school, radical students usually relied on conflict theory or political economy when dealing with macroscopic relationships.[30] By the turn of the millennium, however, a new perspective, *postmodern criminology*, appeared in opposition to these standpoints.

To understand this development, we should recall that the originators of postmodernism were literary critics from the humanities who questioned the a priori existence of 'objective reality' confirmed by scientific methods (Baudrillard, 1981; Lyotard, 1984). These critics argued that endlessly changing conditional social interactions generated human institutions via the medium of language. Presumably, these interactions – and their linguistic mediations – in turn generated social systems, such as capitalism. But a causal analysis of such systems was deemed irrelevant unless it conformed to rules developed by literary criticism rather than science. Scientific methods and causal analysis were no truer than other methods for knowing the world as constructed by novelists, theologians or ordinary people, for instance.

Social relations, for these literary idealists, were composed of relations among 'signs' rather than material relations. Consequently, the deconstruction and reconstruction of discourse is the primary medium through which social reality is originally established. The idealists assumed that language also functioned as the principal agent of social change. However, what passed for objectivity and truth 'was really just one possible story about social reality'. Reality, in this theory of knowledge, is available only as 'texts', read by people in all walks of life (Wonders, 1999: 116).

Fortunately, the veracity of scientific knowledge has never relied upon epistemological procedures developed by literary critics. Granted, the relations between concepts and 'real things' may be arbitrary in so far as they are determined by language conventions. And concepts that purport to be mirror images of 'real things' may be illusions. But does this mean that scientific practices produce nothing but illusions and that scientific theories are merely stories or texts? Scientists cannot be absolutely certain about the truthfulness of their theories but their procedures for falsifying them are more reliable than literary critics are for spotting illusions. They are reliable enough to have contributed substantially to historically unprecedented advances in knowledge and technology; furthermore, since the sixteenth century when scientists were burned at the stake or confined to house arrest, the theories tested by these procedures do not have to be taken on faith merely because an ecclesiastic court believed them.

Therefore, the issue concerning postmodernism is not whether fictional narratives can help social scientists understand reality. Indeed, they most certainly can help scientists understand the world. However, Baudrillard's belief that works of fiction can tell us as much about society as scientific theories implicitly assumes that scientific methods have nothing to do with the ways theories are constructed or that scientific methods are irrelevant for determining truth. This implication cannot be true: if science were merely another form of fiction – if it did not lead to truths that could be put to use – we would lack the vast technology that we employ in daily life such as automobiles, aeroplanes, spectacles, electric power and modern medicine. Writers of fiction may imagine such things but scientific practices help create them.

Hence Baudrillard's theory of language is wrong. Scientific practices profoundly affect the linguistic structures of scientific theories.[31] Furthermore, these practices aim at the *discovery* of social relationships – not just *proving* theories about them. Therefore, they require some understanding of the degree to which methods and logics of discovery differ from the methods and logics of proof. They require an appreciation of the necessity for distinguishing between pre-theoretic and theoretical thinking, which facilitate scientific practices that produce genuinely new theories, and theoretical thinking that can be readily falsified.

Because they serve very different purposes, the language of literary criticism is infinitely less disciplined than the language of science. To advance empirical knowledge, scientists refer to 'useful fictions' but they are not the kinds of ironic, playful and unconventional fictions literary critics have in mind. Postmodernists have evolved qualitatively different types of discourse because they are engaged in qualitatively different kinds of activity.

To some degree elements from postmodern discourse and scientific discourse can be combined, thereby producing a hybrid discourse. Postmodernist variants like 'constitutive criminology' and 'postmodern feminism' usually construct theoretical (i.e. causal) explanations that have little to do with 'narratives'.[32] While Baudrillard is left behind in one regard, he is followed in another, because postmodern criminologists devalue scientific methods for discovering and verifying truth. Despite their 'postmodernity', they occupy a domain once modelled after C. P. Snow's depiction of 'two cultures' in British universities. In criminology, however, the attempt to straddle the cultures, formed by the humanities and natural sciences, is basically forced by a tacit allegiance to the classical (postmodernist) dismissal of research practices devoted to measurement. And it is expressed by the pejorative and indiscriminate use of the word 'positivism', to dismiss any research enterprise or any school of thought (from social Darwinism to Marxism) that takes the epistemological importance of measurement for granted.

This paradoxical stance has confusing consequences. Postmodernist theories are overflowing with metaphors, analogies and literary illusions because their capacity to imagine an infinite number of human possibilities is not reigned in by scientific conventions. Sometimes their imaginations produce astonishing insights into the nature of social reality. At other times, their visions of this reality are totally fictitious. Psychoanalytic propositions regarding the Oedipal complex, penis envy, the unconscious and the interpretation of dreaming and homosexuality, for instance, have been devastated by modern empirical research (Torrey, 1992). Yet, postmodern criminologists go merrily along and use these propositions as if they are true or concoct 'psychoanalytic semiotics' without regard to their empirical track record in psychology.

When employing causal analysis, postmodern thinking usually (but not always) encourages criminologists to study crime and crime control without the aid of macroscopic theories. Unlike traditional criminologists and their sterile survey methods, the postmodern perspective at least promises in-depth examination of subjective relationships and observable social interactions. It favours 'verstehen' (or 'deconstruction') when 'reading' (or 'explaining') these interactions, and it contends that social policies aimed at 'hierarchies of power and inequality' are ineffective unless personal opinion, public discourse, linguistic conventions and culture are 'reconstructed'. 'It is through discourse (language and symbol use) that we conceive of and act to produce our world,' according to Henry and Milovanovic (2001a).

Cultural criminology, another emerging standpoint, has been influenced by postmodernism as well as cultural studies, critical theory and interactionist sociology, according to Jeff Ferrell (1999). Cultural criminology, Ferrell declares, boldly aims at the study of the entire cultural world including 'the stylised frameworks and experiential dynamics of illicit subcultures', the 'symbolic criminalisation of popular culture form', the culturally 'mediated construction' of crime control, the 'representations of crime and crime control in mass media' and the mutually interacting impact of these representations on 'popular audiences and the culture of policing'. Ferrell's postmodernism may tell us why his aims do not refer to structural determinants, but his research agenda does promise to fill the barren landscape left by mainstream theories of subcultural relationships.

In the 1990s, some postmodern criminologists hinted at outright macroscopic theories of social processes. In a fascinating article, Christopher Williams and Bruce Arrigo (2001), for instance, inverted Thomas Hobbes' speculative justification for the state. They posited stateless societies as the 'natural order of things' while the historical abandonment of this order – through the 'artificial insertion' of the state into society – has produced crime, unemployment, inequality and environmental disasters.[33] Their anarchistic inversion may be as speculative as Hobbes' *Leviathan*; nonetheless, it could prove useful because it does not take the legitimating functions of the state for granted and it justifies deeper inquiries into the historical evolution of the destructive consequences of state policies.

Finally, some postmodern criminologists, despite extensive engagement with postmodern linguistic analyses, are experimenting with macro system theories. But, before we justify our paradoxical classification of their writings, recall that systems theory was fashionable in the 1950s and early 1960s when social scientists believed they could explain complex systems where causes and effects all interacted with one another.[34] Because of their interest in managerial problems, the early systems analysts formulated 'cybernetic theories', 'social-control theories' and 'information-flow theories' that emphasised self-regulation, feedback, deviation and conformity, information flows and entropy.[35] To avoid the shortcomings of equilibrium analysis, some even focused on social change and 'open systems' or utilised physical laws such as the second law of thermodynamics as causal mechanisms (i.e. Maggroh, 1968).

Currently, the fashionable analogue of 'chaos' or 'complexity' theory epitomises the macro systems trend among post-modern criminologists. In *The End of Certainty: Time, Chaos, and the New Laws of Nature*, Ilya Prigogine (1997) employs the laws of physics to explain unstable 'time-irreversible' phenomena. Since these physical laws follow empirical scientific conventions, they are expressed by mathematical equations that predict, among other things, the variable motion of fluids, molecules or atomic particles. Furthermore, in dealing with physical realities, Prigogine's theory, among other things, takes note of molecular changes, called 'bifurcations', in atmospheric currents or hydraulic relationships. He assumes that these bifurcations are caused by causal mechanisms having to do, for instance, with the effects of temperature on molecular collisions and thermal diffusion. However, as adapted by postmodern criminologists, 'chaos theory' in our opinion is *a systems analogue* of Prigogine's theory. Hence, even though it is dubbed 'chaos theory' and merely regarded as just another postmodern theory, it is a macro social-system theory. Finally, since Prigogine's theory deals with physical rather than social realities, analogous reasoning in this context relies on similarities in form rather than content, because it cannot credibly substitute the laws of physics for the social mechanisms actually causing changes in the properties of social systems as they move from one phase state to another.

On the other hand, criminology – especially mainstream criminology – overflows with macro theories that have no relation to reality. Analogical reasoning may not conform to 'logics of proof' but it is justified by 'logics of discovery'. This reasoning under certain conditions can help reduce conceptual confusion experienced when researchers, who are confronted with unknown dynamic and complex relationships, realise that their received wisdom is worthless. Consequently, as long as criminologists are aware of its limitations, analogical models such as 'chaos theory' may prompt the discovery of new relationships and advance critical criminology as an empirical science.

Berkeley and Beyond

From 1973 on, some professors at the Berkeley School legitimated the closing. In a confidential memo to the Berkeley Academic Senate Committee on Educational Policy, for instance, Jerry Skolnick expressed agreement that the school ought to be phased out. 'It seems to me', he added, 'that historically the school has suffered from extremes: either the police and correctional orientation of earlier generations, or the antithesis – the grandly systemic, Marxist orientation of a sizeable proportion of the current generation of faculty.' While this estimation undoubtedly pleased the authorities, it was decidedly inaccurate: although other faculty members also fought for civil rights and social justice, only two assistant professors had actually become Marxists.

On the other hand, a 'sizeable proportion' of students at the school had become deeply immersed in a political subculture sparked by teach-ins, publications, speeches, posters and songs. This subculture familiarised students with Marxist ideas about capitalism, class conflict, class ideology and American imperialism. Furthermore, as anyone familiar with American universities would know, students truly interested in Marxism rarely depended on academic staff to learn about historical materialism and the distinctions between 'levels of reality' in Marxist epistemology.[36] Due to its close association with the four-letter word, M-A-R-X, in an inherently conservative discipline, it was inevitable that radical criminology would be attacked by mainstream criminologists like Inciardi. But the attacks featured caricatures of radical ideas and stimulated polemic debates that were politically situated rather than scholarly. For example, the unfounded allegation that radical theory was abstract and could not be subjected to empirical investigation was, in later years, repeated so often that it became accepted. Rather than provide proof for this allegation, mainstream criminologists dismissed the radical challenge especially to structural-functional paradigms without benefit of the scientific canons that supposedly supported the criminological enterprise. Because of their shortage in criminology, Marxian political economists have produced fewer empirical studies than other criminologists; nevertheless their studies provide sufficient proof for the empirical value of their theories.

The phrase 'radical criminology' was often identified with Marxian ideas; consequently, radical criminologists were confronted by criticism from critical criminologists as well as mainstream criminologists. Ten years after the publication of the Inciardi edition was put to rest, Aogan O'Maolchatha and Jim Thomas raised it from the dead. These critical criminologists argued, 'Limited though the outcome [of traditional criminology] has been, it is much more constructive than turning to the new, radical, conflict, or Marxist criminology. After more than 20 years, we suspect that the principal product of that turn has been hot air, heat but no real light (Gibbs, 1987a: 3).'[37]

While O'Maolchatha and Thomas were trying to embalm radical criminology, they remained optimistic about three 'new developments' that were replacing the stale air in their morgue with the sweet smell of spring. Two of them, peacemaking and left realism, were deemed entirely 'new' even though the Berkeley radicals had recommended restorative justice and promoted the capture of rapists through police training, 'street sheets', 'hot lines' and rapid collection of evidence. (These radicals even fought for legislation aimed at reorganising Berkeley police so that it could be more effective in African American communities.) Still, O'Maolchatha and Thomas were right about the striking novelty of the third development: Berkeley radicals were not postmodernists.

We wish to reserve our closing comments, however, to recent work in our own field. The work of Berkeley criminologists continued after the closure of the school. American 'left realism', for example, has an eloquent voice in Elliot Currie (Currie, 1999). By 1989, the number of Marxist criminologists had shrunk. After all, most Marxists were not in a position to teach doctoral students, and the political conditions that had encouraged students to undergo the time-consuming self-study required learning Marxian ideas had abated.

Still, Marxists kept their red flag flying and their empirical studies continued to focus attention on the relationship between economic marginalisation, crime causation and crime control by utilising measures of labour force participation (unemployment rates) and class struggle (economic inequality). Early foundational studies marked an important step in critical model building (e.g. Greenberg, 1977; Gordon, 1971; Box and Hale, 1982; Jacobs, 1981, 1979; Jacobs and Britt, 1979; Jankovic, 1977). As Robert Bohm (1985) points out, there was nothing inherently radical in the connection between unemployment, inequality and crime. Orthodox criminologists also posited a relationship between these social factors and crime (e.g. Freeman, 1983). What made this connection radical was the theoretical context of the argument and data connecting unemployment and inequality to the normal historical development and economic cycles evident in capitalist economies.

Conceptual and methodological innovations featuring uniquely radical measures followed the early work on capital accumulation and crime published by Humphries and Wallace (1980). In addition, the rate of surplus value – an objective measure of labour's alienation, exploitation and marginalisation and an indicator of class struggle – has been repeatedly connected to crime, policing and imprisonment trends (Lizotte, Mercy and Monkkenon, 1982; Lynch, 1987, 1988; Lynch, Groves and Lizotte, 1994; Nalla, Lynch and Leiber, 1997; Lessan, 1991). Furthermore, long-wave theories of capitalist development (Kondratieff, 1935; Gordon, 1980) have been employed to explain trends in criminal justice legislation (Barlow and Barlow, 1995; Barlow, Barlow and Johnson,

1996; Lynch, Hogan and Stretetsky, 1999). Here, an expansion of criminal laws especially designed to control marginal members of the labour force is expected during the contraction phase of economic development. In addition, Raymond Michalowski and Susan Carlson (1999; Carlson and Michalowski, 1997) have extended this premise by adopting the 'social structures of accumulation' perspective to examine the historically conditioned relationship between unemployment, crime and imprisonment trends during different phases of capitalist development.

In addition, recent studies have incorporated themes from the environmental justice literature to examine the relationship between the class and racial composition of areas and their proximity and exposure to hazardous waste sites and wastes (Stretesky and Hogan, 1998; Stretesky and Lynch, 1999a, 1999b). This research uses geographic analysis to highlight three important issues: (1) the effects of race and class conflict on the siting of hazardous waste production and processing facilities and exposure to toxic hazards; (2) the corporate violence and issues of responsibility with respect to class- and race-related exposure patterns (Lynch and Stretesky, 1999; Stretesky and Lynch, 1999b; Lynch, Stretesky and Hammond, 2000); and (3) the relationship between exposure to behaviour-altering toxins such as lead (Pb) and the geography of race and class (Lynch and Stretesky, 1998; 2000; Stretesky and Lynch, 2001).

The studies above use official data and statistical procedures. But the Schwendingers' recent work utilises data and procedures aimed at discovering social psychological and organisational relationships.[38] After describing the historical development of social class, community and school relationships generated by changes in the capitalist mode of production, they employed the analytic 'method of progressive concretion' developed by Marxists (Dos Santos, 1970; Engels, 1939) to explain relationships not distinguished by macroscopic theory. These relationships converge on adolescent subcultures in the US during the second half of the twentieth century.

Unlike postmodernists who tacitly dismiss the need to develop a quantifiable research technology, the Schwendingers' *epistemological stance* forces them to become methodologists as well as theoreticians. They have proposed (1997) a solution to the 'micro/macro sociological divide' that exploits the interplay between ethnographic observations, small group experiments and methods for graphing networks of informal groups. This proposal embodies 'a Galilean strategy' because it recognises the impact of research technologies on the sixteenth-century Galilean revolution in the organisation of science. Science's rapid theoretical advances at that time depended on the invention of telescopes and experiments with inclined planes, for instance, to obtain knowledge about planetary motions and the effects of gravity on the acceleration of rolling objects.

Hence to advance the study of subcultural identities, the Schwendingers developed a comprehensive 'social type rating method' that employed photographs of several thousand students and over 300 rating teams. They constructed a mathematical algorithm that utilised over 20,000 friendship choices to map the social networks sustaining these identities.[39] And they asked adolescent informants to provide information about their best friends in order to estimate the delinquency parameters of their peer networks. The sociographs produced with these procedures are akin to X-rays and other devices for discovering patterns that have advanced knowledge of the physical universe (Schwendinger and Schwendinger, 1997).

To assess the 'modes of moral rhetoric' expressed in peer groups and to refute Sykes and Matza's 'techniques of neutralisation' theory, the Schwendingers conducted small group experiments in the field – in alleys, parks and at a children's camp. To understand how ephemeral markets composed of adolescent demand and supply crowds worked, they constructed marketplace flow diagrams with the help of high-status marketeers. Ethnographic observations of peer groups from middle-class and working-class communities can also be added to these methods. In fact, Herman Schwendinger's four-year record as a participant observer was not broken until Martin Sanchez Jankowski, another critical criminologist, conducted an insightful ten-year study that led to *Islands in the Streets*.

This is a suitably inconclusive note on which to close. For although this chapter has been in part retrospective, the theoretical trajectories arising from the pioneering body of critical scholarship associated with the short-lived but stunning achievements of the Berkeley School of Criminology remain a work in progress.

Notes

1. The course description, evaluation and readings can be found in Barry Krisberg (1974).
2. This course among other things exposed students to ethnography, sociometric analyses, small group experiments and the writings of Charles Pierce and other pragmatists interested in scientific thinking.
3. Including interviews with Marie Bertrand, Richard Quinney, Ian Taylor, Paul Walton and Jock Young.
4. These editors included June Kress, Virginia Engquist Grabiner, Cynthia

Mahabir, Wayne Lawrence, Eleanor Evans, Susan Barnes and Tommie Hannigan.

5. It was also created to delegitimise critics of class-biased justice and to abolish the requirement of 'rotation', thereby unburdening corporate lawyers from defending indigents.

6. A small group from the school attended this conference.

7. To force compliance, the group actually prevented the hospital from receiving a federal grant.

8. Apparently, eight had doctorates but the ninth may not have completed his degree.

9. This phrase is borrowed from Bertram Gross (1980).

10. Using the word 'troubleshooter', for Meese, is derived from Bob Woodward (1999). See his coverage of President Reagan's Irangate and Contragate.

11. Including the Hearst Foundation, Security Pacific National Bank, Western Bancorporation, Broadway-Hale Stores, First Surety Corporation, Stanford Bank, Commonwealth Assurance Corporation, Crown-Zellerbach Corporation, Pacific Lighting Co., Arizona Bancorporation, Southern California Edison, Pauley Petroleum, Del Monte Foods, Irvine Foundation, DiGiorgio Company, Norton Simon Inc., the 230,000-acre Tejon Ranch Co., Safeway Stores, Bell Brand Foods, Dresser Industries, Pan American World Airways, Western Airlines, Air West, F. E. Young Construction Company, Kaiser Steel, Crucible Steel, Atcheson Topeka and Sante Fe Railway Company, Northern Pacific Railroad and more than 20 other large corporations and utilities.

12. The raw power and influence of the Regents extended beyond California. They were also owners or on the boards of directors of corporations that controlled such conservative media as: the Associated Press and King Features Syndicate, the *San Francisco Examiner*, *Saturday Review*, *US News and World Report* and Scholastic Publications. They also owned *McCall's*, *Redbook*, *Popular Science*, *Good Housekeeping*, *Avon Paperbacks*, *Harper's Bazaar*, and so on.

13. An equally notorious case involved Ely Katz, an assistant professor in the early 1960s. He had refused to cooperate with the House Un-American Activities Committee when it asked whether he had been a member of the Communist Party. He was fired from the university because he refused to answer the same question when UCB Chancellor Strong posed it. He then sued the university and forced it to rehire him. However, despite favourable recommendations from his tenure review committee and a Dean, he was denied tenure.

14. Granted, a few Berkeley students (who were not in criminology) may have engaged in vandalism or arson during the 1969 Third World Strike. Also, 'crazies', as they were called, in anti-war demonstrations along Telegraph Avenue and Shattuck Avenues, indiscriminately smashed windows – including windows of merchants who *supported* the anti-war movement. But this gratuitous and disorganised violence pales in comparison with the organised and systematic clubbing and beatings by the police. (The 'crazies' usually lived hand-to-mouth in the residential area or streets south of the campus near Telegraph Avenue and some even set fire to a couple of rooms in the basement of Stephens Hall because, to them, the words 'criminology' and 'repression' may have been synonymous. The basement included the Criminalistics laboratory

and offices, a few graduate student offices and H. Schwendinger's data-processing office.)

15. Similar peaceful tactics were used during the initial days of 'Stop the Draft Week'.

16. A few School of Social Welfare academic staff signed the letter. It was also signed by criminology professors Gordon Misner, Richard Korn, Bernard Diamond, Herman Schwendinger and David Fogel (at that time a graduate student).

17. 'Professors protest brutality', *The Daily Californian*, 19 Thursday October, 1967, p. 8 (editorial page).

18. Don Fach, 'Letter to Joseph Lohman from the Peace Officers Research Association of California', 24 November 1967. (This letter was distributed by Lohman to faculty and staff on 5 December 1967 to get their reactions before he drafted his reply.) Fach also demanded that Dean Lohman publicly repudiate the statements in the *Wall Street Journal* and *The Daily Californian*.

19. But the confrontations were not merely expressed in violent encounters. In fact, to stop the cycle of violence in Berkeley, some radicals at the School of Criminology began to work with the Black Panther Party and Ron Dellums, the black Congressman who represented Alameda County, at finding peaceful solutions. This attempt, however, only deepened the antagonism between the radicals and the police.

20. For the FBI campaign against political dissidents, see Brian Glick (1989).

21. The military withdrawal, however, did not undo the harm done to protesters. At Kent State four students were killed and ten were wounded by gunfire; at Jackson State two students were killed and 12 wounded. In Augusta, Georgia six black students were killed; the police and National Guard wounded twenty. At the University of New Mexico 11 students were bayoneted. Altogether, during May 1970, over a hundred people were killed or seriously wounded by police and guardsmen. More than 2,000 people were arrested in the first two weeks of May alone. A demonstration called by the anti-war groups brought out over 100,000 people to Washington, DC on a week's notice, to be faced with over 25,000 police and soldiers.

22. Anyone still convinced that the Vietnam War was justified should read McNamara's recollections, published in 1999. He called the war 'a mistake'. He said (p. 22) it was started by the US because he and other government leaders believed in the 'domino theory', which never proved true, and because they had *wrongly* believed North Vietnam leaders were Soviet puppets. What they actually found was 'a war in the South [Vietnam] that was fundamentally a war among southerners' (p. 418).

23. The Pentagon Papers showed that the Vietnamese insurgents would have won a democratic election if the US had not sabotaged the 1954 Geneva settlement and ceasefire agreement between the French and Vietminh (which represented insurgents throughout Vietnam).

24. Meanwhile, United States troops on the ground threw suffocating 'tear gases' and other chemical weapons into shelters and underground tunnels where women and children hid from bombs and artillery shells. This country's South Vietnamese allies used poison gas as well.

25. Quoted in Christopher Hitchens (2001: 28–9).
26. Quoted in Hitchens (2001: 31).
27. Mitchell was Attorney General from 1969 to 1972 and, after conviction in the Watergate case, was disbarred in 1975.
28. The radicals tried but failed to get the Society to rectify this unprofessional affair by allowing them to edit a special edition of their own.
29. Entire issues of *Crime and Social Justice* (or *Social Justice*) were published in the 1980s and 1990s on state terrorism, human rights and justice, struggles for justice, dynamics of the informal economy, justice policies in Canada and the US, etc.
30. Conflict theory is not Marxian theory. It is largely composed of pluralist and 'interest group' theories.
31. Among other things, they require that scientific propositions can eventually be expressed by hypothetical constructs.
32. For current postmodern 'threads,' see Milovanovic (2000) and Barak, Henry and Milovanovic (1997).
33. Their 'theory' of what constitutes a 'natural order' also turns St Thomas Aquinas on his head. Aquinas contended that God established 'natural laws' justifying the feudal state (i.e. the rule of the prince). In his view, the abandonment of the state in favour of democratic rule of necessity brought about disorder and destruction. For the concept of natural social law, see Schwendinger and Schwendinger (1974).
34. See, for example, Walter Buckley (1968: xiv).
35. See, for example, Nett (1968), Mackay (1968) and Easton (1968). Most of these types of theories were originally published in the 1950s and early 1960s.
36. Students were offered individual essays in some required readings but no Marxist course had ever been offered at the school.
37. One good turn deserves another. For anyone interested in what Marxists think of postmodernism (in criminology or elsewhere), see Russell's (1997) learned article.
38. In sociology, these are at times referred to as 'mezzodomain' relationships because they lie between macro and microsociological levels of reality.
39. Some sociographs and current writings can be found on their personal (http://home.earthlink.net/~schwendh/) or university homepages.

Bibliography

Arrigo, Bruce A. (ed.) (1999) *Social Justice: The Maturation of Critical Theory in Law, Crime, and Deviance.* CA: Belmont, CA: West/Wadsworth.
Barak, G. (1974) *In Defense of the Poor: The Emergence of the Public Defender System in the United States (1900–1920)* in PhD Dissertation. Berkeley, CA: University of California, School of Criminology.
Barak, G. (ed.) (1991) *Crimes by the Capitalist State: An Introduction to State Criminality.* Albany: State University of New York Press.
Barak, G., Flavin, J. M. and Leighton, P. S. (2001) *Class, Race, Gender and Crime: Social Realities of Justice in America.* Los Angeles: Roxbury.

Barak, G., Henry, S. and Milovanovic, D. (1997) 'Constitutive criminology: an overview of an emerging postmodernist school', in B. MacLean and D. Milovanovic (eds), *Thinking Critically About Crime*. Vancouver: Collective Press.

Barlow, D. and Barlow, M. H. (1995) 'Federal criminal justice legislation and the post-World War II social structure of accumulation in the United States', *Crime, Law and Social Change*, 22: 239–67.

Barlow, D., Barlow, M. H. and Johnson, W. (1996) 'The political economy of criminal justice policy: a time series analysis of economic conditions, crime and federal criminal justice legislation, 1948–1987', *Justice Quarterly*, 13: 223–42.

Baudrillard, J. (1981) *For a Critique of the Political Economy of the Sign*. St. Louis, MA: Telos.

Beckett, K. and Sasson, T. (2000) *The Politics of Injustice: Crime and Punishment in America*. Thousand Oaks, CA: Sage/Pine Forge Press.

Bohm, R. (1985) 'Beyond unemployment: toward a radical solution to the crime problem', *Crime and Social Justice*, 21–2: 213–22.

Box, S. and Hale, C. (1982) 'Economic crisis and the rising prisoner population in England and Wales', *Crime and Social Justice*, 17: 20–35.

Brady, J. P. (1974) Popular Justice: Conflict and Community in the Chinese Legal System (200 B.C.–1974), PhD Dissertation. Berkeley, CA: University of California, School of Criminology.

Buckley, Walter (ed.) (1968) *Modern Systems Research for the Behavioral Scientist*. Chicago: Aldine.

Buel, R. A., Stone, R. (1967) 'Blue power and the control of mobs', *Wall Street Journal*, Friday, 20 October.

Carlson, S. and Michalowski, R. (1997) 'Crime, unemployment and social structures of accumulation: an inquiry into historical contingency', *Justice Quarterly*, 14: 209–41.

Chatfield, C. (1990) 'The antiwar movement and America', in C. Debenedetti and C. Chatfield (eds), *An American Ordeal: The Antiwar Movement of the Vietnam Era*. Syracuse, NY: Syracuse University Press.

Clements, J. M. (1975) *The San Francisco Maritime and General Strikes of 1934 and the Dynamics of Repression*, PhD Dissertation. Berkeley, CA: University of California, School of Criminology.

Coles, F. S. (1974) *Women in Litigation Practice: Success and the Woman Lawyer*, PhD Dissertation. Berkeley: University of California, School of Criminology.

Cooper, L. B. (1976) *Promoting a Stable Environment: the Law Enforcement Assistance Administration*, PhD Dissertation. Berkeley, CA: University of California, School of Criminology.

Currie, E. (1999) 'Radical criminology – or just criminology – then, and now', *Social Justice*, 26: 16–18.

Daly, K. (1999) *Gender, Crime and Punishment*. New Haven, CT: Yale University Press.

Dodd, D. J. (1972) 'The life and times of Albert Alexander: a study of identity formation and disintegration in urban Afro-America', in *School of Criminology*. Berkeley, CA: University of California.

Dos Santos, T. (1970) 'The concept of social classes', *Science and Society*, 34: 166–95.

Easton, D. (1968) 'A systems analysis of political life', in Buckley, W. (ed.), *Modern Systems Reserch for the Behavioral Scientist*. Chicago: Aldine.

Engels, F. (1939) *Herr Eugene Dühring's Revolution in Science (Anti-Düring)*. New York: International Publishers.

Engquist Grabiner, V. (1976) *Woman's Suffrage and Social Control*, PhD Dissertation. Berkeley, CA: University of California, School of Criminology.

Ferrell, J. (1999) 'Cultural criminology', *Annual Review of Sociology*, 25: 395–418.

Ferrell, J. and Sancers, C. R. (1995) *Cultural Criminology*. Boston: Northeastern University Press.

Freeman, R. (1983) 'Crime and unemployment', in J. Q. Wilson (ed.), *Crime and Public Policy*. San Francisco: ICS Press.

Friedrichs, D. (1996) *Trusted Criminals*. Belmont CA: Wadsworth.

Fujimoto, T. (1975) 'Social class and crime: the case of the Japanese Americans', in *School of Criminology*. Berkeley: University of California.

Garofalo, J. (1981) 'Introduction.' *Radical Theory and the Practice of Criminal Justice*, 27 (January): 1–3.

Glick, R. (1969) *Southern Community And New Left Organizers: A Cultural Meeting*, PhD Dissertation. Berkeley, CA: University of California, School of Criminology.

Glick, B. (1989) *War At Home: Covert Action Against U.S. Activists and What We Can Do About It*. Boston: South End Press.

Gordon, D. M. (1971) 'Class and the economic of crime', *Review of Radical Political Economics*, 3: 51–72.

Gordon, D. M. (1980) 'Stages of accumulation and long cycle economics', in T. K. Hopkins and I. Wallerstein (eds), *Processes of the World System*. Beverly Hills, CA: Sage.

Greenberg, D. F. (1977) 'The dynamics of oscillatory punishment processes', *Journal of Criminal law and Criminology*, 68: 643–51.

Greenberg, D. F. (ed.) (1993) *Crime and Capitalism: Readings in Marxist Criminology*. Philadelphia: Temple University Press.

Gross, B. (1980) *Friendly Fascism: The New Face of Power in America*. New York: M. Evans.

Groves, W. Byron, and Corrado, C. (1983) 'Culture as metaphysics: an appraisal of cultural models', *Crime and Social Justice*, 20: 99–120.

Hamm, M. (1993) *American Skinheads: The Criminology and Control of Hate Crime*. Westport, CT: Praeger.

Hamm, M. (1995) *The Abandoned Ones: The Imprisonment and Uprising of the Mariel Boat People*. Boston: Northeastern University.

Henry, S. and Lanier, M. M. (eds) (2001) *What is Crime: Controversies over the Nature of Crime and What to Do about It*. Lanham, MD: Rowman & Littlefield.

Henry, S. and Milovanovic, D. (2001a) Postmodernism and Constitutive Criminology. Unpublished article.

Henry, S. and Milovanovic, D (2001b) Constitutive Criminology Meets Its Critics. Unpublished article.

Hitchens, C. (2001) *The Trial of Henry Kissinger*. New York: Verso.

Humphries, D. (1973) *The politics of abortion: a case study of New York's Abortion Law*, PhD Dissertation. Berkeley, CA: University of California, School of Criminology.

Humphries, D. and Wallace. D. (1980) 'Capitalist accumulation and urban crime, 1950–1971', *Social Problems*, 28: 180–93.

Iadicola, P. and Shupe, A. (1998) *Violence, Inequality and Human Freedom*. New York: General Hall.

Jacobs, D. and Britt, D. (1979) 'Inequality and police use of deadly force: an empirical assessment of the conflict hypothesis', *Social Problems*, 26: 403–11.

Jacobs, D. (1979) 'Inequality and police strength', *American Sociological Review*, 44: 913–24.

Jacobs, D. (1981) 'Inequality and economic crime', *Sociology and Social Science Research*, 66: 12–28.

Jankovic, I. (1977) 'Labour markets and imprisonment', *Crime and Social Justice*, 8: 17–31.

Jankowski, M. S. (1991) *Islands in the Street. Gangs and American Urban Society.* Berkeley, CA: University of California Press.

Kasinsky, R. G. (1972) *Refugees from Militarism: Draft-Age Americans in Canada*, PhD Dissertation. Berkeley, CA: University of California, School of Criminology.

Keller, C. (1974) *Levels of Sanctioning Behavior on Indian Reservations in the Great Plains Area*, PhD Dissertation. Berkeley, CA: University of California, School of Criminology.

Kondratieff, N. D. (1935) 'The long waves in economic life', *Review of Economic Studies*, 17: 105–15.

Krisberg, B. (1974) 'Teaching radical criminology: Criminology 100A–B, Professors Barry Krisberg, Tony Platt, and Paul Takagi', *Crime and Social Justice*, 1: 64–6.

Lessan, G. (1991) 'Macroeconomic determinants of the penal process: estimating the unemployment and inflation influences on imprisonment rate changes in the United States, 1948–1985', *Crime, Law and Social Change*, 16: 177–98.

Lizotte, A., Mercy, J. and Monkkenon, E. (1982) 'Crime and police strength in an urban setting: Chicago 1947–1970', in J. Hagan, (ed.), *Quantitative Criminology.* Beverly Hills, CA: Sage.

Lynch, M. J. (1987) 'Quantitative analysis and marxist criminology: old answers to a dilemma in Marxist criminology', *Crime and Social Justice*, 29: 110–27.

Lynch, M. J. (1988) 'The extraction of surplus value, crime and punishment: a preliminary empirical analysis for the U.S.', *Contemporary Crises*, 12: 329–44.

Lynch, M. J. and Michalowski, R. J. (2000) *The New Primer in Radical Criminology: Critical Perspectives on Crime, Power and Identity*, 3rd edn., Monsey, NY: Criminal Justice Press.

Lynch, M. J. and Stretesky, P. B. (1998) 'Uniting class and race with criticism through the study of environmental justice', *Critical Criminologist*, 1, Fall: 4–7.

Lynch, M. J. and Stretesky, P. B. (1999) 'Clarifying the analysis of environmental justice: further thoughts on the critical analysis of environmental justice issues', *Critical Criminologist*, 9: 5–8.

Lynch, M. J., and Stretesky, P. B. (2000) 'Radical criminology: race, class, inequality, crime and justice', in R. Paternoster and R. Bachman (eds), *Explaining Criminals and Crime: Essays in Contemporary Criminological Theory.* Los Angeles: Roxbury.

Lynch, M. J., Groves, B. W. and Lizotte, A. (1994) 'The rate of surplus value and crime: theoretical and empirical examination of Marxian economic theory and criminology', *Crime, Law and Social Change*, 21: 15–48.

Lynch, M. J., Hogan, M. J. and Stretesky, P. (1999) 'A further look at long cycles, legislation and crime', *Justice Quarterly*, 16: 431–50.

Lynch, M.J., Stretesky, P. B. and Hammond, P. (2000) 'Media Coverage of Chemical Crimes: Hillsborough County, Florida, 1987-1997', *British Journal of Criminology*, 40: 112–26.

Lyotard, J. F. (1984) *The Postmodern Condition: A Report on Knowledge.* Manchester: Manchester University Press.

Mackay, D. M. (1968) 'Towards an informational-flow model of human behavior', in W. Buckley (ed.), *Modern Systems Research for the Behavioral Scientist*, Chicago: Aldine.

McNamara, R. S. (1999) *Argument Without End: In Search of Answers to the Vietnam Tragedy*. New York: Public Affairs.

Maggroh, M. (1968) 'The second cybernetics: deviance-amplifying mutual causal processes', in W. Buckley (ed.), *Modern Systems Research for the Behavioral Scientist*. Chicago: Aldine.

Messerschmidt, J. W. (1997) *Crime as Structured Action*. Thousand Oaks, CA: Sage.

Meyers, R. E. (1974) *Controlling the Poor: the Undeclared Goal of Public Recreation*, PhD Dissertation. Berkeley, CA: University of California, School of Criminology,.

Michalowski, R. (1996) 'Critical criminology and the critique of domination', *Critical Criminology: An International Journal*, 7: 9–16.

Michalowski, R. and Carlson, S. (1999) 'Unemployment, imprisonment and social structures of accumulation: historical contingency in the Rusche-Kirchheimer Hypothesis', *Criminology*, 37: 217–50.

Miles, M. W. (1980) *The Odyssey of the American Right*. New York: Oxford University Press.

Milovanovic, D. (1988) 'Jailhouse lawyers and jailhouse lawyering', *International Journal of the Sociology of Law*, 16: 455–75.

Milovanovic, D. (2000) 'Transgressions: towards an affirmative postmodern criminology', *Australian and New Zealand Journal of Criminology*, 33: 202–20.

Mintz, R. F. (1974) *The Miners Who Tore Down the Walls*, PhD Dissertation. Berkeley, CA: University of California, School of Criminology.

Nalla, M., Lynch, M. J. and Leiber, M. J. (1997) 'Determinants of police growth in Phoenix, Arizona, 1950–1988', *Justice Quarterly*, 14: 115–44.

Napper, G. (1971) *The Black Student Movement: Problems of Unity*, PhD Dissertation. Berkeley, CA: University of California, School of Criminology.

Nett, R. (1968) 'Conformity-deviation and the social control concept', in W. Buckley (ed.), *Modern Systems Research for the Behavioral Scientist*. Chicago: Aldine.

O'Maolchatha, T. and Thomas, J. (1989) 'Reassessing the critical metaphor: an optimistic revisionist view', *Justice Quarterly*, 6: 48–158.

Osborne, L. T. (1973) *The Ethics And Aesthetics of Crime: a Study of Jean Genet*, PhD Dissertation. Berkeley. CA: University of California, School of Criminology.

Petras, J. (2001) 'U.S. banks and the dirty money empire', *Dollars and Sense*, 237 (September/October): 11–13.

Platt, T. and Cooper, L. (ed.) (1974) *Policing America*. Englewood Cliffs, NJ: Prentice-Hall.

Poveda, A. G. (1970) *Drug Use among the Major Social Types in a High School*, PhD Dissertation. Berkeley, CA: University of California, School of Criminology.

Prigogine, I. (1997) *The End of Certainty: Time, Chaos, and the New Laws of Nature*. New York: The Free Press.

Renzetti, C. M. and Goodstein, L. (2001) *Women, Crime, and Criminal Justice: Original Feminist Readings*. Los Angeles: Roxbury.

Ross, J. I. (ed.) (1998) *Cutting the Edge: Current Perspectives in Radical/Critical Criminology and Criminal Justice*. New York: Praeger.

Russel, S. (1997) 'The failure of postmodern criminology', *Critical Criminology: An International Journal*, 8 (Autumn): 61–90.

Rustigan, M. A. (1974) *Toward a Reinterpretation of the Origins of the Classical School of Criminology In England*, PhD Dissertation. Berkeley, CA: University of California, in School of Criminology.

Schwartz, M. D. and Milovanovic, D. (1996) *Race, Gender, and Class in Criminology: The Intersection*. New York: Garland.

Schwendinger, H. and Schwendinger, J. R. (1974) *Sociologists of the Chair: A Radical Analysis of the Formative Years of North American Sociology (1883–1922)*. New York: Basic Books.

Schwendinger, H. and Schwendinger, J. R. (1997) 'Charting subcultures at a frontier of knowledge', *British Journal of Sociology*, 48 (March): 71–94.

Schwendinger, H. and Schwendinger, J. R. (1999) 'The First Edition', *Social Justice*, 26, Summer: 108–13.

Speiglman, R. C. (1976) *Building the Walls Inside – Medicine, Corrections, and the State Apparatus for Repression*, PhD Dissertation. Berkeley, CA: University of California, School of Criminology.

Staff of the Research Center on Criminal Justice (1975) *Iron Fist and the Velvet Glove: An Analysis of the U.S. Police.*, Berkeley: Center for Research on Criminal Justice.

Stretesky, P. and Hogan, M. (1998) 'Environmental justice: an analysis of superfund sites in Florida', *Social Problems*, 45: 268–87.

Stretesky, P. and Lynch, M. J. (1999a) 'Corporate environmental violence and racism', *Crime, Law and Social Change*, 30: 163–84.

Stretesky, P. and Lynch, M. J. (1999b) 'Environmental justice and the predictions of distance to accidental chemical releases in Hillsborough County, Florida', *Social Science Quarterly*, 80: 830–46.

Stretesky, P. and Lynch, M. J. (2001) 'The relationship between lead and homicide', *Archives of Pediatric and Adolescent Medicine*, 155: 579–82.

Swan, L. (1972) *A Study of Race Riots, 1900–1944: a Form of Race Conflict*, PhD Disseration. Berkeley, CA: University of California, School of Criminology.

Torrey, E. F. (1992) *Freudian Fraud: The Malignant Effect of Freud's Theory on American Thought and Culture*. New York: HarperCollins.

Weis, J. G. (1974) *Delinquency among the Well-to-Do*, PhD Dissertation. Berkeley, CA: University of California, School of Criminology.

Williams, C. R. and Arrigo, B. A. (2001) 'Anarchaos and order: on the emergence of social justice', *Theoretical Criminology*, 5: 223–52.

Wonders, N. A. (1999) 'Postmodern feminist criminology and social justice', in B. A. Arrigo (ed.), *Social Justice/Criminal Justice: The Maturation of Critical Theory in Law, Crime, and Deviance*. Belmont, CA: West/Wadsworth.

Woodward, B. (1999) *Shadow: Five Presidents and the Legacy of Watergate*. New York: Simon & Schuster.

Chapter 4

'Losing my religion': reflections on critical criminology in Australia

David Brown

That's me, that's me in the corner,
That's me in the spotlight
Losing my religion

REM, *Losing My Religion*

Introduction

One of the affectations of 1960s and 1970s critical criminology I remember kindly was the tendency to start a paper with a quote from a Bob Dylan song. I start this paper with a quote from REM, *Losing My Religion*, a favourite song which seemed to echo as a background theme to the emerging text: a theme in both the musical and textual senses and one which served to highlight the personal and the biographical in the process of reflecting on three decades of critical criminology. Reflection can of course be a dangerous enterprise, its results sometimes inconsequential, self–indulgent, sanitised and prey to the vagaries of memory. If such tendencies can be kept within acceptable bounds the biographical touch might reprise the central theme of this chapter: the nature of the relationship between law and politics, somewhere beyond the often predictable reaffirmations of 'praxis' or the self-evident virtues of critical theory.

The reflections are, in a sense, of a life of crime, or a life in the discourse of crime, which is of far less popular interest and commercial potential than the reflections of an actual practitioner of crime, in the

Mark Brandon Read, *Chopper: From the Inside* (1991), *Chopper 2: Hits and Memories* (1992) genre. It was fashionable in the 1960s and 1970s to start radical accounts of crime and deviance by noting that academic and legal careers were dependant upon, produced by (and in the more angry accounts, parasitic on) crime and criminals. In as much as such analyses were theorised, the key reference was to a passage in Marx's *Theories of Surplus Value* entitled 'The apologist conception of the productivity of all professions' where Marx wrote: 'A philosopher produces ideas, a clergyman sermons, a professor compendia and so on...The criminal produces not only crimes but also criminal law, and with it the professor who gives lectures on criminal law and in addition to this the inevitable compendium in which this same professor throws his lectures onto the general market as "commodities;" ' (Marx, 1963: 387).

While a few took this to be a central insight into a Marxist theory of crime, Paul Hirst (Hirst, 1975: 221–3) and Taylor, Walton and Young (1973) pointed out that the passage is an ironic attack on functionalism: 'There is no serious attempt to establish crime as a central dynamic in the system of capitalist production and innovation' (Taylor, Walton and Young, 1973: 212). Taylor Walton and Young noted that 'viewing crime in functionalist terms drives one into the absurd position of seeing crime as a necessary feature of society. For Marx and for us it is not' (Taylor, Walton and Young, 1973: 213).

So perhaps we need not flagellate ourselves about making a career out of crime, although Jock Young's admonition in 1975 that 'it is a thousand times easier to become a radical academic than a militant shop steward: the first course of action leads to Penguin Books Ltd and the second to the blacklist' (Young, 1975: 83), while an exaggeration, still contains some truth. In my case the road to Penguin Books Ltd took from 1974 when I was appointed to the University of New South Wales Law Faculty in Sydney, Australia, until 1982 when George Zdenkowski's and my *The Prison Struggle* was published (Zdenkowski and Brown, 1982). The destination wasn't hugely productive in financial terms. Penguin, on realising they had a much more radical and academic book on their hands than they envisaged, pulped 600 out of the already small print run of 1,500, without asking or informing the authors, so we were prevented from buying up the stock (it was clogging shelves in the warehouse apparently) and distributing them ourselves for free to prisoners, students, libraries and dentist's surgeries. I recall receiving annual royalty cheques for sums such as $6.70 for a few years. So that in material terms the road to Penguin Books Ltd hardly turned out to be paved with gold.

The reflections will be presented loosely under three overlapping headings or approaches: the waves of theory, influential books and an ecological approach to the personal library. These somewhat light-hearted and biographically tinged reflections will identify some of the key intellectual resources and influences on critical criminology in Australia as manifest in the establishment of the *Alternative Criminology Journal*, the conduct of the prison movement and other criminal justice oriented social movements, and in the establishment and teaching of criminology courses in Australia in the early 1970s, in law faculties in particular. The aim is to demonstrate both the enduring legacy of critical criminology and to identify some of its problematic features and undesirable tendencies. In telling at least some of the stories of the interconnections between radical criminology and criminal justice politics in Australia in the last thirty years a key theme that emerges is the contingency and specificity of theory and politics. This is important in itself, but it also carries implications for those who ritually assert the importance of 'praxis', or who assume that politics are transparent to critical theory (or vice versa). What emerges is the importance of context over and against forms of critical theory that presume a sort of universal applicability outside space and time.

Waves of theory

One form of reminiscence is to recall the waves of theoretical approaches, each one not superseding but washing over, overlapping, existing understandings and approaches. When I came first to criminology it was to the deviancy theory of the National Deviancy Conference, manifest in publications such as Stan Cohen's *Images of Deviance* (1971), Ian and Laurie Taylor's *Politics and Deviance* (1973), Laurie Taylor's *Deviance and Society* (1973), Paul Rock's *Deviant Behaviour* (1973) and Paul Rock and Mary McIntosh's *Deviance and Social Control* (1974), a field dubbed 'misfit sociologies' by Geoffrey Pearson (Pearson, 1975a: 147; Pearson, 1975a: 49). In the Australian context a similar if less developed and less sophisticated movement was underway, illustrated by Edwards and Wilson, *Social Deviance in Australia* (1975) and later Wilson and Braithwaite, *Two Faces of Deviance* (1978).

The range of subject matter of radical deviancy theory included sport, crime thrillers, mental illness, music, demonstrations and drugs: issues many post-1968 students thought of as lifestyle choices. That these could now be turned into legitimate objects of study and research, entwining the personal, the political and the professional, was a source of amazement, delight and no little envy on the part of friends studying in more settled fields. Pearson described deviancy theory at the time as 'an odd theoretical cocktail, constructed out of sociology, psychiatry, criminology, social administration, media studies, law, social work, political science, cultural criticism, social psychology, and even some strands of popular culture and music' (Pearson, 1975a: 51). 'Strange brew' indeed, and nothing if not 'heady', the dangers of 'voyeurism' and 'zoo-keeping' notwithstanding (Gouldner, 1968: 121–2; Young, 1975: 69–71). The later *New Criminology*-led neo-Marxist, 'radical', 'alternative' or 'critical' criminology tended in its '"immanent critique" of existing theories of crime, deviance and social control' (Pearson, 1975a: 20) to attempt to establish a Marxist hegemony, in the process sacrificing some of the richness and diversity of radical deviancy theory in the name of rigour and totality. While much of the deviancy theory of the time and its later progeny stand up well to a retrospective reading, some of the neo-Marxist work now seems crude and doctrinaire, especially when compared with earlier work in a variety of traditions (compare, for example, Richard Quinney's *Critique of Legal Order* (1974) with Geoffrey Pearson's *The Deviant Imagination* (1975a), or indeed with earlier work by US sociologists and criminologists such as Matza, Becker, Lemert, Goffman, Garfinkel and others).

The emerging Marxist criminology was itself split over whether crime and deviance were legitimate theoretical objects within a Marxist problematic, illustrated in the exchange between Paul Hirst and Taylor, Walton and Young in the sequel to *The New Criminology*, *Critical Criminology* (1975). For Hirst, then working within an Althusserian tradition:

> There is no 'Marxist theory of deviance', either in existence, or which can be developed within orthodox Marxism. Crime and deviance vanish into the general theoretical concerns and the specific scientific object of Marxism. Crime and deviance are no more a scientific field for Marxism than education, the family or sport. The objects of Marxist theory are specified by its own concepts: the mode of production, the class struggle, the state, ideology, etc.
>
> (Hirst, 1975: 204).

For Taylor, Walton and Young:

> What many radical deviancy theorists, Marxists or otherwise, are attempting to do is to move criminology away from a focus on the 'criminality' of the poor, the pathologising of 'deviant' behaviour

into categories derived from biology, psychology or positivistic sociology, and to abolish the distinction between the study of human deviation and the study of the functioning of States, and ruling-class ideologies as a whole.

(Taylor, Walton and Young, 1975: 234).

The *New Criminology* position was more open, more libertarian and more eclectic: in addition to a selective use of 'classic' Marxist texts, inspiration and lineage were drawn from, for example, C. Wright Mills, E. P. Thompson and Alvin Gouldner. Hirst soon renounced his position as flawed by a reliance on a rationalist conception of discourse: 'The discourse written under the sign of an epistemological doctrine is not "logically bound" by it...the relation between these concepts and the other concepts in the text into which they are written is determined by the specific conditions of the writing and by no inherent logical properties in the concepts themselves' (Cutler et al. 1977: 108–9).

In the mid-1980s this debate was revived (Hulsman, 1986; Steinert, 1986; O'Malley, 1982, 1988), with Pat O'Malley arguing that 'the conflicting aims of Marxist theory and the bourgeois legal theory from which "crime" is transferred make it difficult for Marxist criminology to generate a unified theory to guide political practice and research' (O'Malley, 1988: 65). The influence of Foucault led to more modest conceptions of the tasks, boundaries and limits of criminology:

Rather than 'crime in general', what confronts us is a heterogeneous range of conducts embedded in diverse sites of social practice which are most usefully examined by tracing the legal and ideological mechanisms through which particular events, conducts and individuals are constructed as targets of social intervention and objects of knowledge, and the terms in which this is carried out.

(Brown and Hogg, 1992b: 214).

The Althusserian current, which gained a following in the 1970s, was both rigorous and somewhat heavy going. It required pouring over those lovely New Left Books hardbacks by Althusser (1972, 1973, 1977); Balibar (1977), Therborn (1976, 1978, 1980) and Poulantzas (1973, 1974, 1975, 1976, 1978), and in the same series the more Gramscian and my favourite, Laclau (1977) and later Laclau and Mouffe (1985). Althusserianism did not have any substantial spin offs in criminology, and with the exception of Laclau and perhaps Poulantzas, tended to reinforce highly orthodox and 'theoreticist' Marxism, drawing down the wrath of E. P. Thompson in *The Poverty of Theory and Other Essays* (1978), a dispute in turn refereed by

Perry Anderson (1980). Thompson's work in the magisterial *The Making of the English Working Class* (1968) and *Whigs and Hunters* (1977) and that of writers such as Eric Hobsbawm (1959, 1972, 1973), George Rude (1959) and Douglas Hay, Peter Linebaugh and others in *Albion's Fatal Tree* (1975), reflected a more grounded tradition of class-oriented social history which included various historical studies of banditry, riot, revolt and crime, and was influential in the emerging radical criminology and socio-legal studies. A range of publications emanating from the Birmingham Centre for Cultural Studies and culminating with *Policing the Crisis* (Hall et al., 1978) also brought a more historical approach, heavily influenced by the rediscovery of Italian Marxist Antonio Gramsci (1970), to cultural studies in the deviancy and crime fields of scholarship.

More specifically within criminology, in the National Deviancy Conference production, *Capitalism and the Rule of Law*, significantly subtitled 'From deviancy theory to Marxism' (Fine et al., 1979), Jock Young launched a critique of 'left idealism', a key feature of which was said to be that it 'plays down the impact of working–class crime against the working class; it maximizes the anti-working class effects of ruling class crime whilst at the same time stressing its endemic nature' (Young, 1979: 15). Here the seeds of the later turn to left realism and the dichotomy between left idealism and left realism were sown. Also in 1979 *Deviant Interpretations* (Downes and Rock, 1979) appeared, containing some excellent essays in a more sceptical vein, defending the diversity of deviancy theory against the 'new orthodoxies' (Downes and Rock, 1979: viii) of Marxist critical criminology. A similar diversity and the influence of Foucault were also apparent in *Radical Issues in Criminology* (Carlen and Collison, 1980).

Meanwhile Foucault generated a whole new discourse and a range of new domains (Gane and Johnson, 1993) which arguably have had a significant influence in criminology, especially through *Discipline and Punish* (1977) but also through the later work on governmentality (Burchell, Gordon and Miller, 1991), which others such as Nick Rose (1989, 1999; Barry, Osborne and Rose, 1996), Richard Ericson (Ericson and Haggerty, 1997; Stenson and Sullivan, 2001) and, in Australia, Pat O'Malley (1992, 1996b, 1999, 2000; O'Malley and Palmer, 1996; Pratt, 1997; Brown and Pratt, 2000; and see generally Dean, 1999) have elaborated. Feminist influences expanded from the 1970s and Carol Smart's first forays (Smart, 1976). Feminist or feminist influenced criminology now constitutes a significant body of work (i.e. Gelsthorpe and Morris, 1990; Daley, 1994; Naffine 1987, 1997) and has generated a new interest in and emphasis on masculinity and crime (Messerschmidt, 1993; Newburn and Stanko, 1994; Polk, 1994; Jefferson, 1997; Collier, 1998). Poststructuralism, tailing on from Foucault, has influenced criminological theory (Young, 1996) as has postmodernism (Henry and Milovanovic, 1996). Left realism raised its head in the mid-1980s as a political attempt to reorient popular debate around crime and policing away from the hegemony of conservative law and order politics on the one hand and the abstentionism of the left on the other (Mathews and Young, 1992a, 1992b; Brown and Hogg, 1992a, 1992b).

The current waves of theory involve arguments around 'late modernity', 'market society', 'the risk society', 'neoliberalism' and 'governmentality' with no dominant theoretical approach apparent, although the influence of feminism and poststructuralism is strongly evident. The leading work, as represented, for example, in the journals *Theoretical Criminology* and *Punishment and Society*, in Jock Young's *The Exclusive Society* (1999), Ian Taylor's *Crime in Context* (1999), David Garland's *The Culture of Control* (2001) and the collection of essays in Garland and Sparks, *Criminology and Social Control* (2000), first published as a special edition of the *British Journal of Criminology*, manifest an attempt to grapple with the massive social, economic, cultural and political transformations that have taken place in the conditions of late modernity over the last three decades. This involves an opening out to broader social theory and a return to some of its grand themes. Downes and Rock, editors of the series in which *Criminology and Social Control* appears, claim for it a lineage with *The New Criminology*'s 'preoccupation with big ideas and political economy'. Editors Garland and Sparks argue that in 'a culture that is now saturated with images of crime and fear of crime, criminology can no longer hope to dominate the ways in which these issues are analysed.' This social and cultural centrality of crime 'is an opportunity for criminology to embrace a more critical, more public, more wide-ranging role' for 'its fate is to be redefined by the political culture of which it forms a part' and thus its aim must be to 'understand that political culture' (Garland and Sparks, 2000: 19) and engage with 'the theoretical work of contemporary social theory' (Garland and Sparks, 2000: 21).

Influential Books

Another way of reminiscing which covers the same ground but in a more selective way is to nominate the books which were particularly influential: a *High Fidelity*-style (Hornby, 1996) list of your own top five 'most influential'. In chronological order rather than order of merit my list would start with Taylor, Walton and Young's *The New Criminology*

(1973). Having just finished the Diploma of Criminology course at Cambridge in 1973 the discovery of a wholesale alternative perspective, grounded in a neo-Marxism, led students such as myself to become converts and, in my case, a bearer of *The New Criminology* in the Australian context; it became the bible. The finding of partialities and gaps in all the pre-existing criminological approaches, the professed need to 'deal with society as a totality' (Taylor, Walton and Young, 1973: 278) and the formulation of the task ahead as 'to create a society in which the facts of human diversity, whether personal, organic or social, are not subject to the power to criminalize' (Taylor, Walton and Young, 1973: 282) appealed to many left-wing sensibilities at a time of social upheaval and mass opposition to the Vietnam War. Nearly two decades later it still impresses with its sweep and its boldness; but now the desire to point out the deficiencies and partialities of all previous traditions tends to diminish the richness on offer, the claims of totality appear as improbable and indeed suspect, and the almost total lack of influence of feminism seems simultaneously shocking and an indication of how influential feminism has been in the intervening period (see also Chapter 5). For an assessment of the *New Criminology* twenty-five years on from some of its leading practitioners see Walton and Young (1998) and, for an earlier critique, see Downes and Rock (1979).

Chronologically my second choice in the 'very influential' list is Thomas Mathiesen's *The Politics of Abolition* (1974), a detailed account of the strategies of KRIM, KRUM and KROM, the various Scandinavian Prison movement organizations in the 1960s and early 1970s. Mathiesen's 'politics of the unfinished' and his distinction between 'positive' and 'negative' reforms was carried into the NSW Prisoners Action Group (PAG) and became an important touchstone and organising principle for much of the agitation around, and submissions to the Nagle Royal Commission into Prisons, in the late 1970s (PAG, 1979, 1980a, 1980b; Nagle, 1978) in the aftermath of the Bathurst prison riots of 1970 and 1974. The NSW PAG drew on Mathiesen's warning that there is a strong tendency for debate on alternatives to prison to proceed without any departure from the basic premises underlying the existing system (Mathiesen, 1974: 83–4; PAG, 1980b: 6). The attraction of Mathiesen's approach was its realisation that 'completely to avoid any work for short-term reforms is often politically impossible as well as paralysing to action, while short-term reforms often have a corrupting effect on long-term work' (Mathiesen, 1973: 210). The way out of this conundrum was to work for reforms of a consistently abolishing kind: 'not only is it necessary, in order to attain a long-term goal of abolition that you stubbornly insist on abolitions on a short-term basis and in the immediate present; conversely it is just as important, in order to insist on abolitions in the immediate present, that you have to have a long-term goal of abolition to work for' (Mathiesen, 1973: 212). A key notion is that of the 'unfinished', the denial of the aim of achieving any particular final goal, state or position 'at which the policy of abolition ends...the point, therefore, must be precisely that of *not* letting the policy of abolition end' (Mathiesen, 1973: 208; adapted in Brown, 1977: 491). Russell Hogg and I were later to challenge the centrality given to productivist criteria in locating prisoners as essentially unproductive, and question the useful-ness of the positive/negative distinction (Brown and Hogg, 1985: 56), more of which later (see also Chapters 2 and 9 in this volume).

My third choice is Michel Foucault's *Discipline and Punish* (1977) which I read in a hardback version, with a mixture of amazement and excitement, entranced by the sheer poetic beauty of the text, the brilliance of the exposition, the way it seemed to open up new domains of thought, strategy and politics. The rethinking of power away from functionalist and instrumentalist understandings, conceiving it not as a property to be possessed but as a strategy to be exercised, the effects of power no longer to be thought in negative terms of exclusion, repression, masking and concealing but as productive, producing 'reality', 'domains of objects and rituals of truth' (Foucault, 1977: 194) was a lasting and incisive intervention which immeasurably improved the ability to think more imaginatively about the politics of various struggles. *Discipline and Punish* gave a major fillip to the prison movement; the analysis of the 'micro-physics of power' which is centred on and invests the body through detailed practices of discipline which seek to produce 'docile and useful' bodies had a grounded feel that was easily recognisable to activists working in the minutiae of prison struggle. My first instinct (Brown, 1981) was, like many others (Fine, 1979, 1980; Poulantzas, 1978), to reinscribe it within Marxism. But further readings and the numerous commentaries which emerged on this and the later Foucault, suggested that Foucault was, without rejecting notions such as class, mapping a road out of Marxism, a direction also indicated by more orthodox examinations such as Hindess and Hirst's *Mode of Production and Social Formation* (1977) and Cutler et al.'s *Marx's Capital and Capitalism Today*, Vol. 1 (1977) which effectively demolished the base/superstructure model of Marxist analysis. On top of this was the increasingly obvious fragility and undesirability of actually existing communist regimes.

My fourth choice is Stuart Hall et al., *Policing the Crisis* (1978) (Tony Jefferson, one of the co-authors of this text, also has a chapter in this volume). I first came across this in a photocopy first draft, almost samizdat form, when visiting Ian Taylor in Hamilton in Canada in 1977.

Ian Taylor's death from cancer in January 2001 is a sad loss to criminology of one of its central figures and to those of us who knew him as a friend. I recall sitting in the guest bedroom, snowed in, soaking up the rigorous and detailed analysis and enjoying the Gramscian 'Marxism without guarantees', with its emphasis on culture, race and the authoritarian populism as a way of explaining the emergence of and state reaction to the social phenomenon of 'mugging' in Britain in the 1970s. Thus the emergence of mugging is placed first in the context of a social history of a moral panic, with detailed analysis of the social production of news and the orchestrating of public opinion. The book then examines 'why and how the themes of race, crime and youth – condensed into the image of "mugging" – comes to serve as the articulator' of a crisis of social order and how these themes serve 'as a mechanism for the construction of an authoritarian consensus' (Hall et al., 1979: viii). The moves between the media construction of mugging, the crisis in hegemony and the exhaustion of consent ushering in a law and order society are carefully constructed, theorised and empirically detailed. It is a wonderful work, rich in all sorts of ways, albeit that in retrospect the 'authoritarian populism' argument was overplayed and too readily exported and imported to other national contexts without the necessary local grounding and specific historical and cultural analysis exemplified in the original.

My fifth choice is Stan Cohen's *Visions of Social Control* (1985) (a major piece of influential scholarship considered in John Pratt's chapter in this volume) although the drift of it appeared in earlier articles, particularly 'The Punitive City: Notes on the Dispersal of Social Control' (1979), which all demonstrated a breadth of vision and a reflexive, open and engaging style. The strength of this work lies in the way Cohen analyses 'social control talk' and its languages, vocabularies, stories and metaphors as specific forms of discourse with their own varied conditions of existence, rejecting the notion of 'demystification' and assuming that in the relations between words and deeds there will be 'anomalies, incongruence, lack of fit, contradictions, paradoxes, impurities' (Cohen, 1985: 156). Cohen called for a 'looser' model to capture the 'deep structures' of various 'stories of change', 'not the simple idealist, nor the simple materialist, nor even Foucault's complex spiral of power and knowledge' (Cohen, 1985: 158). Among those deep structures are: 'consequences so different from intentions; policies carried out for reasons opposite to their stated ideologies; the same ideologies supporting quite different policies; the same policy supported for quite different reasons' (Cohen, 1985: 158). Arguably, Cohen's dispersal of social control thesis tends in the direction of seeing the wide range of differentiated developments in regulation and control (disciplinary, normative and risk-based strategies and programmes, carried out by a variety of public and private agencies) as 'essentially repressive and undesirable, and hence to detect a common and singular underpinning to them in preference to recognising their diverse and differentiated nature' (Hogg, 1979: 111).

If I were allowed a reserve sixth, I would nominate David Garland's *Punishment and Modern Society* (1990) as a brilliant critical review of debates and theories around penality.

These are highly personal choices of key works that were influential on me; obviously everyone could formulate their own, different list. Looking at the choices the list is concentrated in the 1970s: perhaps a function of age and conjuncture; perhaps in the 1980s and 1990s it is harder to single out specific works as against a range of scholarship; perhaps more of the current influential work is in journal form? It does not include any Australian book, although clearly John Braithwaite's *Crime, Shame and Reintegration* (1989b) would be up there on any international list in terms of international influence. My list does not include any specifically feminist work, although there are many excellent works to choose from. Pat Carlen's *Women's Imprisonment* (1983), for example, was very influential in NSW in women's penal reform debates in the 1980s (Brown, Kramer and Quinn, 1988). The purpose of the list is only to illustrate key influences within a specific context in one individual's criminological career.

An Ecological Analysis of Library Shifts

Another way of coming at these reminiscences, materialising the influential books and waves of theory, would be to chart the changes in one's personal library, whether at home or work. Let us imagine, for example, a time series photographic record of the growth, modification and rearrangement of personal/professional libraries over the last few decades, rather like those time frame series which condense the life of a flower or eight hours' sleep to a one minute video – what would it reveal?

From such a time series video might be constructed an ecological, Chicago-school type analysis, with the acquisition and arrangement of books being marked by conflict, assimilation, succession, symbiosis, cooperation and invasion. A zonal analysis might be made, with the desk or now personal computer being the central zone and proximity to this zone being graded in terms of accessibility (a function of distance from the desk or computer, placement on high, middle or low shelves, with the high and low being reserved for those books less and less often used) and those obscured by furniture or piles of photocopied materials and administrative documents and reports, including the ever-expanding Strategic Plans and Vision Statements.

In my own case it might reveal the migration of the large volumes of hardback, handsome but very cheap (heavily subsidised: $3–5 for 500 plus pages of good paper and hardcover) Progress Publisher volumes of Marx's *Capital*, *Theories of Surplus Value*, the assorted works of Engels, Lenin, Trotsky, Mao, through to various lesser lights, to a lower level shelf in my office library some distance from the computer, after being in pride of place on a middle shelf of my lounge room in the 1970s and 1980s. Assorted commentaries on these works are one shelf up, with Gramsci and Gramscian influenced work still appearing in a position of reasonable accessibility. The other major movement through zones of transition to the periphery and even to the second-hand bookshop have been the shelves of political economy, a sad move from their heyday when some criminology courses, including one I taught, did not contain anything much about traditionally defined crimes but only phenomena such as unemployment, racism, sexism and the political economy of almost everything.

Assorted social history, particularly convict history, has maintained a reasonably central location, as have the shelves of general criminology and penology, with the critical work tending to gravitate to the best-placed middle shelves. Feminist work with a particular influence on sexual violence and feminist theory has both expanded rapidly and moved to a prime position. A solid policing section is mid way, overrun a little by a rapidly expanding section of media and cultural studies which fringes into poststructuralism and post-modernism, both in general treatments and specific accounts. Closer to hand comes Foucault and a shelf of Foucauldian studies and governmentality, surrounded above and below by numerous accounts of miscarriages of justice and specific case studies, critical psychiatry, crime prevention, indigenous studies and the Black Deaths in Custody Royal Commission, assorted journals including both discontinued numbers such as the *Alternative Criminology Journal*, and current journals (*Theoretical Criminology*, *Punishment and Society*, the *Australian and New Zealand Journal of Criminology* and *Current Issues in Criminology*) flanked by an ever expanding and increasingly utilised section on government and law reform commission reports.

Another wall shows jurisprudence moving slowly out of reach, criminal justice holding place flanked by criminal law texts. Closest to the computer are dictionaries and crime statistics. Times have changed from when *The Prison Struggle* could be written in the late 1970s, with little reference, as one hostile reviewer fairly pointed out, to statistical material – a small example of what the governmentality tradition calls the statisticalisation of knowledge. Statutes have increasingly moved into a transition zone as on-line web databases such as Austlii and Butterworths are used to check statutory provisions and have largely replaced hard copy. The storage of large amounts of information and sources on disk, particularly in law, together with increased access to governmental and research institute reports on websites and databases, suggests that the academic library of the future will be less dependent on hard copy and more electronically based without entirely supplanting the book and journal. But the type of 'time series' exercise just conducted will leave less obvious physical evidence of change, less overt 'footprints in the sand'.

While personal and mundane, reflection on the ecology of the personal/professional library raises in a material way issues of the flux of theory, the shifting boundaries and fortunes of different disciplines and traditions, the nature of the seams or sutures which stitch them together, transition and supersession, the opening up of new domains.

Theory and Politics

These three forms of reminiscence – waves of theory, influential books and an ecological analysis of the personal library – have been ways of illustrating some of the key intellectual resources of critical criminology. The strengths of these legacies have been briefly asserted and some of the deficiencies hinted at. The following sections will attempt to demonstrate some of the difficulties and problems which emerged as criminologists and social movements attempted to carry some of these theoretically oriented works into practice in the Australian context. In the process the contingency and specificity of theory and politics in local settings will be elaborated, along with the argument that theory and politics are not transparent or reducible to each other.

Among the joint strengths of the works just discussed is their theoretical reach; in different ways these leading texts in critical criminology all exhibited a sophisticated grasp of social theory that was compelling and influential. Followers often tended to treat these texts as theoretical manuals; all that was required was to adopt and propagate the essential theoretical core and apply that in the specific local context.

The New Criminology tended to authorise a dismissive and at times denunciatory approach to non-Marxist traditions of radical deviancy theory, let alone to 'mainstream' and later 'administrative' criminology, that was and to some extent still is problematic. The sense of certainty generated out of the 'religion' of Marxism tended to manifest itself in an often rather denunciatory style common to much leftist politics in earlier decades: that 'nightmare' voice (which was sometimes mine) from the back of the hall in question time, informing the speaker and the audience that the talk or paper had evinced no coherent theory of the state, before moving on to identify 47 other flaws. Meaghan Morris (1988) describes a lecture in Sydney by Juliet Mitchell, following the publication of her book *Psychoanalysis and Feminism*.

> Mitchell completed a generous and enlightening lecture on her work, only to be greeted with that voice, that nightmare voice of the left, yelling boldly from up the back of the room, 'Yeah, Juliet, what about Chile?' As it happens, I think Juliet Mitchell at that time was one of the feminists most equipped and able to deal with precisely that kind of political question. But the point at issue is not her competence, but the way that voice from the back could so smoothly inscribe itself – and politics – as a perfect non sequitur (Morris, 1988: 180).

Another common practice was that of clearly differentiating, over-endowing and mythologising so called 'official', 'mainstream' or 'administrative' criminology. Apart from the suspect virtues of crude 'us and them' forms of identity, in the Australian context there is not a monolithic 'mainstream' criminology, as a glance at recent issues of the official journal of the main criminological professional association, the *Australian and New Zealand Journal of Criminology*, will reveal. My assessment would be that never, in the three decades of the journal's existence, has broadly 'critical' work been so much to the fore. Further, it may be important in particular contexts to utilise 'mainstream' or 'administrative' criminological work and enter into alliance with its practitioners in public debate and struggles over issues such as mandatory sentencing. 'Critical' criminologists are not self-evidently the most able or the best placed to influence public debate or lead opposition to law and order excesses. In relation to mandatory sentencing, for example, the role played by traditional conservative and liberal judges, Northern Territory magistrates, state Law Societies and Bar Associations, former Liberal Party Prime Ministers, and so on, has arguably been far more significant than the rather muted collective voice of 'critical' criminology, individual contributions notwithstanding.

Mathiesen's *The Politics of Abolition* defined prisoners in classic Marxist fashion by their (non) relation to the means of production and accordingly as largely powerless unless in alliance with their inherent allies, the 'radical part of the working class'. Such formulations tended to 'determine a priori agents of change, levels of effectiveness in the field of the social and privileged points and moments of rupture' (Laclau and Mouffe, 1985: 178–9), to assert an underlying relation of unity which is merely to be realised. Brown and Hogg (1985) in a reconsideration of abolitionism give a number of examples which illustrate Laclau and Mouffe's argument that 'social movements and struggles derive their progressive character through their discursive constitution, not by virtue of some essentialist subjectivity or particular location in a topography of groups oppressed under capitalism' (Brown and Hogg, 1985: 65). Mathiesen's specification was less problematic when applied to the alliance forged in NSW in the 1970s between the NSW PAG and the NSW Builders Labourers' Federation (BLF), an organisation which consciously pursued a policy of constructing and constituting concrete interests in common with a diversity of groups such as students, middle-class environmentalists, feminists, low-income earners in inner-city housing and prisoners, through their policy of 'green bans'. These involved widespread consultation with affected constituencies and local resident action groups prior to proceeding with development projects, and on occasions the withholding of labour on projects such as prison construction at Katingal, university buildings in support of women's studies courses and against the expulsion of a gay student from an Anglican residential college on campus, Aboriginal housing, the destruction of bush land and the planned demolition of traditional low-income urban areas in favour of large-scale high-rise commercial development (Burgmann and Burgmann, 1998: 121–45). The NSW BLF and the green ban policy were eventually smashed by a combination of a massive downturn in the building industry and a violent take-over by the Maoist-led federal branch of the BLF based largely in Victoria, which had entered into an alliance with major employers. The Victorian PAG had close ties with the Victorian BLF during this period, and actively promoted the prison struggle as one against 'US owned multinationals', which allegedly held state power in Australia, and later against 'soviet social imperialism'. For prisoners, which alliance is it to be? Such examples demonstrate the limitations of constituting subject positions in terms of particular privileged locations; the absence of a unified subject: prisoners; and the dangers of subordinating the interests of autonomous social movements to the dictates of particular political party 'lines'.

Foucault's *Discipline and Punish* seemed to cut through approaches that reduced the prison struggle to an epiphenomenon of some more general aim. For Foucault, what sustained the discourses, memories and invectives of revolts were the 'minute material details'. Rather than merely blind demands or the products of 'alien strategies' these revolts were 'revolts, at the level of the body, against the very body of the prison. What was at issue was not whether the prison environment was too harsh or too aseptic, too primitive or too efficient, but its very materiality as an instrument and vector of power' (Foucault, 1977: 30). However the metaphor of Bentham's panopticon was often generalised into an all encompassing 'carceral' or 'disciplinary society' in which local and specific struggles tended to disappear or were rendered futile. A similar consequence tended to follow from Stan Cohen's tendency to see in the diversity of shifting and blurred boundaries the unitary hand of state social control. The risks of net-widening became an a priori basis for refusal to support various alternatives to imprisonment, precluding a detailed analysis of their specific local conditions of operation.

A thorough-going 'unfinished' abolitionism, as waged through the pursuit of 'negative' reforms which oppose the underlying tenets of the existing system, tended to render all sorts of practical penal politics an 'incorporation' which would strengthen the system, and the positive/ negative distinction became increasingly difficult to draw in practice. Brown and Hogg give a number of local examples of these difficulties (Brown and Hogg, 1985: 71–4). For example, in relation to prison internal disciplinary hearings, 'is the provision of rights to legal representation, to call witnesses, to be given reasons for a decision, a right of appeal etc., to be regarded as breaking down (negative) or shoring up and making more tolerable (positive)?' (Brown and Hogg, 1985: 72). For Balbus the answer is clear: such demands not only are contained within the 'bourgeois legal form' but actually strengthen it, contributing to a 'declassification of politics which militates against the formation of ... class consciousness' (Balbus, 1977: 577; for a critique of this position see Zdenkowski and Brown, 1982: 28–40). Such examples illustrate perhaps that reform measures or lines of advance cannot be adequately specified or evaluated a priori by reference either to some positive/negative calculus or to some general theory of law, state, capital, legitimation or legal right.

Similarly the adequacy of the principle of 'voluntariness' as a guide to what is a genuine alternative as against that which merely reproduces or augments the prison system proved to be problematic in practice. The NSW PAG after initially opposing the introduction of Community Service Orders (CSO) on abolitionist and net-widening lines later offered the Breakout printing works, run by the PAG, as a CSO placement option, the advantage being that offenders serving such a placement could be drawn into and schooled in the techniques, practices and arguments of prison movement political activism. Later Department of Corrective Services finance was accepted in relation to a PAG-run halfway house.

The earlier assertion of the test of 'voluntariness for alternatives...so that the individual can come and go and take it or leave it as he/she pleases, free from any coercive control by agencies of the state' (PAG, 1980b: 9) was superseded or undercut by rather more precise and tactical calculations on the basis, not of regulation or non-regulation but rather, as Garland and Young suggest, of 'the specific nature of regulatory conditions' (Garland and Young, 1983: 33).

The notion of 'authoritarian populism' in *Policing the Crisis* seemed apt to describe the situation in Australia, and in NSW under the Greiner government in particular. From 1986 onwards law and order became an increasingly significant political and electoral issue exploited first in opposition and then as Prisons Minister by Michael Yabsley, who attempted, in his own words, to 'put the value back in punishment' (Brown, 1990, 1991, 1998). However, in time the danger became that 'authoritarian populism' explained both too much and too little, especially in the period of the Hawke-Keating federal Labour governments. Used as an all-purpose 'one size fits all' analysis it lost much of its detailed explanatory force and proved insufficient in explaining the multitude of developments owing more to neoliberal 'autonomisation' and 'responsibilisation' strategies, those 'adaptions' to 'the myth of sovereign crime control', and the ensuing volatility in law and order policies characteristic of many western democracies (Garland, 1996).

Policing the Crisis sustained the centrality to leftist analysis of the leitmotif of the 'crisis', albeit this was not the usual rhetorical 'crisis of capitalism' and the 'capitalist state' but a 'crisis of hegemony or "general crisis of the state"' which 'marks a moment of profound rupture in the political and economic life of a society, an accumulation of contradictions'. The 'crisis of hegemony' necessitated a modification in the 'modes of hegemony' in the direction of a 'tilt in the operation of the state away from consent towards the pole of coercion' (Hall et al., 1978: 217). The 'moment of mugging' thus needed to be located within the 'exhaustion of consent' and a shift to an authoritarian populism and a 'law and order society'. The difficulty in retrospect is that both the cruder 'crisis of capitalism' and the more specific 'crisis of hegemony' went on and on and on for decades, rather devaluing any explanatory force in the notion of crisis and ultimately the crisis rather manifested itself in capitalism's chief international rival system, which eventually went belly up in the Soviet Union and is in the process of being heavily modified along market lines in countries such as China. That does not mean we have to lie back and love it, but involvement in the actual politics of social change, especially as influenced by social movements, is to talk in more concrete terms of specific crises, rather than a crisis in capitalism or hegemony, for example in legal aid funding, or in prison overcrowding, or in intergenerational unemployment, or in levels of intra community violence, injury and death in particular Indigenous communities, and so on.

It is unfair to blame the various problematic features connected with these major works, works which embody much of the best of the established resources of critical criminology, on their specific authors and the specific texts. Sometimes the weaknesses were indeed in the original theory, as in the weaknesses of an essentialist Marxism. More often the weaknesses emerged in the way in which the works were used. Several tendencies are apparent here. The first is the assumption that politics can be directly conducted in accordance with theory, in this case criminological theory; that the problems are merely those of choosing the right theory and then applying it with sufficient steadfastness and commitment to 'principle'. This is the theory as template notion, the search for the theoretical fix, the Holy Grail, the night vision goggles which suddenly enable seeing in the dark. The second is that theory, which is developed in particular national contexts, can be readily applied in different national and local contexts. A third and related tendency is that of seeing local instances as manifestations of a universal totality, such as late modernity, governmentality, globalisation, neoliberalism, etc. These three tendencies are often closely linked and help to produce a criminological convergence in which national, regional, local and cultural difference is downplayed or subsumed into forms of exceptionalism. The neglect of the pertinence of race in the specific histories of penality in western colonial settler societies such as Australia is in part a consequence of the metropolitan and Eurocentric orientation of leading criminological and penological work (see Finnane and McGuire, 2001; Hogg, 2001).

The convergence of these three tendencies – choose the right theory and apply it across the board because we are all subject to the 'logic', 'mentalities', 'forces' of globalisation, neoliberalism, late modernity, the market, etc. – produces an underestimation of the complexity of the relationships between theory, government and politics. Theory, government and politics are all semi-autonomous domains which have their own conditions of existence, rationalities, institutional means, technologies, languages, modes of deportment, practices and limits which are not reducible 'to the realisation of any philosophy of rule, sovereign legal form or extrinsic interest (that of a ruling class or patriarchy, for example)' (Hogg, 1996: 46). Criminological theory cannot be simply implemented in governmental programmes or practice without careful attention being paid to its translation into political programmes which are in turn justified at least in part within or against prevailing popular media discourses of, for example, harm, risk, safety, cost, efficiency, desert, equity, cohesiveness, victimisation, reward, fear, horror, anxiety, autonomy, community, exclusion, and so on. The political process involves not only fashioning 'messages' which attempt to justify and explain the need for particular types of programme within a political party and the broader voting and media consuming public, but also the attempt to adhere the messages to particular constituencies or 'populations' which will promote the message and work in detail on fashioning operational programmes within the specific civil, bureaucratic, fiscal, inter-governmental and inter-agency means and limits prevailing.

Precisely what this translates into is often a mish-mash of competing and contradictory theories, messages and political programmes, as Stan Cohen's 'anomalies, incongruence, lack of fit, contradictions, paradoxes, impurities' and unintended consequences come into play. A recent attempt to 'purify' this unruliness is the claim in Britain that under New Labour criminal justice reform will now be 'evidence driven', a prescription backed up by bureaucratic controls over research grant funding. Here is a clear attempt to provide a rationalist, empirical basis to criminal justice policy and curb the irrationalism of policies formulated often overnight in response to the visceral vicissitudes of media and popular reaction. This understandable and well-intentioned policy, however, falls into the same trap: the assumption that politics can be made answerable to criminological rationality, rendered amendable and ruly through the dictates of reason. The limits to the claims of 'evidence-driven' criminal justice research and policy are all too evident once the *Sun* launches a campaign against this or that 'hooligan' or 'other'.

'Criminologies of Catastrophe'

O'Malley notes the current, end-of-millennium tendency, for what he calls 'criminologies of catastrophe' (O'Malley, 2000: 153) which propose a 'more or less complete transformation in criminal justice and penality', citing: 'diagnoses of the end of penal modernism and the rise of post-modern penality and criminal justice; the emergence of the risk society and actuarial justice; and the "death of the social" and the displacement of modernist welfare sanctions by neo-liberal penality' (O'Malley, 2000: 154). He argues, correctly in my view, that in many such accounts 'there has been a tendency to envisage criminal justice and penality as overdetermined by structural shifts. In this process, little room is left for the impact of contestation and resistance'. He adds that while we can detect the main tendencies at play in contemporary criminal justice, the future is not given in one or other of the logics of social or governmental transformation. However we read these, they create spaces for relational politics, hybridisation and governmental innovation. The theoretical models with which we work, in this sense are tools for politics rather than criminologies of catastrophe (O'Malley, 2000: 164).

Admittedly the shadow of the events of 11 September 2001 and their immediate aftermath hang over us and serve to bolster analyses, which emphasise rupture, catastrophe and insecurity. The likelihood is that security concerns and the 'war on terrorism', like the 'war on drugs' before it, will license a substantial relegitimation and expansion of state and private intelligence agencies, military and police powers, curbs on freedom of movement and traditional civil liberties. Like a particular fatal Great White shark attack in Western Australia at Cottesloe beach in 1999 which Robert Drewe argues has entered the national psyche and comes to mind whenever one enters the water, so plane travel is, as everyone says, never going to be quite the same again. The world is, in various ways many as yet unknown, a different place.

The extraordinary spectacle of the hijacked passenger jets ploughing into the twin towers of the World Trade Center in New York, captured on film and endlessly replayed, like that earlier film from the grassy knoll, will likely fuel analyses of catastrophe in its various forms: the 'epistemological break', the 'paradigm shift', the 'essence' or 'logic' of an overwhelming force, be it 'terrorism', 'capital', 'patriarchy', 'risk', 'neoliberalism', 'governmentality', 'late modernity', 'globalisation' or whatever. The 11 September 2001 will also bolster the passion for periodisation, which tends to accompany the view of history as a set of ruptures, the supersession of the new driving all before it. For those not of the 'first world' there have been other '11 Septembers', among them 11 September 1973 in Santiago, Chile, when, as Ariel Dorfman notes, 'planes came from the sky and rained death down upon national monuments and innocent people', followed by a reign of terror, torture and mass murder under General Pinochet (Morgan, 2001). The irrevocability of rupture and the Eurocentrism are evident in Jock Young's otherwise exciting excursion into cultural criminology in his *The Exclusive Society*. For Young and many others, some time in the 1960s there occurred a 'transition' from 'the Golden Age of the post-war period within the First World to the crisis years of the late 1960s onwards', 'a movement from modernity to late modernity', from an 'inclusive to an exclusive society' (Young, 1999: 1). The less apocalyptic among us are left with the rather more fragmented world of amalgams, hybrids, contestation and above all politics. The 'eclipse of the solidarity project' (Garland, 1996: 466) is partial and while 'the social' has taken a terrible battering, announcements of its 'death' (Rose, 1996) are exaggerated.

One of the great liberations from the myths of May 1968 has been the withering away of the limiting rhetoric of 'the barricades' and of the all-purpose revolution/reform dichotomy. Pleasure, delight and a sense of worth were no longer reserved for only the most cataclysmic overthrows of the existing order: the election of the Whitlam government in Australia after 23 years of Liberal/National Party coalition rule, the victory of the Vietcong, the defeat of apartheid and the release of Nelson Mandela, for example. Delight could be taken in more modest and local victories: the release of the Ananda Marga Three and later the final acquittal of Tim Anderson (Anderson, 1992; Carrington et al., 1991); the release of particular prisoners after campaigns such as those over Sandra Willson and Violet and Bruce Roberts; the establishment of the first community legal centres in the early 1970s, which have now multiplied into a network of general and specialist centres such as Women's Legal Centres, Welfare Rights, and the various Aboriginal Legal Services; the closure of Katingal prison in 1978, the exposure of brutality, incompetence and corruption in various state and now private agencies through a myriad of local campaigns across all states; the recent taking of Deer Park private women's prison in Victoria back into public ownership; the transmuting of the NSW PAG into Justice Action, a financially secure and successful lobby group founded on a printing business which employs a significant number of ex-prisoners; the continued efficient and professional production of the *Legal Service Bulletin/Alternative Law Journal*, the *ANZ Journal of Criminology*, and so on. Pat Carlen tells the story of being challenged to cite one thing her book on Cornton Vale prison, *Women's Imprisonment* (1983), had changed and replying that it ended the use of chamber pots – a small victory but one of great significance in the lives of those forced to endure such indignities.

A feature of many of these delights or victories, however small scale, is that they were achieved not by that one brilliant book, article, exposé or speech, but by specific social movement campaigns within which some criminologists, academics and students worked, often for many years. Involvement or association with criminal justice-oriented social movements has numerous benefits, one of which is as an antidote to what we used to call 'theoreticism', and in particular to sweeping claims of some new paradigm, theory, analysis, prediction. Pat O'Malley gives the example of Andrew Scull's (1977) 'discovery of decarceration', which – on the eve of probably the longest period of sustained and massive increase in imprisonment in most of the English-speaking world – predicted the mass closure of prisons and their displacement by cost-effective community corrections' (O'Malley, 2000: 153). Perhaps if Andrew Scull had been working more closely with particular criminal justice social movements in the actual politics of decarceration movements and programmes, as distinct from deriving its inevitability from an economistic analysis of the fiscal imperatives of the state, his prediction might have been rather more modest and rather less wrong.

Alliance Building

One of the key issues that has emerged then, in the Australian context, is the relationship between critical criminologists and criminal justice-oriented social movements. Politics is by its very nature a realm of conflict, compromise and contingency. All effective politics – whether electoral or issues based – involves coalition building, often among interests and groups who share limited common ground. Therefore the actual direction, composition, priorities, strategies and chosen allies in movements, campaigns and projects for progressive reform are likely to vary enormously for different issues and contexts. The fragmentation so often bewailed by those nostalgic for a collectivist past need not be a recipe for demoralisation, an indication of weakness, if that fragmentation of issues, identities, politics is accompanied by identification with and involvement in the various social movements in a very broadly defined criminal justice arena and beyond. Examples which spring to mind in the recent Australian context include:

- the S11 protests in Melbourne;
- the opposition to the building of a new women's prison in NSW;
- the taking of Deer Park private prison back into public ownership;
- widespread national opposition to mandatory sentencing policies in the Northern Territory and Western Australia, leading in late 2001 to their repeal in the NT by the newly elected ALP government.

Critical criminology can and should align itself with and be a part of such movements. However, it should also be acknowledged that social movements do not only occur on the left: witness the rise of the One Nation Party in the Australian context. A task of critical criminology then becomes not of aligning itself to One Nation, but, as Hogg and Carrington's work (1998) on rural crime and arguments for a spatial, geographically informed criminology illustrate, in contesting One Nation's simplistic accounts of the origins, manifestations and appropriate responses to rural discontent and anxiety.

Attention should also be devoted to the style of political involvement in social movements. In some quarters there is a persistence of the 'take-over' style of politics, manifest in a desire to occupy all the space and to ensure that all those involved share a common set of values and approaches, not only in relation to specific issues but more broadly. There have been elements of this approach in NSW recently in the movement to stop the building of a new women's prison at Windsor. Here more organised and radical groups tended to assert a self-appointed leadership role and insist on certain (abolitionist) lines of argument, undermining the strength and unity of a movement which relies precisely on the very broad alliance of predominantly women's groups and organisations not traditionally directly involved in prison or criminal justice issues, but from sectors such as health, community services, drug rehabilitation, homeless services, education and so on.

Such groups have settled on a more tactical, less ideological argument, adopted in the New South Wales Legislative Council Select Committee on the Increase in Prisoner Population, *Interim Report: Issues Relating to Women* (2000). The tactical argument is that plans for building a new women's prison should be suspended pending the implementation of a range of specific diversionary measures, followed by the monitoring of both the cost and effectiveness of those measures in comparison with the costs of building a new women's prison. Such an approach is more likely to garner support and is more attractive to a wide range of non-government and government-oriented women's organisations than either an approach which starts from explicitly abolitionist foundations, or a secondary approach which insists that there should be no increase in prison beds, as though the current ratio of beds to population holds some sort of magic. The danger of the latter approach is that, absent changes in practices and processes of criminalisation, prosecution and sentencing, can amount to a recipe for severe overcrowding and deteriorating conditions (for a similar argument in the British context see Mathews, 1999: 139–40). It is worth noting that both the Carr government and the Coalition state opposition immediately repudiated the Legislative Council Report, so that the task ahead is a formidable one. Nevertheless, a line of argument which has an open 'let's see' character, rather than one which appears to be driven by a foundationalist ideological approach, has most chance of gaining organisational and broader public support.

Such alliance building requires a rather different concept of resistance to that held by many leftist groups and individuals. As argued by Pat O'Malley (2000: 162), resistance has to be reconceived away from the romantic 'property of the left' notion of heroic struggle against dominant forces to encompass tensions and struggles within those dominant forces. Arguably the key political dynamic in contemporary western democracies (whatever the governing political parties) is the unstable alliance between neoliberal and neoconservative forces. O'Malley usefully sees this instability at the core of Garland's 'volatility' in governmental responses to the myth of sovereign crime control: 'adaption' through responsibilisation and crime prevention on the one hand and 'denial' in the form of excessive law and order politics on the other. Powerful neoliberal forces provide a major brake or resistance to tendencies to barbarism contained in current conservative law and order policies such as the death penalty, mandatory sentencing and selective incapacitation and 'zero tolerance' policies.

There is a need then for alliance building in relation to particular issues to be much broader and to take in the full potential of the political spectrum. Other examples of this are in the drug debate over issues such as heroin trials, safe-injecting rooms, drug courts, where groups such as the Australian Medical Association can make major contributions. Similarly in the fight against mandatory sentencing regimes the role of the churches can be significant – see, for example, the recent *A Statement of the Catholic Bishops of the United States, Responsibility, Rehabilitation, and Restoration: A Catholic Perspective on Crime and Criminal Justice* (2000). There is a need also to become more adept at using human rights arguments and to be able to give them a practical and specific operation, embodied in actual standards of practice, for example in how to actually run a prison system (Wilkie and Brown, 2002). There is a tendency for many on the left, myself included, to retain a residual hostility to what are seen as 'rhetorical' and 'abstract' human rights arguments, rather than to enter more constructively into debates around how human rights concepts might be made more concrete and operationalised. It is precisely the feeling that human rights arguments are abstract and 'over there', nothing to do with us, restricted to despotisms, that enable John Howard to thumb his nose at the United Nations Human Rights Committees and refuse to accept any international criticism of mandatory sentencing policies.

The Engaged Character of Australian Critical Criminology

Clearly there is an increasing international dimension, linkages and evident similarities across nation states, such as the diminishing and fragmentation of any organised political force to the left of so-called third-way politics in the western liberal democracies. Yet there are still significant differences in national contexts. Russell Hogg and I attempted in *Rethinking Law and Order* (1998) to look at law and order politics from both an international and a specifically Australian perspective. And in earlier contributions we sought to offer a brief history of postwar

Australian criminology from the establishment of criminology departments at Melbourne (1951) and Sydney (1959) Universities, the Australian
and New Zealand Society of Criminology (1967) and *ANZ Journal of
Criminology* (1968), the Criminology Research Council and the Australian
Institute of Criminology (1971), through to the emergence of radical
criminology in the early 1970s (Brown and Hogg, 1992a, 1992b; and see
Carson and O'Malley, 1989; Finnane, 1998). Among the key elements in
the emergence of radical criminology in Australia we identified
abolitionism (PAG, 1979, 1980a, 1980b; Brown and Hogg, 1985); a strong
Australian stream of social history particularly evident in work on
convicts, policing and punishment (e.g. Sturma, 1983; Hirst, 1983;
Daniels, 1983; Garton, 1988; Hughes, 1988; Neal, 1991; Van Krieken,
1991; Finnane, 1987, 1997; Oxley, 1996); an emphasis on the definition of
crime and criminology; and feminism (e.g. Allen, 1988, 1990; Carrington,
1990, 1993, 1998a; Howe, 1987, 1991, 1994; Naffine, 1987, 1997).

One of the characteristic features of Australian criminology has been
its engaged and reformist stance. Its unofficial motto might well have
been 'philosophers have explained the world, the point is to change it'.
With some exceptions such as Braithwaite, O'Malley, Hogg and Naffine,
critical criminology in Australia has not been marked by major theoretical
advances. Theoretical exposition has nearly always been connected to
specific criminal justice campaigns, often waged in conjunction with
various criminal justice social movements and groups. There are many
examples that illustrate the point. One is the prison movement and the
close involvement of academic criminologists schooled in *The New
Criminology, The Politics of Abolition* and later *Discipline and Punish*, in
alliance with ex and serving prisoners in the NSW PAG, in agitating for
the Nagle Royal Commission into prisons and helping to create the
conditions for a period of reform in penal practice, including the closure
of the then most recently built 'intractable' prison, Katingal (Zdenkowski
and Brown, 1982; Findlay, 1982; Vinson, 1982). Criminologists in Australia
have been heavily involved in agitation around the issues of miscarriages
of justice, both in general (Carrington et al., 1991) and in specific
campaigns such as those around the Ananda Marga Three (Molomby,
1986), Tim Anderson (Anderson, 1992) and Leigh Leigh (Carrington and
Johnson, 1994; Carrington, 1998b; Armstrong-Byrne et al., 1999) cases, to
mention only a few.

There was less need in Australia for an explicitly 'left realist'
reorientation in order to 'take seriously' crimes of violence against women
in particular, because many criminologists were already heavily involved
in campaigns to reform sexual assault laws, draw attention to the
prevalence of domestic violence, and establish rape crisis and other

support services for women victims of violent crime (Scutt, 1980, 1983; O'Donnell and Craney, 1982; Stubbs, 1994; Chappell and Egger, 1995; Cunneen and Stubbs, 1997; Easteal, 1998; Cossins, 2000). Academic criminologists have regularly taken up positions in State and Federal Law Reform Commissions on references such as Sentencing Reform (ALRC, 1988; Victoria, Sentencing Task Force, 1989; NSWLRC, 1996), conducted inquiries into aspects of criminal justice, written major reports for or provided policy advice to government and non-government agencies as consultants on a range of issues (O'Malley, 1996a: 34 cites 'almost every member of the Melbourne University Criminology Department...including Alder, James, Polk, White and Sutton, to name a few'; Chan, 1997; Chan et al., 1998), including police–Indigenous relations (e.g. Cunneen and Luke, 1995; Cunneen and Robb, 1987; Cunneen, 1990, 1991).

Criminologists have consistently taken a high profile in various public and media campaigns against police verbal, corruption, violence and killings (Harding, 1970; Flemington/Kensington Community Legal Centre, 1992; Dixon, 1999), white collar crime and business regulation (Hopkins, 1978; Braithwaite, 1984; Grabosky and Braithwaite, 1986; Grabosky, 1989; Ayres and Braithwaite, 1992; Fisse and Braithwaite, 1993; Haines, 1997; Findlay, 1999; Braithwaite and Drahos, 2000), industrial injury and disease (Hopkins, 1989; 1992; Grabosky and Sutton; Gunningham and Johnstone, 1999), deaths in custody (Hogan, Brown and Hogg, 1988; Biles and McDonald, 1992), mandatory sentencing (Harding, 1995; Johnson and Zdenkowski, 2000; Flynn, 2000; Morgan, 2000; Freiberg, 2001), juvenile justice (White, 1990; Youth Justice Coalition, 1990, 1994; White and Alder, 1994; Cunneen and White, 1995), policing of particular ethnic communities (Maher et al., 1998; Collins et al., 2000), criminal justice and Indigenous communities (Wilson, 1982; Gale, Bailey-Harris and Wundersitz, 1990; Purdy, 1996; Broadhurst, 1999; Cunneen, 2001), private prisons and policing (Moyle, 1994, 2000; Harding, 1997), crime prevention (O'Malley and Sutton, 1997), and sentencing (Zdenkowski, 2000) to list but some examples. Despite what is said below about the link between political engagement in criminal justice issues and the location of Australian criminology predominantly in law faculties, many examples of politically engaged work involve criminologists from other disciplines such as sociology (e.g. John Braithwaite and Paul Wilson), social work (e.g. Tony Vinson and Eileen Baldry), social policy (e.g. Janet Chan), geography (e.g. Fay Gale and Joy Wundesitz), history (e.g. Mark Finnane) and many feminists who would not identify themselves as criminologists.

Even one of the leading theoretically oriented works of Australian criminology, John Braithwaite's *Crime, Shame and Reintegration*, can be used to illustrate this point. Rather than just a theoretical intervention Braithwaite's text was used to argue for a series of reorientations in the practice of the sentencing of juveniles in particular by way of the development of concrete schemes of youth justice conferencing in NSW and elsewhere. In the ACT a series of reintegrative shaming sentencing experiments (RISE) have been carried out, overseen by Braithwaite and colleagues, with some interesting outcomes (Strang and Braithwaite, 2000, 2001). These various developments have increasingly been seen as part of an emerging international movement for restorative justice that draws strongly on Indigenous practices of youth conferencing in New Zealand and circle sentencing in Canada. While such a label condenses a range of very different schemes which are not without their critics, both conservative and radical (e.g. Cunneen, 1997; Blagg, 1998), the point here is that possibly the best known theoretically oriented work of Australian criminology has both been operationalised in the interests of criminal justice reform and has emerged as a major challenge to the dominance of retributive theory and practice. Here is an example of paying attention to the specificities of theory and politics and managing the process of political, bureaucratic, fiscal and legal translation.

Arguably distinctive local traditions, milieux and networks affected these possibilities. While the NDC/New Criminology in Britain and similar developments in the USA centred on sociological criminology, criminology in Australia remained closely connected with the law, both in its academic and its political manifestations. In part this is what oriented it to practical arenas of struggle around a whole array of criminal justice issues. Law students wanted not only to understand but also to change, to assist in the various struggles of prisoners, Indigenous people, tenants, psychiatric patients, welfare recipients, battered women, youth, etc. They did this by assisting in establishing and staffing the wave of community legal centres, which has grown into a national network. The law faculty in which I work, the University of NSW, has a twenty-year-old community legal service, operating as a clinical teaching programme that still attracts committed and idealistic students into social justice-oriented legal practice. Students can gain experience at one of a range of eight centres, including the National Children's and Youth Law Centre which assists young people hassled by police, families and government, through campaigns, test cases, media work and a highly sophisticated and successful website; the Indigenous Law Centre; and the Centre of Public Law which promotes debate on issues such as law reform, a bill of rights, Indigenous land rights, a republic, and so on.

Many other law faculties in Australia have similar programmes. So, the location of critical criminology predominantly in law faculties in

Australia, while it may have inhibited the development of theoretical sophistication, operated to ensure an ongoing and practical commitment to law reform which has been client or social movement driven. A further consequence of the location of academic criminology in law faculties is the close association between criminology, criminal justice and criminal law scholarship and teaching. Individual academics tend to write and teach across these areas, leading not only to the more engaged and practical involvement in criminal justice campaigns mentioned above but also to a more politicised, contextual and criminologically informed criminal law teaching and scholarship (see e.g. Brown et al., 1990, 1996, 2001; Byrne, 1993; Rush, 1997; Bronnit and McSherry, 2001) and a rich stream of criminal justice studies (Basten et al., 1982; Findlay, Egger and Sutton, 1983; Sallmann and Willis, 1984; Zdenkowski et al., 1987; Findlay and Duff, 1988; Findlay and Hogg, 1988; Chappell and Wilson, 1977, 1986, 1994, 2000; Settle, 1995; Findlay, Odgers and Yeo, 1999).

Another distinctive aspect of Australian criminology has been in part produced by the (relatively) small population size and the focus on the largely metropolitan capital cities. This has meant that there has been much cross-over and interaction between academic life and activism, working in 'the system', in law reform commissions, on inquiries and as media commentators. Such cross-over and interaction militates against rigid divisions between critical and administrative criminology (O'Malley, 1996a: 34; Israel, 2000: 10; Chan, 2000: 131). It also promotes a recognition of the different modes of deportment, vocabularies, calculations and forms of ethical practice (Meredith, 1993: 228; Hunter et al., 1991, 1992) specific to different contexts. Even within the one context, academics are called upon to be teachers, researchers and administrators. It is increasingly difficult to move between these different contexts, statuses and subjectivities without both a recognition of their differential nature, limits and requirements and the flexibility required to move between them. Such flexible movement is, as Meredith points out, particularly difficult within the 'characteristic posture of transcendent vision seeking adopted as part of the repertoire of critical exercises. Staying too long in the position of far-seeing intellectual can make it difficult to sustain the ethical stamina and the flexibility required to move between the increasingly demanding roles of teacher, researcher and administrator' (Meredith, 1993: 228).

A further consequence of the small population size that engenders interaction with social movements, government and media is that there is not likely to be a sustainable academic market for a critical criminology cut off from other activist and reform and policy-oriented constituencies. The pulping of nearly half the small print run of *The Prison Struggle* (1982) mentioned in the introduction may be a case in point. Further, the locus of research is still predominantly in the university sector, rather than in research institutes; research is not, as in the UK, managed in such a highly centralised way – we have no equivalent of the Home Office operating as a gatekeeper over research funding, requiring adherence to a range of current prescriptions such as 'evidence-based policy'. The Australian Research Council research grant process operates in a far more chaotic and disparate way, although Israel (2000) has warned of the increasing commercialisation of university-based criminological research and Presdee and Waters (1998) offer a case study of the 'perils and politics' of criminological research. The Australian Institute of Criminology has at various times been subject to threats of closure and in 1994 its budget and operations were substantially trimmed and its research programme was reined in to provide 'timely, policy-relevant advice to the Commonwealth and other key clients' (Israel, 2000: 13; Geis, 1994; Brown, 1994).

The Return to Social Theory

In the 1970s and 1980s debate over the definition of crime and the appropriate boundaries or subject matter of criminology was intense. Some leading criminologists mounted a critique denouncing or rejecting the legitimacy of criminology as a discipline (Smart, 1990; Cohen, 1988). Others like myself took seriously the Schwendingers' (1975) call for a redefinition of the criminal law based on the notion of 'historically determined human rights' and ran criminology courses which rejected current definitions of crime and focused entirely on issues such as unemployment, imperialism, racism and sexism, the uncriminalised crimes of the powerful, ignoring traditional working-class crime (Brown, 1977: 489). The impact of feminism and left realism, together with the demands to be relevant and engage in the politics of various criminal justice struggles, made such militant postures appear increasingly evasive and abstract, albeit that deconstructionists have continued to argue, following Derrida rather than Mathiesen, for a 'post-disciplinary reconfiguration of criminology' based on 'unhinging post-disciplinary criminologies from a commitment to realist conceptions of crime' via attention to the processes of 'accusation' and a version of critique which valorises the 'undecided' (Pavlich, 2000: 138, 147).

So the notion of the 'failure of criminology' is a well-established theme, pursued from diverse positions, including lack of relevance to policy-makers (Braithwaite, 1989a), anti-criminology (Cohen, 1988: 8) and left realism (Young, 1986). As Hogg has pointed out, the various rhetorical purposes at work here 'to exhort criminologists, with the lure of governmental and political relevance and receptivity, to greater theoretical rigour or to the abandonment of "left idealism"' are 'served only at the expense of a rather impoverished conception of government and a serious underestimation of the complexity of the relationships between "science", power, government and politics'. For 'neither the "abject failure" of criminology...nor its complete renunciation, has served to seriously inhibit its life – the flow of research funds, the development of tertiary courses of study, the establishment of institutes, the demand for expert policy advice and critical criminology...' (Hogg, 1996: 47).

Paradoxically perhaps, crime and criminal law are likely to both retain their centrality and become increasingly peripheral to criminology. They remain central because crime provides a key site for the growing politics and spectacle of affect, through which stories of usually spectacular and uncommon crime saturate the media, providing an embodiment of feelings of outrage, disgust, fascination, transgression. The confession of deviance and perversion as public spectacle and commodity cut through claims of expertise so that everyone becomes an expert and voyeur in the dimensions of good and evil. This public ownership of crime issues, as constructed through the media, is likely to continue and multiply. Simultaneously criminal law becomes less important as criminal law based regulation gives way to a host of other civil, administrative and governmental forms of regulation, privatisations, normative regimes operating through neoliberal notions of choice and freedom, a govern-ance of the self assisted by the heightened production of all manner of statistical information.

Even within criminal law itself there is a clear shift away from the classic conception of common law general principles, the presumption of *mens rea* and the burden of proof on the prosecution, to an increasing swathe of statutory offences created by legislatures which found liability in strict terms, either minimising fault elements to due diligence or negligence-based liability or restricting them to defences of honest and reasonable mistake of fact. The traditional burden of proof has been supplemented or undermined by reverse onus and deeming provisions and civil standards of proof (Ashworth, 2000: 228). The shift in areas such as social security and taxation to administrative and civil penalties, levied by bureaucracies for breaches of regulations, can be seen clearly. In 2000 for example, in Australia over 200,000 unemployed citizens were fined up to $1,300 for failure to attend interviews or answer correspondence. In medicare, white-collar and business regulation we see the proliferation of forms of civil regulation, the suspension of licences or registration and the suggestion that police investigation for fraud and white-collar crime be outsourced and privatised (Brown et al., 2001: 24–5).

What these developments indicate is that criminology needs to be able to follow the shifts in regulation, which it cannot do if it remains wedded to the traditional focus on crime as defined by the state. There is a need to encompass the broader concept of regulation, its justifications in relation to specific behaviours and processes, its techniques and its effects. Braithwaite and Drahos (2000) provide a good example of this type of work in their recent mammoth examination of regulation across a wide range of industries at an international level. Thus criminology needs a broader focus to encompass regulation, but for different reasons to those of the 1970s when a refusal to accept state definitions of crime as the basis of criminology was for the predominantly ideological reasons that the 'crimes of the powerful' (Pearce, 1976), the most socially damaging and widespread harms were largely outside a criminal law which focused on traditional working-class crime. The argument now is less ideological and more descriptive, that such activities and practices are still largely outside the criminal law, but have now been caught up in myriad forms of normative regulation under conditions of neoliberal governance, globalisation, the 'universalism of the market' (Beck, 1992: 104), the development of local, regional and international codes of practice, and forms of self- and industry-specific regulation. Such a broadening of focus will be assisted by a closer attention to an understanding of political culture and 'the theoretical work of contemporary social theory' (Garland and Sparks, 2000: 21), assisted also by a greater breadth, eclecticism and flexibility in analysis, in disciplinary resources and in the subject matter of research. Braithwaite (2000: 63), for example, argues that to become an 'educated scholar of the new regulation' requires the ability to 'sweep across the disciplines'.

Conclusion

This discussion has rehearsed some of the great strengths of critical criminology over the last thirty years and suggested a need to mitigate some of the undesirable features demonstrated in my recollections and elaborate the features of openness, eclecticism and flexibility as we follow the divergent trails of crime, law and order and regulation.

Let me return to REM's refrain, *Losing My Religion*, which seemed to echo in the waves of theory, the influential texts, the shifting library shelves and the realms of reminiscence. The refrain echoes a personal questioning, a scepticism towards a self-identified critical criminology or criminologist. That scepticism arises in part from what now (with the benefit of hindsight) seem to be some of the undesirable features of the critical criminology of the last three decades. These include an at times denunciatory and sectarian style and approach; the attempt to establish a hegemony for a particular approach at the expense of diminishing or dismissing other approaches which did not fit the prescribed 'critical' set of requirements of the time; the tendency for 'critical' to become a cipher or code word for a set of exclusionary practices and for a moral posture of critical intellectual seer; and a tendency to assume that critical theory had a universal applicability, over and above context, outside time and place.

A scepticism born not of a 'coming to truth', but of a 'losing my religion', a leeching of a previous faith derived from a belief in the self-evident correctness of particular 'critical' positions and identities. 'Losing my religion' has derived in part from a reflexive questioning of the 'heroic' texts of critical criminology, in part from engagement in the minutiae of criminal justice campaigns and social movement struggles in the Australian context, and in part from engagement in teaching criminal law, criminal justice and criminology in an Australian law faculty across three decades and across very different institutional and political circumstances.

Bibliography

Allen, J. (1988) 'The "masculinity" of criminology: interrogating some impasses', in M. Findlay and R. Hogg (eds), *Understanding Crime and Criminal Justice*. Sydney: Law Book Company.

Allen, J. (1990) *Sex and Secrets: Crimes Involving Australian Women Since 1880.* Melbourne: Oxford University Press.

ALRC (1988) *Sentencing.* Canberra: Australian Government Printer.

Althusser, L. (1972) *Politics and History.* London: New Left Books.

Althusser, L. (1973) *Essays in Self Criticism.* London: New Left Books.

Althusser, L. (1977) *For Marx.* London: New Left Books.

Anderson, P. (1980) *Arguments within English Marxism.* London: Verso.

Anderson, T. (1992) *Take Two.* Sydney: Bantam Books.

Armstrong-Byrne, H., Carmody, M., Hodge, B., Hogg, R. and Lee, M. (1999) 'The risk of naming violence: an unpleasant encounter between legal culture and feminist criminology', *Australian Feminist Law Journal*, 13: 13–37.

Ashworth, A. (2000) 'Is the criminal law a lost cause?', *Law Quarterly Review*, 116: 225–6.

Ayres, I. and Braithwaite, J. (1992) *Responsive Regulation.* Oxford: Oxford University Press.

Balbus, I. (1977) 'Commodity form and legal form: an essay in the "relative autonomy" of the law', *Law and Society Review*, 11: 571–88

Balibar, E. (1977) *On the Dictatorship of the Proletariat.* London: New Left Books.

Barry, A., Osborne, T. and Rose, N. (eds) (1996) *Foucault and Political Reason*. London: UCL Press.

Basten, J., Richardson, M., Ronalds, C. and Zdenkowski, G. (1982) *The Criminal Injustice System*. Sydney: Australian Legal Workers Group and Legal Service Bulletin.

Beck, U. (1992) *Risk Society: Towards a New Modernity*. Newbury Park, CA: Sage.

Bianchi, H. and Van Swaaningen, R. (eds) (1986) *Abolitionism*. Amsterdam: Free University Press.

Biles, D. and McDonald, D. (eds) (1992) *Deaths in Custody Australia, 1980–1989. Research Papers of the Criminology Unit of the Royal Commission into Aboriginal Deaths in Custody*. Canberra: Australian Government Printer.

Blagg, H. (1998) 'Restorative visions and restorative justice practices: conferencing, ceremony and reconciliation in Australia', *Current Issues in Criminal Justice*, 10(1): 5–14.

Braithwaite, J. (1984) *Corporate Crime in the Pharmaceutical Industry*. London: Routledge & Kegan Paul.

Braithwaite, J. (1989a) 'The state of criminology: theoretical decay or renaissance?', *Australian and New Zealand Journal of Criminology*, 22: 129–35.

Braithwaite, J. (1989b) *Crime, Shame and Reintegration*. Cambridge: Cambridge University Press.

Braithwaite, J. (2000) 'The new regulatory state and the transformation of criminology', in D. Garland and R. Sparks (eds), *Criminology and Social Theory*. Oxford: Oxford University Press.

Braithwaite, J. and Drahos, P. (2000) *Global Business Regulation*. Cambridge Cambridge University Press.

Broadhurst, R. (ed.) (1999) 'Crime, justice and Indigenous peoples', Special Issue of *The Australian and New Zealand Journal of Criminology*, 32(2).

Bronnit, S. and McSherry, B. (2001) *Principles of Criminal Law*. Sydney: Law Book Company.

Brown, D. (1977) 'Criminal justice reform: a critique', in D. Chappell and P. Wilson (eds), *The Australian Criminal Justice System*, 2nd edn., Sydney: Butterworths.

Brown, D. (1981) 'A note on Michel Foucault's *Discipline and Punish*', *Alternative Criminology Journal*, 4: 114–29.

Brown, D. (1987) 'The politics of reform', in G. Zdenkowski, C. Ronalds and M. Richardson (eds), *The Criminal Injustice System, Vol. 2*, Sydney: Pluto Press.

Brown, D. (1990) 'Putting the value back into punishment', *Legal Service Bulletin*, 15(6): 177–85.

Brown, D. (1991) 'The state of play in the prisons under the Greiner government: definitions of value', *Journal of Studies in Justice*, 4: 27–60.

Brown, D. (1994) 'Facing the knife: the Australian Institute of Criminology', *Alternative Law Journal*, 19: 15–18.

Brown, D. (1998) 'Penality and Imprisonment in Australia', in N. South and R. Weiss (eds), *Comparing Prison Systems*. Amsterdam: Harvester Wheatsheaf.

Brown, D. and Hogg, R. (1985) 'Abolition reconsidered', *Australian Journal of Law and Society*, 2(2): 56–75.

Brown, D. and Hogg, R (1992a) 'Law and order politics – left realism and radical criminology: a view from "down under"', in R. Mathews and J. Young (eds), *Issues in Realist Criminology*. London: Sage.

Brown, D. and Hogg, R. (1992a) 'Essentialism, Radical Criminology and Left Realism', *Australian and New Zealand Journal of Criminology*, 25(3): 195-230.

Brown, D., Kramer, H. and Quinn, M. (1988) 'Women in prison: task force reform', in M. Findlay and R. Hogg (eds), *Understanding Crime and Criminal Justice*. Sydney: Law Book Co.

Brown, D., Farrier, D. and Weisbrot, D. (1996) *Criminal Laws*, 2nd edn., Sydney: Federation Press.

Brown, D., Farrier, D., Egger, S. and McNamara, L. (2001) *Criminal Laws*, 3rd edn. Sydney: Federation Press.

Brown, D., Farrier, D., Neal, D. and Weisbrot, D. (1990) *Criminal Laws*. Sydney: Federation Press.

Brown, M. and Pratt, J. (eds) (2000) *Dangerous Offenders*. London: Routledge.

Burchell, G., Gordon, C. and Miller, P. (1991) *The Foucault Effect: Studies in Governmentatlity*. London: Harvester Wheatsheaf.

Burgmann, M. and Burgmann, V. (1998) *Green Bans, Red Union*. Sydney: UNSW Press.

Byrne, P. (1993) *Criminal Law and Colonial Subject*. Cambridge: Cambridge University Press.

Carlen, P. (1983) *Women's Imprisonment*. London: Routledge & Kegan Paul.

Carlen, P. and Collison, M. (eds) (1980) *Radical Issues in Criminology*. Oxford: Martin Robertson.

Carrington, K. (1990) 'Feminist readings of female delinquency', in J. Grbich (ed) *Feminism, Law and Society*. Melbourne: La Trobe University Press.

Carrington, K. (1993) *Offending Girls: Sex, Youth and Justice*. Sydney: Allen & Unwin.

Carrington, K. (1998) 'Postmodernism and feminist criminologies: fragmenting the criminological subject', in P. Walton and J. Young (eds), *The New Criminology Revisited*. London: MacMillan Press.

Carrington, K. (1998b) *Who Killed Leigh Leigh?*. Sydney: Random House.

Carrington, K. and Johnson, A. (1994) 'Representations of crime, guilt and sexuality in the Leigh Leigh rape/murder case', *Australian Feminist Law Journal*, 3: 3–29.

Carrington, K., Dever, M., Hogg, R., Bargen, J. and Lohrey, A. (eds) (1991) *Travesty! Miscarriages of Justice*. Sydney: Pluto Press.

Carson, K. and O'Malley, P. (1989) 'The institutional foundations of contemporary Australian criminology', *Australian and New Zealand Journal of Sociology*, 25(3): 333–55.

Catholic Bishops (2000) *A Statement of the Catholic Bishops of the United States. Responsibility, Rehabilitation, and Restoration: A Catholic Perspective on Crime and Criminal Justice*. Available on <http://www.nccbuscc.org/sdwp/criminal/htm>.

Chan, J. (1997) *Changing Police Culture*. Cambridge: Cambridge University Press.

Chan, J. (2000) 'Globalisation, reflexivity and the practice of criminology', *Australian and New Zealand Journal of Criminology*, 32(2): 118–35.

Chan, J., Dixon, D., Maher, L. and Stubbs, J. (1998) *Policing in Cabramatta. Final Report to the NSW Police Service* (unpublished).

Chappell, D. and Egger, S. (1995) *Australian Violence, Contemporary Perspectives II*. Canberra: Australian Institute of Criminology.

Chappell, D. and Wilson, P. (1977) *The Australian Criminal Justice System*. Sydney: Butterworths.

Chappell, D. and Wilson, P. (1986) *The Australian Criminal Justice System. The Mid 1980s*. Sydney: Butterworths.

Chappell, D. and Wilson, P. (1994) *The Australian Criminal Justice System. The Mid 1990s*. Sydney: Butterworths.

Chappell, D. and Wilson, P. (2000) *Crime and the Criminal Justice System in Australia: 2000 and Beyond*. Sydney: Butterworths.

Cohen, S. (ed.) (1971) *Images of Deviance.* London: Penguin Books.

Cohen, S. (1979) 'The punitive city', *Contemporary Crises,* 3: 339–63.

Cohen, S. (1985) *Visions of Social Control.* London: Polity Press.

Cohen, S. (1988) *Against Criminology.* New Brunswick, NJ: Transaction Books.

Collier, R. (1998) *Masculinities, Crime and Criminology.* London: Sage.

Collins, J. et al. (2000) *Kebabs, Kids, Cops and Crime: Youth, Ethnicity and Crime.* Sydney: Pluto Press.

Cossins, A. (2000) *Masculinities, Sexualities and Child Sexual Abuse.* The Hague: Kluwer Law International.

Cunneen, C. (1990) *Aboriginal–Police Relations in Redfern: With Special Reference to the 'Police Raid' of 8 February 1990,* Report Commissioned by the National Inquiry into Racist Violence. Sydney: Human Rights and Equal Opportunity Commission.

Cunneen, C. (1991) *A Study of Aboriginal Juveniles and Police Violence,* Report Commissioned by the National Inquiry into Racist Violence. Sydney: Human Rights and Equal Opportunity Commission.

Cunneen, C. (1997) 'Community conferencing and the fiction of Indigenous control', *Australian and New Zealand Journal of Criminology,* 30(3): 292–311.

Cunneen, C. (2001) *Conflicts, Politics and Crime.* Sydney: Allen & Unwin.

Cunneen, C. and Luke, G. (1995) *Aboriginal Over-representation in Discretionary Decisions in the NSW Juvenile Justice System.* Sydney: Juvenile Justice Advisory Council.

Cunneen, C. and Robb, T. (1987) *Criminal Justice in North-West New South Wales.* Sydney: New South Wales Bureau of Crime Statistics and Research, Attorney-General's Department.

Cunneen, C. and Stubbs, J. (1997) *Gender, Race and Legal Relations.* Sydney: Institute of Criminology, School of Law.

Cunneen, C. and White, R. (1995) *An Australian Perspective on Juvenile Justice.* Sydney: Oxford University Press.

Cutler, A., Hindess, B., Hirst, P. and Hussain, A. (1977) *Marx's Capital and Capitalism Today.* London: Routledge.

Daley, K. (1994) *Gender, Crime and Punishment.* New Haven, CT: Yale University Press.

Daniels, K. (ed.) (1983) *So Much Hard Work: Women and Prostitution in Australian History.* Sydney: Fontana.

Dean, M. (1999) *Governmentality.* London: Sage.

Dixon, D. (ed.) (1999) *A Culture of Corruption.* Sydney: Hawkins Press.

Downes, D. and Rock, P. (1979) *Deviant Interpretations.* Oxford: Martin Robertson.

Downes, D. and Rock, P. (1982) *Understanding Deviance.* Oxford: Clarendon Press.

Easteal, P. (ed.) (1998) *Balancing the Scales: Rape Law Reform and Australian Culture.* Sydney: Federation Press.

Edwards, A. R. and Wilson, P. (1975) *Social Deviance in Australia.* Melbourne: Cheshire.

Ericson, R. and Haggerty, K. D. (1977) *Policing the Risk Society.* Oxford: Oxford University Press.

Findlay, M. (1982) *The State of the Prison.* Bathurst: Mitchellsearch.

Findlay, M. (1999) *The Globalisation of Crime.* Cambridge: Cambridge University Press.

Findlay, M. and Duff, A. (1988) *The Jury Under Attack.* Sydney: Butterworths.

Findlay, M. and Hogg, R. (eds) (1988) *Understanding Crime and Criminal Justice.* Sydney: Law Book Company.

Findlay, M., Egger, S. and Sutton, J. (eds) (1983) *Issues in Criminal Justice Administration*. Sydney: Allen & Unwin.

Findlay, M., Odgers, S. and Yeo, S. (1999) *Australian Criminal Justice*. Melbourne: Oxford University Press.

Fine, B. (1979) 'Struggles against discipline: the theory and politics of Michel Foucault', *Capital and Class*, 9: 80–98.

Fine, B. (1980) 'The birth of bourgeois punishment', *Crime and Social Justice*, 13: 19–26.

Fine, B., Kinsey, R., Lea, J., and Picciotto, S. (eds) (1979) *Capitalism and the Rule of Law*. London: Hutchinson.

Finnane, M. (1987) *Policing in Australia: Historical Perspectives*. Sydney: NSW University Press.

Finnane, M. (1994) *Police and Government*. Oxford: Oxford University Press.

Finnane, M. (1997) *Punishment in Australian Society*. Oxford: Oxford University Press.

Finnane, M. (1998) 'Sir John Barry and the Melbourne Department of Criminology: some foundations of Australian criminology', *Australian and New Zealand Journal of Criminology*, 31(1): 69–81.

Finnane, M. and McGuire, J. (2001) 'The uses of punishment and exile: Aborigines in colonial Australia', *Punishment and Society*, 3(2): 279–98.

Fisse, B. and Braithwaite, J. (1993) *Corporations, Crime and Accountability*. Cambridge: Cambridge University Press.

Flemington/Kensington Community Legal Centre and the families of Mark Militano, Graeme Jensen and Jedd Houghton (1992) *Police Shootings in Victoria, 1987–1989*. Melbourne: Fitzroy Legal Service.

Flynn, M. (2000) 'International law, Australian Criminal law and mandatory sentencing: the claims, the reality and the possibilities', *Criminal Law Journal*, 24(3): 184–97.

Foucault, M. (1977) *Discipline and Punish*. New York: Pantheon.

Freiberg, A. (2001) 'Three strikes and you're out – it's not cricket: colonisation and resistance in Australian sentencing', in M. Tonry and R. Frase (eds), *Sentencing and Sanctions in Western Countries*. New York: Oxford University Press.

Gale, F., Bailey-Harris, R., and Wundersitz, J. (1990) *Aboriginal Youth and the Criminal Justice System*. Melbourne: Cambridge University Press.

Gane, M. and Johnson, T. (1993) *Foucault's New Domains*. London: Routledge.

Garland, D. (1990) *Punishment and Modern Society*. Oxford: Clarendon.

Garland, D. (1996) 'The limits of the sovereign state: strategies of crime control in contemporary society', *British Journal of Criminology*, 36(4): 445–71.

Garland, D. (1997) '"Governmentality" and the problem of crime', *Theoretical Criminology*, 1(2): 173–214.

Garland, D. (2001) *The Culture of Control*. Oxford: Oxford University Press.

Garland, D. and Sparks, R. (eds) (2000) *Criminology and Social Theory*. Oxford: Oxford University Press.

Garland, D. and Young, P. (eds) (1983) *The Power to Punish*. London: Heinemann.

Garton, S. (1988) *Medicine and Madness*. Sydney: University of NSW Press.

Geis, G. (1994) '"This sort of thing isn't helpful": the dilemmas of the Australian Institute of Criminology', *The Australian and New Zealand Journal of Criminology*, 27: 282–98.

Gelsthorpe, L. and Morris, A. (eds) (1990) *Feminist Perspectives in Criminology*. Buckingham: Open University Press.

Gouldner, A. (1968) 'The sociologist as partisan: sociology and the welfare state', *The*

American Sociologist, 3 May, 103–16; reprinted in J. D. Douglas (ed.), (1970) *The Relevance of Sociology*. New York: Appleton-Century-Crofts.

Grabosky, P. (1977) *Sydney in Ferment*. Canberra: ANU Press.

Grabosky, P. (1989) *Wayward Governance: Illegality and Its Control in the Public Sector*. Canberra: Australian Institute of Criminology.

Grabosky, P. and Sutton, A. (eds) (1989) *Stains on a White Collar – Fourteen Studies in Corporate Crime or Corporate Harm*. Sydney: Hutchinson.

Grabosky, P. and Braithwaite, J. (1986) *Of Manners Gentle: Enforcement Strategies in Australian Business Regulatory Agencies*. Melbourne: Oxford University Press.

Gramsci, A. (1970) *Prison Notebooks*. London: Lawrence & Wishart.

Gunningham, N. and Johnstone, R. (1999) *Regulating Workplace Safety: Systems and Sanctions*. Oxford: Oxford University Press.

Haines, F. (1997) *Corporate Regulation: Beyond Punish or Persuade*. Oxford: Clarendon Press.

Hall, S., Critcher, C., Jefferson, T., Clarke, J. and Roberts, B. (1978) *Policing the Crisis*, London: Macmillan.

Harding, R. W. (1970) *Police Killings in Australia*. Ringwood, Victoria: Penguin Books.

Harding, R. (ed.) (1995) *Repeat Juvenile Offenders: The Failure of Selective Incapacitation in Western Australia*, 2nd edn., Perth: Crime Research Centre UWA.

Harding, R. W. (1997) *Private Prisons and Public Accountability*. Buckingham: Open University Press.

Hay, D. et al. (eds) (1975) *Albion's Fatal Tree*. London: Allen Lane.

Henry, S. and Milovanovic, D. (1996) *Constitutive Criminology*. London: Sage.

Hindess, B. and Hirst, P. Q. (1975) *Pre-Capitalist Modes of Production*. London: Routledge.

Hindess, B. and Hirst, P. Q. (1977) *Mode of Production and Social Formation*. London: Macmillan.

Hirst, J. B. (1983) *Convict Society and its Enemies*. Sydney: Allen & Unwin.

Hirst, P. Q. (1975) 'Marx and Engels on crime, law and morality', in I. Taylor, P. Walton and J. Young (eds), *Critical Criminology*. London: Routledge.

Hirst, P. (1994) *Associative Democracy – New Forms of Economic and Social Governance*. Cambridge: Polity Press.

Hobsbawm, E. J. (1959) *Primitive Rebels*. Manchester: Manchester University Press.

Hobsbawm, E. J. (1972) *Bandits*. London: Penguin Books.

Hobsbawm, E. J. and Rude, G. (1973) *Captain Swing*. Suffolk: Penguin University Books.

Hogan, M., Brown, D. and Hogg, R. (eds) (1988) *Death in the Hands of the State*. Sydney: Redfern Legal Centre Publishing.

Hogg, R. (1979) 'Criminal justice and social control: contemporary developments in Australia', *Journal of Studies in Justice*, 3: 89–122.

Hogg, R. (1996) 'Criminological failure and governmental effect', *Current Issues in Criminal Justice* 8(1): 43–59.

Hogg, R. (2001) 'Penalty and Modes of Regulating Indigenous Peoples in Australia', *Punishment and Society*, 3(3) 355–79.

Hogg, R. and Brown, D. (1998) *Rethinking Law and Order*. Sydney: Pluto Press.

Hogg, R. and Carrington K. (1998) 'Crime, rurality and community', *Australian and New Zealand Journal of Criminology*, 31(2): 160–81.

Hopkins, A. (1978) *Crime, Law and Business*. Canberra: Australian Institute of Criminology.

Hopkins, A. (1989) 'Crime without punishment: the Appin Mine disaster' in P. Grabosky and A. Sutton (eds), *Stains on a White Collar*. Canberra: Australian Institute of Criminology.

Hopkins, A., Easson, H. and Harrison, J. (1992) 'The legal response to work-related fatalities in NSW', *Australian and New Zealand Journal of Criminology*, 25(2): 135–55.

Hornby, N. (1996) *High Fidelity*. London: Indigo.

Howe, A. (1987) 'Toward critical criminology – and beyond', *Law in Context*, 5: 97–111.

Howe, A. (1991) 'Postmodern penal politics? – further footnotes on women prisoners', in K. Carrington and B. Morris (eds), *Politics, Prisons and Punishment, Special Issue, Journal for Social Justice Studies*, 4: 61–72.

Howe, A. (1994) *Punish and Critique: Towards a Feminist Analysis of Penality*. London: Routledge.

Hughes, R. (1988) *The Fatal Shore*. London: Pan Books.

Hulsman, L. (1986) 'Critical criminology and the concept of crime', *Contemporary Crises*, 10: 63–80.

Hunter, I. (1992) 'Auditing the critique department: on the humanist understanding of bureaucracy', in D. Stockey (ed.), *Melbourne Studies in Education*. Melbourne: La Trobe University Press.

Hunter, I., Meredith, D., Smith B., and Stokes, G. (1991) *Accounting for the Humanities*. Brisbane: Institute of Cultural Policy Studies.

Israel, M. (2000) 'The commercialisation of university-based criminological research in Australia', *Australian and New Zealand Journal of Criminology*, 33(1): 1–20.

Jefferson, T. (1997) 'Masculinities and crime', in M. Maguire, R. Morgan and R. Reiner (eds), *The Oxford handbook of criminology*, 2nd edn. Oxford: Clarendon Press: 535–58.

Johnson, D. and Zdenkowski,G. (2000) *Mandatory Injustice: Compulsory Imprisonment in the Northern Territory, Report Submitted to the Senate Legal and Constitutional References Committee, Inquiry into the Human Rights (Mandatory Sentencing of Juvenile Offenders) Bill, 1999*.

Laclau, E. (1977) *Politics and Ideology in Marxist Theory*. London: New Left Books.

Laclau, E. and Mouffe, C. (1985) *Hegemony and Socialist Strategy*. London: Verso.

Maher, L., Dixon, D., Swift, W. and Nguyen (1998) *Anh Hai: Young Asian Background People's Perceptions and Experiences of Policing*. Sydney: UNSW Faculty of Law.

Marx, K. (1954) *Capital, Vols 1, 2 and 3*. Moscow: Progress Publishers.

Marx, K. (1963) *Theories of Surplus Value*, Parts 1, 2 and 3, Moscow: Progress Publishers.

Mathiesen, T. (1974) *The Politics of Abolition*. London: Martin Robertson.

Mathews, R. (1999) *Doing Time*. London: Macmillan Press.

Mathews, R. and Young, J. (1992a) *Rethinking Criminology: The Realist Debate*. London: Sage.

Mathews, R. and Young, J. (1992b) *Issues in Realist Criminology*. London: Sage.

Meredith, D. (1993) 'Twenty minutes for the heart: facing the exercise of critique' in D. Bennett (ed.), *Cultural Studies: Pluralism and Theory*. Melbourne: Department of English, University of Melbourne.

Messerschmidt, J. (1993) *Masculinity and Crime*. Lanham, MD: Rowman & Littlefield.

Molomby, T. (1986) *Spies, Bombs and the Path of Bliss*. Sydney: Potoroo Press.

Morgan, J. (2001) 'A survivor of that other September 11', *Sydney Morning Herald*, 6 November, 18.

Morgan, N. (2000) 'Mandatory sentences in Australia: where have we been and were are we going?', *Criminal Law Journal*, 24(3): 164–83.

Morris, M. (1988) *The Pirate's Fiancee*. London: Verso.

Moyle, P. (1994) *Private Prisons and Police*. Sydney: Pluto Press.

Moyle, P. (2000) *Profiting from Punishment*. Sydney: Pluto Press.

Naffine, N. (1987) *Female Crime*. Sydney: Allen & Unwin.

Naffine, N. (1997) *Feminism and Criminology*. Sydney: Allen & Unwin.

Nagle, J. (1978) *Report of the Royal Commission into NSW Prisons*. Sydney: NSW Government Printer.

Neal, D. (1991) *The Rule of Law in a Penal Colony*. Cambridge: Cambridge University Press.

Newburn, T. and Stanko, E. A. (1994) *Just Boys Doing Business?*. London: Routledge.

New South Wales Law Reform Commission (1996) *Report No. 79: Sentencing*. Sydney: NSW Government Printer.

New South Wales Legislative Council, Select Committee on the Increase in Prisoner Population (2000), *Interim Report: Issues Relating to Women NSW*. Sydney: Government Printer.

O'Donnell, C. and Craney, J. (1982) *Family Violence in Australia*. Melbourne: Longman.

O'Malley, P. (1982) 'Historical practice and the production of Marxist legal theory', *Crime and Social Justice*, 18: 53–61.

O'Malley, P. (1988) 'The purpose of knowledge: pragmatism and the praxis of Marxist criminology', *Contemporary Crises*, 12: 65–79.

O'Malley, P. (1992) 'Risk, power and crime prevention', *Economy and Society*, 21(3): 252–75.

O'Malley, P. (1996a) 'Post social criminologies. some implications of current political trends for criminological theory and practice', *Current Issues in Criminal Justice*, 8: 26–38.

O'Malley, P. (1996b) 'Risk and responsibility', in A. Osborne, T. Barry and N. Rose (eds), *Foucault and Politics*. London: UCL Press.

O'Malley, P. (1999) 'Volatile and contradictory punishment', *Theoretical Criminology*, 3(2): 175–96

O'Malley, P. (2000) 'Criminologies of catastrophe?: understanding criminal justice on the edge of the new millenium', *Australian and New Zealand Journal of Criminology*, 33(2): 153–67.

O'Malley, P. and Palmer, D. (1996) 'Post Keynesian policing', *Economy and Society*, 27: 135–47.

O'Malley, P. and Sutton, A. (1997) *Crime Prevention in Australia*. Sydney: Federation Press.

O'Malley, P., Weir, L. and Shearing, C. (1997) 'Governmentality, criticism, politics', *Economy and Society*, 26: 501–17.

Oxley, D. (1996) *Convict Maids*. Cambridge: Cambridge University Press.

Pavlich, G. (2000) 'Forget crime: accusation, governance and criminology', *Australian and New Zealand Journal of Criminology*, 33(2): 136–52.

Pearce, F. (1976) *Crimes of the Powerful*. London: Pluto Press.

Pearson, G (1975a) 'Misfit sociologies and the politics of socialization', in I. Taylor, P. Walton and J. Young (eds), *Critical Criminology*. London: Routledge & Kegan Paul.

Pearson, G. (1975b) *The Deviant Imagination*. London: Macmillan.

Pearson, G. (1983) *Hooligan: A History of Respectable Fears*. London: Macmillan.

Polk, K. (1994) *When Men Kill*. Cambridge: Cambridge University Press.

Poulantzas, N. (1973) *Political Power and Social Classes*. London: New Left Books.
Poulantzas, N. (1974) *Fascism and Dictatorship*. London: New Left Books.
Poulantzas, N. (1975) *Classes in Contemporary Capitalism*. London: New Left Books.
Poulantzas, N. (1976) *The Crisis of the Dictatorships*. London: New Left Books.
Poulantzas, N. (1978) *State, Power, Socialism*. London: Verso.
Pratt, J. (1997) *Governing the Dangerous*. Sydney: Federation Press.
Presdee, M. and Waters, R. (1998) 'The perils and politics of criminological research and the threat to academic freedom', *Current Issues in Criminal Justice*, 10(2): 156–67.
Prisoners Action Group (PAG) (1979) 'Prisoners Action Group submission on the knowledge of crime and its causes', *Alternative Criminology Journal*, 3(2): 8–74.
Prisoners Action Group (PAG) (1980a) 'Prisoners Action Group 2nd submission to the NSW Royal Commission into Prisons: contemporary penal practices', *Alternative Criminology Journal*, 3(3): 1–67.
Prisoners Action Group (PAG) (1980b) 'Prisoners Action Group 3rd submission to the NSW Royal Commission into Prisons: abolition', *Alternative Criminology Journal*, 3(4): 1–74.
Purdy, J. (1996) 'Postcolonialism: The emperor's new clothes', *Social and Legal Studies*, 5(3): 405–26.
Quinney, R. (1974) *Critique of Legal Order*. Boston: Little, Brown.
Read, M. B. (1991) *Chopper: From the Inside*. Smithfield, NSW: Sly Ink.
Read, M. B. (1992) *Chopper 2: Hits and Memories*. Smithfield, NSW: Sly Ink.
Rock, P. (1973) *Deviant Behaviour*. London: Hutchinson.
Rock, P. and McIntosh, M. (1974) *Deviance and Social Control*. London: Tavistock.
Rose, N. (1989) *Governing the Soul: the Shaping of the Private Self*. London: Routledge.
Rose, N. (1996) 'The death of the "social"? Refiguring the territory of government', *Economy and Society*, 26: 327–46.
Rose, N. (1999) *Powers of Liberty*. Cambridge: Cambridge University Press.
Rude, G. (1959) *The Crowd in the French Revolution*. London: Oxford University Press.
Rush, P. (1997) *Criminal Law*, Sydney: Butterworths.
Sallmann, P. and Willis, J. (1984) *Criminal Justice in Australia*. Melbourne: Oxford University Press.
Scull, A. (1977) *Decarceration, Community Treatment and the Deviant*. Englewood Cliffs. NJ: Prentice Hall.
Scutt, J. (ed.) (1980) *Rape Law Reform*. Canberra: Australian Institute of Criminology.
Scutt, J. (1983) *Even in the Best of Homes*. Ringwood, Victoria: Penguin Books.
Settle, R. (1995) *Police Informers*. Sydney: Federation Press.
Smart, C. (1976) *Women, Crime and Criminology*. London: Routledge.
Smart, C. (1990) 'Feminist approaches to criminology or postmodern woman meets atavistic man', in L. Gelsthorpe and A. Morris (eds), *Feminist Perspectives in Criminology*. Buckingham: Open University Press.
Steinert, H. (1986) 'Beyond crime and punishment', *Contemporary Crises*, 10: 21–38.
Stenson, K. and Sullivan, R. E. (eds) (2001) *Crime, Risk and Justice: the Politics of Crime Control in Liberal Democracies*. Cullompton: Willan Publishing.
Strang, H. and Braithwaite, J. (eds) (2000) *Restorative Justice: From Philosophy to Practice*. Cambridge: Cambridge University Press.
Strang, H. and Braithwaite, J. (eds) (2001) *Restorative Justice and Civil Society*. Cambridge: Cambridge University Press.
Stubbs, J. (ed.) (1994) *Women, Male Violence and the Law*. Sydney: Institute of Criminology, Sydney University Law School.
Sturma, M. (1983) *Vice in a Vicious Society*. St Lucia: Queensland University Press.

Taylor, I. (1981) *Law and Order: Arguments for Socialism*. London: Macmillan.

Taylor, I. (1999) *Crime in Context*. London: Polity Press.

Taylor, I. and Taylor, L. (1973) *Politics and Deviance*. London: Penguin.

Taylor, I. and Walton, P. (1975) 'Radical deviancy theory: a reply to Paul Q. Hirst', in I. Taylor, P. Walton and J. Young (eds), *Critical Criminology*. London: Routledge & Kegan Paul.

Taylor, I., Walton, P. and Young, J. (1973) *The New Criminology*. London: Routledge & Kegan Paul.

Taylor, I., Walton, P. and Young, J. (1975) *Critical Criminology*. London: Routledge & Kegan Paul.

Taylor, L. (1973) *Deviance and Society*. London: Nelson.

Therborn, G. (1976) *Science, Class and Society*. London: New Left Books.

Therborn, G. (1978) *What Does the Ruling Class Do When It Rules?* London: New Left Books.

Therborn, G. (1980) *The Ideology of Power and the Power of Ideology*. London: Verso.

Thompson, E. P. (1968) *The Making of the English Working Class*. London: Penguin.

Thompson, E. P. (1977) *Whigs and Hunters*. London: Penguin.

Thompson, E. P. (1978) *The Poverty of Theory and Other Essays*. London: Merlin Press.

Van Krieken, R. (1991) *Children and the State*. Sydney: Allen & Unwin.

Victoria, Sentencing Task Force (1989) *Review of Statutory Maximum Penalties*. Melbourne: Victoria Government Printer.

Vinson, A. (1982) *Wilful Obstruction*. Sydney: Methuen.

Walton, P. and Young, J. (1998) *The New Criminology Revisited*. London: Macmillan.

White, R. (1990) *No Space of their Own: Young People and Social Control in Australia*. Cambridge: University of Cambridge Press.

White, R. and Alder, C. (1994) *Police and Young People in Australia*. Melbourne: Cambridge University Press.

Wilkie, M. and Brown, D. (eds) (2002) *Prisoners as Citizens* (forthcoming). Sydney: Federation Press.

Wilson, P. (1982) *Black Death, White Hands*. Sydney: Allen & Unwin.

Wilson, P. and Braithwaite, J. (eds) (1978) *Two Faces of Deviance*. St Lucia: University of Queensland Press.

Young, A. (1996) *Imagining Crime*. London: Sage.

Young, J. (1975) 'Working class criminology', in I. Taylor, P. Walton, and J. Young (eds), *Critical Criminology*. London: Routledge & Kegan Paul.

Young, J. (1979) 'Left idealism, reformism and beyond: from new criminology to Marxism', in NDC/CSE (eds) *Capitalism and the Rule of Law*. London: Hutchinson.

Young, J. (1986) 'The failure of criminology: the need for a radical realism', in R. Mathews and J. Young (eds), *Confronting Crime*. London: Sage.

Young, J. (1999) *The Exclusive Society*. London: Sage.

Youth Justice Coalition, (1990) *Kids in Justice*. Sydney: Youth Justice Coalition.

Youth Justice Coalition, (1994) *Nobody Listens. The Experience of Contact Between Young People and Police*. Sydney: Youth Justice Coalition.

Zdenkowski, G. (2000) 'Sentencing trends: past, present, and prospective', in D. Chappell and P. Wilson (eds), *Crime and Criminal Justice in Australia: 2000 and Beyond*. Sydney: Butterworths.

Zdenkowski, G. and Brown, D. (1982) *The Prison Struggle*. Melbourne: Penguin.

Zdenkowski, G., Ronalds, C. and Richardson, M. (eds) (1987) *The Criminal Injustice System, Volume Two*. Sydney: Pluto Press.

Chapter 5

Feminism and critical criminology: confronting genealogies

Kerry Carrington

Introduction

Just as there is no single critical approach to criminology, feminist approaches to research on criminology are equally diverse (see Naffine, 1997: 29; Carrington, 1994: 263; Young, A., 1996: 34). The impetus for both feminist and critical versions of criminology grew broadly out of a constellation of cultural, material and ideological changes that swept the western world from the 1960s that 'gave courage to attack the Big Enemies: scientism, dehumanisation, determinism, reification, fake neutrality, [and] the denial of politics' (Cohen, 1998: 103). This was a time when intellectual critics were seized by deconstructionist impulses to propose radical critiques of knowledge, power and the state. This chapter reviews the substantial and often neglected contribution of feminist research and theory to the development of critical approaches to criminology. Feminism is located in my analysis as a vital and vibrant part of critical criminology, not as some add-on or afterthought. In doing so it examines areas of compatibility and contestation in and between feminist approaches and other critical approaches to the study of crime, law and criminal justice. It identifies tensions that arose around a number of key issues, among these: the role and status of the victim, the politics of reform versus revolutionary transcendence, and the dispute over the salience of class or gender in explanations of crime and criminalisation. I argue that, apart from tension being a welcome aspect of reflexive and dynamic approaches to intellectual analysis, these anxieties have waned with the growing influence of poststructuralism on critical approaches to criminology and with it thankfully the once obligatory necessity to demonstrate one's radical or feminist credentials through essentialist denunciations of the state, patriarchy, knowledge and the law. Nevertheless, there is, I argue, a continuing and deeply problematic denial of the legitimacy of victimisation still prevalent among much contemporary critical criminology. I conclude with some observations about the future prospects and challenges for the intellectual and political projects of feminist criminological research.

Challenging Criminology, Correcting False Images and Inserting Gender

Feminists began to challenge criminology's neglect of gender around the time feminists elsewhere were challenging the misogynist content and masculinist bias of history, law, sociology, politics, philosophy, literature, geography and other disciplines (Grosz, 1989). It should not be at all surprising therefore that developments within feminist criminology have resembled those in feminism more broadly, with the initial critiques of criminology emerging out of the woman-centred feminist radicalism of the late 1960s.

In 1968 Francis Heidensohn described the analysis of women and crime as 'lonely uncharted seas'. The initial feminist incursions into the field of criminology criticised both the omission of women as well as their misogynist representation within the discipline (Adler, 1975; Adler and Simon, 1979; Bertrand, 1967, 1969, 1979; Heidensohn, 1968; Klein, 1973). The first sustained critique of the discipline of criminology was Carol Smart's pioneering analysis published more than a quarter of a century ago in *Women, Crime and Criminology* (1976). This text took issue with the biologically reductionist and ideologically loaded accounts of women's offending produced by classical studies of female criminality. She took the works of Lombroso and Ferrero (1895), Thomas (1923) and Pollak (1950) as her objects of deconstruction (Smart, 1976:27), exposing the culturally biased assumptions about women that underscored their studies of female criminality. She exposed how criminal women were represented as not only prey to their 'inferior' biology and individual pathologies, and prone to hysterical sex-strivings and other equally absurd physiological urges, but as doubly deviant because they transgressed not only the law but their gender roles as well. Smart's analysis demonstrated how the same ideological ingredients that slotted women into sexist stereotypes were essentially present in the contemporary studies of female criminality that also fraudulently claimed to be objective and scientific (Smart, 1976: 54–70).

As for the innumerable studies that fail to even acknowledge women or the significance of gender to their criminological analyses, Smart observed; 'They are written largely by men, on the subject of men, for an audience of men' (Smart, 1976: 178). When contemplating future directions for feminist research in criminology, Smart warned of the risk of ghettoisation on the one hand and co-option on the other (Smart, 1976: 179–80). The task at hand as she saw it some twenty-five years ago now was how to conceptualise women's experiences and specificities without subsuming them within an overarching framework of criminology. This particular, and particularly incisive, insight was the focus of much subsequent theoretical work in feminist criminology (Allen, 1988, 1989; Carlen, 1992; Cain, 1990; Edwards, 1981; Heidensohn, 1985; Leonard, 1982; Daly and Chesney-Lind, 1988; Rafter and Stanko, 1982; Naffine, 1987, 1997; Gelsthorpe and Morris, 1990; Van Swaaningen, 1989; Smart, 1989; Young, A., 1996).

Because gender played such a significant role in patterns of offending, with far more men than women appearing before the courts and in prisons in Britain, Canada and the US, during the 1970s pioneering feminist scholars in this field such as Smart (1976), Heidensohn (1968), Klein (1973) and Bertrand (1967, 1969, 1979) questioned criminology's neglect of this fundamental fact. That women comprised only a small proportion of the criminal population compared to men did not, they argued, justify their total neglect. Arguing for the inclusion of women in studies of crime and punishment, the resolution at this time was primarily one of adding 'real women' to balance the gender blindness of traditional criminology (Naffine, 1987: 2–5, Rafter, 2000: xxv). However impressive and important as a new body of feminist critique, these initial feminist incursions did not adequately challenge the underlying epistemological assumptions of criminology's theories, categories or methods (Cousins, 1980: 111). This project was to become the major focus of a second wave of feminist challenges to criminology to which I shall return later.

The Rise of Feminist Victimology

Alongside the initial feminist challenges to criminology, a constellation of quite distinct feminist intellectual and political work centred around women as victims of violence (mostly male).[1] This work rendered visible women and girls as victims of crime, challenging the hidden and privatised nature of much violence against women (Gelsthorpe and Morris, 1990: 3). These intellectual feminist challenges were inspired by a great deal of feminist activism around the definition of rape, child abuse and wife battering as well as the treatment of women prisoners (Rafter, 1990). That the personal was political was painstakingly obvious to feminists working with victims.

From the outset there has been a close, enduring and symbiotic connection between the intellectual and political projects of feminist criminology. Reflecting this 'praxis' feminists (who mostly did not identify with criminology) embarked on studies to expose the experiences of victimisation so readily disqualified by masculinist prejudices. They studied date rape (Lees, 1997), incest (Bell, 1993), sexual assault (Breckenridge and Carmody, 1992), domestic violence (Dobash and Dobash, 1979; Scutt, 1983), child sexual assault, violence against Aboriginal women (Greer 1994), gang bangs (Carrington, 1998) and violence against women more generally (Stubbs, 1994; Cook and Bessant, 1997; Wilson, 1983; Stanko, 1985; 1990). Feminists extended their analyses to the treatment of women as victims, of the criminal justice system and the law as well (Edwards, 1981; Smart, 1989; Threadgold, 1993; Naffine, 1991; Carrington, 1998). Their research sought to demonstrate how women's victimisation was exacerbated in many instances by their subsequent treatment by the police, prison, legal and judicial authorities, such that they experienced a double victimisation.

By studying the experience of victimisation feminist scholars sought to demonstrate how the justice system 'sees and treats women' and girls from the perspective of the male gaze, continually repositioning and measuring them in relation to men. This is not only the case with female criminals who tend to be represented as doubly monstrous, as gender deviant and socially deviant, but also especially the case with female victims of crime who are routinely treated with contempt, ridicule and deep suspicion, culminating in their representation in terms of a simple dyad, as either deserving or undeserving depending on how good they are at doing their gender. A range of rich gendered symbols and signifiers, such as dress, manner, conduct, appearance, associates, place and time are called upon in a variety of insinuation strategies to imbue the female victim with contempt and suspicion. She asked for it, she nagged him too much, she acted like a temptress, she walked home alone, she didn't resist enough, and so on. Men who are the victims of crime, especially crimes involving interpersonal violence, are rarely scripted into such narrow victim-blaming typologies, unless of course they happen to be gay or transsexual, that is outside identifiable hegemonic forms of masculinity. These were such important insights into the workings of criminal justice that feminism can rightly claim that it has played a key role in the emergence of a relatively new field of inquiry, victimology.

Transgressing the Boundaries of Criminology

During the late 1980s and throughout the 1990s a second wave of feminist challenges to criminology rejected outright its disciplinary boundaries and claims to knowledge. This deconstructionist feminist agenda promoted a radical scepticism about the disciplinary project of criminology, questioning its key concepts, its methods of inquiry, its common sense assumptions, its claims to neutrality and its epistemological approach to studying crime. The positivist and empiricist methods, which had hitherto dominated mainstream criminology, were rejected largely in favour of qualitative research methods that elevated the experiences of women as subjects (Naffine, 1997: 45–8; Gelsthorpe, 1990: 86; Cain, 1986). Criminology's epistemological claims to neutrality and objectivity were also debunked. For how could criminology be neutral when it assumed the norm was male, then unproblematically proceeded to measure women as deviance from a masculine norm? Feminist encounters with criminology consequently had to be more than corrective. They had to do more than just add women to the criminological agenda of existing conceptual frameworks. Feminist criminology had to be transgressive of the discipline of criminology and its ideological and methodological assumptions (Cain, 1990: 6) for:

> From the prism of criminology, women are only another interest group to be acknowledged, and gender is just another variable to be included.
>
> (Klein, 1995: 219)

In a historically significant speech to the American Society of Criminology (subsequently published in the *International Journal of the Sociology of Law*) Maurine Cain proposed that a truly transgressive criminology entailed the triple project of reflexivity, deconstruction and re-construction (Cain, 1990: 8), proposing that feminist research 'starts from outside criminological discourse' (Cain, 1990: 10). This proposition has become an article of faith among contemporary feminist scholars (Klein, 1995: 217) for whom criminology is considered a constraining rather than an enabling or creative space for feminist research (Gelsthorpe and Morris, 1990: 2).

For this kind of feminism, the discipline was beyond redemption. Criminology and feminism were contradictory enterprises irreconcilable into a coherent project of 'feminist criminology', for criminology not only ignored or misrepresented half of humanity, it mistakenly took the other half for the whole of humanity, universalising its theories based largely as they were on observations of male criminality, it being so much more preponderant than female criminality. Criminology was a hopelessly compromised form of masculinist thinking which assumed a false universal validity for its phallocentric theories (Allen, 1989: 20). So much so that masculinity was conveniently neutered leaving it completely untheorised for over a century of criminological thought and research. The central failing of criminology was now recognised as its inherent phallocentricism and its obliviousness to the highly sexualised nature of its empirical referents (Allen, 1989: 20–1; Van Swaaningen, 1989: 288; Cain, 1990: 11; Gelsthorpe and Morris, 1990: 4).

While carving out a new and exciting territory for feminist scholarship on its own terms, and not those limited by the conventions of mainstream criminology, this approach was not, however, without its own internal conceptual and political difficulties. In theoretical terms the critique of biologism was overstated, and a faith in sociology as a remedy for biological reductionism over-rated (Brown, 1990: 41). One form of biologism – the mistaken representation of femininity told by classical criminology and retold on a daily basis within the criminal justice system – was replaced with an inverted form of biologism within feminism that sought to correct false images by retelling what it claimed was the truth or essence of femininity (Young, A., 1996: 38). It was too confidently assumed within such analyses that the diversity of women's experiences of criminalisation and victimisation could be represented by merely adopting a feminist standpoint, leading to essentialist forms of analysis which themselves erased the intra-sex specificities among women and led to fervent internal feminist critique, particularly over questions related to race and indigenousness (Rice, 1990; Carrington, 1994; Naffine, 1997).

Critical Feminist Incursions of a Postmodernist/Poststructuralist Kind

Over the last decade feminist engagements within and across the field of criminology have diversified as they have become more and more influenced by postmodern and poststructuralist forms of deconstruction and scepticism about universalist notions of identity and politics. These influences upon critical approaches to criminology are not, however, as new as frequently thought. As early as the 1960s elements of postmodernism – the focus on language, discourse, plurality, representation, relativism and indeterminism – were present in a variety of radical approaches to deviance theory such as labelling theory and symbolic interactionism (Cohen, 1998: 115–19). These influences only later became articulated within a discourse of postmodernism.

The postmodern critique of the enlightenment project of modernism has been wide-ranging: deconstructing modernist notions of the transcendental unitary subject, essentialist notions of society, power and politics, evolutionary notions of history and progress, utopian solutions to the problems of modernity, and teleological searches for origins that they claim do not exist (Chambers, 1986; Lyotard, 1986; Baudrillard, 1992; Bauman, 1992). There is no new modern reality to be discovered or researched, only a profusion of re-representations of representations, alongside an implosion of relentless simulacra. Postmodernism spelt an end to the grand narratives and certainties once taken so much for granted within the academy. According to this perspective, those bodies of modernist intellectual thought that believed they could make a difference, an improvement, discover causes or suggest remedies for the problems of modernism were just kidding themselves.

Given that modernism has nurtured the sociological forms of radical thinking in which much of the history of feminism is enmeshed, postmodernism has received a rather cool reception from feminists. Few believe that we have entered a post-feminist period of history in which sexual difference is so diverse and fragmented that it no longer makes any sense to speak with any persuasion or coherency about gender issues. Even fewer believe that feminism made no appreciable difference to the modern world. On the contrary, the effects and achievements of feminism, while certainly not complete, have been substantial. Nevertheless following the critique of totalising theories and politics, 'Feminism had to abandon its early frame-work and to start to look for other ways to think which did not subjugate other subjectivities' (Smart, 1990: 83). Unlike standpoint feminism, postmodernist approaches to feminism reject universalist solutions and ways of knowing. They seek to reveal subjugated knowledges and tell different stories of diverse specificities rather than impose a fictive unitary reality upon a sisterhood interlaced with immense cultural and historical diversity (Smart, 1990: 82).

Poststructuralism has received a warmer welcome among feminists because it refrains from pre-empting the pessimistic polemics of postmodernism, yet offers a similar constructive toolbox of ideas and methods with which to deconstruct the discourses of the present. The construction of sexual difference in political, psychological, criminological, sociological and philosophical discourse has become the primary target of methodological and theoretical deconstruction in poststructuralist feminism. This kind of feminism no longer insists on any singular relation between sexual difference, law, crime and social power and seeks instead to locate its specificity in relation to the exercise of power. The aim of this kind of feminism is not to construct a more correct feminist version of the truth, but to deconstruct and analyse the power effects of truth claims (Smart, 1990: 82). Nor does this kind of feminism restrict its focus to the Women question. Their objects of deconstruction differ widely but tend to concentrate on constructions, images and representations of masculinity, power and other statuses deployed in the criminolegal complex. One welcome consequence of this shifting focus has been the rise of intellectual interest in the specific issue of the relationship between masculinity and crime (Newburn and Stanko, 1994; Jefferson, 1997; Messerschmidt, 1993; Collier, 1998).

A particularly good example of poststructuralist feminist deconstruction can be found in Alison Young's work, for which femininity is the enigma of criminology, which must remain closeted (othered) such that masculinity can masquerade as the sexless neutral norm. Femininity is simultaneously the essential yet prohibited couplet of masculinity (Young, A., 1996: 48). The closet to which Young sees femininity being consigned is also enigmatic – simultaneously a place of control and a place beyond its canonical boundaries to control (Young, A., 1996: 47). More recently, Alison Young has deployed the tools of deconstruction to take issue with the discursive constructions of the rape victim during the cross-examination process. Her analysis illustrates with specific examples from transcripts of cross-examination just how the discursive strategy of demanding yes and no answers to a barrage of accusations and loaded insinuations, silences the rape victim's answers to the drum of the 'brisk and authoritative' defence narrative (Young, A., 1998: 458). Her analysis powerfully reveals how these discursive strategies accumulate throughout the rape trial to produce an asymmetry of power the effect of which is the silencing of the voice of the rape victim (Young, A., 1998: 460). Much of Young's feminist deconstruction of the way the legal system systematically disqualifies the testimony of the female sexual assault victim draws upon Goodrich's poststructuralist reading of law.

Goodrich argues that law is a monologic language 'better fitted to expressing the power or authority of law' (Goodrich, 1986: 187) than a form of exchange between different discursive positions. Its principle aim is to produce 'incontestable truths' and impose unitary meanings. Legal discourse does this through a number of mechanisms: by privileging the voice of the judicial author 'as the supreme arbiter of meaning'; by asserting uniform meanings; by denying that words can have contested or multiple meanings; by precluding dialogue; by producing fictive 'closures', and employing 'distancing devices' (Goodrich, 1986: 189); by invoking 'devices of exclusion' (Goodrich, 1986: 191); by asserting the sovereignty of law; and finally by refuting the need to justify its rationale outside a narrowly constructed axiomatic episteme which arrogantly assumes, rather than demonstrates, its own objectivity. The monologue of law seeks to control discourse through the exercise of power, not persuasion, argument or dialogue, that is, 'coercively rather than dialectically' (Goodrich, 1986: 194), to command obedience and deference. Young's use of Goodrich's postmodern reading of law in her innovative analysis of sexual assault trials presents an illustrative example of the effective intermingling of feminist and poststructuralist tools of deconstruction in contemporary forms of critical analysis. Her analysis goes much further, however, in demonstrating the masculinist dimensions and effects of the discourse of law. It makes little sense to characterise this intellectual work as singularly feminist or poststructuralist, for it is simultaneously both and more.

Poststructuralist feminist analyses have been especially effective in exposing how the monologic reasoning of disciplines like law and criminology exclude sexual difference by privileging masculinity (Naffine, 1991: 20–1) and othering women (Kirkby, 1995: xviii). Deconstruction is not, however, an end itself. It does not necessarily undermine the power of dominant discourses, such as law (Cohen, 1998: 118). There is a danger that women's experience, subjectivity and affectivity may disappear in a whirlpool of discursive constructions, representations, texts and images.

Concerned to move beyond the postmodern impasse haunting feminist scholarship, Kathy Daly and Lisa Maher have encouraged a feminist project of reconnecting 'real women' with the 'women of discourse' in feminist criminological endeavours (Daly and Maher, 1998: 6). Their edited collection of articles has been carefully chosen to reflect their concern to focus on the cross-roads between 'real women' and 'the women of discourse'. They conclude that, 'Feminist work in and against criminology must move on two fronts: building feminist knowledges and continuing to challenge and correct a nonfeminist field for its gender blindnesses, ethnocentricisms, and theoretical rigidities' (Daly and Maher, 1998: 12). They note that early feminist research agendas were primarily concerned with discovering women as victims and criminals. But today, after two decades of this kind of research, they acknowledge the importance of studying women as both subjects of and producers of knowledge as well as the discursive and real effects of law and criminal justice. I return to a discussion of the future prospects and challenges that arise from the pursuit of such an ambitious intellectual and political project in my conclusion.

Feminism and critical criminology: Confronting Genealogies

The origins of critical criminology are usually associated with the 1968 National Deviancy Conference in the UK. In such accounts *The New Criminology* (Taylor, Walton and Young), first published in 1973, is the text often identified with the origins of critical criminology (Muncie, 1998: 221). There are good reasons to think this given that *The New Criminology* set out an ambitious manifesto to radically alter the nature of criminological research, to shift it from a focus on correctionalist crime control and the positivist study of pathological behaviour, to the manner in which social control and criminalisation processes embody class relations which systematically discriminate against the powerless by criminalising their behaviour, while turning a blind eye to the transgressions of the corporate and bourgeois world. This account, however, underplays the genealogical significance of feminism (and other theoretical/political movements) and overrates the importance of Marxism in the development of critical perspectives in criminology.

As with feminist criminology, radical criminology gained much of its impetus from the wider deconstructive fervour of the 1960s to rethink, to push boundaries, to defy limits and to refuse to accept the status quo. As Stan Cohen reminds us, the emergence of critical criminology was part of a wider scepticism of science, modernism and rationality (Cohen, 1998: 115). The feminist critique of patriarchy was very much part of this genealogical impetus – it was not an afterthought.

Critical Tensions

Early versions of what became regarded as critical criminology showed negligible interest in rethinking the gendered boundaries of criminological theories, practices and concepts. Little attention was paid, for example, to gender issues in the National Deviancy Conferences convened during the 1960s and 1970s (Heidensohn, 2000: 78) that were so important to mapping out the foundations for neo-Marxist versions of critical criminology (Young, J., 1998: 16). It was here that the twin influences of labelling theory and sub-cultural theory met with a neo-Marxism to form the basis for a radical criminology variously referred to as new, critical, radical or alternative criminology (Cohen, 1998: 100). It was also here that class relations initially emerged as the centrepiece of the theoretical innovation of the new criminology. From here a number of critical tensions between feminist and left radical projects in criminology became patently obvious.

Early versions of critical criminology shared with mainstream criminology a masculinist gaze that assigned the woman question to the closet. The unabashed recourse to male pronouns and references to 'a socialist conception of man' (Taylor, Walton and Young, 1975: 23) and the radical criminologist as unequivocally male (Taylor, Walton and Young, 1975: 36) in the writings of the early critical criminologists is a legacy of the profoundly masculinist nature of radical criminology only a little more than a quarter of a century ago. While the neglect of gender is a valid criticism of the new criminology, it would be unfair not to point out that its initial development pre-dated much of the work in second-wave feminism as well as the emergence of a discernable body of work in feminist criminology (Young, J., 1998: 27–8). Nevertheless this seems a lame excuse for the continued marginalisation of questions of gender in contemporary critical criminological research. Marginalisation, incorporation and tokenism have historically characterised criminology's dealing with gender issues and feminist concerns and examples of it in both radical and mainstream approaches are not difficult to find (for analysis of concrete examples see Gelsthorpe and Morris, 1990:7; Rafter and Heidensohn, 1995: 4–5; Scraton, 1990: 17).

Just as radical and mainstream criminology can be criticised for their neglect of gender, feminist approaches to criminology can be legitimately criticised for their historical neglect of class and race. By focusing on gender as the primary category of analysis and source of female oppression early feminist critiques frequently failed to take into account the historical, cultural and material specificities of women's offending and victimisation (Gelsthorpe, 1989: 152). They presumed that commonalities shared among the female sex made it possible to analyse and represent women as a singular unitary subject of history (Allen, 1990: 88), despite their astonishing historical, cultural and racial diversity. More attention to these specificities would have revealed little in common between women and girls drawn into the orbit of the criminal justice system with those who live their lives unaffected by it. We know from more recent detailed empirical studies (Chesney-Lind and Sheldon, 1998; Carlen et al., 1985; Carlen, 1988; Daly, 1994; Gelsthorpe, 1989; Carrington, 1993; Maher, 1997) that the vast majority of the female population rarely come into contact with the criminal justice agencies. Those who do (mostly women and girls who are poor and from racial minorities) have very little in common with the vast majority of women insulated from the effects of criminal justice. Not all women are equally vulnerable to victimisation either. For instance, women from public housing neighbourhoods and rural areas are more vulnerable to forms of domestic assault than women who live in the leafy urban spaces of the city. These differences demand a genuine recognition of the complex ways in which gender interlaces with other dimensions of experience, history and identity to shape the diversity of women's experiences.

Class or sex?

Many of the critical tensions within and between feminist and other critical approaches to criminology arose from modernist forms of analysis that privileged certain conceptual categories such as sex or class. Just as there was much debate in the 1970s and 1980s over the salience of sex or class in structuring oppression and inequality in capitalist patriarchal societies, there was a similar corresponding tension within critical approaches to criminology of which feminism was one. Is the criminal justice system inherently masculinist – in that the law sees and treats women how men do (Mackinnon, 1987)? Or is the criminal justice system an instrument of capitalism, a social control apparatus that functions to effectively supervise, apprehend, police and punish the lumpen-proletariat, to repress the rising of the masses, the resistance of youth subcultures and counter-cultural movements to their domination by a society divided primarily by class, wealth and opportunity? Certainly the major thrust of the political and intellectual project of feminist criminology had been focused on exposing the sexism and masculism of criminology, the law and the criminal justice system. By contrast the major focus of the New Criminology was to expose the relationship of class to the selective processes of criminalisation. The issue was not so much the class distribution of crime, but the class relations of the criminalisation process that selectively policed and criminalised the behaviour of the lower working classes (Young, J., 1998: 27). The flip side of this selectivity was the almost wholesale neglect in criminology, and criminal justice policy, of the crimes of the middle and corporate classes, of the rich and powerful (Fattah, 1997; Schwendinger and Schwendinger, 1975). Legal definitions of crime simply excluded human rights abuses, sexism, racism, war, economic crimes and environmental sabotage as acts of criminality. Hence one of the important tasks identified by early critical criminologists was the need to redefine crime, to broaden the objects of criminological analysis and to redefine criminologists, 'no longer to be the defenders of order but the guardians of human rights' (Schwendinger and Schwendinger, 1975: 138). These were very important insights with lasting effects on the areas of study undertaken by critical criminologists.

There is no easy way of resolving the impasse over which is more important – sex or class – unless one steps outside of the overarching determining structuralist modes of thought that construct such unnecessarily oppositional binaries. Surely sex and class intersect with other dimensions of psychosocial life to produce a tapestry of social phenomena interlaced with similarity *and* diversity. Just as the debate between radical and socialist feminists waned along with the post-structuralist critique of universalising theories, so has the tension between feminists and critical criminologists over the salience of class or gender. Forms of critical analysis no longer need pre-empt where class or gender relations are to take precedence over the other. Critical scholars are now relieved of having to entrench their analyses with obligatory essentialist denunciations about patriarchy or capitalism. Race, age and sexual preference may be just as important, so too might be geography and post-coloniality in such analyses.

Victim or offender?

Perhaps the most significant and recurring of tensions between feminist and other critical approaches to criminology have centred on the role of the victim. The victim (male or female) was almost entirely absent from discussions about crime, deviance and criminal justice within the radical frameworks of much of the early critical criminology. Victims were largely considered the concern of conservatives in criminology and politics, not radicals. Women were, as Carol Smart pointed out in 1976, not only the unrecognised victims of criminal acts such as rape but also the silent victims of 'criminal law, penal policy and criminological theories' (Smart, 1976: 180), even radical ones. The emergence of radical deviance theory and the new criminology did not initially alter any of this, for its focus was directed at the analysis of victimless crimes, such as drug crimes, homosexuality, prostitution and participation in working-class youth subcultures, within a non-utilitarian framework that rejected instrumentalist views of crime (e.g. Young's drug-takers, Cohen's mods and rockers, Becker's outsiders). The anti-utilitarianism of early radical criminology was primarily interested in the expressive, rather than the instrumental qualities of deviance, and in particular 'illicit drug use, bohemian crime in general and "sexual deviance"' (Taylor, Walton, Young, 1975: 16). By 'sexual deviance' I presume they obviously meant sex outside marriage, adultery, promiscuity, homosexuality, transsexuality and a vast array of other sexual practices and preferences considered 'deviant' to the moral guardians of bourgeois sexuality. Presumably they were not referring to rape, incest or other varieties of sexual violence.

Influenced heavily by the insights of labelling theory and symbolic interactionism, critical emphasis in radical deviance theory at that time was placed very much on understanding the social reaction to deviance, analysing this social reaction as a process and not an act, and representing the meaning making of those labelled deviant, mad or bad. The psychosocial dimensions of deviance were considered irrelevant. Offenders bearing the labels of deviance were frequently romanticised as representatives of oppressed sexual, racial or class minorities effectively criminalised for their cultural diversity, their deviation from the norms of white, Anglo middle-class society. So the juvenile delinquent was really just an ordinary working-class kid resisting through rituals the dislocation of working-class culture in postwar Britain (Hall and Jefferson, 1976) and Australia (Cunneen et al., 1989; White, 1990; Stratton, 1993). The petty thief was not committing crime, but surviving in a world that denied them equal opportunities to access wealth and prosperity. The schizophrenic was only deviant to those who measure normality through a rigid grid of bourgeois values. Psychiatrists made people mad through the imposition of their value judgements implemented with the aid of psychometric testing and neo-Lombrosian forms of analysis focused on the signs of individual pathology. The crime control authorities made people bad, initially by labelling as such, and then by imprisoning them in criminogenic institutions, such as lock-ups, prisons and juvenile detention centres, escalating the spiral from primary to secondary deviation.

To problematise the taken for granted notion of crime by analysing it as an effect of a criminalisation process, and not just a quality inherent in an act, has been an insight of immense and fundamental importance to contemporary critical perspectives in criminology (see also Chapter 2). This insight has allowed for much more scrutiny to be placed upon the abuses of state power alongside the discriminatory processes of labelling and criminalisation. However, such a singular focus, with an over-emphasis on the processes of criminalisation was at the expense of a regard for the reality of the *experience* of victimisation, in addition to the psychosocial dimensions of offending. As Tony Jefferson's piece in this book argues, conceptions of the subject within critical and traditional criminology have been hopelessly inadequate. Only the experience of those doing the criminalising (i.e. the state) seemed to matter. Within these kinds of critical frameworks the lines between the victim and offender were almost meaningless. The offender was the victim of some overarching structure of class, sexual or racial exclusion, domination, repression or oppression. This may well be the case in some if not many, instances. No doubt young people participating in street-based leisure activities, such as mods and rockers, bikies, teddies, bodgies and widgees, and young people participating in the drug culture of the counter cultural revolution were victimised by the moral entrepreneurs, conservative institutions, the press and the police. No doubt a great many people jailed for petty property crimes do not deserve to be treated as such in an unequal society. However, not all offenders can be conflated with such neat and romantic images of the offender as victim. For instance, where do men (many of whom are working-class and from disadvantaged backgrounds) who inflict crimes of violence upon children and women fit into such an analysis. Basically they don't and they didn't. Crimes with 'real' victims tended to be either overlooked or downplayed. Consequently the theoretical framework, empirical attention and political focus of much of radical deviancy theory and critical criminology rendered the victim not only invisible but worse – an apparition of false consciousness on the part of the politically incorrect.

Consequently feminist research on women and children as victims of crime fitted uneasily alongside the radical insistence that underplayed the effects of crime and the concerns of victims as merely the social constructions of police targeting, moral panics, and law and order nonsense (Young, J., 1988: 298). Feminist research required politicians, policy-makers and criminologists (of critical and traditional orientation) to rethink the notion that the fear of crime was just an irrational response to media and political beat-ups, and to reconsider the validity of crime statistics by acknowledging the dark figure of crime which rendered so many women and children the hidden victims of family, domestic and sexual violence.

These insights of feminism led to a significant rethinking of the role of the victim in some versions of critical criminology. So much so that the progressive reconstruction of criminology since the 1960s cannot even begin without recognising the implications of feminist scholarship (Sumner, in Gelsthorpe and Morris, 1990: xii). Indeed, as Stan Cohen has pointed out, it was the feminist critique of the romantic notion of the criminal that led to a reconstruction of idealist models of crime that characterised early versions of radical deviancy theory (Cohen, 1998: 106). The fear of crime was real for women, not just some ideologically externally imposed construct of Thatcherism or conservative law and order agendas. Real women were the victims of male violence, and the men who inflicted violence could not be romanticised as resisters to capitalism. Nor were they necessarily incorrectly labelled as deviant by the social control authorities. Those who committed crimes against the weak, the marginal and the vulnerable were not working-class heroes. Their violence could not be glossed over, excused, tolerated or ignored by criminologists on the left or the right. Feminist concerns about the victims of domestic violence and sexual assault deserved to be taken seriously.

The agenda for critical criminology had to be reconstructed to take on board these and other omissions that arose from its initial concentration on class as the defining feature of the political economy of crime and criminal justice. Left realist criminology subsequently did take these feminist concerns seriously, at least at the level of rhetoric, leading one of its most quoted exponents to write: 'The importance of feminist work in the recent development of radical criminology cannot be overestimated' (Young, J., 1988: 301).

Nevertheless I believe a deep residual tension between feminism and radicalism over the legitimacy of the experience of victimisation simmers not far beneath a thin veneer of pretences to the contrary. The ferocity of this tension flared to the surface during a recent fierce and boisterous public debate about the chronic and epidemic levels of sexual violence in some Aboriginal communities in Australia[2]. It began when several women (all of them Aboriginal) exposed their shared experiences of rape by a Koori man, who just happened to be a national leader of the Aboriginal rights movement (ATSIC) (*Sydney Morning Herald*, 14 June 2001). These women were subsequently condemned as politically suspect – and likened more generally to stereotypical rape victims – and not to be believed. Australia's first Aboriginal female magistrate with a long list of 'radical' credentials publicly attacked the motives of the women alleging '"a lot of women manufacture a lot of stories" about sexual assault, and told "bleating feminists" they lived in fantasy land' (*Sydney Morning Herald*, 16 June 2001). Somewhat ironically activists among left justice action groups (historically associated with the history of critical criminology in Australia – see David Brown's Chapter 4) invoked a classic traditional rights defence – that Koori men are innocent of these allegations of sexual violence until proven guilty by a criminal justice system – that in other instances they would denounce for its inherent inability to deliver anything remotely resembling justice or the protection of rights for indigenous peoples. Why should it be any different for Koori women who as rape complainants have very little if any prospect of receiving justice through the same legal system? It was left largely to white feminists as journalists, academics and politicians to defend these women.[13]

Then the issue of sexual violence in Aboriginal communities was opportunistically seized upon by the ideologues on the right (in the media and in politics) to derail the reconciliation process by constructing Aboriginal people as atavistic, untamed savages who deserve no apology. The politics of this debate translated the legitimate expression of concern about sexual violence in Aboriginal communities into the occasion to orchestrate a racist attack on Aboriginal culture, on the one hand, and on the other, a masculinist discourse that dismisses women's allegations of rape as fantasy. In such a hostile cultural climate around the politics of race it is not difficult to see why so few Aboriginal women are prepared to report rape, why the issue tends to be defensively deflected by Aboriginal leaders, and why it presents such a dreadful dilemma for critical criminologists. For to expose the chronic levels of victimisation among Aboriginal women runs the risk of turning it into a feeding frenzy for racists, but to ignore it feeds into the silencing of the real and tragic consequences of sexual violence for the lives of so many Aboriginal women and children.

The debate about sexual violence in Aboriginal communities (which is roaring again as I write with revelations before a Coronial Inquiry of a 15-year-old-girl found hanged in an Aboriginal community in Western Australia, two weeks after she complained to police of having been raped by a Koori elder and his son[4]), powerfully illustrates just how salient tensions over the 'legitimacy' of the victims of violence remain several decades after feminists first raised them. So despite reassurances that a reconstructed contemporary critical criminology has learnt about the experience of victimisation from feminist research, I have little confidence that this enlightened understanding extends much beyond rhetorical gestures.

Essentialism

Many of the tensions between feminism and other versions of critical criminology can be traced to the effects of the tendency to essentialise the victim and the criminal, one according to gender the other according to class. For feminists victims were nearly always assumed to be women, and perpetrators nearly always men. Meanwhile among the various versions of radical criminology the gender of offenders rarely rated a mention. It was their status as resisters, working-class youth and members of oppositional cultures and marginalised social groups that mattered, not their gendered behaviour. Categories of analysis were homogenised and oversimplified. Heterogeneous behaviours were attributed to essentialist categories such as maleness or working-classness, which led 'to bland abstractions of breathtaking lack of utility' (Young, J., 1998: 33). Because identity is much more varied, fluid, fragmented and dynamic, essentialist categories such as class, race or gender impose a fictive unity upon complex social phenomena through the attribution of a singular universal set of presumed interests, characteristics or essences which are unnecessarily totalising and homogenising (Hindess, 1977). Most early versions of feminist and radical criminology engaged in this kind of sociological structuralism particularly fashionable during the 1970s and 1980s.

The difficulty with deploying an essentialist analysis in feminist criminology may be more readily understood by analysing a specific instance in its application. Appeals to essentialism are – for example – readily apparent in the opportunistic denunciation of the fear of rape as an occasion to construct *all* women as victims of the monolithic structures of patriarchal sexual power (Brownmiller, 1975; Easteal, 1994: 1). While most victims of rape are female, and their perpetrators male, rape victimisation is very unevenly spread throughout the female population, with adolescent girls having by far the greatest risk (Salmelainen and Coumarelos, 1993). These intra-gender discrepancies are erased by accounts that universalise rape. Rape is reduced to the structural effects of some totalising source of oppression (i.e. patriarchy), over which individual women are constituted as almost completely helpless. Women are incapable of exercising sexual autonomy and thus incapable of consent. Consent, according to this discourse, is then nothing more than a farce, a product of coercion and male dominance (Vega, 1987: 77–8).

The flip side of this universal model of female victimisation is the even more dubious attribution to the male species of a neo-Lombrosian form of dangerousness, which makes every male body a potential rape zone, despite the fact that not all men rape or benefit from it, and that some men (e.g. gays and transsexuals in prisons) are especially vulnerable to rape by other men. Such an overarching negative conception of masculinity as 'dangerous' is not only misleading (see Connell, 1995; Jefferson, 1997; Messerschmidt, 1993), but leads to a number of other serious methodological and conceptual difficulties (Collier, 1998: 177). This approach fails to take into account the multiple ways in which masculinity is cross-culturally and trans-historically variable (see Collier, 1998: 6–33). It also fails to challenge the biologically reductionist discourse that normalises male sexual violence as inherently uncontrollable and thus unpreventable. In closing off the possibility of men being able to fashion ethical sexual practices, women are for ever poised waiting to be raped, and men for ever prey to their uncontrollable biological urges (Carmody and Carrington, 2000: 346). The inference is that women must be made responsible for avoiding their victimisation, for men can't avoid their destiny as potential rapists (a point made also by Tony Jefferson in this volume). Rape is misconstrued as ungovernable conduct – a dangerous manifestation of an alleged entrenched structure of sexual relations, not amenable to any form of contemporary reconstruction (Carrington and Watson, 1996: 256). If, however, it is possible, indeed

Critical Criminology

desirable, that men negotiate consenting and mutually pleasurable sexual practices, then those who are sexually violent have no excuse for their conduct. They are not exaggerations of normal men. And women have no responsibility for their victimisation by such men. Importantly such an approach requires the abandonment of radical feminist essentialist denunciations of male sexuality as inherently dangerous.

Essentialism is a problem for feminism, but not one over which it has a monopoly. Elements of essentialism are also readily detectable in many other versions of critical criminology. For instance, appeals to essentialism are very much present in the radical theory that crime is an expression of class inequality and crime control a totalising form of capitalist state control, the conditions of which can only be altered through a radical transformation to socialism (Brown and Hogg, 1992: 196). That crime has no necessary essence, but is rather constituted as an object in a range of domains, discourses and practices, 'disrupts any notion of criminology as a unified discipline or discourse or as a vehicle for applying a general body of theory' (Brown and Hogg, 1992: 196).

The critique of essentialism has called for a different kind of feminist and critical intellectual engagement with criminology to the one that totalises conceptions of social control attributing to them a false unity of purpose to the law and criminal justice (i.e. patriarchy for feminism and capitalism for Marxism). There are healthy signs of this occurring. Many feminists working broadly in the field of criminology have become much more aware of the effects of race and colonialisation which they had once ignored (see Rafter and Heidensohn, 1995; Rice, 1990). Feminists are also working hard to correct their tendencies to essentialise masculinity and femininity – to demonise one and romanticise the other (see Carmody and Carrington, 2000), and much contemporary feminist research has displaced its once essentialist focus on gender to analyse how a complex tapestry of racial, colonial, gender and class inequalities intersect to position women differently in relation to the operation of criminal justice and law (i.e. Alder and Baines, 1996; Allen, 1987; Carlen et al., 1985; Carlen, 1988; Bell, 1993; Carrington, 1993; Chesney-Lind and Sheldon, 1998; Howe, 1994; Gelsthorpe, 1989; Daly, 1994; Lees, 1997; Maher, 1997). This is especially the case with indigenous women and girls in countries like Canada and Australia who are massively overrepresented before the courts and in our prisons and figure disproportionately as victims of crime as well (Cunneen, 1992). To reduce all this to the exercise of some overarching form of patriarchal power erases the fundamental salience of the racialisation of crime and punishment in the western world in the twentieth century (Hogg, 2001). The solution to this problem is not, however, to erect race as a higher form of essentialism (Harris, 1990; Rice,

132

1990) but to reject essentialist forms of analysis that attribute a false unity to complex social phenomena such as crime and criminal justice. And feminists over the last decade have increasingly done so in response to the challenges of coloured, postcolonialist and black feminists to their formerly profoundly essentialist tendencies.

Utopianism and the Politics of Revolution or Reform

One of the legacies of the essentialist feminist critique of the discipline of criminology has been a deep reluctance to engage with the politics of criminological knowledge leading to a self-sustaining remoteness from the workings of criminal justice. If the state is patriarchal, the legal system masculinist and criminology so hopelessly phallocentric then what's the point of any contemporary political or intellectual engagement with it? If patriarchal structures of power are so overwhelmingly hegemonic any reform efforts are destined to doom, failure, tokenism or co-option, mere tinkering at the edges, band-aid solutions or worse more masculinist control disguised as SNAG[5] benevolence.

Arguably the distance between the political and intellectual project of feminism widened considerably during the second wave of feminist challenges to the discipline. This was often justified by a romantic clinging to utopian notions of revolutionary transcendence, that it was just a matter of waiting for the feminist revolution to dissolve gender categories, to overthrow the patriarchal power of the state and the judiciary, to reinvent masculinist culture and so on. This revolutionary politics led to a self-imposed marginalisation of feminist perspectives within mainstream criminology and criminal justice policy, and too ready denunciations of feminist attempts at political engagement in and on the present, such as the femocratisation of corrections, policing and the judiciary, the reduction of women in custody, improvements in the conditions in women's prisons, the introduction of services for sexual and domestic assault victims and the decriminalisation of prostitution to name a few.

When taken to the extreme, this radical feminist politics could even converge with the politics of the radical religious right, as it did for instance during the intense debate over prostitution in the 1980s, arguing for it to be outlawed as a form of sexual exploitation of *all* women. Some even regarded sex-workers as the parasites of patriarchal forms of sexuality. It is with some humour that I now recall being asked to account for my involvement in the establishment of the first *Australian Prostitutes Collective*[6] in 1983 with transsexual activist Roberta Perkins and 'Rose' an ex-sex-worker. Wasn't such a collective parasitic on patriarchal forms of sexual relations – the exchange of money for the objectification of women's bodies? How could I continue to call myself feminist for assisting its establishment and calling upon the government to decriminalise sex-work? That was my last attendance at a Women's Collective Meeting.

The tension between radical critique and political strategy in feminist criminology shares similarities with the tension between idealist and realist critical criminology. Should critical criminologists take crime seriously, or should they leave such interventions to the conservative agenda of administrative criminology? For critical criminologists in the early 1970s abolitionism was a realistic ideal. Just as the state would whither away under socialism, so too they thought would the material basis for the commission of crime and 'the material necessity to criminalize crime' (Taylor, Walton and Young, 1975: 20). A decade later, for left realist criminologists wanting to take crime seriously, abolitionism was utopian. The intra-class victims of much crime committed among the working classes could not be erased as depictions of false consciousness, nor be expected to whither away along with the state and all others things bad under socialism, which itself was withering away at that time. The experiences of victimisation (which came to be 'measured' quite problematically through victim surveys) were just as real as the experiences of rape victims and deserved the attention of critical criminologists. As Stan Cohen reminds us, there is no perfect fit between theory and politics:

> All we can do, is find the best guide to each one – then confront the tension that results. This is hard going. In the end the only guides are first, our sense of social justice, and second, whatever time we have in the twenty-four-hour-day.
>
> (Cohen, 1998: 123)

The Future of Contemporary Feminist Criminological Research

The last decade of the millennium is perhaps best described as a state of flux. During this turbulent period an increasingly divergent range of feminist perspectives has emerged. While a growing body of work in an identifiably dynamic field of feminist criminology has continued to concentrate on gender and social justice issues, as Nicole Rafter and Francis Heidensohn suggest, 'feminist' may no longer be an appropriate way of describing the diversity of the intellectual work and political effort undertaken by those interested in issues of gender, justice and equality (Rafter and Heidensohn, 1995: 3). Much contemporary feminist work has abandoned femininity as its singular focus, adding to it concerns about the power effects of age, sexuality, sexual difference, social class, geographic location and race (Rafter and Heidensohn, 1995: 4). Questions of gender and justice have also broadened to include studies of masculinity and crime (Jefferson, 1997; Messerschmidt, 1993; Newburn and Stanko, 1994; Carmody and Carrington, 2000).

Looking back, much has been achieved for which we can feel proud. Feminist work can rightly claim to have revitalised radical criminology and to have added an entire new subdiscipline of victimology to the canon of criminology. As Carol Smart suggests, 'It might be that criminology needs feminism more than the converse' (Smart, 1990: 84), while warning that feminist criminologists can expect to remain marginal to criminology (Smart, 1990: 71). Consequently a number of key issues face the future of feminist scholarship. Perhaps the most challenging is still how to institute feminist approaches to the study of crime, victimisation and sexual difference without surrendering to the canonical hierarchy of criminology (Young, A., 1996: 33). Feminist criminology is itself enigmatic, unthinkable yet thinkable. In this sense feminism is a subterranean postmodern project within criminology, one that makes 'the formerly unpresentable presentable' (Lyotard, 1986: 81). Its disruptive effects are unknowable yet felt and feared. Consequently criminology as a discursive practice has had to constantly contain feminist incursions from leaping out of the cupboard. Chapters on gender and crime have had to be added to criminology texts and sections of conferences organised around the concerns of feminist criminology (Young, A., 1996: 47). Yet the overall outward symbolic imagery of criminology as a science has been little altered by feminism's challenge to its foundational categories based as they are on masculine norms. Rather than seeing this as one of the most significant renovations to the foundations of criminological discourse over the last thirty years feminist criminology still tends to be marginalised, and gender treated as an add on rather than an integral feature of the commission of crime, criminalisation processes and the experience of victimisation. How to negotiate feminism's conundrum, to be simultaneously inside, yet outside – influential within yet unconstrained by – criminology will require the crossing of boundaries along with the reinvention of borders around criminological knowledge, and not just their transgression or outright rejection.

Another major challenge facing feminist criminological work is how it can better deal with the ethnocentrism that plagues not only criminology, but second-wave essentialist versions of feminist criminology as well. This is not a simple matter of adding black women to a feminist analysis of women and crime, for their experiences are not homogeneous (Rice, 1990: 68). Nor is it a simple matter of erecting race as a higher form of essentialism. It requires the abandonment of universalising categories such as women and race altogether and the pursuit of the more humble tasks undertaken by the specific intellectual. As truth cannot be emancipated from power, the task of the specific intellectual is to detach or deconstuct its production from forms of hegemony (Foucault, in Rabinow, 1984:75). This is precisely what I see feminist research in criminology increasingly doing when it challenges, exposes and deconstructs the taken-for-granted, self-evident categories of law, crime and the justice system. And it does so especially effectively when it connects specific instances with the more general discursive regimes that construct these masculinist processes as 'objective, just and true'. The tasks of the specific intellectual also sit comfortably with the robust tradition of critical criminological scholarship that contests the truth claims of 'law', by exposing its injustices as well as the unchecked exercise of judicial authority and police power (Walton and Young, 1998).[7]

Objections to taking on the mantle of the specific intellectual usually include fears of losing an independent standpoint, especially the ability to criticise from a position outside power. This of course assumes there is indeed such an ideal position and that somehow, quite remarkably, the critic is free from the constraints of the politics of representation that afflicts others. Specific feminist objections include a concern that feminism will have to surrender the right to represent the interests of women and that its voice will be politically reduced as a consequence. This fear is, I think, unfounded. The more specific the challenge to masculinist expressions of power and phallocentric constructions of knowledge (e.g. Young's deconstruction of the rape trial), the more dangerous and compelling the feminist intervention precisely because it operates within a concrete field of specificity rather than at a level of comfortable abstraction more readily confined to the cupboard as an irrelevance, annoyance or distraction. The risk of being specific may, however, come at a high personal cost in a twenty-first century academic world that increasingly lacks the means and motivation to defend instances of research critical of dominant institutions and practices (see, for example, Byrne-Armstrong et al., 1999).

Lastly feminists working in criminology and criminal justice policy may need to confront how much of that work is implicated in what Rafter and Heidensohn refer to as 'the construction of hierarchies based on gender, race, class and sexuality' (Rafter and Heidensohn, 1995: 11). This may not be a comfortable experience. Regardless of differences that fragment feminist criminologies, they will undoubtedly continue to share at least one commonality, namely that their scholarship is both 'political and intellectual' (Naffine, 1997: 28) and this is what has made feminist scholarship integral and not incidental to the larger project of critical criminology.

Notes

1. Significant and influential works include Dobash and Dobash's (1979) study of family violence; Hamner and Maynard's (1987) analysis of women and violence; Russell's (1975, 1982) exposé of rape, including rape in marriage; to name only a few.
2. *Sydney Morning Herald*, 14 June 2001: 'Tears of the women haunted by the sneering face of Geoff Clark'.
   Sydney Morning Herald, 15 June 2001: 'Clark denies rape: "Absolutely Outrageous"'.
   Sydney Morning Herald, 16 June 2001: 'O'Shane turns her fire onto "bleating" feminists, but could lose sex cases'.
   Sydney Morning Herald, 18 June 2001: 'O'Shane Lashes out at rape hypocrisy'.
   Sydney Morning Herald, 18 June 2001: 'Why it was right to air the claims of rape'.
   Sydney Morning Herald, 20 June 2001: 'O'Shane's words could destroy decades of progress'.
   Sydney Morning Herald, 21 June 2001: 'For O'Shane, sexism is the lesser of two evils'.
   Sydney Morning Herald, 23 June 2001: 'How the law fails women in rape cases'.
   The Australian, 18 June 2001: 'Women Convicted in Trial by Media: Pat O'shane has undermined decades of feminism'.
   The Australian, 18 June 2001: 'O'Shane defies critics'.
   The Australian, 16–17 June 2000. 'Hatred at the heart of Clark family' 'ATSIC commissioners stick by leader'.
   The Australian, 20 June 2001: 'ATSIC Board stands up for Clark'.
3. i.e. *Sydney Morning Herald*: 'MP attacks "frauds" for not tackling sex crimes, 20 June 2001; *The Australian*, 18 June 2001: 'Women convicted in trial by media'.
4. Of course both the elder and his son have strenuously denied the allegations, claiming they were orchestrated by racist outsiders not from their community. The main external exponent for the girl has been an indigenous doctor employed by the Aboriginal Medical Service in that state.
5. SNAG – Sensitive New Age Guy.
6. I did my honours thesis on prostitution as a form of sex-work, and my 'intellectual project' became entangled with the political project of decriminalising sex-work and setting up the first Australian Prostitutes Collective, much to the obvious disgust of my colleagues (then in industrial relations, and my 'sisters' in the collective).

7. There is an abundance of examples here: the analysis of miscarriages of justice; the exposure of wrongful executions; the brutality of allegedly humane punishments; the racialisation of crime in indigenous communities; law and order driven policing of young people, soccer fans and the like; the injustice of mandatory sentencing; the futility of imprisonment for most categories of crime; the net-widening effect of diversion programmes; the violation of prisoner's rights; the mistreatment of suspects in police custody; the targeting of ethnic minorities; the criminalisation of victimless activities; discrimination against sexual, religious and racial minorities before the courts. And the list goes on.

Bibliography

Adler, F. (1975) *Sisters in Crime: The Rise of the New Female Criminal*. New York: McGraw-Hill.
Adler, F. and Simon, R. J. (eds) (1979) *The Criminology of Deviant Women*. Boston: Houghton Mifflin.
Alder, C. (1994) 'The Policing of young women', in R. White and C. Alder (eds), *The Police and Young People in Australia*. Melbourne: Cambridge University Press.
Alder, C. and Baines, M. (eds) (1996) *...and When She Was Bad? Working with Young Women in Juvenile Justice and Related Areas*. Tasmania: National Centre for Youth Studies.
Allen, H. (1987) *Justice Unbalanced: Gender, Psychiatry and Judicial Decisions*. Buckingham: Open University Press.
Allen, J. (1988) 'The masculinity of criminality and criminology: interrogating some impasses', in M. Findlay, R. Hogg, (eds), *Understanding Crime and Criminal Justice*. Sydney: Law Book Co.
Allen, J. (1989), 'Men, Crime and Criminology: Recasting the Questions', *International Journal of the Sociology of Law*, 17: 19–39.
Allen, J. (1990) *Sex and Secrets: Crimes Involving Australian Women Since 1880*. Melbourne: Oxford University Press.
Baudrillard, J. (1992) 'Simulations', in A. Easthorpe and K. McGowen (eds), *A Critical and Cultural Studies Reader*. Sydney: Allen & Unwin.
Bauman, Z. (1992) *Intimations of Postmodernity*. London: Routledge.
Bell, V. (1993) *Interrogating Incest: Feminism, Foucault and the Law*. London: Routledge.
Bertrand, M. (1967) 'The myth of sexual equality before the law', *Proceedings of the Fifth Research Conference on Delinquency and Criminality*. Montreal: Quebec Society of Criminology.
Bertrand, M. (1969) 'Self-Image and delinquency: a contribution to the study of female criminality and women's image', *Acta Criminologica*, 2: 71–144.
Bertrand, M. (1979) *La Femme et le Crime*. Montreal: L'Aurore.
Breckenridge, J. and Carmody, M. (eds) (1992) *Crimes of Violence: Australian Responses to Rape and Child Sexual Assault*. Sydney: Allen & Unwin.
Brown, B, (1986) 'Women and crime: the dark figure in criminology', *Economy and Society*, 15(3): 355–402.
Brown, B. (1990) 'Reassessing the critique of biologism', in L. Gelthorpe and A. Morris (eds), *Feminist Perspectives in Criminology*. Buckingham: Open University Press.

Brown, D. and Hogg, R. (1992) 'Essentialism, radical criminology and left realism', *Australian and New Zealand Journal of Criminology*, 25: 195–230.

Brownmiller, S. (1975), *Against Our Will: Men, Women and Rape*. London: Penguin.

Byrne-Armstrong, H., Carmody, M., Hodge, B., Hogg, R. and Lee, M. (1999) 'The risk of naming violence: an unpleasant encounter between legal culture and feminist criminology', *Australian Feminist Law Journal*, 13: 13–37.

Cain, M. (1986) 'Realism, feminism, methodology, and law', *International Journal of the Sociology of Law*, 14: 255–67.

Cain, M. (1990) 'Towards transgression: new directions in feminist criminology', *International Journal of the Sociology of Law*, 18(1): 1–18.

Carlen, P. (1988) *Women, Crime and Poverty*. Buckingham: Open University Press.

Carlen, P. (1992) 'Criminal women and criminal justice: the limits to, and potential of, feminist and left realist perspectives', in R. Matthews and J. Young. (eds), *Issues in Realist Criminology*. London: Sage.

Carlen, P. (1998) *Sledgehammer: Women's Imprisonment at the Millennium*. London: Macmillan.

Carlen, P., Hicks, J., O'Dwyer, J., Christina, D. and Tchaikovsky, C. (1985) *Criminal Women*. Cambridge: Polity Press.

Carmody, M. and Breckenridge, J. (eds) (1992) *Crimes of Violence: Australian Responses to Rape and Child Sexual Assault*. Sydney: Allen & Unwin.

Carmody, M. and Carrington, K. (2000) 'Preventing sexual violence?', *Australian and New Zealand Journal of Criminology*, 33(3): 341–61.

Carrington, K. (1990) 'Aboriginal girls and juvenile justice: what justice? white justice', *Journal for Social Justice Studies*, 3: 1–18.

Carrington, K. (1993) *Offending Girls: Sex, Youth and Justice*. Sydney: Allen and Unwin.

Carrington, K. (1994) 'Postmodernism and feminist criminologies: disconnecting discourses', *International Journal of the Sociology of Law*, 22: 261–77.

Carrington, K. (1998) *Who Killed Leigh Leigh?*. Sydney: Random Press.

Carrington, K. and Watson, P. (1996) 'Policing sexual violence: feminism, criminal justice and governmentality', *International Journal of the Sociology of Law*, 24: 253–72.

Chambers, I. (1986) *Popular Culture*. London: Methuen.

Chesney-Lind, M. and Sheldon, R. (1998) *Girls, Delinquency and Juvenile Justice*. Belmont, CA: West Wadsworth.

Cohen, S. (1998) 'Intellectual scepticism and political commitment: the case of radical criminology', in P. Walton and J. Young (eds), *The New Criminology Revisited*. London: Macmillan; New York: St. Martin's Press.

Collier, R. (1998) *Masculinities, Crime and Criminology*. London: Sage.

Connell, R. W. (1995) *Masculinities*. Sydney: Allen & Unwin.

Cook, S. and Bessant, J. (eds) (1997) *Women's Encounters With Violence: Australian Experiences*. New York: Sage.

Cousins, M. (1980) 'Men's rea: a note on sexual difference, criminology and law', in P. Carlen and M. Collison (eds), *Radical Issues in Criminology*. London: Martin Robertson.

Cunneen, C. (ed.) (1992) *Aboriginal Perspectives on Criminal Justice*, The Institute of Criminology Monograph Series No. 1. Sydney: Institute of Criminology.

Cunneen, C., Lynch, R., Tupper, V. and Findlay, M. (1989) *The Dynamics of Collective Conflict*. Sydney: Law Book Co.

Daly, K. (1994) *Gender, Crime and Punishment*. New Haven, CT: Yale University Press.

Daly, K. and Chesney-Lind, M. (1988) 'Feminism and Criminology', *Justice Quarterly*, 5(4): 498–538.

Daly, K. and Maher, L. (1998) *Criminology at the Crossroads: Feminist Readings in Crime and Justice*. New York: Oxford University Press.

Dobash, R. and Dobash, R. (1979) *Violence Against Wives*. London: Open Books.

Easteal, P. (1994) *Voices of the Survivors*. Sydney: Pinnifex Press.

Edwards, S. (1981) *Female Sexuality and the Law*. Oxford: Martin Robinson.

Fattah, E. (1997) *Criminology: Past, Present and Future*. London: Macmillan.

Gelsthorpe, L. (1989) *Sexism and the Female Offender*. Aldershot: Gower.

Gelsthorpe, L. (1990) 'Feminist methodologies in criminology: a new approach or old wine in new bottles', in L. Gelsthorpe and A. Morris (eds), *Feminist Perspectives in Criminology*. Buckingham: Open University Press.

Gelsthorpe, L. and Morris, A. (1990) 'Introduction: transforming and transgressing criminology', in L. Gelsthorpe and A. Morris (eds), *Feminist Perspectives in Criminology*. Buckingham: Open University Press.

Gelsthorpe, L. and Morris, A. (eds) (1990) *Feminist Perspectives in Criminology*. Buckingham: Open University Press.

Goodrich, P. (1986) *Reading the Law*. Oxford: Basil Blackwell.

Greer, P. (1994) 'Aboriginal women and domestic violence in NSW', in J. Stubbs (ed.), *Women, Male Violence and the Law*. Sydney: Institute of Criminology Monograph Series.

Grosz, L. (1989) 'The in(ter)vention of feminist knowledges', in *Crossing Boundaries: Feminisms and the Critique of Knowledges*. Sydney: Allen & Unwin.

Hall, S. and Jefferson, T. (eds) (1976) *Resistance Through Rituals*. London: Hutchinson.

Hanmer, J. and Maynard, M. (eds) (1987) *Women, Violence and Social Control*. London: Macmillan.

Harris, A. P. (1990) 'Race and essentialism in feminist legal theory', *Standford Legal Review*, 42: 581–61.

Heidensohn, F. (1968) 'The deviance of women: a critique and an enquiry', *British Journal of Sociology*, XIX (2): 160–75.

Heidensohn, F. (1985) *Women and Crime*. London: Macmillan.

Heidensohn, F. (2000) 'Feminist criminology, Britain', in N. H. Rafter (ed.), *Encyclopedia of Women and Crime*. Phoenix, AZ: Oryx Press.

Hindess, B. (1977) 'The concept of class in Marxist theory and Marxist politics', in J. Bloomfield (ed.), *The Communist University of London*. London: Lawrence and Wishart.

Hogg, R. (2001) 'Penality and modes of regulating indigenous peoples in Australia', *Punishment and Society*, 3(3): 355–79.

Howe, A. (1994) *Punish and Critique: Towards a Feminist Analysis of Penality*. London: Routledge.

Jefferson, T (1997) 'Masculinities and crime', in M. Maguire, R. Morgan and R. Reiner (eds), *The Oxford Handbook of Criminology*. Oxford: Clarendon Press.

Kirkby, D. (ed.) (1995) *Sex, Power and Justice*. Melbourne: Oxford University Press.

Klein, D. (1973) 'The etiology of female crime: a review of the literature', *Issues in Criminology*, 8(2): 3–30.

Klein, D. (1995) 'Crime through gender's prism: feminist criminology in the United States', in N. Rafter and F. Heidensohn. (eds), *International Perspectives in Feminist Criminology*. Buckingham: Open University Press.

Lees, S. (1997) *Ruling Passions: Sexual Violence, Reputation and the Law*. Philadelphia, PA: Open University Press.

Leonard, E. (1982) *Women, Crime and Society: A Critique of Criminology Theory*. New York: Longman.

Lyotard, J. (1986) *The Postmodern Condition: A Report on Knowledge*. Manchester: Manchester University Press.

MacKinnon, C. (1987) 'Feminism, Marxism, method and state: toward feminist jurisprudence', in S. Harding (ed.), *Feminism and Methodology*. Buckingham: Open University Press.

Maher, L. (1997) *Sexed Work: Gender, Race and Resistance in a Brooklyn Drug Market*. Oxford: Clarendon Press.

Messerschmidt, J. W. (1993) *Masculinities and Crime*. Lanham, MD: Rowm & Littlefield.

Muncie, J. (1998) 'Reassessing competing paradigms in criminological theory', in P. Walton and J. Young (eds), *The New Criminology Revisited*. London: Macmillan; New York: St. Martin's Press.

Naffine, N. (1987) *Female Crime*. Sydney: Allen & Unwin.

Naffine, N. (1991) *Law and the Sexes*. Sydney: Allen & Unwin.

Naffine, N. (1997) *Feminism and Criminology*. Sydney: Allen & Unwin.

Newburn, T. and Stanko, E. (eds) (1994) *Just Boys Doing Business: Men, Masculinities and Crime*. London: Routledge.

Rabinow, P. (1984) *The Foucault Reader*. New York: Pantheon Books.

Rafter, N. (1990) *Partial Justice: Women, Prisons and Social Control*, 2nd edn. New Brunswick, NJ: Transaction Books.

Rafter, N. (2000) 'Preface', in N. H. Rafter (ed.), *Encyclopedia of Women and Crime*. Phoenix, AZ: Oryx Press.

Rafter, N. and Heidensohn, F. (eds) (1995) *International Feminist Perspectives in Criminology*. Buckingham: Open University Press.

Rafter, N. and Stanko. E. (eds) (1982) *Judge, Lawyer, Victim, Thief: Women, Gender Roles and Criminal Justice*. Boston, MA: Northeastern University Press.

Rice, M. (1990) 'Challenging orthodoxies in feminist theory: a black feminist critique', in L. Gelsthorpe and A. Morris, (eds), *Feminist Perspectives in Criminology*. Buckingham: Open University Press.

Russell, D. (1975) *The Politics of Rape: the Victim's Perspective*. New York: Stein & Day.

Russell, D. (1982) *Rape in Marriage*. New York: Macmillan.

Salmelainen, P. and Coumarelos, C. (1993) 'Adult sexual assault in NSW', *Crime and Justice Bulletin*, no. 20. Sydney: NSW Bureau of Crime Statistics and Research.

Schwendinger, H. and Schwendinger, J. (1975) 'Defenders of order or guardians of Human Rights', in I. Taylor, Pl Walton and J. Young (eds), *Critical Criminology*. London: Routledge & Kegan Paul.

Scraton, P. (1990) 'Scientific knowledge or masculine discourses? Challenging patriarchy in criminology', in L. Gelsthorpe and A. Morris (eds), *Feminist Perspectives in Criminology*. Buckingham: Open University Press.

Scutt, J. (1983) *Even in the Best of Homes: Violence in the Family*. Australia: Penguin.

Smart, C. (1976) *Women, Crime and Criminology*. London: Routledge & Kegan Paul.

Smart, C. (1989) *Feminism and the Power of Law*. London: Routledge.

Smart, C. (1990) 'Feminist approaches to criminology – or postmodern woman meets atavistic man', in L. Gelsthorpe and A. Morris (eds), *Feminist Perspectives in Criminology*. Buckingham: Open University Press.

Stanko, E. (1985) *Intimate Intrusions: Women's Experiences of Male Violence*. Boston, MA: Routledge.

Stanko, E. (1990) *Everyday Violence*. London: Pandora.

Stratton, J. (1993) *The Young Ones*. Perth: Black Swan Press.

Stubbs, J. (ed.) (1994) *Women, Male Violence and the Law*. Sydney: Institute of Criminology.

Taylor, I., Walton, P. and Young, J. (1973) *The New Criminology*. London: Routledge & Kegan Paul.

Taylor, I., Walton, P. and Young, J., (eds) (1975) *Critical Criminology*. London: Routledge & Kegan Paul.

Threadgold, T. (1993) 'Critical theory, feminisms, the judiciary and rape', *Australian Feminist Law Journal*, 1: 7–25.

Van Swaaningen, R. (1989) 'Feminism and abolitionism as critiques of criminology', *International Journal of the Sociology of Law*, 19: 287–306.

Vega, J. (1987) 'Coercion and consent: classic liberal concepts in texts on sexual violence', *International Journal of the Sociology of Law*, 16: 75–89.

Walton, P. and Young, J. (eds) (1998) *The New Criminology Revisited*. London: Macmillan; New York: St. Martin's Press.

White, R. (1990) *No Space of Their Own: Young People and Social Control in Australia*. Sydney: Cambridge University Press.

Wilson, E. (1983) *What Is to Be Done About Violence Against Women?*. London: Penguin.

Young, A. (1996) *Imagining Crime*. London: Sage.

Young, A. (1998) 'The waste land of the law, the wordless song of the rape victim', *Melbourne University Law Review*, 22(2): 442–65.

Young, J. (1988) 'Radical criminology in Britain', *British Journal of Criminology*, 28(2): 159–83.

Young, J. (1998) 'Breaking windows: situating the new criminology', in P. Walton, and J. Young (eds), *The New Criminology Revisited*. London: Macmillan; New York: St. Martin's Press.

Part II
New Directions and Challenges for
Critical Criminology

Chapter 6

For a psychosocial criminology

Tony Jefferson

Introduction

In criminology, whose subject matter must surely include the criminal actor, or offender, there has been surprisingly little interest in (usually) him, especially since the arrival of critical criminologies in the 1960s and 1970s. Where s/he has appeared it has been in a depleted and unrecognisable form: a travesty of a human subject. Deconstructing this should have been the job of a critical criminology. This was happening elsewhere. In psychology the authors of *Changing the Subject* (Henriques et al., 1984/1999), the spearhead of a critical psychology movement, offered an exciting new understanding of human subjectivity. In the humanities, subjectivity was being rethought, not only in the light of structural linguistics, Marxist semiology or Foucaultian discourses, but also in relation to feminist re-readings of Freud and Freudianism (e.g. Mulvey, 1975). In sociology the emergence of questions to do with difference and identity increasingly involved encounters with the complexity of subjectivity (Du Gay, Evans and Redman, 2000). But, despite the important changes within criminology precipitated by all the 'posts' (-modernism, -structuralism, -Marxism and -feminism) the offender or criminal subject remains largely untouched by these developments. The result is that the (explicit or implicit) subject of critical criminology is as inadequate as that bequeathed by traditional criminology. None of this is to suggest that things were better before critical criminology transformed the intellectual landscape, merely that the advent of a critical criminology promised better. Worse still, by ignoring the offender for its own theoretical reasons, critical criminology left a gap which came to be plugged largely by traditional psychology's re-entry into criminological discourse (cf. Hollin, 1989) and by journalism. Surely critical criminologists should not hand over the responsibility for explaining the causes of serious criminal acts committed by particular individuals to a discipline that they have tended to hold in contempt, and to journalists who are trained fundamentally as investigative reporters and not as social scientists.

All this has serious implications for any criminological theorising which requires (and most does) presumptions about human subjectivity, a point which delivers my three objectives in this chapter. The first is to reveal the criminal subject presumed by various theoretical approaches within contemporary criminology. This will involve demonstrating that the widespread practice of ignoring the individual offender does not eliminate the theoretical need to presume a subject, if only implicitly. The second is to propose a psychosocial notion of the subject that is informed by recent developments in critical 'post'-theorising. Finally, I begin to show where within criminology such a notion is beginning to have a presence, and to explore how it might help answer a series of criminological questions and thus make a difference to some criminological debates which otherwise appear to be terminally stuck.

The Subject in Contemporary Criminology

The birth of critical criminology in the UK is usually credited to the publication of Taylor, Walton and Young's seminal *The New Criminology* (1973). However, its authors would be the first to acknowledge their debt to symbolic interactionism and labelling theory. Although the idea of labelling transformed much within criminology, the subject presumed by symbolic interactionism was essentially Meadian, namely that we are 'looking-glass' selves: what others see and reflect back to us, we become. But what happens when reflections fail to fit? Like the oft-noted failure of Becker's (1963) labelling theory of deviance to explain the category of the secret deviant, Meadian psychology cannot account for the subject who sees her (or him)self differently from the self reflected back by others, what we might call the misreflected or misrecognised self. Consequently, the labelling approach was always happier explaining the adoption of the labelled identity than resistance to labelling, which tended to end up suggesting, lamely, that the take up of a label was not automatic – individuals could choose not to adopt the label. At that point symbolic interactionism's latent voluntarism manifests itself.

If *The New Criminology* was indebted to symbolic interactionism, it can be said also to have acted as midwife to Marxism within criminology. Its concluding call 'for a fully social theory of deviance', with its Marxist accent on 'fully' (surface and depth, appearance and what is hidden), gave birth to a critical Marxist reconstruction within criminology. It also marked the end of any interest in the causes of crime, in the traditional sense of understanding offending as to do with the behaviour of concrete individuals. The macro-sociological focus of Marxism, especially after its structuralist turn in the 1970s, left little space for interactional factors, never mind individual ones (despite the insistence in *The New Criminology* of the importance of social psychology as well as political economy). The same criticism could be made of *Policing the Crisis* (Hall et al., 1978), a Marxist text partly inspired by *The New Criminology*. Its primary focus was on the reaction to mugging, not the behaviour of muggers. When it did address the latter briefly in the final chapter it did so by introducing the importance of the biographical level (in addition to the structural and the cultural). Even here though, the focus, as Goodey (2000: 486–7) notes approvingly, is on the 'typical biography', the social (or structural/cultural) within the biographical (but not the biographical within the social).

While the criminological left in its Marxist variant was busy settling accounts with (bourgeois) individualism and, in consequence, effectively writing off the criminological subject altogether,[1] traditional criminology was mutating into what came to be known as administrative criminology. Paradoxically, both criminologies were agreed that crime is widespread under capitalism, although for different reasons and hence with different consequences. For Marxists, the criminogenic nature of capitalism accounted for the normality of crime and hence the need to focus elsewhere, on unequal social arrangements and not individual actors. For administrative criminologists, the empirical fact of the ubiquity of crime rendered explanation largely a matter of faith, about which they preferred to remain agnostic. In any event, their interest in explanation was always secondary to the practical goal of prevention. However, a theory of prevention has to presuppose a motivated individual who must be prevented, at which point a criminological subject is required. What then gets drawn on to meet this requirement is rational choice theory, that curious amalgam of the rational unitary subject of traditional psychology and the free-willed 'choosing' subject of classical criminology (and contemporary economics), selfishly pursuing his or her own interests. The preventive goal is to alter the balance of interests so that, manifestly, 'crime doesn't pay'.

A notoriously conservative take-up of this position is that by the North American sociologist Charles Murray in his theory of the underclass (Murray, 1984, 1990). Essentially, Murray argues that underclass boys choose crime over work because our 'generous' treatment of the unemployed encourages worklessness and our 'lenient' treatment of criminals makes crime attractive. A similarly voluntaristic argument is used to explain pregnancies among underclass teenage girls. Change the balance of opportunities, the reward/punishment ratio, the theory implies, and you can change behaviour – though Murray's own solution is to ghettoise the 'feckless' and allow them to govern themselves, a solution which, whatever its democratic pretensions, is based on an exclusionary rather than an inclusive logic.

So many words have been expended on control theory (Hirschi, 1969; Gottfredson and Hirschi, 1990) that it seems redundant to produce yet more.[2] But, since control theory is interested in the causes of crime and is committed to understanding criminal behaviour, even to the extent of proposing a general theory of crime, it is necessary to address its version of the criminological subject. In a nutshell, control theory argues that the weaker a person's ties to the conventional social order the more a person is likely to revert to crime, and vice versa. This has always struck me as tautologous, as others have also argued (Akers, 1991), although this does not seem to trouble Hirschi for whom 'tautologies are at the heart of much of what we do' (quoted in Taylor, 2001: 382). If a child's social ties or 'bonds', of attachment, involvement, beliefs and commitments, are crucial to whether s/he is more or less likely to become delinquent, it is obvious that the parents and their bonds with the conventional order are also crucial. In other words, upbringing and experiences within the family are crucial. Traditional sociology used to talk of a 'cycle of disadvantage', a reference to the structural disadvantages 'inherited' by the children of the poor. Control theory can read like a cultural version of this with delinquent children the inheritors of the weak social ties to conformity of their parents. The problem is how to explain 'resistance' to the cycle, its non-reproduction. This would require moving beyond the mere presence or absence of strong social bonds to an account of motivation, but within the theoretical terms available this is just not possible.[3]

If Charles Murray's thesis about the underclass has often been taken as a contemporary conservative tirade against fecklessness, the work of David Farrington, the only Professor of Criminological Psychology in the UK to my knowledge, can be read as a liberal version. His longitudinal study of over 400 London males aged from 8 to 32 (Farrington and West, 1990; Farrington, 1995) seems only to have produced the depressing conclusion that badly behaved parents tend to produce badly behaved boys, or fecklessness begets fecklessness – although he does recognise that 'more research is needed on factors that vary within individuals' (Farrington, 1997: 399). Now few would deny the (depressing) strength of such a connection, but it is clearly not the whole story – as is well known by all those books, films and songs depicting families and friends split by the law (law breaker/law enforcer, brother as gangster-hero versus brother as priest). The dramatic potential of such stories is obvious,[4] but their power to pull in audiences suggests an interest in exploring and understanding why and how similar circumstances produce dissimilar outcomes: how conformity and deviance are reproduced and/or resisted. This appears to exceed the curiosity of most criminologists.

The problem that I am addressing here, that of the missing or inadequately conceptualised criminological subject, has not gone entirely unnoticed. In 1986 Jock Young talked of the 'crisis of aetiology' afflicting criminology. But he did not rectify it in his transition from 'new criminologist' to 'left realist'. Denouncing his old self and Marxist criminology generally as 'idealist', the new 'realist' stricture became 'to take crime seriously' – by which was meant, effectively, the victims of crime. Although, theoretically, Young's 'square of crime' (the offender, the victim, the state, informal social controls) includes 'the offender', it is never developed (Young, 1992: 27).[5] Moreover, the victim (implicitly) is a risk-averse individual (in contrast to the risk-taking offender, we might add) whose fear level is a 'realistic' response to the likelihood of being a victim of crime. While this may be true of some people,[6] it is, once again, far from the whole story. Less fearful people of all ages are easily found in high-risk areas and more fearful people in low-risk areas, as recent research has shown (Hollway and Jefferson, 2000a).

Left realism's commitment to the victims of crime stems partly from an identification with the poor and disadvantaged who populate high-crime areas and for whom crime is yet another disadvantage. Feminism's commitment to women stems from a similar identification; in this instance with women as victims of male violence. This laudable political commitment has had two unfortunate theoretical consequences. The first is a tendency to take women's apparently higher fear of crime at face value – as a 'realistic' response to (male) threats. In this it echoes and endorses left realism's version of the subject: risk-averse, with (high) fear levels 'rationally' matching (high) risk levels. The second has been to equate man and men – to tar all men with the brush of patriarchal commitment to power over and control of women, read through a social constructionism that effectively removes the need for psychology altogether. In this way, differences between men become erased as the idea of a continuum of violence embracing all men makes every man, at least potentially, an abuser, an assaulter, a molester, and so on. It is only a question of degree, of inhabiting a different point on the same continuum. Politically, this idea was addressed to a traditional criminology, and its common sense variants, whose interest in violent men of various kinds was motivated by a search for their difference from other, non-violent men. Within this context, early feminist writing about male violence against women wanted to 'bend back the stick' and emphasise how widespread and culturally acceptable such violence was. This now seems uncontentious, and still true. However, the problem of explaining the non-violent male remains, since whatever figures are used – official, criminal victimisation or self-report – he is in the majority (Levi, 1997: 881). Even if he were a minority, this would still present a theoretical problem. To regard the non-violent male as merely inhabiting a different point on the same continuum of violence seems to add very little by way of explanation. Moreover, speaking as a man, there does seem to me to be a difference of some importance between me and all the men I know, and Peter Sutcliffe, Jeffrey Dahmer, Ed Gein, Fred West, Dennis Nilsen and their ilk.

Let me conclude this section of the chapter by summarising the various notions of the criminal subject or offender presumed within contemporary criminology and the theoretical assumptions underpinning these. In broad terms these amount to three: traditional Freudian, rational-unitary and social constructionist.

Traditional Freudian

The defining feature of this version is its individualistic focus: the self as a unique product of instincts, drives, learning and developmental processes, anxieties and the resulting defences. Although not much in evidence now within academic criminology, having been washed out partly by the critical deluge from the 1960s onward, its common-sense legacy lives on in the (widespread) notion of the disturbed or abnormal offender often attributed to so-called senseless crimes which seem to defy rational explanation.[7] This traditional version of the offender was prominent in the trial of Peter Sutcliffe. There, the question of his plea hinged on whether he was to be regarded as mentally ill or not. In the event, the psychiatrists adjudged him to be suffering from paranoid schizophrenia, only to be overruled by the trial judge who thought the jury should decide. In finding him 'guilty to murder' in all 13 cases, they decided, effectively, he was normal, not insane: bad not mad. Subsequently he was sent to Broadmoor, a prison hospital for the criminally insane, as a diagnosed paranoid schizophrenic. For our purposes, two things are interesting about this battle to define Sutcliffe's subjectivity: it is a good example of a traditional Freudian view of the offender confronting a version of offender as normal man (at the extreme end of the continuum of violence); it demonstrates neatly the inadequacy of either version (Sutcliffe as mentally ill, Sutcliffe as normal) to understand his offending.

Rational-unitary

Like the traditional Freudian version, this too is individualistic in focus. But, whereas the common-sense version of the Freudian legacy within criminology is the abnormal or 'disturbed' offender, the equivalent version of, for example, rational choice theory is Mr and Mrs 'Normal': the self-interested, cognitively-driven, rational, unitary subject of classical criminology, traditional psychology and contemporary economics. S/he is the opportunist offender of administrative criminology, the female or male of Charles Murray's underclass, and the 'realistic' victim presumed by left realism and many feminists.

Social Constructionist

The defining feature here is the notion of the self as essentially a product of social forces. These can be social interactions (symbolic interactionism), attempts to balance means and ends (strain theory), structural (class/ Marxism, patriarchy/feminism), a poor family environment (control theory), or, most recently, discursive (Foucaultian-inspired). For example, offenders such as burglars or drug users have tended to be viewed largely as victims of 'strain' or (class) structural disadvantage, whereas male sexual abusers are products of the structural advantages of patriarchy. Where agency is required (if only implicitly) by these theories, the agent is broadly the rational unitary subject.

It would seem fair to conclude on the basis of the above that not only is work on offenders a minority interest in contemporary, especially critical, criminology, it is also misleading. If you want to know why he, or she, 'did it', don't ask a criminologist. Given this bleak picture, in the next section I begin the process of constructing a more adequate psychosocial subject, one who is hopefully more recognisable and who might in consequence help us answer better this question of motivation.

Towards a Psychosocial Subject

One practical result of these inadequate conceptualisations of the subject is the inability of criminology to contribute constructively to topical debates such as offender profiling or the compulsive nature of serial killing, topics which cannot be called trivial or unimportant. One consequence, as I have suggested above, has been the reappearance within criminology of traditional psychology with its cognitively driven, information-processing subject, partly one suspects to plug some of these gaps. The other has been the rise of the journalist/writer specialising in murder.[8] This case-based work attempts to place a particular individual in a social setting. In doing so, in attending to both the psychic and the social influences on their subjects, these writers appear to assume a psychosocial subject. But this is never spelled out theoretically. So let me, in schematic outline, try to do just that.

Human behaviour is not the product of cognition alone but of reason and emotion. That much should be uncontentious, which makes the peculiarly passionless subject of criminology hard to comprehend. Often our reason and our feelings are in conflict: what we know 'rationally' is contradicted by how we feel about something – a situation that can cause us discomfort or distress. If it is common to consign our emotions to the realm of the irrational, psychoanalysis tells us that there is a 'logic' to the latter, though one that is not fully accessible to our conscious selves. In other words, psychoanalysis posits a non-unitary subject, one char-acterised by conflicts between motivations arising from a reasoning consciousness and others which remain hidden or unconscious. At a general level, these conflicts are the result of experiences which are difficult, painful and disempowering and which invoke too much anxiety for the conscious mind to contemplate. They will in consequence be defended against – by repressing them, splitting them off and projecting them elsewhere, or by denial.

A number of unavoidable early life experiences are crucial to the development of a defended self. These include the timing and manner of separation from the mother (or substitute), a process which produces the first, early sense of an independent self, and the way in which the father (or substitute) 'interrupts' the mother–child dyad. This latter process is what propels the child into triangular relationships of self, mother, other(s) – to which s/he must thereafter accommodate, and is infused with both threat and desire. In other words, the blissfulness of early union with the mother is twice broken as each child is forced to recognise the (sometimes) conflicting needs of mother, and of father/others. This inevitably conflict-ridden process is strewn with anxiety. Unconscious defences against anxiety originate here. The way a sense of self emerges from these processes is different for each and every one of us. Although we all go through the same processes, we each do so differently: nobody shares our biographical experiences in all their particularity; these are always unique. This is why it is essential to hold onto a psychic dimension to subjectivity and not simply dissolve it into the social. Although it will not remain 'fixed' throughout life (although it can get 'stuck'), our subjectivity can never escape these unique, early influences which will affect:

- our particular pattern of defences against anxiety;
- our particular identifications and resulting sexuality;
- our 'core personality',[9] in terms of our general capacity for empathy, basic sense of security, ability to tolerate difference, etc.[10]

If traditional psychoanalysis has come to be construed as an intra-subjective or individualistic theory (a not entirely unwarranted construction though now is not the time to argue the point), the object relational school of psychoanalysis, upon which much recent theorising relies (Chodorow, 1978, 1994; Benjamin, 1995, 1998; Layton, 1998), is intrinsically inter-subjective, hence unavoidably social.[11] Which means none of what takes place does so in a social vacuum. Whatever our particular, biographically unique experiences of early life processes, with their resulting patterns of defences, identifications and so on, these are always also simultaneously social (which is not, for reasons outlined above, to say they can be reduced to the social: they are psychosocial). They are simultaneously social in several senses. The social world impacts directly on these early processes of identity formation, thus shaping them somewhat. The ability of the mother to protect the child from external, traumatic events – physical accidents, physical or sexual abuse, nightly bombing raids, witnessing frightening events – is variable. But, however loving and attentive she may happen to be, such traumatic events will have an impact regardless, as those dealing with children from war zones know only too well.

The social world impacts indirectly on the child through the mediation of the mother, then of others. The mother's relation to the social world – happy or unhappy, distracted or attentive, loving or resentful, worn-down or energetic, consistent or inconsistent, etc. – will affect how she is with the child, how she is experienced by the child, hence the process of separation. The same is true of the father and how his social world gets mediated to the child. In other words, the sense of self held by both mothers and fathers, their identifications, sexuality, 'personality', etc. provide an important early social context for the child. This brings us to the other crucial mediator, namely discourse.

Although the social world can be experienced directly as frightening (e.g. a loud noise) or soothing (e.g. a gentle touch), most of what takes place in the social world is meaningless in itself. Praying, shaking hands, writing a cheque, exchanging food for banknotes, reading a newspaper, talking, watching moving images, painting a picture, taking photographs – all these and other activities only make sense through discourse, since discourse is what gives meaning to 'things' and practices. Given the centrality of language to rendering things socially meaningful, especially in literate, developed cultures, it is the most important discursive medium. Hence our limited ability to make sense of things where we lack the appropriate language, and why the development of language is such a crucial moment in a young child's social development. The acquisition of language, then, propels the child into a vast, new world of significance. Differences become saturated with social meanings. Sexual difference acquires the significance of gender, with its endless coding of the social world into masculine and feminine and their associated behavioural 'imperatives' for each sex. Differences of pigmentation and where one is from are transformed into the social discourses of race and ethnicity, with their tales of in-groups and out-groups, of envy and fascination and fear and loathing, of multicultural toleration and racist rejection. Differences of possession become stories about the rich and the poor, 'us' and 'them', the class structure. Different practices, like saying one's prayers or reading the Koran, enter narratives of religion with their infinite variations on the holy and the non-believer, the righteous and the damned, good and evil.

Given the psychic processes outlined above and given the social context in which all this necessarily takes place, the big question of course is how the two are connected in a non-reductive fashion. Schematically, we can say that the way in which early life processes are managed and their resulting patterns of anxieties, defences, identifications and so on will have effects on the adoption of particular discursive positions. This means, for example, that our adoption of particular discursive positions is not something we rationally choose as a result of a purely cognitive cost-benefit analysis, as rational choice theorists would have it, since this eliminates both inner conflict and the social world. Nor is our take-up of particular positions determined by the social meanings espoused by our parents, our neighbourhood, our peers, our class, etc. as the social constructionists would have it, since this erases the psychic realm altogether. Rather, it means that our adoption of particular discursive positions can only be fully understood once account is taken of both conscious and unconscious motivations and, crucially, the conflicts among them.

Although the relation between the social and the psychic is more complex than I have space for here (see Jefferson, 2002 for a fuller account), I hope this schematic outline at least indicates the importance of the idea of a subject whose motivations and behaviour are always psychosocial: irreducibly psychic and simultaneously social. To attempt to reduce the psychic to the social, and vice versa, would be to do the subject, and any theory requiring a subject, an injustice, as would be a failure to think these irreducible elements in their simultaneity. With this established, we can now begin to explore how such a notion of the subject might be used to advance some debates within criminology.

Deploying a Psychosocial Subject in Contemporary Criminological Debates

Rape and Serial Killing

Let us start where some progress has been made. Given the connection with sexuality and given that psychoanalysis offers the most sophisticated current theory of sexuality, perhaps this is not surprising. The involvement of feminists in this area – not always criminologists – certainly rectified criminology's gender-blindness and pointed out that most violent offenders are men and their victims are women and children. However, having said that, radical feminist commitment to the 'normality' of male violence and abuse, together with hostility to traditional Freudianism, has rendered certain ideas unthinkable. The result has been to produce a blindness to contemporary psychoanalytic theorising. The idea, for example, that 'rape is rape' makes it difficult to attempt to understand the difference between various types of rape. Statistically speaking, date rape (a term that some feminists object to because 'rape is rape') is more widespread than the grotesquely violent rapes followed by murder of certain serial rapists, though neither may be as common as rapes committed within war. The behaviour involved in each type of rape is manifestly different, especially in terms of the level of violence enacted. In the cases of killer rapists, what we might call the 'non-utilitarian' aspects of their behaviour (gouging genitals, dismembering corpses, etc.), has no counterpart in the behaviour of date rapists and usually lacks the group element of much wartime rape. My contention is that these (and other) different types of rape are accompanied by different psychosocial dynamics that it is unrealistic to ignore.[12] My own work on date rape (Jefferson, 1997), some with Wendy Hollway (Hollway and Jefferson, 1998; see also, on sexual harassment, Hollway and Jefferson, 1996), is trying to address these dynamics. This work uses a psychoanalytically informed understanding of ambivalence – the idea that we often entertain contradictory feelings, of love and hate, towards the same object – and the idea of unconscious defences against anxiety, especially the tendency to split off unwanted parts of the self when anxieties become too uncomfortable to manage, in an effort to interpret the complex, shifting, psychosocial, inter-subjective dynamics of particular, high-profile case examples.[13]

This 'new realism' about feelings should alter the way we approach another canonical slogan within the rape debate, namely the idea that 'no means no'.[14] More generally, a psychosocial approach might shed light on many currently ignored or unexplained aspects of rape: the obsession with washing yet never feeling clean that rape victims often attest to; the way rape by a known other can be more traumatic than rape by a stranger, even when the latter is more violent; or the relation between fantasy and rape. Both men and women, it appears, entertain rape fantasies. This would seem to connect up with the role of violence and aggression in sex, especially the relation between the two (e.g. Bataille, 1962; Benjamin, 1988). Without wishing to ignore the obvious differences between violent fantasies, the 'violence' in consensual sex (of which sadomasochistic sex is but one example) and rape, there would seem to be much to be gained by looking at possible points of connection. That this has not happened says something, again, about the general blindness of feminism in this area, typified in this case by the insistence on wanting to see rape purely as violence (and not also about sex).[15] By redefining male, including sexual, violence against women as fundamentally to do with 'power and control' feminists introduced a missing element into the rape debate; but, in excluding sexuality, it also misses something crucial.

Most academic writing on serial killing relies upon or contributes to the practice of offender profiling.[16] Whatever its merits as a tool of detection, this has little to offer in terms of understanding why the offender raped and murdered. The implicit subject becomes simply an artificial amalgam of all the information contained in the profile. Partly depending on the definitions of serial murder deployed, different authors at different times have produced portraits of the serial killer that traverse the spectrum from insanity and psychopathy, through instability, trauma, anti-social personality and sexual sadism to various versions of 'normality': 'a small, well-dressed, sociable and charming man in his forties, who neither smokes, drinks nor is inclined to swear and is often a practising Christian' is how Lester (Lester, 1995: 49) summarises the 'typical serial murderer' described by Dickson (1958) in an early study. Given these variations from insanity to banal ordinariness, it is little wonder that Lester is forced to conclude that, 'with the present state of knowledge, it is virtually impossible to construct a solid profile of serial killers' (Lester, 1995: 189). Predictably, he then calls for '[m]uch more research...to be conducted on the psychological and behavioural characteristics of serial killers, as well as the reasons why people turn to this type of murder' (Lester, 1995: 189). Since he has reviewed the many existing studies, and many previous reviews of the scholarly literature, perhaps the problem lies not with the quantity of research but with the approach: the attempt to produce 'typical' profiles from reviewing numerous cases. Given this situation, it is small wonder that journalists have stepped in with their detailed examinations of particular cases. A similar situation of journalists plugging the gaps left by academic writings on the subject characterises the topic of child killers. And although the work of David Smith (1994) on the Bulger killers and of the writer Gitta Sereny (1972/1995 and 1999) on Mary Bell is exemplary, it still falls short at the explanatory level. A psychosocially informed approach could begin to advance this morally difficult and intellectually conflicted debate, something I have attempted in a lengthy review of this work (Jefferson, 1996).

Burglary and Drug-taking

Although burglary and drug-taking can be connected offences, as in the case of the burglary undertaken to fund a drug habit, that is not the reason I choose to consider them together here. Rather, this is because the criminological portrait of the burglar or the drug (ab)user is all but identical, namely a young working-class male from a poor background who is undereducated, unqualified, unemployed and bored.[17] This seems to be an important starting point but hardly the endpoint of an inquiry. Once again, we know that many boys with such a profile will neither commit burglary nor take drugs, that some will be drug users but not burglars, a minority will burgle, some taking drugs. As well as having limited portraits of those who burgle and of drug-users,[18] there are several questions a psychosocial approach might help answer. For example, there are many 'non-utilitarian' dimensions in certain burglaries that nobody has properly addressed. Why do some burglars crap on the carpet? Why do some use more violence than would appear to be 'necessary'? Why do some rape as well as burgle their victims? Tony Kearon and Rebecca Leach (2000) have begun to look at the 'non-utilitarian', emotional dimensions of being victims of burglary – feeling defiled, uncontrollably upset, etc. I am suggesting that a similar look at the non-utilitarian dimension of offending could be illuminating.[19]

The same would be true for questions to do with drug-taking. The 'over-normalised' portrait of the drug user that emerges in the best work on drug use within criminology (Parker, Newcombe and Baxx, 1988; Parker, Aldridge and Measham, 1998; Pearson, 1987) is undoubtedly partly an understandable overreaction to the media's pathologisation of the 'junkie'.[20] However, the result is that there is much we don't know that a psychosocial approach could inform. Speaking of a high-risk activity like taking heroin, who is attracted to such risks, who is turned off by them? Who is attracted to the idea of 'escape' which is intrinsic to drug use? Who is attracted to the particular pleasure/pain calculus involved in drug-taking, with its balancing of 'getting high' and 'coming down'? Who is attracted to the element of self-destruction which is intrinsic to drug use? In general, the debate would benefit if, in conjunction with the pains of drug-taking, we took more seriously the pleasurable dimension of hard drug use. For example, heroin is addictive partly because it is indescribably pleasurable, pleasures that for some make such extreme risks 'worth it', psychosocially speaking. Since Jack Katz's ground-breaking book, *Seductions of Crime* (1988), where the focus is on the immediate sensuous and pleasurable dynamics of enacting particular crimes, the emergence of cultural criminology has begun to take seriously the pleasures involved in the commission of crime – crime as carnival, to use Presdee's (2000) term. This is a welcome antidote to the condescension of criminal-as-victim (of disadvantageous circumstances). However, Katz's book and cultural criminology more generally would make for more insightful reading if contextualised within a psychosocial framework. For, though Katz's analysis of the killer Gary Gilmore is illuminating, ultimately it was the superb journalistic biography by Gilmore's brother (Gilmore, 1994) that added a necessary level of psychic complexity missing from Katz. As with all such journalistic accounts though, it remains undertheorised.

The idea that the psychosocial risks in being a burglar are different from the psychosocial risks in being a heroin user emerges clearly in work Wendy Hollway and I did on a fear of crime project. Our psychosocial case study of 'Ron', the intrepid burglar with a fear of needles and of ingesting poisonous substances generally, should at least serve to convince that the two forms of risk-taking, burglary and taking heroin, are dissimilar (Hollway and Jefferson, 2000a: Ch. 7). The idea of risk-taking young males accomplishing masculinity in the performance of both activities, while useful in some respects, cannot begin to address the particularity of Ron.

The Criminology of War

The criminology of war is in its infancy (see also Chapter 8). Consequently, it carries less baggage than other areas of criminology. However, the same over-sociological tendency is evident. One of the things we think we know about torture, for example, is how ordinary men (usually men, it would seem), through repeatedly being subjected to, and witnessing, acts of brutality that thus become 'normal', are transformed into dehumanised, unfeeling torturers. I find that less than fully convincing. Let me say why by drawing on a symptomatic example from a cognate field, namely the role of individual soldiers in genocidal atrocities. Bilton and Sim (1992), journalists not criminologists, have produced an account of the My Lai massacre, the most infamous single atrocity in the war in Vietnam. At My Lai hundreds of defenceless villagers, women, children and old men, were beaten, tortured and slaughtered by American troops in a four-hour orgy of brutality and violence. As with sociological accounts of the socialisation of torturers, Bilton and Sim's broad explanation of My Lai is dependent on the idea of a culture of war 'socialising' normal American men into killers. They argue against the army view that My Lai was an aberration (which the army did its best to cover up), attributable to the malign influence of the only soldier subsequently convicted of an offence, Lt Calley, and to the 'delinquency of some of his men'. This psychological explanation Bilton and Sim reject as 'perverse' (Bilton and Sim, 1992: 18). Against this they argue that My Lai became possible, not simply because of a culture of war in which brutality and contempt for human life had become commonplace, but specifically because a particularly barbaric culture had developed within the company responsible for the atrocity, namely Charlie Company. This, in turn, had to be understood in relation to the particularly harrowing and brutalising experiences the company had lived through. Their particular experiences, together with a growing inwardness, eventually produced the moral vacuum, the 'moratorium on restraint and self-control' (Bilton and Sim, 1992: 79), that characterised My Lai.

This probably chimes broadly with criminological common sense in this area. Now, I do not wish to challenge the idea that the horrific experiences of war can and do dehumanise participants, but I do wish to question its adequacy as an explanation for something like My Lai. There are, as we know, other responses to a brutal culture of war – from desertion to shell-shock, alcoholism and drug addiction. Moreover, killing the enemy in battle is not quite the same thing as the gratuitous killing of unarmed women, children and old men. Perhaps most importantly there are the specific features of My Lai. Not everyone killed at My Lai, and, at many critical moments, Calley's actions seemed crucial to the ensuing brutality and murder. One example must suffice to illustrate both points (though Bilton and Sim offer many more). At some stage the platoon had rounded up some 40–50 villagers. Calley was impatiently questioning a monk, who was aiding an elderly sick woman, about the whereabouts of the Vietcong. The monk's tearful denial of knowledge was met with a violent assault, then three cold-blooded murders by Calley: of a child, the monk and the sick woman. As other soldiers arrived with more villagers, Calley began pushing their captives into an irrigation channel, and indicating that he wanted them all killed. Some of the soldiers were clearly shocked by the order; others simply refused to obey it. ' "He can send me to jail but I am not going to kill anybody", said Dursi. ' "I'm not going to do that" ', said Maples to a direct order from Calley to ' "Load your machine gun and shoot these people" ' (Bilton and Sim, 1992: 122–3). At that point 'Calley turned his M-16 on Maples as if to shoot him', but 'some of the other soldiers interposed to protect him', at which point 'Calley backed off'. Then, '[s]econds later he [Calley] and Meadlo began firing'. Others clearly joined in, but 'Dursi stood completely frozen, watching disbelievingly, as the Vietnamese tried frantically to hide under one another, mothers protecting babies' (Bilton and Sim, 1992: 123).

What the grisly details of this mass execution clearly reveal is that not all the men in C Company followed orders and did what others were doing. On the contrary, some resisted the company's culture of callous brutality and remained in touch with the horror they were unwittingly a part of. Had Maples or Dursi been in charge at that moment, the outcome would surely have been different. What all this points to is the need to attend to both the particularity of the cultural conditions surrounding the event and the particularity of the psychological individuals involved: not culture or psychology but culture and psychology – a psychosocial explanation. To suggest this is not to want 'to trace My Lai back to the psychology of a single inadequate officer' (Bilton and Sim, 1992: 18), a move which I agree would be 'perverse' (Bilton and Sim, 1992: 18). But it is to insist that a psychosocial understanding of Calley's role in the affair would enlighten as to how such horrors can happen.

Fear of Crime

The debate is still dominated by the risk–fear calculus despite the now obvious empirical fact that risk and fear are never simply related (as in high risk = high fear and low risk = low fear). Challenging that domination, my own work with Wendy Hollway has been an ongoing attempt to advance the debate by making central to it an anxious, defended, psychosocial subject. The results of introducing this alternative, psychosocial 'logic' have begun to answer the question of why risk and fear are never simply related but are always mediated by anxiety (Hollway and Jefferson, 1997a, 2000b and 2000c). We also spell out the methodological prescriptions that follow from the assumption of such a subject (Hollway and Jefferson, 1997b and 2000a).

Conclusion

I am writing this in the aftermath of 11 September. The meanings of what happened on that fateful day are manifold. However, for my present purposes, the responses to the day's events present a symptomatic case study of my central argument, namely a reminder of the inadequacies of our thinking about the criminal subject. As we all know there has been a deluge of reporting, comment and analysis. Inevitably, one of the themes has been 'why did they do it?' Writers of all kinds – journalists, cultural commentators, political scientists, experts in international relations and Islam, historians, novelists, poets and others – have all had their say. But I have yet to come across any comment or analysis from a criminologist. Remember, whatever the political and other meanings of the day's horrific events, the acts were undeniably criminal. So, why no criminological voices? One reason, undoubtedly, was the early definition of the event as an act of war – which immediately fingers the political scientists, historians, military strategists and writers on international relations as the appropriate experts. Another was the difficulty of grasping the scale and horror of the human dimension, despite watching it endlessly on 'live' television. This perhaps accounts for the presence of poets and novelists. With their practiced imaginative capacities they are, arguably, our experts on the human heart (why psychologists are not so regarded speaks volumes about the state of mainstream psychology). But one reason, as I have been arguing throughout this chapter, is that criminologists have nothing to contribute to such debates. The criminology of war is still in its infancy and 'why did they do it' is not of serious interest to contemporary criminologists, especially those of the critical variety. The result, as we have seen with other areas of serious deadly crime like serial killing, is that journalists and writers of fiction are called upon to answer the question.

Predictably, the answers to this particular question proposed by journalists and novelists, though eloquently expressed and interesting, have been theoretically inadequate. Let me cite two examples from journalists and two by novelists. In an otherwise excellent article (*Guardian*, 18 September), Safire gropes towards an explanation. He talks of 'theological brainwashing' creating 'human missiles' – but this is merely a particularly deterministic rendering of a now discredited socialisation theory. It fails to address the issue of susceptibility, of which Islamic fundamentalists are, and which are not, liable to succumb to such destructive doctrines (the equivalent of which soldiers did, and which did not, join in the orgy of destruction in the case of My Lai). In short, it offers an essentially sociocultural explanation, devoid of a psychological dimension. Ian Buruma offered a more developed explanation when he compared the suicidal terrorists of 11 September with the Japanese kamikaze pilots of the Second World War (*Guardian G2*, 25 September: 5), but this too, for all its thoughtful drawing of a useful historical parallel, was an entirely sociocultural explanation. By contrast, Martin Amis's attempt, an assertion that '[t]error always has its roots in hysteria and psychotic insecurity' (*Guardian G2*, 18 September: 4), drifts too far towards a purely psychological explanation, one, moreover, which aligns too readily terror and mental illness. Only Ian McEwan, in my fairly comprehensive reading of *The Guardian*, managed to link the cultural and the psychological. But although he does this with enviable succinctness – 'The hijackers used fanatical certainty, misplaced religious faith and dehumanising hatred to purge themselves of the human instinct for empathy' (*Guardian*, 15 September: 1) – there is no attempt to spell out how the connections between a culture of faith and certainty and a psychology of hatred are secured (to do which would have to make empathy a (variable) human achievement, not an 'instinct' as it is for McEwan).

In summary, we have here four explanations of why they did it: two are too cultural; one is too psychological; and only one is properly psychosocial, and that is theoretically underdeveloped. I do not blame the writers for their failures in this respect. The discipline that should have been there to answer the question is simply not up to the task. It is about time criminology became so. Understanding why they did it could be criminology's indirect contribution to the effort to prevent other such atrocities. It may not be much. But it is more than we as a discipline have contributed so far to analyses of this monstrous crime. Let me end finally with a moving quotation from a 'survivor' from My Lai, Vernado Simpson. He was one of the American soldiers. He killed 25 people. According to him, his mind 'just went' and he became a 'killing machine'. Now, years after, he is depressed, suicidal and in pain because he is compelled to remember what he would rather forget. His words cannot be forced into a purely sociological frame of reference but require a psychosocial approach to even begin to make sense of their poignancy, paradoxicality and sheer contradictoriness:

> There's a part of me that's kind and gentle. There's another part of me that's evil and destructive. There's more destructiveness in my mind than goodness. There's more wanting to kill or to hurt than to love or to care. I don't let anyone get close to me. The loving feeling and the caring feeling is not there.
>
> (Bilton and Sim, 1992: 8)

Notes

1. Pat Carlen, for example, once praised *The New Criminology* for, among other things, producing 'a criminology that is without a crime and without a criminal' (Carlen, 1980: 12).

2. According to a study of mainstream criminology journals by Cohen and Farrington (1998), Hirschi was the most cited criminologist between 1991 and 1995. See Taylor (2001) for a recent assessment of this work, which differentiates between early and later control theory.

3. Once again, I am not the first to criticise control theory for its inadequate theory of motivation underlying offending behaviour (see Smith, 1995: 39); and, once again, Hirschi has never seen this as a problem. As he puts it, 'the question "why do they do it?" is simply not the question the theory is designed to answer' (Hirschi, 1969: 34).

4. Try Bruce Springsteen's 'State Trooper', which pits Sgt Joe Robert, who 'always done an honest job/As honest as I could', against ' a brother named Johnny/And Johnny ain't no good', for a wonderful example from the genre.

5. To the extent that a criminological subject is presumed in Young's writings, it is the sociological subject of Mertonian strain theory.

6. Although the survey-based data upon which this conclusion is based remains thin, contradictory and methodologically suspect. See Farrell et al. (1997) and Gilchrist et al. (1998).

7. This is the secular version of the notion of evil, which is the equivalent term within religious discourses.

8. For example, Brian Masters on Dahmer (1993) and Nilson (1995), Gordon Burn on Sutcliffe (1984) and the Wests (1998), Gitta Sereny on Mary Bell (1972/1995 and 1999), David Smith on the Bulger killers (1994). This trend arguably originated with Colin Wilson (e.g. 1992).

9. An unpopular notion I know in these postmodern times but for a contemporary (and to my mind successful) defence of the notion, see Layton (1998).

10. In a much neglected book in the field of gender studies, MacInnes (1998) called these unique early influences 'sexual genesis'. He distinguished these generational issues – the result of being born *of* a man *and* a woman, an experience common to all – from the cognate notion of 'sexual difference', i.e. the result of being born *as* a male *or* a female and the basis for the social production of gender differences, and explored how we have come to confuse the two terms. This distinction enables us, as I have argued elsewhere (Jefferson, 2002), to begin seriously to think about the relation between the psychic and the social in gender development.

11. However, it differs from a Meadian version of inter-subjectivity in its acceptance of Freudian notions of the unconscious and defences against anxiety, and hence of a unique psychic realm.

12. See, for example, Box (1983) for a fuller consideration of different types of rape. However, his explanations, thoughtful and interesting though they are, remain entirely social.

13. The idea of ambivalence could also help explain why it is that many women choose to stay in violent relationships, not because they have nowhere else to go

or cannot afford to leave, but because, in their own words, they 'love him'. Feminists often find this idea difficult to accept – in marked contrast, ironically, to their general willingness to listen to women and help give them a voice. See Gadd (2000) for a text on male perpetrators of violence against women that adopts a psychosocial approach.

14. But see Phillips (2000) and Kitzinger and Frith (2001) for recent examples of feminist texts that do challenge this orthodoxy, albeit using social constructionist approaches.

15. Exemplified by the success of some feminist campaigns in certain jurisdictions (e.g. Canada) to get rape redefined as a violent assault in order to make convictions easier to secure (Smart, 1989: 45–6).

16. But see Cameron and Frazer (1987) and Ward Jouve (1988) for two excellent exceptions to this general rule.

17. Admittedly, the class profile of the drug-taker is more complex than this, being different for different drugs at different times in different places.

18. In most cases, researchers seem happiest recounting what offenders do, using offenders' own words where possible, and constructing typologies, rather than addressing why they offend (e.g. Pearson, 1987; Cromwell, Olson and Avary, 1991; Walsh, 1980; Wright and Decker, 1994).

19. This point has been recognised by others. As long ago as 1980, Walsh was 'arguing the case for more small-scale psychological studies of burglars, particularly in relation to anxiety, excitement and destruction' (1980: 57). More recently, Wright and Decker concluded their interview-based study of 105 active burglars in St Louis, Missouri with a critique of rational-choice explanations. To explain their burglars' offending behaviour they resurrect a psychosocial model first promoted by Lofland (1969). While clearly a step in the right direction, the emotional dimension of the psychosocial remains underdeveloped and, as interpreted by Wright and Decker (1994: 196–206), still over-social.

20. Although, to be fair, the current debate about decriminalisation and legalisation of 'soft' drugs is changing things a little.

Bibliography

Akers, R. L. (1991) 'Self-control as a general theory of crime', *Journal of Quantitative Criminology*, 7: 201–11.

Bataille, G. (1962) *Eroticism*. London: Calder & Boyars.

Becker, H. (1963) *Outsiders*. New York: Free Press.

Benjamin, J. (1988) *The Bonds of Love: Psychoanalysis, Feminism and the Problem of Domination*. New York: Pantheon.

Benjamin, J. (1995) *Like Subjects, Love Objects: Essays on Recognition and Sexual Difference*. New Haven, CT: Yale University Press.

Benjamin, J. (1998) *Shadow of The Other: Intersubjectivity and Gender in Psychoanalysis*. New York: Routledge.

Bilton, M. and Sim, K. (1992) *Four Hours in My Lai: A War Crime and its Aftermath*. London: Viking.

Box, S. (1983) *Power, Crime and Mystification*. London: Tavistock.

Burn, G. (1984) *Somebody's Husband, Somebody's Son: The Story of Peter Sutcliffe*. London: Heinemann.

Burn, G. (1998) *Happy Like Murderers: The True Story of Fred and Rosemary West*. London: Faber & Faber.

Cameron, D. and Frazer, E. (1987) *The Lust to Kill: A Feminist Investigation of Sexual Murder*. Cambridge: Polity.

Carlen, P. (1980) 'Radical criminology, penal politics and the rule of law', in P. Carlen and M. Collison (eds), *Radical Issues in Criminology*. Oxford: Martin Robertson.

Chodorow, N. J. (1978) *The Reproduction of Mothering: Psychoanalysis and the Sociology of Gender*. Berkeley. CA: University of California Press.

Chodorow, N. J. (1994) *Femininities, Masculinities, Sexualities: Freud and Beyond*. Lexington, KY: The University Press of Kentucky.

Cohen, E. G. and Farrington, D. P. (1998) 'Changes in the most-cited scholars in major international journals between 1986–1990 and 1991–1995', *British Journal of Criminology*, 38(1): 156–70.

Cromwell, P., Olson, J. and Avary, D. (1991) *Breaking and Entering: An Ethnographic Analysis of Burglary*. Newbury Park, CA: Sage.

Dickson, G. (1958) *Murder by Numbers*. London: Robert Hale.

Du Gay, P., Evans, J. and Redman, P. (2000) *Identity: A Reader*. London: Sage.

Farrell, S., Bannister, J., Ditton, J. and Gilchrist, E. (1997) 'Questioning the measurement of the "fear of crime" ', *British Journal of Criminology*, 37(4): 658–79.

Farrington, D. P. (1995) 'The development of offending and anti-social behaviour from childhood: key findings from the Cambridge Study in Delinquent Development', *Journal of Child Psychology and Psychiatry*, 36: 929–64.

Farrington, D. P. (1997) 'Human development and criminal careers', in M. Maguire, R. Morgan and R. Reiner (eds), *The Oxford Handbook of Criminology*, 2nd edn. Oxford: Clarendon Press, pp. 361–408.

Farrington, D. P. and West, D. J. (1990) 'The Cambridge Study in Delinquent Development: a long-term follow-up of 411 London males', in H.-J. Kerner and G. Kaiser (eds), *Criminality: Personality, Behaviour, Life History*. Berlin: Springer-Verlag, pp. 115–38.

Gadd, D. (2000) *Deconstructing Male Violence: A Qualitative Study of Male Workers and Clients on an Anti-Violence Programme*. Unpublished PhD, Keele University.

Gilchrist, E., Bannister, J., Ditton, J. and Farrell, S. (1998) 'Women and the "fear of crime": challenging the accepted stereotype', *British Journal of Criminology*, 38(2): 283–98.

Gilmore, M. (1994) *Shot in The Heart: One Family's History in Murder*. London: Penguin.

Goodey, J. (2000) 'Biographical lessons for criminology', *Theoretical Criminology*, 4(4): 473–98.

Gottfredson, M. R. and Hirschi, T. (1990) *A General Theory of Crime*. Stanford, CA: Stanford University Press.

Hall, S., Critcher, C., Jefferson, T., Clarke, J. and Roberts, B. (1978) *Policing the Crisis: Mugging, The State and Law and Order*. London: Macmillan.

Henriques, J., Hollway, W., Urwin, C., Venn, C. and Walkerdine, V. (1984/1999) *Changing the Subject: Psychology, Social Regulation and Subjectivity*. London: Methuen.

Hirschi, T. (1969) *Causes of Delinquency*. Berkeley, CA: University of California Press.

Hollin, C. (1989) *Psychology and Crime: An Introduction to Criminological Psychology*. London: Routledge.

Hollway, W. and Jefferson, T. (1996) 'PC or not PC: sexual harassment and the question of ambivalence', *Human Relations*, 49(3): 373–93.

Hollway, W. and Jefferson, T. (1997a) 'The risk society in an age of anxiety': situating fear of crime', *British Journal of Sociology*, 48(2): 255–66.

Hollway, W. and Jefferson, T. (1997b) 'Eliciting narrative through the in-depth interview', *Qualitative Inquiry*, 3(1): 53–70.

Hollway, W. and Jefferson, T. (1998) '"A kiss is just a kiss": date rape, gender and subjectivity'. *Sexualities* 1(4): 405–23.

Hollway, W. and Jefferson, T. (2000a) *Doing Qualitative Research Differently: Free Association, Narrative and the Interview Method*. London: Sage.

Hollway, W. and Jefferson, T. (2000b) 'The role of anxiety in fear of crime', in T. Hope and R. Sparks (eds), *Crime, Risk and Insecurity: Law and Order in Everyday Life and Political Discourse*. London: Routledge, pp. 31–49.

Hollway, W. and Jefferson, T. (2000c) 'Anxiety and the experience of locality', in P. Chamberlayne, J. Bornat and T. Wengraf (eds) *The Turn to Biographical Methods in Social Science: Comparative Issues and Examples*. London: Routledge, pp. 167–80.

Hollway, W. and Jefferson, T. (2002) 'Heterosexual relating, unconscious inter-subjectivity and fear of crime', *Journal for the Psychoanalysis of Culture and Society* (forthcoming).

Jefferson, T. (1996) 'The James Bulger case: a review essay', *British Journal of Criminology*, 36(2): 319–23.

Jefferson, T. (1997) 'The Tyson rape trial: the law, feminism and "emotional truth"', *Social and Legal Studies*, 6(2): 281–301.

Jefferson, T. (2002) 'Subordinating hegemonic masculinity', *Theoretical Criminology*, 6(1): 63–88.

Katz, J. (1988) *Seductions of Crime*. New York: Basic Books.

Kearon, T. and Leach, R. (2000) 'Invasion of the "body snatchers": burglary reconsidered', *Theoretical Criminology*, 4(4): 451–72.

Kitzinger, C. and Frith, H. (2001) 'Just say no? The use of converstion analysis in developing a feminist perspective on sexual refusal', in M. Wetherell, S. Taylor and S. J. Yates (eds), *Discourse Theory and Practice: A Reader*. London: Sage, pp. 167–85.

Layton, L. (1998) *Who's That Girl? Who's That Boy? Clinical Practice Meets Postmodern Gender Theory*. Northvale, NJ: Jason Aronson.

Lester, D. (1995) *Serial Killers: The Insatiable Passion*. Philadelphia, PA: The Charles Press.

Levi, M. (1997) 'Violent crime', in M. Maguire, R. Morgan and R. Reiner (eds), *The Oxford Handbook of Criminology*, 2nd edn. Oxford: Clarendon Press, pp. 841–89.

Lofland, J. (1969) *Deviance and Identity*. Englewood Cliffs, NJ: Prentice Hall.

MacInnes, J. (1998) *The End of Masculinity: The Confusion of Sexual Genesis and Sexual Difference in Modern Society*. Buckingham: Open University Press.

Masters, B. (1993) *The Shrine of Jeffrey Dahmer*. London: Coronet.

Masters, B. (1995) *Killing for Company: The Case of Dennis Nilsen*. London: Arrow.

Mulvey, L. (1975) 'Visual pleasure and narrative cinema', *Screen*, 16(3): 6–18.

Murray, C. (1984), *Losing Ground*. New York: Basic Books.

Murray, C. (1990) *The Emerging British Underclass*, Choice in Welfare Series No. 2. London: Health and Welfare Unit, Institute of Economic Affairs.

Parker, H., Aldridge, J. and Measham, F. (1998) *Illegal Leisure: The Normalisation of Adolescent Recreational Drug Use*. London: Routledge.
Parker, H., Newcombe, R. and Baxx, K. (1988) *Living With Heroin*. Buckingham: Open University Press.
Pearson, G. (1987) *The New Heroin Users*. Oxford: Blackwell.
Phillips, L. M. (2000) *Flirting with Danger: Young Women's Reflections on Sexuality and Domination*. New York: New York University Press.
Presdee, M. (2000) *Cultural Criminology and the Carnival of Crime*. London: Routledge.
Sereny, G. (1972/1995) *The Case of Mary Bell*. London: Pimlico.
Sereny, G. (1999) *Cries Unheard: The Story of Mary Bell*. London: Papermac.
Smart, C. (1989) *Feminism and the Power of Law*. London: Routledge.
Smith, D. J. (1994) *The Sleep of Reason: The James Bulger Case*. London: Century.
Smith, D. (1995) *Criminology for Social Work*. London: Macmillan.
Taylor, C. (2001) 'The relationship between social- and self-control: tracing Hirschi's criminological career', *Theoretical Criminology*, 5(3): 369–88.
Taylor, I., Walton, P. and Young, J. (1973) *The New Criminology: For a Social Theory of Deviance*. London: Routledge.
Walsh, D. (1980) *Break-ins: Burglary from Private Houses*. London: Constable.
Ward Jouve, N. (1988) *'The Street-Cleaner': The Yorkshire Ripper Case on Trial*. London: Marion Boyars.
Wilson, C. (1992) *Serial Killers: A Study in the Psychology of Violence*. London: True Crime.
Wright, R. T. and Decker, S. (1994) *Burglars on the Job: Streetlife and Residential Break-ins*. Boston, MA: NorthEastern University Press.
Young, J. (1986) 'The failure of criminology: the need for a radical realism', in R. Matthews and J. Young (eds), *Confronting Crime*. London: Sage.
Young, J. (1992) 'Ten points of realism', in J. Young and R. Matthews (eds), *Rethinking Criminology: The Realist Debate*. London: Sage.

Chapter 7

Critical criminology and the punitive society: some new 'visions of social control'

John Pratt

Introduction

As the title of this chapter clearly indicates, it has as its main referent Stan Cohen's (1985) *Visions of Social Control*. My purpose here, however, is neither to offer some belated critique nor review of such an important contribution to the critical criminology canon. Indeed, I think due reference should be made to the massive impact this book has made – and not just on critical scholarship: even the most administrative of administrative criminologists overseeing penal policy development is almost certainly going to be conscious of the way in which their careful planning is likely to be subverted by 'net-widening' tendencies, even if they may not be aware that it was that most unadministrative criminologist Stan Cohen (1979) who coined the term in the article which was the precursor to his book, 'The punitive city: notes on the dispersal of social control'. Having said this, though, and in a bid to put Cohen's contribution to critical analysis of contemporary penal trends in its appropriate light, what I want to suggest here is that it is also now possible to discern 'visions of social control' which were not anticipated in his book – and some emerging patterns of control which seem to depart from the 'master patterns' hitherto implicit in modern penal development.

In these respects, if there is substance to the arguments I will be setting out in this chapter, then perhaps Cohen's book should now be seen as an emblem for a phase in modern penal development which has now passed – or is at least undergoing a process of significant reconfiguration.

Cohen's 'Visions' of Social Control

Let us first recap the main arguments set out in *Visions of Social Control*. The book is based on the premise that there have been two phases in the development of modern penal control. The *first* took place at the end of the eighteenth century, when the master patterns of penal modernity were set in place. These took the form of:

- an increasing involvement of the state in the business of deviancy control;
- an increasing differentiation and classification of deviant and independent groups into separate types and categories, each with its own body of scientific knowledge and its own recognised and accredited experts;
- increased segregation;
- the decline of punishment involving the public infliction of physical pain.

The *second* phase begins in the 1960s with the alleged destructuring of penal control that was then set in place, involving decentralisation, de-professionalisation and de-institutionalisation. *But* (and this is where Cohen's book became so central to critical criminology since it provided a penetrating glimpse of what was really happening behind the screen of official penal discourse):

> instead of any destructuring, however, the original structures have become stronger; far from any decrease, the reach and intensity of state control have been increased; centralization and bureaucracy remain; professionals and experts are proliferating dramatically and society is more dependent on them; informalism has not made the legal system less formal or more just; treatment has changed its forms but certainly has not died
>
> (Cohen 1985: 37).

So, in effect, the book deconstructed the destructuring process – it unpacked the alleged humanitarian justifications for penal development in the 1970s and 1980s and found instead that 'the benevolent-sounding destructuring package had turned out to be a monster in disguise, a Trojan horse' (Cohen, 1985: 38). The alternatives to prison that had been set up in the name of destructuring had merely left us with 'wider, stronger, different nets', which then became the basis for the other wonderful metaphors that adorn the book such as 'thinning the mesh' to describe the development of new trends: once one became enmeshed in this net of social control that now operated in the community beyond the prison where one was supposed to be free, then, like a fish that had been caught, it became increasingly difficult to slip out of the net. Indeed, it was as if the net itself was getting ever more extensive: alternatives to custody projects were being supplemented by further programmes designed to assist in the move from community control to freedom by offering, as it were, a 'transitional phase' – with built-in penalty clauses as well. These acted as a kind of 'snakes and ladders', game, only there did not seem to be many ladders which one could climb to expedite one's way out of the net: only snakes, which one could slide down with the effect, in some cases, that 'the game' started all over again – and, of course, took much longer to finish (for examples, see Cohen, 1985, also Pratt, 1987).

And thus, notwithstanding all the talk of humanitarian destructuring, informalism, control in the community rather than the prison, nothing much was changing, save for an *enhancement* of the existing master patterns of social control. Prison populations remained, at best, largely untouched despite the frenzied growth of the alternatives to them being constructed in the community; indeed, it was with great irony that this period in the mid-1970s, with all its emphasis on decarceration (Scull, 1977), was the moment that the United States prison population which had been relatively stable at a rate of around 110 per 100,000 of population for most of the twentieth century, began to accelerate into 'hyper-drive' (Simon, 2000), so that it in 1999 it stood at around 500 per 100,000 of population if one just counts prisons, or 709 per 100,000 if one counts prisons and local gaols (Christie, 2000). And, of course, this pattern has since been followed, admittedly at a less furious pace, by the escalation of prison populations in other western societies.

And yet, beyond the prison, the community itself was turning into a kind of quasi-prison, or, to use the vernacular, a halfway house where, in Kafkaesque fashion, no one really knew who was a quarter of the way in or three-quarters of the way out, such was the complex web of control in the community. This sector in turn was likely to be policed through the deployment of the new technology of surveillance; video cameras would be able to record one's every movement, 24 hours a day; computerized record-keeping and electronic security devices would tell 'the controllers' exactly where one had been and where one was.

In certain respects, Cohen was offering a vision of social control that was largely in keeping with the pessimistic predictions of writers such as George Orwell (*Nineteen Eighty Four*), Aldous Huxley (*Brave New World*) and Anthony Burgess (*Clockwork Orange*). As Cohen himself wrote (Cohen, 1985: 141), 'the nightmare was a new psychological technology with which the benevolent (or not so benevolent) eye of the state would be able to know and control all'. What seems to unite all these writers is a sense of loss: as if, in Rousseau (1754) tradition, the inherent goodness of man is suppressed or perverted by the inexorable growth of state power that marked the second half of the twentieth century; and the more the state touches, the more it seems to pervert and make malignant, whether this be through the forced feeding of drugs (Huxley, 1952), lobotomization (Burgess, 1962), sheer terror and brute force (Orwell, 1949), or suffocating layers of community control, camouflaged by mellifluous 'psychobabble' (Cohen, 1985). Even today, under the development of a political ethos which views state power with distaste and is committed to 'getting the state out of people's lives', it still controls us, except that it now does so (with even more fiendish cunning) 'at a distance', as Peter Miller and Nikolas Rose (1990) so ably argued. And, as Cliff Shearing and Philip Stenning (1984) demonstrated in relation to Disney World, we fall into line and take our place in the queue 'automatically'. Such a growth of state power – controlling by means of both prison and the community – is indeed something to be feared.

Nor was Cohen the only criminologist to make such assumptions about the future of social control. He thus quotes Gresham Sykes (1980: 7):

> it is possible to envision, on the one hand, a society marked by increasing violence and attacks on property, by intolerance of any deviation from an obsessive morality, and by far reaching police surveillance coupled with a loss of civil liberties in a totalitarian social order. It is also possible...to envision a society with widespread acceptance of and conformity to the criminal law, a modest view of the proper reach of the state, and methods of law enforcement that are just, humane and effective.

So here too there is a dualism which inevitably seems to grip intimations of the future of social control: the menace of the totalitarian, overarching state on the one hand; rational, humane, community governance on the other, where the uncorrupted human spirit can be trusted to act in accordance with these values.

Vision and Reality

To what extent have these visions materialised? I think it should be acknowledged, first, that there are significant differences in the power and efficiency of the social control apparatus in modern societies from that envisioned by these various commentators. Thus, unlike the paramilitary modality of control in the totalitarian society of Orwell's (1949) *Nineteen Eighty Four*, the reality of social control in modern democratic societies is much more in the form of a 'soft machine' – as opposed to its articulation by Orwell: 'if you want a picture of the future, imagine a boot stamping on a human face – forever' (Orwell, 1949: 206). Cohen (1985: 185) thus writes:

> My vision of social control is much more mundane and assuring. It is the eternal case conference, diagnostic and allocation board or pre-sentence investigation visit... the more negative the results, the more manic and baroque the enterprise of selection becomes: more psychological tests, more investigation units, more pre-sentence reports, more post-sentence allocation centres, more contract forms, more case summaries, more referral notations, more prediction devices.

A very familiar picture is conjured here: the more intractable the problem, the more obvious the failure of the criminal justice organisations to deal with it, the more they are able to soak up resources to try and make them work more efficiently – of which the history of the prison is surely one of the best examples of the way in which failure comes to justify ever increasing investment (see Rothman, 1971; Foucault, 1978). At the same time, some of the technology of control which features predominantly in the work of Cohen (1985), but in a variety of other futuristic studies as well, such as computerised security checks, data collection banks hidden away in cyberspace, surveillance systems and so on, have become very familiar to most of us in the course of our everyday lives. And in most cases they do not seem to have been particularly threatening; even if they provide new boundaries around the policing of everyday life, even if they can become intrusive, this in itself does not seem to be a cause of any great concern. The lives of most of us have been touched on only marginally or incrementally as we internalise the new normative expectations of our conduct without difficulty, as we gain access to our workplaces with swipe cards rather than keys, as we give out one of the range of pin numbers we are now likely to possess to gain access to our bank, as we make a telephone transaction or use a money machine. We may periodically wonder where all the real banks and bankers have gone, but by and large, the electrification and computerisation of increasing areas of everyday life in this way seems relatively untroubling to most of us. Indeed, electronic security systems may in fact, for many, be a welcome badge of security – the identifying logo of the particular organisation displayed on the control box over our front door acts as a new kind of gargoyle specific to late modernity to those who would seek to threaten our security. And it may even prove to be the case in time that this new technology of surveillance and crime prevention has been in some way responsible for the decline in crime which now seems well established in some modern societies at least.[1] In these respects, the computerisation and electrification of everyday life – thereby encircling most of us with new systems of control – need not in itself be threatening and sinister.

In other respects, the efficiency of the control apparatus envisaged by Cohen and other writers in the genre was always, I think, overrated and overestimated. Where systems of control have been set in place, it is as if some people get caught up in them and stuck in them as if they are quicksand: particularly if they possess certain crucial identifying characteristics that seem to trigger the system into action – with frequently unhelpful results for them. Crime mixed with attributes such as homelessness or unemployment may well lead to prison, as may drug use and sexual promiscuity among young women (see Carlen, 1983, 1996; Carlen and Worrall, 1987). Prison hides away such problem groups for a time, while leaving the difficulties underlying their crimes untouched – and making their return to prison all the more likely. These groups, of course, with such characteristics, have been the staple diet of prison for generations. And yet the same control system can ignore very many others whose problems are of such a nature that they fail to send out the right signals and do not trigger it into action – those with mental health problems for example. Such people may actually want to get caught up in the system, may want it to run their lives for them – which it steadfastly refuses to do, referring them instead to some flimsy circuit of assistance masquerading as community care.

At times a strange kind of logic seems to be at work in the modern world that denies control to those who say they are most in need of it. In New Zealand, in April 2000 Taffy Hotene was released from prison after serving two-thirds of a 12-year jail term for violent and sexual offences: he was entitled to one-third statutory remission and the state had no power to keep him in jail, even though he was released very much against his will: '[he] did not want to leave maximum security prison, and had tried to kill himself. The only life he knew was on the inside, and it has been suggested that his committing a murder would mean he would be returned to jail for the rest of his days' (*New Zealand Herald*, 19 August 2000: 13). On release he was referred to after-care services. Within a few weeks he had raped and murdered a young woman and he is now serving a sentence of life imprisonment (with a minimum non-parole period of 18 years) for these new crimes. At his trial the judge stated that it might be that he will never be let out of prison. The denial of control to some can lead too much more extensive forms of control being applied later on.

Where does this differentiated pattern of control leave us? Even if we accept the worrying prognostications of Cohen (1985), then social control itself is simultaneously more subtle and clumsy, more welcome and more threatening, more extensive and more scrupulously rationed than the inexorable machinery of surveillance and discipline that it could appear to be in some of the contributions to the social control genre of critical criminology.

New Visions

And yet, in other ways, it is possible to see very different trends of social control emerging at the present time, emerging out of possibilities that were hinted at by Cohen himself. Most of the attention given to that book was taken up with the tantalising machinery of control that he saw being constructed at that time – the construction of that new apparatus of control in the community, staffed not by prison officers but, in the main, social workers, armed not with guns or batons but the impenetrable language of psychobabble. However, in what seems to have become one of the lesser known sections of the book, Cohen (1985: 210) acknowledged that 'the fear is that the machine is breaking down by itself, and that "outside" in the chaos of urban life, in the desolate city streets abandoned to the predators, lies the ultimate horror – chaos, disorder, entropy.' This particular kind of fear – that the machinery of control is breaking down, or that, more generally, the familiar structures of certainty and security which provided the glue to hold modern society together up to a couple of decades or so ago are fragmenting and crumbling – is a familiar theme in all the contemporary sociological literature on risk (see Giddens, 1990; Beck, 1992); accompanying all the emphasis on self-enhancement, self-presentation and self-development that we find in modern societies today, there is also a pervading sense of anxiety, fear and tension. The new opportunities we have for pleasure and self-fulfilment bring with them their own attendant anxieties as we venture into unknown avenues of experience (see Pratt, 1997). At the same time, the more our knowledge of the world increases, the more risks and insecurities are brought home to us. And with social developments over the last two or three decades, traditional support systems which could have provided reassurance or instructed us on how to resolve these worries no longer seem to be in place.

This decline of the local community and its replacement with more abstracted systems of protection and order has inevitably led to a much greater privatisation of everyday life. In relation to our understanding of a particular phenomenon such as crime, this has meant a reliance on more remote sources of news and information – reliance on the mass media rather than neighbours, for example. In this way the presentation of the risks and threats from the phenomenon of crime become both more globalised and more localised (Giddens, 1990). The sexual murder of a child in England (as in the July 2000 case of eight-year-old Sarah Payne) is immediately flashed around the world – and at the same time turned into a local possibility, particularly in those societies similar in many ways to Britain: if it could happen 'there' then it could happen 'here' as well. As is well known, the presentation of information about crime to us makes it appear to be 'everywhere' and at the same time localises its particular threat to us, however much the *real* threat of crime is unequally distributed across the population, and however much the threat of *particular* crimes varies enormously. Nonetheless, the fact that our sources of information about crime highlight the existence of 'dangerous criminals' makes them a potential threat to all of us, however oblique and far removed the distance between 'them' and 'us'. In this way, it is as if a 'chronic and sporadically acute anxiety about crime' (Sparks, 1992: 12) has become an institutionalised feature of modern society: the contemporary opportunities to enhance pleasure in life have been accompanied by the immanence of personal threats to it.

Our anxieties about such threats are then likely to be exacerbated by the fact that the state itself is prepared to acknowledge that there are limits to the assistance it can give us in such matters (Garland, 1996) – there are avenues of everyday existence which are beyond its orbit of intervention. In such areas we must look towards 'taking care of ourselves'. In these respects, we do indeed become fearful when it appears to us that the machinery of state control is breaking down, or that the state no longer seems to have much interest in coming to our assistance when needed, or that neither the state nor its organisations seem to have the solutions to our fears of disorder and personal threat. It cannot even recognise the dangers to us, however obvious they may appear to the general public – as in the New Zealand Hotene case.

That we are actually fearful of the machinery breaking down or that, in certain respects, it may even no longer exist in itself tells us of the differing relationship of citizens to the state than that which exists in most versions of critical criminology: for most, the state is seen as neither oppressive nor threatening but as a welcome force whose presence can assure us that 'the machine' is still capable of functioning. Perhaps more so than for a long time in the modern world, forms of social control that have an ostentatious presence and are calculated to bring out the emotive sentiments of a watching public are gaining ascendancy, precisely because of the growing demands on the central state to show that the machine is still working; in a time of insecurity they become symbols of security for those on the outside of the control apparatus. Thus the reintroduction of chain gangs is justified in the United States because 'I recall seeing chain gangs as a child...the impression I had was one of hard labour and a law-abiding state. That's the image Florida needs today – instead of one of innocent citizens being robbed and raped everyday' (Crist, 1996: 178). Hence the introduction of punishments in parts of the United States and Australia that are deliberately designed to shame and humiliate: the Northern Territory Punitive Work Order, introduced to that Australian jurisdiction in 1996, compels offenders to perform community work while wearing a black and orange bib: those serving a punitive work order will be clearly obvious to the rest of the community. 'They will be identifiable as Punitive Work Offenders either by wearing a special uniform or some other label. It is meant to be a punishment that shames the guilty person...from my discussions the community [want] to see the punishment so that it is both a warning and deterrent to others and a shameful experience for the offender' (Ministerial statement on the Criminal Justice System and Victims of Crime, 20 August 1996). And if, twenty or thirty years ago, those countries with low prison populations were thought to be among the leaders of the civilised world, with a high level of imprisonment thought shameful or 'uncivilised', now high prison populations have become important indicators of political virility (see Pratt, 2000).

Developments such as these seem to represent something more than just a change of emphasis in the social control apparatus: there is no subtlety nor seamless web; they are not hidden; they are not even particularly intrusive. Their coercive, sometimes brutalising nature is not camouflaged anymore by mellifluous psychobabble and there is an increasingly thick (not thin) dividing line being drawn between criminals and non-criminals: our suspicion of and hostility towards criminal 'others' becomes increasingly intensified (Garland, 1996; Bauman, 2000). In other words, a different pattern of social control may be emerging from that which formed the basis of Cohen's *Visions*. At the same time, the growing importance of these expressive, ostentatious forms of punishment allow us the possibility of some new visions of social control: what modalities of punishing are likely to emerge when the machinery of control which sustained us for so long in the modern world begins to break down, or at least when we think it is breaking down?

It has only been in the last few years that the contours of this new arena of punishment have come into focus. They seem to involve elements of the following:

- New patterns of control where the state sets limits to what it can achieve and where it is prepared to be involved: our protection, our security in various ways, increasingly depends on ourselves – hence the significance of the investment in private security noted above.

- Much more simplistic and binary classification of populations: divisions based around 'us' – 'normal', law abiding citizens against demonised 'others' (Garland, 1996) – who are made known to the rest of us not through the pseudo-scientific classifications of experts who have some sort of monopolistic control of knowledge over them (in fact very few such experts exist) but instead through representations of them in the popular press, for example the campaign against paedophiles that began last July in Britain, largely through the offices of the *News of the World*, that country's most popular Sunday paper. After publishing the names and localities of those whom it claimed were known paedophiles, it followed the story for several weeks, with such headlines as:

DOES A MONSTER LIVE NEAR YOU?
We have begun the biggest public record of child sex offenders ever seen in this country. We do so in memory of Sarah Payne, whose murder broke every heart in this country. There are 110,000 proven paedophiles in the UK, one for every square mile of the country.[2] We have started identifying these offenders and make a pledge that we will not stop until all 110,000 are named and shamed.
(*News of the World*, 23 July 2000: 2)

- Increased segregation – but accompanied by inexorable demands for still more segregation and confinement: from being formally regarded as a 'last resort' penal option when *Visions* was published, it as if the prison estate is now set on a course of expansion which, at the present time at least, has no end in sight.

- Growing public participation in the process of punishment. This trend has been gathering momentum for a number of years, initially perhaps in granting victims the right to be 'heard' when assessing how much harm a particular crime had caused, or in allowing them to make representation to parole board hearings when determining the release date of applicants. Increasingly, however, a broader public seems to be assuming a vicarious interest in the criminal. For example, they demand the right to be notified of the movements of sex offenders, in particular on their release from prison: this was the momentum behind the formulation of Megan's Law in the United States (Simon, 1998) and lay at the heart of the above campaign in Britain started by the *News of the World*. It had insisted that it was not providing a charter for vigilantes. However, it did not need to provide a charter for this to happen: what it had done, through its campaign, was to act as a catalyst for an outpouring of emotional turmoil which burst through the straitjacket of self-restraint and indifference that might have hitherto held such anger in check. At the same time, governments more and more insistently try to tap into this mood of 'populist punitiveness' (Bottoms, 1995) by formulating penal policy which, again, is predicated on significant increases in imprisonment: hence new proposals in New Zealand for longer prison terms and non-parole periods in the aftermath of a 1999 referendum where 92 per cent voted in favour of such measures – and which was one of the justifications by the government for these changes (Ministry of Justice, 2001).

In these particular respects, perhaps one of the most obvious departures from the master pattern of control in Cohen (1985) re-emphasises the prison at the expense of the range of community alternatives to it. But there is at the same time the increasing emphasis on public participation in the process of punishment. Here this does more than simply readjust the balance between prison and community alternatives to it – it would seem to have the potential to take us into a new arena of punishment altogether.

The Vigilantes

Public participation – community involvement in punishment – has regularly been seen as the antidote to overarching state power and totalitarian modes of control – from Nils Christie's work in the mid-1970s to that of the current restorative justice proponents: the realignment of state power and forces allows the formation of new social movements with the ability to change consciousness and values through reintegrative shaming (Braithwaite, 1989). Thus: remove the state, give power back to the people, and some inherent goodness which they are presupposed to possess will then drive the process of punishment, turning it away from the non-productive retributive characteristic of modern penal philosophy and, in practice, the stigmatic, disqualificatory imposition of punishment towards a penality that draws on intrinsic community values and is thereby productive and utilitarian. I am not saying that this will not happen; what I am saying is that this is by no means the only possibility of what will happen when state power is withdrawn, or when, as at the present time, the state, as it were, shrugs it shoulders and informs its citizens that it can only do so much – the rest is up to them.

Under these circumstances, a new vision of social control emerges which seemed to have no foundation in reality when Cohen's book was published in 1985. Indeed, perhaps the most significant literary text to articulate a vision of social control where state power has been removed – William Golding's (1954) *Lord of the Flies* – receives no mention at all in that book. And yet it provides us with a very clear if disturbing vision of the future of social control: the concern here is not the shift towards a totalitarian state, but instead of state power in retreat. In this book, a plane crash maroons a group of English public schoolboys on a remote desert island – all accompanying adults have been killed in the crash. The schoolboys then attempt to construct a form of social organisation that initially is based around internalised school rules and hierarchies, but which, in the absence of any central, affirming authority, begins to disintegrate, ultimately leading to rule by terror: outcasts – those who disagree with the mob the schoolboys have by now turned into, or who have some identifying weakness – are hunted down and, in some cases, murdered. In this parable, when state power is removed or weakened, then it is just as possible that new social movements based around the rule of the mob will emerge rather than some humane form of community or restorative justice: the rule of the mob, whether it masquerades as community justice or whether it simply brushes to one side anything that represents 'justice' as this term is understood in the modern world, as it begins to seek out those who might have offended the mob in some way or other.

This is not mere speculation: it is a possibility to which a range of writers have drawn our attention in the last few years (see Rose, 1994; Johnston, 1996). And it should be emphasised that the most glaring manifestation of this possibility which emerged in Britain in the summer of 2000 – the vigilante[3] attacks against supposed paedophiles – is by no means the only possibility of activating these tendencies; others are related to vigilante type activities against troublesome young people (Girling et al., 1998), or against unwanted ethnic minorities (Dawes and Hil, 1998). Not only this, but in addition, if we examine the history and sociology of vigilantism in the United States (see, for example, Williams, 1959; Hall, 1979; Bartley, 1983) where this kind of extra-penal community action was used to terrorise black communities (and some whites) in its Deep South from around 1870 to 1950, some disturbing parallels emerge. All the conditions necessary to activate this modality of community action at that time would seem to be present to reactivate it in the modern world today. These are:

- a weakened central state authority;

- dissatisfaction with the existing criminal justice and penal systems, which seem too remote and inefficient and non-responsive to the interests of ordinary people;

- a sense of vulnerability, from perceptions that the traditional solutions to crime no longer seem to keep it in check, to a growing range of insecurities whereby the world seems less certain and less orderly;

- socially and ethnically homogeneous communities which facilitate communication and trust between participants and which encourage subsequent involvement with their victim(s);

- a weakening of the norms of self-restraint and a raising of the threshold of embarrassment that had been central to the development of the cultural values of modern, civilised societies (Elias, 1939, 1984): once a strong, central state relinquishes its previous monopolistic control over the management of crime and punishment, then local citizens begin to look to their own resources to resolve such matters; this enables them to breach the previous boundaries of self-restraint.

Once this combination of forces coalesces, then participation in the vigilante-type actions against any troublesome or demonised group becomes a possibility, although not a necessity, as it did recently in New Zealand, reported in the following terms:

> Vigilantes force five from homes. Three prostitutes, a convicted paedophile and a repeat burglar have shifted from their Auckland homes amid vigilante 'name and shame' tactics. The unknown people behind the campaign have struck twice in the past month, with letter-drops giving the convicted paedophile's name and address and inciting residents to 'do something about' prostitutes

working from a house on the same road. Two years ago a concerted campaign was waged against a youthful burglar living in a neighbourhood street. It forced his family to move.

(*The Dominion*, 22 August 2000: 13)

In Britain, a feature of one of the most prominent vigilante groups formed, from July to September 2000 to hunt out paedophiles in the aftermath of the sexual assault and murder of the child Sarah Payne, was their claim to possess a self-constructed, self-styled 'list of power' – the names and addresses of local people whom they suspected of such activities. The state would not provide the forms of community notification in the manner of Megan's Law that they were demanding, so their response was to provide their own systems of notification and action. One woman who was later interviewed about her involvement with this group seemed to scarcely believe what she had found herself doing – but showed at the same time how easy it is to become involved in such activities once the conditions for them are set in place. She told *The Observer*:

There is no list. I asked for it when I discovered that they were going to target someone in my sister-in-law's road. They said to me the list's all mental. I said, 'No way, you could not have a mental list, that you know every house and every road that has a paedophile.' The [woman] ... feels ashamed because she enjoyed walking up the street with a gang of women, all shouting to get the paedophiles out. 'I can't help it but this is how I felt. Walking the streets with all the noise, I got a buzz out of it. I know it sounds really childish. But when I came back here and thought "what have I done." ... Now, I think if we have been to innocent people's homes, then I am ashamed. I do think it has got a bit hysterical. And because of what's happened we have been made to look like riff-raff'

(*The Observer*, 13 August 2000: 4).

Hobbes v Rousseau?

In these respects, my own discomforting vision of the future is rather different to that of Orwell (certainly not so terrifying, so it involves a modality of control that is nothing like so all inclusive), and also to that of Cohen (unfortunately not so reassuring), with his benignly inefficient case conference taking place. Instead, my vision centres around one of those local citizen's groups in possession of their 'list of power', as if this becomes a form of empowerment, in response to the state's own reluctance to act as such groups think appropriate, then deciding for themselves who is on the list, and what they may or may not have done to warrant inclusion. I am not, however, restating a kind of Hobbesian version of the possibilities of human behaviour, in contrast to the Rousseau tradition. What we should beware of, though, is essentialism. It would, instead, seem that humanity is neither inherently good nor bad, but is capable of being shaped by predominant social and cultural forces and acting accordingly. Given the context of these determining factors of the last two decades or so – the emphasis on taking care of oneself, above all, at a time of insecurity and uncertainty, and the instruction that we should no longer look to the state to resolve such matters for us, even if its own withdrawal from the centre of public life exacerbates them – it is hardly surprising that this creates the potential for the kind of vigilante-type activities that we are once again becoming familiar with in the modern world. The above events should serve as a warning to us as to what we are capable of doing, and the fragility and the contingency of what we like to think is the civilised world, where there should be no place for mob rule ('it cannot happen here').

Where, though, does this leave us? If the case conference possibility of the future of social control has been over taken by events, does this mean we are left with a choice between the new western-style gulags on the one hand (Christie, 1992), or, where even this is no longer sufficient to soak up the weight of punitive sentiment that now exists, mob rule on the other? However unpalatable to us they may be, in the form of a new kind of dualism, these are the visions of social control it is now possible to have in modern, western societies, visions which probably were not possible when Cohen's book was written in 1985.

Perhaps my worries are totally unjustified and that humanity's capacity for goodness will gain the upper hand; mob rule will be replaced by restorative justice, which will in turn have the potential to dismantle the gulags that western governments are now building for us (Braithwaite, 1996)? Perhaps this different set of visions will come into existence, in a triumph of Rousseau over Hobbes? Perhaps. All that I would say by way of conclusion is that I do not think that there is any certainty or necessity for this, and that the future may contain other, rather less reassuring eventualities for us. And because we like to think that we live in modern, civilised societies, that in itself is not sufficient to insulate us from the possibilities of social control that have more association with totalitarianism (the gulag) or anarchy (the mob).

Notes

1. For example, reported crime in England has declined from 5,591,717 offences in 1992 to 4,598,327 in 1997 (www.homeoffice.gov.uk); in New Zealand, from 525,622 offences in 1991 to 455,552 in 1999 (Statistics New Zealand, 2000). In the United States from 14,872,900 in 1991 to 12,475,600 in 1998 (Sourcebook of Criminal Justice Statistics 1999, 266–7). In Canada, crimes known to the police declined from 2,737,388 in 1995 to 2,476,210 in 1999 (http://www.statcan.ca.80/english/Pgdb/State/Justice/legal02.htm).
2. These claims were subsequently described as 'total nonsense' by the head of the English probation service and 'totally misleading... no one knows all the sex offenders in Britain. For the *News of the World* to claim it can publish a list is absolute nonsense' (*The Independent*, 30 July, 2000, 1). However, she also went on to say that many people 'are not even aware of the probation service and don't understand the work we do' (idem). This is the problem. And most people are aware of the *News of the World* and its claims to truth that it makes.
3. Vigilantism obviously means more than people simply taking the law into their own hands. For the purposes of this chapter, I have relied on the definition of it provided by Johnston (1996). He argues that there are six necessary features to it: (1) planning and premeditation; (2) voluntary involvement of private citizens; (3) it is a form of 'autonomous citizenship', thereby constituting a social movement; (4) it can involve the use of force; (5) it arises out of perceived threats to the established order; (6) it purports to control law-breaking by offering assurances to its participants and onlookers.

Bibliography

Bartley, N. (1983) *The Creation of Modern Georgia*. Athens, GA: University of Georgia Press.

Bauman, Z. (2000) 'Social issues of law and order', *British Journal of Criminology*, 40: 205–21.

Beck, U. (1992) *Risk Society*. London: Sage.

Bottoms, A. E. (1995) 'The politics and philosophy of sentencing', in C. Clarkson and R. Morgan (eds), *The Politics of Sentencing*. Oxford: Clarendon Press.

Braithwaite, J. (1989) *Crime, Shame and Reintegration*. Cambridge: Cambridge University Press.

Braithwaite, J. (1996) *Restorative Justice and a Better Future*. Paper presented at the Dorothy J. Killam Memorial Lecture, Dalhousie University, Canada.

Burgess, A. (1962) *A Clockwork Orange*. London: Heinemann.

Carlen, P. (1983) *Women's Imprisonment: A Study in Social Control*. Oxford: Blackwell.

Carlen, P. (1996) *Jigsaw: A Political Criminology on Youth Homelessness*. Buckingham: Open University Press.

Carlen, P. and Worrall, A. (eds) (1987) *Gender, Crime and Justice*. Buckingham: Open University Press.

Christie, N. (1992) *Crime Control as Industry*, 1st edn. London: Martin Robertson.

Christie, N. (2000) *Crime Control as Industry*, 3rd edn. London: Martin Robertson.

Cohen, S. (1979) 'The punitive city: notes on the dispersal of social control',

Contemporary Crises, 3: 339–60.

Cohen, S. (1985) *Visions of Social Control*. Cambridge: Polity Press.

Crist, C. (1996) 'Chain gangs are right for Florida', *Corrections Today*, 58(2): 178.

Dawes, G. and Hil, R. (1998) Racialised Vigilantism: Notes on Cultural Identity and Localised Crime Control'. Paper presented at 13th Annual Australian and New Zealand Criminology Conference, Queensland University of Technology, Brisbane.

Elias, N. (1984) *The Civilizing Process*. [1939] Oxford: Basil Blackwell.

Foucault, M. (1978) *Discipline and Punish*. London: Allen Lane

Garland, D. (1996) 'The limits of the sovereign state: strategies of crime control in contemporary society', *British Journal of Criminology*, 36: 445–71.

Garland, D. (2001) 'The meaning of mass imprisonment', *Punishment and Society*, 3: 5–8.

Giddens, A. (1990) *The Consequences of Modernity*. Cambridge: Polity Press.

Girling, E., Loader, I. and Sparks, R. (1998) 'A telling tale: a case of vigilantism and its aftermath in an English town', *British Journal of Sociology*, 49: 474–90.

Golding, W. (1954) *Lord of the Flies*. London: Faber & Faber.

Hall, J. (1979) *Revolt against Chivalry*. New York: Columbia University Press.

Huxley, A. (1952) *Brave New World*. London: Vanguard Library.

Johnston, L. (1996) 'What is vigilantism?', *British Journal of Criminology*, 36: 220–36.

Miller, P. and Rose, N. (1990) 'Governing economic life', *Economy and Society*, 19: 1–31.

Ministry of Justice [New Zealand] (2001) *Sentencing and Parole Reform Details Released*. Wellington: Ministry of Justice, press release.

Orwell, G. (1949) *Nineteen Eighty Four*. London: Secker & Warburg.

Pratt, J. (1987) 'A revisionist history of intermediate treatment', *British Journal of Social Work*, 17(4): 417–39.

Pratt, J. (1997) *Governing the Dangerous*. Sydney: Federation Press.

Pratt, J. (2000) 'Emotive and ostentatious punishment: its decline and resurgence in modern society', *Punishment and Society*, 2: 417–40.

Rose, D. (1994) *In the Name of the Law; the Collapse of Criminal Justice*. London: Vintage.

Rothman, D. (1971) *The Discovery of the Asylum*. Boston, MA: Littlejohn.

Rousseau, J. J. (1964) *Discourse on Inequality*. [1754] NewYork: St Martin's Press.

Scull, A. (1977) *Decarceration*. Englewood Cliffs, NJ: Prentice Hall.

Shearing, C. and Stenning, P. (1984) 'From the Panopticon to Disney World: The development of discipline', in A. Doob and E. Greenspan (eds), *Perspectives in Criminal Law*. Toronto: Canada Law Books.

Simon, J. (1998) 'Managing the monstrous: sex offenders and the new penology', *Psychology, Public Policy and Law*, 4: 452–67.

Simon, J. (2000) 'The society of captives in the era of hyper-incarceration', *Theoretical Criminology*, 4: 285–308.

Sparks, R. (1992) *Television and the Drama of Crime*. Buckingham: Open University Press.

Sykes, G. (1980) *The Future of Crime*. Washington, DC: National Institute of Mental Health.

Williams, J. (1959) *Vogues in Villainy*. Columbia, SC: Columbia University Press.

Chapter 8

Criminology beyond the nation state: global conflicts, human rights and the 'new world disorder'

Russell Hogg

Introduction

This chapter was shaped by a number of contemporary local and global events. My initial intention was to develop some points made in a brief review essay published a few years ago entitled 'Criminology, violence and the nation state' (Hogg, 1998). The essay reviewed, among other works, the third edition of *The State of War and Peace Atlas* (*WPA*) published by the International Peace Research Institute in Oslo (Smith, 1997), reflecting on its relevance to criminology at a time when there are signs of a blurring of boundaries between domestic and external security, civil and military power, crime and war.

I pointed out in the essay that, unlike one of the other books under review – a compendium of crime and justice facts in Australia (Mukherjee and Graycar, 1997) – *WPA* was not the type of source routinely consulted by western criminologists. Despite the criminological preoccupation with statistics (which now extends to most critical criminology too), the catalogue of violence in *WPA* is symptomatic of a condition that eliminates or subjects to extreme contingency the taken-for-granted foundations of western criminology in a secure nation state system. It is arguably the case that these foundations are now being disturbed by a number of forces – globalisation, people movements, terrorism, drug trafficking and transnational crime, the global NGO movement, and the spread of human rights consciousness to name a few. These developments link regions of conflict and regions of prosperity in new and significant ways. Needless to say these thoughts did not prepare for the events of 11 September and their aftermath, in whose shadow this chapter was written.

Local/Global: from Auburn to Afghanistan

In the mid-western Sydney suburb of Auburn the New South Wales Service for the Treatment and Rehabilitation of Torture and Trauma Survivors has a small office in the main street. Between 1996 and 2000 the number of Afghani clients referred to the service rose from ten to 366. More people fleeing Taliban persecution were seeking asylum in Australia and settling in suburbs like Auburn with its existing Muslim population and local mosque. The service counsels people who had loved ones or neighbours brutally killed by Taliban militia, often before their eyes, or who fled Afghanistan after family members were arbitrarily arrested and disappeared.[1]

A parliamentary by-election was held in the state seat of Auburn on 8 September 2001. A Muslim man was poised to become the first Muslim member of an Australian parliament until the Labour Party head office intervened and prevented him from becoming the Labour candidate.[2] As with many state elections in Australia in recent times, the major issue was crime. Law and order, though, also afforded a coded way of voicing anxieties that stemmed from much more than local crime. Racial and cultural fears have been pervasive and overt in current street-level discourse and on the talkback airwaves, even while politicians and newspaper editors resolutely deny that it in any way inflects their own choice of words and policies. Less than three years before in a neighbouring suburb to Auburn the local council stopped the Bangladeshi Islamic Society from using a former Presbyterian church as a mosque, arguing that the development approval for the building's original occupants issued in 1954 was for a 'church' and that this term did not encompass a Muslim place of worship. The Land and Environment Court accepted the council's argument, although it was later overturned on appeal.[3] Now other more recent developments would crowd onto the local stage upon which political events like the Auburn by-election unfolded.

> ...the whole immigration system needs to be looked at because people come to this country, and don't respect our lifestyle.
> (Talkback caller on Sydney 2SM, August 2001).

On the weekend of 18–19 August 2001 Australia's only national daily newspaper, *The Australian* reported in a front-page 'inside story' that Sydney's southwestern suburbs were experiencing 'a new and shocking phenomenon that is probably without precedent in Australian criminology': groups of young men of Middle Eastern and Muslim background were deliberately selecting young Caucasian women as targets of their sexual attacks.[4] Enormous popular anger was generated during the course of the next week when three young Lebanese-Australian men pleaded guilty and were sentenced for sexually assaulting two young women in a western Sydney suburb.[5] Submerged in what some politicians and senior police defended as a rational and necessary debate about the role of ethnic descriptors in the investigation of crime there was a visceral appeal to cultural and religious prejudice. Some commentators were less inhibited in suggesting that these were cases of the innocent daughters of Australian nationhood being subjected to crimes of racial hatred with their roots in the culture and religion of the perpetrators.[6] Sexual assault – that most under-policed and normalised of crimes in Australian history and culture (Carrington, 1998) – suddenly assumed the status of an instrument of cultural violence, a marker of civilisational difference and an expression of alien, cruel and barbaric values.[7]

This was merely the latest in a long stream of news stories relating to 'ethnic gangs' in western Sydney and right-wing political interventions that sought to link crime and the spectre of increasing civil strife to the presence of non-European immigrant groups in Australia, especially those of Asian and Middle Eastern background. This of course is an old and familiar story across the western world, as old as criminology itself. It is a story, however, that is currently being told with renewed vigour and with some new twists. Aside from the usual symbolic, draconian (and useless) measure of rushing through tougher sentencing laws, the NSW premier had already explicitly linked the problem of 'ethnic crime' with migration laws and immediately placed the issue on the agenda of a meeting with the national immigration minister with a view to ensuring more stringent screening of immigrants to keep criminals out of the country. Not (one might think) a measure that would have had much effect in the case at hand where two of the three offenders were born in Australia and the other emigrated with his family when he was eight.

...it is invasion day again.

(Talkback caller on Brisbane 4BC, 23 August 2001)

The 'ethnic gangs' issue was unexpectedly subsumed within other events in the last week of August, events represented in political quarters and popular discourse as a national emergency – a threat to Australia's sovereignty and the integrity of its national borders. A Norwegian container ship, the *Tampa*, had at the request of Australian Search and Rescue gone to the aid of a boat in distress in the Indian Ocean north west of Christmas Island, an Australian territory, and rescued more than 430 asylum seekers, most of them minority Hazari Afghanis fleeing the persecution of the Taliban. When the *Tampa* – licensed to carry less than 30 people – sought to deliver its human cargo to Christmas Island the Australian government refused it entry to Australian waters. The captain of the *Tampa* anchored his ship in international waters off Christmas Island and refused to budge. He sought supplies and medical care for the passengers (which were denied by the Australian government for 36 hours). The Australian Prime Minister, John Howard, declared: 'That boat will never land in Australia, never!'[8] The stand-off ensued for several days as the Australian government (with overwhelming domestic public support) prepared to force the ship back out to sea if it entered Australian territorial waters, in defiance of obligations under international law and even although (as is now clear) the UN had secured the agreement of a number of countries to take all or most of the *Tampa* refugees if they were processed in Australia.[9] The government, however, facing an election by the end of 2001, was determined, as it put it, to send a message to undocumented people who were tempted to travel by boat to Australia and to the people smugglers who organised their passage that Australia was no 'soft touch'.

Australian governments from both sides of politics had in the years before adopted a range of increasingly draconian measures to deter 'boat people'. The most prominent was the policy of mandatory detention of 'illegal arrivals' (as the government invariably refers to them) without reference to a court. Australia is the only country in the world with such a policy. It has led to an expanding network of detention centres, many of them located in remote, outback locations of Australia (see Mares, 2001). Many more illegal residents remain in the community but they are people who have overstayed visas and are more likely to be European or North American. The asylum seekers coming by boat are overwhelmingly from the most strife-torn regions of the world, the Middle East and central Asia. Although refugees from these regions number in the millions, those arriving in Australia in recent years have numbered only in the low thousands. The mandatory detention policy differentiates on the basis of mode of arrival, but where everyone knows that it is not Americans or French or English that arrive on overcrowded and leaky old fishing boats the policy embodies a thinly veiled racial agenda. Again in everyday talk such racialised anxieties are expressed openly and unapologetically while politicians and officials studiously avoid referring to particular ethnic or religious groups. Demonisation is coded in endless references to 'illegals' and 'queue jumpers' with 'suitcases full of money', falsehoods which are belied by the numbers who are found to be legitimate refugees and by the improbability of finding orderly queues on the borders of Afghanistan or Iraq. Maintaining asylum seekers in complete isolation also facilitates their demonisation and the denial of their suffering and needs, for it condemns them always to be represented predominantly by and through the dehumanising categories employed by the powerful.

The captain of the *Tampa* was faced with the prospect of taking an unseaworthy ship with several unconscious passengers and inadequate supplies back to his home port in Norway if he accepted the edict of the Australian government. Left therefore with no choice he entered Australian waters after two days. Armed members of the Australian Special Air Services immediately boarded and took control of the ship with a view to forcing it back out to sea. This proved to be legally impossible despite the government's best efforts to rush border protection legislation through the parliament, the purported effect of which would have been to exempt government personnel involved in the *Tampa* operation, and any similar future operation, from *all* forms of criminal and civil liability. The government hastily arranged for the small and impoverished Pacific Island nation of Nauru (population 11,000) to receive the asylum seekers in exchange for a $20 million package of benefits. The asylum seekers were transported by Australian armed forces to Nauru without setting foot on Australian soil and are to be 'processed' in camps financed and managed by the Australian government. Since the *Tampa* crisis the government has entered into similar arrangements with a number of other small Pacific nations to establish offshore detention camps to which asylum seekers bound for Australia can be diverted.

This expensive, temporary and wildly popular contrivance for managing asylum seekers pending the national election bore further witness to the visceral fears that are summoned by alien cultures threatening violation of Australia's national borders and way of life and the keenness of governments to cultivate and exploit them. The talkback lines ran hot. Mostly there was enthusiastic support for the government's stand and many directly linked the asylum seeker issue back to the gang rapes involving 'ethnic gangs' in western Sydney.[10]

What better reason to be ever so careful as to what boatloads of people we allow to enter Australia.

(Talkback caller on 612 ABC Brisbane, 13 September 2001).

The *Tampa* was the biggest international news story involving Australia since the Sydney Olympics a year before. The only accolades this time though came from a few English tabloids, which were then also raging against the arrival of asylum seekers on England's shores. At home the *Tampa* was the hottest political issue in a very long time and it seemed there was little that could push it off the front pages. Then on the night of 11 September (Australian time) late-night television programmes were interrupted as channels crossed to live CNN coverage in New York. Viewers were presented with the horrific image of a huge burning building with people leaping to their deaths from its upper floors to escape the intense heat. Apparently a freak accident had occurred: a plane had crashed into the north tower of the World Trade Center in New York, one of the tallest buildings in the world. This hardly prepared shocked viewers for what was about to happen. The hijackers must have carefully timed this part for maximum global effect, but being reliant on the vagaries of domestic passenger flight schedules there could be no guarantee of success. The hijackers on United Airlines flight 175 probably only had a short time to know and savour the scale of their achievement. A global audience watched as a second aircraft hove into view and ploughed into the second tower. Soon after one tower collapsed and then the other.

The terrorists, as one commentator later noted, had managed to turn the everyday institutions and technologies of the most modern, powerful and prosperous nation in history back on itself. Foremost among these institutions were the media themselves, for if terror is a form of political theatre increasingly played out on a global stage to maximum visible effect then it is this, rather than the sheer loss of life and physical destruction, that marks these events out from anything that has gone before.

Such an audacious and destructive assault on its citizens and on the symbols of US power guaranteed certain retribution and on a huge scale. The chief suspect was quickly identified – Osama Bin Laden and his Al-qa'ida network. Bin Laden is now a ubiquitous global image but he remains in every other sense a highly elusive figure. And networks are amorphous things. They cannot be combated by war, only by slow, patient, mostly unspectacular police work whose fruits are likely to come, if at all, over the long term. The impulse to retaliate is impatient with investigations and the processes of evidence gathering that would justify the use of force in a conventional legal context. A target more befitting the logic and means of warfare was therefore needed. Conventional warfare – even involving smart weapons – requires a territorial theatre in which to operate and an enemy state to defeat. A 'war on terror', like a 'war on drugs', is, if it is anything more than metaphor, oxymoronic. One term must give way to the other. The US possesses the most powerful war-making machine in the world. One of its core symbols was directly attacked by the terrorists. Affirmation of its military potency probably ensured that this conflict would be forced into the template of war, however inappropriate this may be to deal with the problem of terrorism. But if the only tool you have is a hammer everything looks like a nail. The 'asymmetry' in this new type of conflict is apparent then not only in the manner in which the terrorists chose their means, but also in the way in which their antagonists appear to be ensnared by theirs. This may prove disastrous for many members of the 'coalition against terror'. Of course it already is for the peoples of Afghanistan and Pakistan.

The confused and shifting objectives of this 'war against terror' are evidence of the bizarre mix of passion, symbolism and military might that is driving it. Emile Durkheim's argument that punishment was in the end a passionate, emotional and vengeful expression of feeling at the outrage to collective feelings and symbols, whatever the rational ends super-imposed on it, remains no less apposite in a global context, as does his observation that punitive reactions '...are so much the result of instinctive, irresistible feelings that they often spread to innocent objects...' to '...a more widely diffused repression...' in which the community of the guilty or suspect are made to 'share in the opprobrium heaped upon him..' (Durkheim in Lukes and Scull, 1984: 63).[11]

Back in Australia the Australian Defence Minister, other members of the government and belligerent talkback hosts wasted no time in linking the *Tampa* and asylum seekers with the 'war on terror'. In at least three interviews two days after the US attacks the defence minister suggested that boat people might include terrorists. A few days later one of his colleagues suggested: 'There is an undeniable linkage between illegals and terrorists.'[12] The Prime Minister later took up the theme. Victims fleeing the state terror of the Taliban and Saddam Hussein were all of a sudden made over into terrorists and 'sleepers' themselves, contrary to all the evidence concerning the profile of the hijackers and the backgrounds of boat people like those picked up by the *Tampa*. The only thing that the terrorists and most of the asylum seekers arriving in Australia by boat have in common is that they are Muslim and they come from parts of the Middle East or central Asia.

From 'ethnic gangs' in the southwest of Sydney to global terror and the war in Afghanistan: in a world made small by new communications technologies and by the mass movements of goods, people and ideas on an unprecedented scale the local and the global are increasingly intermingled. The symbolic and real effects of events ramify backwards and forwards across boundaries – geographical, political, cultural and intellectual – that once kept them separate, or at least gave the illusion of doing so. Terror attacks and wars on one side of the world do not simply push aside local concerns and news stories on the other; they serve to further dramatise and contextualise them, to add new dimensions to widely felt anxieties and to prompt draconian political responses.

Is this a case of the empire striking back? The return of violence from the 'periphery' to the 'centre'? A weakening of the nation state system and perhaps the advent of 'civilisational conflicts' which erode familiar boundaries between civil and military conflicts, domestic and foreign policy, crime and war?

Hobbesian Criminology: the Nation State and Criminology

Criminology is a creature of the modern state and its characteristic forms and practices of rule (Foucault, 1979; Garland, 1994). This does not mean by any stretch that it has developed no life apart from this association or that it can be simply dismissed as a handmaiden of state social control (Hogg, 1996). But in so far as the term 'crime' and some of its immediate neighbours – like law, justice, punishment – remain of central importance they have set the taken-for-granted intellectual parameters and political horizons of criminology. Among them:

- the notion of *crime* as a form of conduct or act 'defined, prohibited, and punishable' by state criminal laws;

- the idea of *justice* as a system of impersonal, public authority – of rules, agencies, procedures, and sanctions – claiming sovereign power over the definition and punishment of crime and offering legal protection to *all* members of society according to principles of equality and impartiality;

- the idea of *the nation* which defines the territorial boundaries and political unity of the sovereign authority of the state and the jurisdiction of the criminal law and the justice system.

This set of assumptions has been questioned only rarely in the past from within criminology. It might usefully be described as the Hobbesian framework of criminology (Hobbes, 1968 [1651]). There is much to suggest that the Hobbesian framework is under stress in the face of emerging conflicts, disorders and divisions as we enter the twenty-first century.

Norbert Elias has shown that a correlate of the rise of state-centred societies in many parts of the world – especially the West – was the progressive internal pacification and collectivisation of social life in these nations and the spread of mutual identification among their citizens, what he depicted as a long-term 'civilising process'. These large-scale historical, social and psychological changes entailed a growing internalisation of restraints on personal behaviour, a broadening in the moral universe of those whose suffering commanded recognition and sympathy beyond immediate family and community members to include distant others, an increasing aversion to open expressions of hostility and a long-term decline in the role of violence in everyday life (Elias, 1978, 1982).

Elias's thesis involved a limited generalisation about the role and scale of interpersonal violence in the domestic life of certain, predominantly western, societies. The pacification and individualisation processes and the forms of mutual identification that he examined related to the social relations between citizens within the 'imagined communities' (Anderson, 1991) of certain nation states. In other words, moral obligations and restraints were organised between strangers strictly *within* national borders. This carried no necessary implications for the manner in which different national communities might relate to each other or for the manner in which states interacted (Elias, 1988; Glover, 2001: 21). In the international arena of course no such monopoly on the exercise of violence was (or is) invested in any overarching agency. At best, in international organisations like the United Nations, states cooperate to selectively intervene in trouble spots to keep the peace where a peace can first be established, and, as history shows, with very mixed results (Shawcross, 2000; Parsons, 1995). Nor did Elias depict the 'civilising process' as in any sense an even, linear or irreversible process. He recognised that societies were subject to 'decivilising' processes at certain times, Nazi Germany being a striking example Elias studied in depth (Elias, 1996). And, as Spierenburg (1996) in particular argues, in so far as the 'civilising process' is concerned with the increasing regulation of the effects, of impulses to aggression and other outward displays of emotion, it is likely to influence the *form* of violence as much or more than its incidence. It is in this respect perfectly consistent with an increase in violence in its more rationalised and premeditated forms.

The bureaucratisation of violence, having concentrated the capacities for organised and rationalised force in a few, official hands, also created the conditions for the hitherto unprecedented exercise of murderous powers by states in conflicts with other states, in the building of colonial empires and on occasions against their own (or sectors of their own) populations. Hence the progressive internal pacification of some societies over the early modern period was no safeguard against the twentieth century becoming 'the century of megadeath' (Brzezkinski, 1993).

The Hobbesian framework can be summarised therefore as order *within* states and conflict (or anarchy) *between* them. The two essential functions of the state, internal order and external defence are distinct though mutually supportive in the making of an international order of states. The system of internal order and social protection based on shared national sentiments was seen as essential to the capacity of states to mobilise their domestic populations to fight wars with other states where necessary. Paradoxically it might also contribute to the preservation of domestic order in *other* states. As Paul Hirst has argued the Treaty of Westphalia (1648), which ended the thirty years war, laid the foundation for the subsequent development of the territorial sovereignty and monopoly on internal violence of states by establishing the principle of external non-intervention in the affairs of other states. Agreement between states not to interfere in the internal affairs of other states and to prevent their populations from doing so paved the way for states 'to gain control of their societies' in the face of what had been the pervasive 'international religious conflict' of the Reformation (Hirst, undated: 3). This afforded the basis for the subsequent 'invention' of nationalism as the 'natural' foundation of the internal unity of states, involving the coincidence of territory and culture. Confessional allegiances and identities that hitherto crossed frontiers were subjugated to national ones. Hirst's crucial point is that the principles underpinning the modern nation state – territorial sovereignty, the monopoly on violence and so on – were importantly *international* in origin and the fate of these principles cannot be considered apart from their global or international context. In other words, an important condition for the internal order of states is the capacity of other states to regulate and support their populations and to suppress externally directed violence and other threats emanating from within their territorial boundaries (see also Thompson, 1994).

Therefore the state system meant that international conflicts were also to be organised through, and exclusively controlled by, states, not other groups. In time such conflicts were subjected to other institutional constraints and conventions such as the laws of war which, for example, safeguarded civilians in wartime. Michael Ignatieff has argued, however, that 'Throughout the twentieth century, humanitarian law has been running an uneven race with the demonic inventiveness of military technology and the protean and ever-changing face of modern war. (Ignatieff, 1998: 128; see also Robertson, 2000: 167–203).

As has often been pointed out criminology has largely taken the form of a technical-rational project in the diagnosis and management of crime and marginal disorders *within* the state, a loyal servant and occasional mild critic of Leviathan, but one largely untroubled by the question of the historically contingent (often violent) social and political conditions of formation and maintenance of states.

What happens to the conceptual apparatus of criminology and how salient are its taken-for-granted terms – crime, law, justice, state, sovereignty – at a time when global change and conflict may be eroding some elements at least of the international framework of states it has taken for granted: when the absence or breakdown of Hobbesian order in some regions has not only unleashed disorder within those societies but also predatory and chaotic forces beyond them such as transnational crime, political terror and uncontrolled people movements. How is the language of criminology to be applied, if at all, to events like the *Tampa* and the US terrorist attacks and their aftermath? Are they better left to other established disciplines like politics and international relations? Criminology might want to claim for itself, not some belated interest in the study of 'war' and international conflict, but at least a critical analytical and normative stake in the examination of events and developments which increasingly merge or blur local and global, internal order and external security, and that do not readily fit these old vocabularies and disciplinary boundaries (Cohen, 1996: 16–18).

War, Conflict and Crime at the End of the Cold War

When the Soviet Union imploded at the end of the 1980s many imagined a new world order based on peace, free markets and the extension of liberal democracy (cf. Fukuyama, 1992, who recently maintained that he saw no reason to amend this view in the light of the 11 September events: Fukuyama, 2001). For others, however, the end of the Cold War, the expansion of capitalist markets, the rise of a globally networked world, the advance of neo-liberalism and the growth of inequality are producing new insecurities, new divisions and a qualitative shift in the nature of social conflicts across the planet (see van Creveld, 1999: 336–414). While the threat of a nuclear confrontation between superpowers has been removed, many detected much to be anxious about in the post-Cold War world: a proliferation of new forms of local and global conflict, instability and crime; a weakening of the nation state from above as a result of global technological and economic change and the creation of a 'borderless world'; and a weakening from below with the release of ancient religious and ethnic hostilities, widespread secessionism, a proliferation of new feeble states and the weakening of many already vulnerable ones. The collapse of Yugoslavia and the former Soviet Union and conflicts in the Middle East, Central Asia and Africa are pointed to as evidence of these trends. At the same time the rise of 'postmodern' identity politics and multiculturalism in the West are seen by many as fostering new divisions and new cultures of complaint, victimisation and resentment within established liberal democratic states, weakening their capacity to sustain moral consensus and mobilise domestic populations for national goals. For others it is not so much cultural as economic and social change, growing inequalities and the retreat of social democratic politics in the face of neoliberalism that is creating these new divisions.

Many also point to the manner in which the convergence of regional political conflicts, weakening states and economic and technological globalisation is fuelling new patterns of transnational crime and blurring the boundaries between politics and crime, political and criminal violence (Kaplan, 1997). Thus ethnic, religious and other conflicts in places like Russia, Central Asia, West Africa and parts of Latin America are increasingly intermingled with drug trafficking, people smuggling and other forms of organised crime. The growing international trade in illegal (as well as legal) goods and services and the global diasporas of displaced and stateless peoples connects, in manifold ways, conflicts in 'the periphery' with the conditions of life at the prosperous 'centre'. Thus the arrest in 1999 of the PKK leader Abdullah Oculan reverberated in far-away countries where local Kurdish emigrés protested in the streets and attacked consulates. Struggles for national liberation and a national homeland are conducted on a global canvas. The US wages one of its other wars – the 'war on drugs' – not only within and at its own borders, but also by giving substantial, direct military aid to the government and armed forces of source countries like Columbia.[13] Domestic and foreign policy agendas – fighting crime and protecting national security – converge, as with Australia's asylum seeker policy. For many 11 September might be taken as powerful confirmation that all these elements of a new global disorder have arrived.

The immediacy and horror of contemporary violent events – accentuated, if not generated, by instant, incessant, global media coverage – may, however, lead us to overstate the novelty and significance of current developments and to pay less attention to areas of continuity. There are no doubt also strategic oversights in many current depictions of global disorder: for example, much more urgent attention is given by the West to the flow of refugees across their borders than the flow of weapons in the other direction. It is important therefore to consider more carefully some of the principal themes in the analyses of contemporary global conflict and order.

The 'New Anarchy'?

The statistics of conflict, war and death at the end of the twentieth century yield abundant evidence suggestive of a new global disorder.[14] The International Peace Research Institute in Oslo, for example, records that between 1990 and 1995 five and a half million people died in 93 wars across 70 states. Robert Cooper (1997) paints a grim portrait of what he refers to as contemporary 'pre-modern states': the world of 'pre-state, post-imperial chaos' to be found in places like Somalia, Afghanistan, West Africa and parts of the former Soviet Union. These are states that have lost the monopoly on the means of violence within their societies, or in many instances had never effectively wrested it from other groups. According to Cooper such internal order as they have enjoyed at various times was usually enforced by their colonial or superpower masters, but in a post-Cold War world where power is no longer tied to territory (barring crucial exceptions like access to oil resources) former colonial states are no longer interested in the burdens of empire:

> No one wants to pay the costs of saving distant countries from ruin. The pre-modern world belongs, as it were, in a different time zone: here, as in the ancient world, the choice is again between empire or chaos. But today, because none of us see the use of empires, we have chosen chaos.
>
> (Cooper, 1997: 318)

Such claims refer to the nature, pattern and methods of violence in the contemporary world and not merely its scale. For many commentators what is new is that war between states – 'cultivated war' fought between regular, disciplined armies according to well-established conventions and the laws of war – has given way to civil (or perhaps what, following Keane (1996), might more accurately be called 'uncivil') wars and conflicts involving warlords, militias and often what amount to little more than criminal gangs and death squads who resort to terror and other overtly cruel methods. There is, it is claimed, a new dimension or level of barbarism and uncivilised behaviour in contemporary conflicts (Enzensberger, 1994; Ignatieff, 1998).

The wars of the 1990s surveyed by Smith (1997) certainly bear many of these features. With the exception perhaps of the Balkan wars most occurred at some distance from the 'zones of prosperity' in the West and many in the vacuum created by the absence of viable and legitimate central authority in many parts of the world. Most involved irregular rather than regular combatants. In many of them children were forced to fight and so grow to maturity in a milieu of violence in which the distinction between civil and military life, between violent self-help and deference to some form of organised legal authority, can have little meaning (Smith, 1997: 64–5; Hobsbawm, 1998). The vast majority of the deaths in the wars of the 1990s involved civilians (about 75 per cent) and about a million of them were children (Smith, 1997: 24–5).

As grim as the picture is, there remain questions as to how new and how widespread this supposed new global disorder really is. The process of 'barbarisation' might be a much longer-term one, a legacy of the twentieth century rather than of any more recent post-Cold War order (Hobsbawm, 1995; Glover, 2001).

Early in the twentieth century no more than 10–15 per cent of war deaths involved non-combatants. By the Second World War this rose to 50 per cent (Smith, 1997: 14). As Jonathon Glover has shown this in part reflected 'advances' in the technologies of warfare, but also the way in which the changing modalities of conducting war, both technological and political, had served to progressively weaken moral inhibitions against the mass slaughter of 'enemy' civilians, especially where they were able to be demonised as less than human. Technology and the capacity to kill at a distance (through aerial bombing for example) served to remove some of the ordinary psychological restraints on violence (such as identification with victims and their suffering), echoing the need, voiced by Elias and Spierenburg, to distinguish the form from the scale of violence. The growing bureaucratisation of war both diluted responsibility and progressively transformed moral questions about killing into technical-instrumental ones concerned with war aims and outcomes. This was a long-term process, a 'moral slide', in which what was treated as an *exceptional* but necessary measure at a peculiar moment in time was invoked as a precedent at a later one, thus normalising the recourse and descent into extreme measures (Glover, 2001: 69–88). The mass slaughter of civilians became accepted as a legitimate instrument of military strategy and policy in wars between states long before the end of the Cold War, although the means of such killing usually served to distance perpetrators from the full meaning and consequences of their acts.

Torture also enjoyed a long and largely uninterrupted history in the twentieth century as an instrument of states and colonial regimes (Hobsbawm, 1998; Peters, 1996). France is only now publicly and officially acknowledging its systematic use of torture during the Algerian war (Vidal-Naquet, 1963).[15]

The date of 11 September resonates for many people for reasons other than the crimes against humanity perpetrated in the US in 2001. Eighteen years earlier on that day General Augusto Pinochet staged a military coup with US backing against the popularly elected Socialist government of Salvadore Allende in Chile, and thereafter initiated his 'caravan of death' which employed torture, death squads and 'disappearances' against radicals across Latin America (Corradi et al., 1992; Robertson, 2000: 368–400; and see Ariel Dorfman's (1998) wonderful memoir of the Allende period, the coup and its aftermath).

Mass slaughter of innocent civilians, political terror and other cruel methods are not therefore new to the post-Cold War world. And at the turn of the millennium many parts of the world – much of Latin America and East and South East Asia – are more stable and more open politically than they were ten years before even if they are not exactly havens of democracy and human rights (Holsti, 1999). And many of the most intractable conflicts of the present day did not begin after the end of the Cold War: Kashmir, Sri Lanka, Palestine, Angola, Columbia, East Timor and Northern Ireland, to name a few. These are long-standing conflicts, invariably the complex legacy of past colonialisms.

A problem with some of the analyses of the *new* global disorder, as Holsti (1999) has argued, is that they perpetuate in a new form the intellectual and political biases of the Cold War and an imperialist mindset. Conflicts, as in the past, are not acknowledged and understood in terms of the local problems, interests and forces which generate them or the suffering of those who experience them, but only or primarily by reference to their impact on western interests and sensibilities. This is what underlay the history of superpower-directed or -sponsored intervention, destabilisation and repression in Africa, South East Asia and Latin America throughout the Cold War.

The images of passenger aircraft soaring into the World Trade Center, of women and children in Sierra Leone with both arms hacked off and of the genocide in Rwanda are readily (and perhaps understandably) taken as evidence of the cruelties and decivilising tendencies of contemporary war and conflict. But there are many varieties of barbarism in the contemporary world. Landmines and cluster bombs, for example, are much more sophisticated weapons than machetes, but they are only more 'civilised' in that most superficial (and perhaps western) of senses that they maim, decapitate and kill at a distance, both spatial and temporal (Keane, 1996: 159–63; Smith, 1997: 28).

Before the current 'war on terrorism' in Afghanistan began there were already an estimated ten million landmines scattered throughout about 80 per cent of the country, the legacy of twenty years of conflict involving Russia and the West. An estimated average of five to ten Afghanis were victims of landmines every day in 1999, dropping to an average of about three in 2000 (Landmine Monitor, 2001). The presence of landmines on such a scale also renders impossible the secure and orderly conduct of everyday life and the economy, especially agriculture. Confirmed reports that the US is using cluster bombs in the current war (as Nato did in Kosovo) ensure that the burden of unexploded ordnance in Afghanistan will increase further and that this war will inflict injury and terror long after open hostilities have ceased. Unexploded cluster bombs effectively become landmines that detonate and cause massive injury on contact. Many of them are bright yellow in colour and about the size of drink cans. Afghani children who see these objects as further evidence of American generosity and humanity – air-dropped beverage to accompany the food parcels and notes of reassurance that this is a war on terrorism not on them – are likely to be at particular risk. The relative indifference to these forms of terror and atrocity in western media and political discourse makes a striking contrast with the coverage given anthrax attacks in the US and other terrorist threats there and elsewhere.

Such devices may be delivered to their destinations by US bombers or more circuitously via a lucrative global market in weapons. These more recent technologies of war and atrocity and their deployment are part of that longer twentieth-century tradition of killing traced by Jonathan Glover and others. The idea that we confront some new global anarchy is problematised. What seems confirmed by the events of 11 September and asylum seeker controversies throughout much of the West is that the domestic populations and ways of life of western nations in the 'zones of prosperity' are no longer effectively sealed off from contemporary global disorders as they once believed themselves to be.

A 'Clash of Civilisations'?

Samuel Huntington (1996) has argued that the end of the Cold War witnessed a fundamental shift in the international order and patterns of conflict. The struggle between the superpowers, between the two great ideological protagonists, capitalism and communism, gave way to multipolar tensions and conflicts between civilisations according to Huntington. Ethnic and religious wars and conflicts in the Balkans and elsewhere lend credence to Huntington's thesis (Juergensmeyer, 1993) and it must have been confirmed in the minds of some by the events of 11 September. As an intellectual framework for understanding contemporary global conflict it is likely to have much appeal or at least to coincide with widespread public and political sentiment in many parts of the world inside and perhaps outside the West regardless of its validity as description and explanation of contemporary trends.

It shares many of the problems noted above. There are conflicts in the contemporary world or from the recent past that can be readily fitted to civilisational specifications but there are many that cannot. Co-religionists,

Iran and Iraq, fought a bitter and costly war in the 1980s for example. It produces oversimplification even for those conflicts that appear to more readily fit the thesis. Many of the contemporary wars of belief and identity – wars in Africa, in the Middle East and in the Asian subcontinent – stem less from civilisational tensions as such than from the past creation of territorial borders to coincide not with ethnic, religious or other communities, but the interests of imperial states and superpowers. To reduce the war in Bosnia for example to being an ethnic conflict driven by ancient hatreds, let alone a clash of civilisations, ignores all its complex local and regional political dimensions (Silber and Little, 1995).

And on closer examination it appears that Huntington's real preoccupation was with the clash of two civilisations in particular, the Christian West and the Islamic world. Islamic fundamentalism has replaced communism as the new enemy of western civilisation. Once again diverse local problems, interests and conflicts are subsumed within a new global bipolarity that may, as in the Cold War, be self-fulfilling in certain respects. Quite apart from the significant variations within Islam its political role in many parts of the world – Turkey, Egypt, Pakistan, Iraq and Indonesia, to take several examples – is strongly oriented towards reform of the local nation state (van der Veer, 1999). The conflation of local and global, of civil society and state, in the civilisational thesis overlooks (and in important respects legitimises) the role of political repression in these Islamic societies. Repressive secular political regimes in countries like Egypt, Turkey and (until Saddam Hussein invaded Kuwait) Iraq have enjoyed enormous military and other aid from the West. This support is often motivated by the desire to contain political Islam, as well as to safeguard oil supplies. The civilisational thesis conveniently overlooks western support for domestic political repression in Islamic societies as a source of grievance in those societies whose priority is domestic reform rather than a global war against western infidels. Such oversight and denial plays into the hands of extremists like Osama Bin Laden who exploit such legitimate grievances to advance their own version of the clash of civilisations.

Huntington has elaborated a new principle of 'social war' for the contemporary world. Although as *description* it is simplistic this does not prevent it, or local variants of it, from serving as an influential principle of action. This is apparent, for example, in the resurgence and growing respectability of xenophobia in the West (Fraser, 2000; Markus, 2001), in political and popular attacks on domestic multiculturalism (which appears to be one of Huntington's major though unstated targets) and in policies, such as those of the Australian government, directed at the demonisation, segregation and exclusion of asylum seekers as a threat to national security. It also permeates the interpretive frameworks and inflects the popular punitiveness that increasingly governs the domestic politics of law and order and social policy.

Smith's (1997) global survey coupled with Kaplan's (1997) close-up reportage from many of the most troubled regions suggests that armed conflict in the 1990s belongs (as it did before) on a continuum with other forms of politically inspired violence and human rights abuses, such as genocide, extra-judicial execution, terrorism, torture, political violence and arbitrary arrest and detention. Smith points out that: 'Two-thirds of the armed conflicts in the 1990s involved states that sanction the killing of political opponents and those whom they regard as socially undesirable. Of these states, almost 80 per cent were involved in armed conflict in the 1990s' (Smith, 1997: 97). There are clear links between armed conflict and the efforts of states to suppress, displace or eliminate (to 'ethnically cleanse') minority populations and cultures. These conflicts were disproportionately concentrated in the poorest and least 'developed' regions of the world. Smith's calculations relying on the United Nations Human Development Index (which combines measures of wealth, health, education, etc.) indicate that a majority (57 per cent) of 'low human development' countries and more than a third of 'medium human development' countries experienced wars in the 1990s, but only 14 per cent of 'high human development' countries did so (Smith, 1997: 48). The general seeds of armed conflict and other extreme forms of violence thus seem clear – weak and divided states, poverty, political tyranny, xenophobia, the suppression of identity and belief, the absence of democratic institutions and a democratic culture, and the denial of human rights.

No doubt there are limits to how much change for the better can be advanced by simply blaming history or 'the West'. On the other hand, the civilisational thesis and its variants run the opposite risk of implying that the baleful and often still deteriorating life conditions in which so many continue to live are somehow intrinsic to their cultures and have nothing to do with past and present global economic, social and political arrangements.

'Sovereign Individuals' of Global Capitalism

For the individual explosive power is cheap; for the state the power to counter terrorism is expensive and usually ineffective. Society is vulnerable, like the plate glass skyscrapers of the World Trade Center.

(Davidson and Rees-Mogg, 1998: 5)

For many contemporary commentators a central feature of the changing times in which we live is the weakening of nation states and the nation state system in an increasingly 'borderless world', even as the number of states has actually proliferated. This view has adherents across the intellectual and political spectrum. The erosion of the frameworks of social control and protection afforded by strong and stable states disturbs many. Others see this – even with all its attendant conflicts and insecurities – in positive, even utopian, terms: the triumph of freedom and the 'sovereign individual' over the compulsions of the state, made possible by new information technologies. Davidson and Rees-Mogg (1998: 5) point to the impact of these technologies in making power, both that of 'the word' and that of 'the gun', 'cheaply available' to the individual and groups below the level of the state who thereby become sovereign. According to them computer power will, while empowering individuals and groups, destroy or substantially erode the taxing capacity of states, make state welfare and social provision unaffordable and consequently produce widening gaps in wealth and income. Choice and voluntary association will become much more important political resources in the absence of effective state compulsion and coordination. States and governments will be constrained to behave more like commercial enterprises – 'competitive territorial clubs' – competing with other public and private entities for individual and corporate customers in a global marketplace. The modern framework of politics – state sovereignty, citizenship, and the rule of law – will become progressively outmoded.

Violent, as well as economic, power will be diffused in this new global order. There are of course changed technologies of warfare that are conducive to this, such as biological and chemical warfare (Heisbourg, 1997), but also the information technologies that empower individuals to engage in vastly increased numbers of economic transactions unrestricted by geography and the supervision of state authorities also facilitate the organisation of violence by individuals and groups outside central control. They reduce the returns on organising violence on a large scale and thus undermine the capacity of states and other large-scale organisations to efficiently protect their members and conversely increase the accessibility, utility and potency of violence in the hands of smaller groups: warlords, militias, gangsters, drug cartels, renegade security agencies, terror networks and so on. Weakening the capacity of states to provide social and physical protection will lead many (particularly those outside the new information elites) to retreat into membership of other subgroups – ethnic, religious, clan-based, etc. – for mutual aid, protection and psychological support.

Protection will thus also be increasingly organised through non-state actors and treated as a private rather than a public good. There is already much evidence to support this argument: the rapid growth and massive size of the private security sector in western states, the increasing tendency of states to contract out the security function (policing, prisons, detention centres for asylum seekers) to private companies or even, as with Australia and its asylum seekers, to poor neighbour states, the spread of completely privatised residential communities (walled housing estates and the like) organised around the provision of security, the signs of a return to vigilante activity in many places (see Pratt in Chapter 7 of this volume), and the growing role of global mercenary organisations and military companies like Sandline International (employed by the Papua New Guinea government in its civil war in Bougainville: O'Callaghan, 1999) and Executive Outcomes (which has had a role in wars in West Africa). The line between predatory and protective violence exercised by the various non-state actors may under many circumstances become increasingly blurred, pointing to a scenario in which 'anarchy' or, at best, some level of localised 'micro-government' are more likely than new forms of governance at the transnational or supra-local level (Davidson and Rees-Mogg, 1998: 32).

Davidson and Rees-Mogg, the authors of this foreboding (if overstated and overreductive) prognosis, circumvent their own analysis when they (unconvincingly) posit the rise of a new global market morality and suggest this will ultimately domesticate the forces of reaction and predatoriness. Rising violence is thus consigned to the status of a temporary, transitional phase in their analysis of the rise of the information age (Davidson and Rees-Mogg, 1998: 369–71). There seems no compelling reason, however, to accept such reassurances about a happy outcome in the long run: to accept, for example, that global technological, economic and social change that weakens states, casts people adrift from state regulation, sharply intensifies inequality and insecurity and, at the same time, increases access to the means of violence will not simply lead to growing disorder and very unfavourable market conditions. The reactions they treat as short term and transitional in nature – the 'revenge of nations' as states seek to reassert and display their sovereignty through repression (Garland, 1996), 'the return of the luddites', gangsterism, vigilantism and ethnic and religious fundament- alism – are more likely, on their own analysis, to define the shape of the future than is the triumph of the global market nirvana they optimistically forecast for the long run.

It is these tendencies that so disturbed Eric Hobsbawm at the close of his 'short' history of the twentieth century, *Age of Extremes* (1995; also see

Hobsbawm, 2000). Minus the tendencies to overstatement and free market utopianism Davidson and Rees-Mogg's analysis of the role of violence in the new information age nevertheless seems genuinely prophetic in relation to the events of 11 September and other developments. The continuing state of emergency generated by the bio-terrorist incidents in the US demonstrates the vulnerability of modern states and their limited capacity to provide effective security for their citizens. It also provides an inkling of the economic as well as psychological impacts of pervasive fear and uncertainty, when citizens cannot take for granted the security of their everyday environments and routines. The US desire to find and target 'rogue states' in the immediate aftermath of the attacks manifests a longing for some old military certainties while obscuring what is distinctive about this new 'asymmetric' brand of warfare/crime: that it is networked rather than state administered or sponsored and that the technologies that work against states – missiles, aircraft carriers, tanks, etc – are of limited effect in a 'war against terrorism'.

Problems and Logics of Collective Action

Some of the trends surveyed above point to a commonplace theme of contemporary social analysis – the hollowing out of the state from above and below. The fact, however, that the general implications of an analysis like that of Davidson and Rees-Mogg – of an end to nationalisms and the rise of the sovereign individual – varies so dramatically from that of Huntington – who foresees individuals becoming increasingly absorbed into civilisational identities – is cause to be sceptical of overblown, single-factor interpretations. States and governments may in certain respects be on the 'defensive' in the face of globalisation (although see Hirst and Thompson, 1996), the advance of political neoliberalism, the rise of identity politics and so on but they are, as Hobsbawm and others point out, far from 'redundant' or 'ineffective' (1995: 576). They remain crucial collective actors in the life of their own domestic populations and societies and in the context of what unquestionably remains an international system dominated by nation states (Hall and Paul, 1999). We are witnessing, though, at least two sets of related changes: first in the logics and devices of rule, both domestic and external; and second, the growing role of other actors, both at the subnational and supranational levels. Explanatory and normative social analysis (in criminology and elsewhere) needs to take account of these changes while avoiding the either/or choice of treating the state as redundant in the face of globalisation or implicitly affirming it in its old status as the taken-for-granted framework and horizon of analysis.

Bill Jordan (1996) has analysed the growth of inequality, poverty and social exclusion in the contemporary world and the corresponding intensification of the 'politics of enforcement' within a framework that pushes beyond conventional analytical parameters. Jordan points out that hitherto the analysis of poverty and social exclusion has been mainly concerned with 'the dynamic between markets and states' and has omitted 'a more comprehensive view of how groups form, organise and act collectively in pursuit of their interests, and how vulnerable individuals come to be excluded and marginalised in such interactions' (Jordan, 1996: 4). Such modes of organisation can be either formal (as in trade unions or friendly societies) or informal (as in clans, criminal gangs, terror networks). From this standpoint nation states appear as merely one, albeit highly formalised and invariably powerful, form of collective organisation among many others (households, neighbourhoods, communities, local governments, professional associations, private insurance schemes, sporting associations, transnational organisations, etc. designed to confer benefits on members and exclude non-members. The nation state is thereby unseated from its typically privileged (if invariably taken-for-granted) status in social scientific analysis, as is the conceptual baggage of citizenship and social rights that usually accompanies such forms of analysis. The state is treated as one form of organisation among a variety of others operating at the subnational and the supranational level and its dual face, as a crucial mechanism of exclusion as well as inclusion, is made clear.

This also has the effect of placing the analysis of such issues in a *global* context. This is relevant for considering how global markets and forces are related to the *internal* life of nation states: the fragmentation of the state, the retreat from (claimed) principles of universality and inclusion in social provision, the tendency for people to retreat into narrower, tighter groupings with more 'homogeneous memberships', whether based on cultural identity, wealth, lifestyle or some other factor (Jordan, 1996: 27–33, 65–8). Of equal importance, though, it focuses attention on the global as the site of collective action for the poor, the alienated and those displaced by war and environmental destruction as much as for transnational corporations and information elites. The latter groups may be the ones who are most obviously realising the potential to maximise economic benefits by avoiding national tax and regulatory laws, but the mobility of people (as of goods, services, information) across national borders (through all manner of schemes, both legal and illegal) is also one of the defining features of the new global age. The voluntary or forced movement of people across national borders (like the historical constitution and reconstitution of the borders themselves) provides a solution to certain problems of collective action – security, access to the resources of survival and to opportunities for economic development, etc. It has done for a long time. And yet this has been obscured by the focus on the internal life of the state at the expense of its external conditions, the assumption being that the absolute principle of national sovereignty guaranteed control over the relationships and movements between these self-contained entities. This assumption may have been valid in a practical sense for a minority of (principally western) states for the last century, but it no longer holds as it once did.

This is because of crumbling states and wars – and more particularly the nature of these wars – in regions of political chaos. War in the latter part of the twentieth century in effect tends to treat the entire society of the enemy as the target and theatre of armed conflict, making no meaningful distinction between civilian and military targets and losses. This is by definition the case in those 'uncivil wars' fought by militias and gangs in parts of Africa that conscript children and torture and maim civilians. It is no less true, however, of the aerial bombing campaigns used by risk-averse western governments in the Gulf War, in Kosovo and now in Afghanistan. In these latter cases the cost of minimising risk to one's combatants and reassuring domestic public opinion is the mass destruction of civilian life and infrastructure in the 'enemy' state. The civilian casualties caused directly by precision bombing may be relatively limited. The full destructive impact is more likely to be felt in the humanitarian crises generated by such wars. Calling these forms of atrocity 'collateral damage' and claiming that the war is being waged against the Taliban or Saddam Hussein rather than the people of Afghanistan or Iraq is simply a cultivated form of denial designed to assuage western opinion. This also requires a concerted effort to censor the images and accounts that would contradict it.[16]

These conditions produce chaos, not just military defeats. And in the absence of genuine reconstruction programmes, like the Marshall Plan after the Second World War, the world of prosperous states cannot easily insulate itself from its by-products: civil breakdown, intensified repression, humanitarian crisis, refugee movements, the proliferation of transnational criminal networks involved in drug trafficking, people smuggling and the like and the growing risks of global terror.

It is clear, for example, that in pursuit of a measure of security and economic opportunity increasing numbers are willing to migrate legally or illegally, to risk much (oppression, exploitation, death) to get to western countries and to sacrifice political, social and other citizenship rights if and when they get there: to suffer detention, to work undocumented, to accept disentitlement to social benefits, etc. These new forms of collective action are taking place *outside* the framework of formal political institutions, rights and citizenship. Jordan points to evidence in Britain that shows this trend is not confined to immigrants, but includes a growing number of other groups: young people among the structurally unemployed, the homeless, travellers, those involved in drug and other illegal and semi-legal economies and so on. He argues that such groups have in effect 'traded in their formal political rights in favour of the freedom to organise in new ways' (Jordan, 1996: 84). The radicalism in such developments may stem less from any demands that are made on the state to alleviate poverty, extend social provision or provide jobs as from resigned acceptance to, or even a positive embrace of, survivalist strategies outside the framework of the legal, political and social institutions of the state.

The response of western governments to these developments has been dominated by a 'politics of enforcement' at home and abroad (Jordan, 1996). This is apparent in the everyday drift into progressively more draconian law and order policies to deal with domestic crime, in the intensification of exclusionary measures against asylum seekers in which Australia now leads the way with its 'Pacific solution' and in the resort to foreign military intervention to suppress terror networks or the drugs trade. As the latter two examples indicate, the pursuit of *internal* order in one state involves governments in dangerous, uncertain and often destabilising interventions into the affairs of *other* states. The politics of enforcement is likely to create a vicious spiral, the more dangerous because the different realms of collective action of governments and peoples – local, national, international – are increasingly interconnected. In Australia's case the war in Afghanistan in which it has joined has brought threats from the Taliban of a jihad against Australia and will also increase the flow of refugees towards its shores. The US-led coalition claims the war is not a war against Islam or the Afghani people but at home in Australia the rhetoric and policies of the major political parties, left and right, are at one in tapping into and fostering visceral fears and prejudices which condense crime in the suburbs, asylum seekers from Asia and the Middle East, Islam and international terror into one alien wedge threatening Australia's national security and way of life. As these fears grow in the face of global forces over which governments acting unilaterally and repressively exercise no effective control the logical resort will be to more concerted measures of exclusion and repression. In order to assuage domestic insecurities the symbols of sovereignty and cultural closure will be displayed with ever more vigour for want of effective political strategies to address the changed international conditions and the new global risks.

Beyond 'the Politics of Enforcement'?

The fundamental challenge this poses, as Jordan points out, is to the closed distributive and solidaristic logics of western welfare states (Jordan, 1996: 73–4). To whom are we obligated and what is the scope of the 'social contract' – the 'imagined community' – to which we belong in an increasingly global world? Richard Rorty has argued that the most 'deeply divisive' issue that will confront the American left in the twenty-first century is whether to give primacy to the reduction of inequalities *between* nations or to redress disadvantage at home (Rorty, 1998: 88, 148). On the other hand, he regrets his own lack of any good ideas about how to resolve this dilemma.

In Australia many believe this question underpins a reconfiguration of politics, the opening up of a new division between 'the elites' composed of left liberals, professionals, the corporate class and other sectors of the 'information rich' who are comfortable with globalisation on the one hand and 'battlers' among the poor, working and middle classes, the small business sector and farmers who are struggling and insecure in the face of economic and social change. 'The elites' are said to be insulated from and unconcerned by the major issues that affect ordinary people: crime in the streets, immigration, welfare cheats, handouts to minorities and making economic ends meet.

Michael Ignatieff (1998) has explored some of the practical ways in which individuals and institutions, including aid workers and organisations, peacekeepers, human rights bodies and parts of the media, traverse these boundaries and manage to embody a sense of global conscience. Robert Cooper (1997) has shown how some states have begun to unhitch questions of security from assertions of national sovereignty. 'Postmodern' states, as he calls them (such as the states of western Europe), have turned the experience of mutual vulnerability in the twentieth century – two world wars fought primarily in Europe followed by the threat of nuclear holocaust – into a new principle of security based less on national sovereignty than on a shared sovereignty involving cooperation, transparency, monitoring and multilateralism between states and respect for international law. National sovereignty is subject, or subjects itself, to 'constraint and supervision' (Cooper, 1997: 316).

Many see hopeful signs in the international human rights movement. Human rights practice has in some important ways begun to catch up with the sort of human rights-based criminological agenda set by Julia and Herman Schwendinger in their justly influential article from the 1970s, 'Defenders of order or guardians of human rights?' (1975; see also their contribution in Chapter 3 of this volume). There has been an extension and strengthening of national, regional and international human rights regimes around the globe. Truth commissions and other 'transitional justice' measures have been adopted in many countries to address human rights violations and state crimes committed under previous regimes. More recently there have been the practical efforts to bring the erstwhile Chilean dictator, Augusto Pinochet, to justice for crimes against humanity, the establishment of ad hoc international tribunals to try war crimes in the former Yugoslavia and Rwanda, the indictment of Slobodan Milosevic and moves to establish a standing International Criminal Court to try crimes against humanity (Robertson, 2000).

Yet the manner in which human rights standards are invoked still frequently belies a number of difficult questions: of the specificity with which definitions can be operationalised as anything more than rhetorical devices in ideological and political debate; of how to establish viable mechanisms of enforcement; and of how to foster peace as well as deliver justice. These issues in turn raise the question of the embeddedness of human rights norms and concepts in day-to-day democratic dialogue, practice and culture in the civil societies of the contemporary world, the point as Michael Ignatieff has put it that even though a human rights-based moral universalism is showing signs of advance, it still remains a 'weak and inconstant ethic' (Ignatieff, 1998: 20). And, one might add, an ethic that has trouble competing with or modulating the appeal of nationalism and other passions and sources of identity that pervade contemporary global and local conflicts and that fuel a hardening of familiar solidarities in the face of fear and insecurity.

Arguments for a sort of extended juridification of conflicts overlook, and harbour the conceit that they might override, the realms of thought and feeling that are importantly constitutive of bonds and relations between peoples. Human rights discourse has done little, for example, to mitigate the rise of a punitive common sense throughout much of the West and beyond or to prevent the massive expansion of prison populations, the spread of mandatory sentencing regimes and so on.

There is also the question of resources and means. Much human rights debate is conducted in the language of moral absolutes as if respect for and implementation of human rights is somehow resource neutral and self-executing once the obstacle presented by states and their narrow political interests is surmounted. In his account of the Rwandan genocide and its aftermath Philip Gourevitch (2000: 242–9) describes the horrific conditions in which many thousands of Hutus involved in the genocide were imprisoned after the Rwandan Patriotic Front took power. These were conditions that would not comply with any human rights standards. On the other hand the alternative may have been to conduct summary executions or leave them to the revenge of the surviving families and communities of those who were slaughtered. What is an impoverished state that has just suffered the horrors of a mass genocide to do? Even incarcerating people in the worst imaginable conditions involved a diversion of much needed resources from reconstruction and care and support of the destitute civilian population. Political despotism and human rights abuses are major problems, but some crumbling states simply lack the political infrastructure and resources to address the rudimentary needs and problems of civil conflict and 'exploding urban populations'. The legacy of colonialism and the circumstances of their creation may have been such that they never enjoyed all the essential attributes of states (Holsti, 1999: 296). Such problems will not be addressed through the establishment of formal human rights machinery but only through political solutions that are centrally concerned with a redistribution of resources. States, as well as other agencies, will be crucial actors in any such process.

This in turn points back to the issue of under what conditions humanitarian aid – compassionate, parsimonious, optional – might assume more the status of an obligation in the international community. This presents conceptual and research (and of course political) challenges for any radical, human rights-based project in criminology. Scholars like Ignatieff (1998), Stan Cohen (2000) and Jonathan Glover (2001) have been addressing these challenges in recent work. These revolve around the central question of the ethical, psychological and sociological conditions under which people come to recognise (or deny) the suffering and needs of others.

There is no easy resolution of these issues where it most matters – in the moral and political life of nations and civil societies. Rorty suggests, following John Dewey, that there is 'nothing bigger, more permanent and more reliable behind our sense of moral obligation to those in pain than a certain contingent historical phenomenon – the gradual spread of the sense that the pain of others matters, regardless of whether they are of the same family, tribe, colour, religion, nation or intelligence as oneself' (Rorty, 1999: 14). If societies do not mechanically evolve – cohere, polarise, re-cohere – according to specifiable historical laws of motion, if we accept the contingent and hybrid character of such forms of solidarity and governance as may be achieved at any given time, and if we further accept that societies are therefore complex amalgams of civic, market, governmental, welfare and other elements, then no single system of thought will be privileged to discern, and no single agency to carry, the forces of history.

Concluding Comments

In making its small, but not unimportant, contribution to understanding the conditions of modern social life criminology has largely assumed the Hobbesian conception of political community: of sovereign states securing within their own borders the conditions of domestic peace by monopolising the means of internal violence. Even critics who often saw the state predominantly in its repressive aspect shared this perspective. Justice was also for the most part, and tacitly, conceived within the framework of national societies, even where universalist values (such as equality and freedom) were invoked. Radicals (like contemporary market utopians) often imagined a self-regulating society in which the state was superseded or radically transformed as a political actor, but social justice was still implicitly conceived within the framework of national boundaries. I have suggested in this chapter that the image of internally self-governing states and societies to which the criminological project has – in its various forms – been tied has never been entirely convincing. State sovereignty was born and sustained in a particular international context and pattern of relationships. This has been more obvious to those in the modern world – the stateless, the conquered, the colonised – whose daily lives are a constant reminder of the contingent, fragile and chimerical qualities of national sovereignty. However, on 11 September, as Noam Chomsky (2001) put it, the guns were pointed the other way. Global terror, transnational crime and the world refugee problem are reminders that attempts to guarantee the internal peace and security of western states by assertions of sovereignty rooted in 'exclusionary nationalism' (Manne, 2001) are likely to prove self-defeating in the long, if not also in the short, term. A reliance on the 'politics of enforcement', as the most powerful symbolic expression of national sovereignty, is likely to set in train a vicious spiral, as much in the regional and international as in the local and national context. Repression will exacerbate rather than relieve problems of security that confront contemporary states. This surely poses some interesting and urgent challenges for criminology as it looks beyond its conventional conceptual and political horizons.

In times like these, Michel Foucault counselled, we should avoid the adoption of 'projects that claim to be global or radical'. He reminded us 'that the claim to escape from the system of contemporary reality so as to produce the overall programmes of another society, of another way of thinking, another culture, another vision of the world, has led only to the return of the most dangerous traditions.' He suggested our 'historico-critical attitude' be 'experimental', and always subject itself to the test of 'contemporary reality' (Foucault, 1997: 126). I take this to mean that we must build on what we have available to us by way of an ethics of recognition and action. In the context of the events that shaped this chapter cause for optimism is difficult to find, although we should look to and build on that which affords hope.

When Arne Rinnan, the captain of the *Tampa*, was informed that close by in the Indian Ocean a boatload of people (mainly Afghani asylum seekers as it turned out) were in distress he immediately changed course, went to their rescue and thereafter assumed responsibility for delivering them to a place of safety. His only (and temporary) bond with these people lay in their helplessness and his capacity to help. He did not, however, act simply out of compassion or conscience. The custom of the sea dictated that he take the action that he did. The custom reflects a recognition of the vulnerability, and thus mutual interdependence, of *all* who travel on the high seas between what we (at least in the prosperous West) have hitherto taken to be islands of sovereignty and security. Perhaps the example of the Norwegian sea captain offers an ethic that more nearly fits the new conditions of insecurity that attend the world in the early twenty-first century.

Notes

1. Pilita Clark, 'The anguish of the Afghans', *Sydney Morning Herald*, 22–23 September 2001:8.
2. Luke McIlveen, 'Carr in race row over poll', *The Australian*, 23 August 2001:6.
3. *House of Peace Pty Ltd & Anor v Bankstown City Council* [2000] NSWCA 44, 16 March 2000. See J. Marsh, 'Why is this church not a church?' *Sydney Morning Herald*, 29 October 1998:1.
4. Martin Chulov, 'Rape menace from the melting pot', *Weekend Australia*, 18–19 August 2001:1.
5. The Australian media monitoring organisation, Rehame, records it as being one of the national top three issues raised by callers on talkback radio for each of the last two weeks of August.
6. *The Daily Telegraph*, Sydney's and Australia's most popular tabloid, published as its front page headline on 24 August 2000: 'Victim tells how rapists taunted her "You deserve it because you're an Australian"'.
7. The media claims that this amounted to a shocking new 'phenomenon', specific to a particular geographical area with a high population of residents of Middle Eastern descent and of the Muslim faith and involving determinate categories of offender and victim, commanded little evidentiary support, let alone the

aetiology ascribed to the crimes. Media reporting of the court hearing registered and helped trigger a 'moral panic', but the events to which it referred occurred a year before. According to the NSW Bureau of Crime Statistics and Research at the time of these reports recorded sexual assaults in the relevant area were in numbers and profile little different to what they were anywhere else in the city or the state. This information was ignored or buried in press reports.

8. Reported Matt Price and Robert Garran, 'PM weighs his anger in stormy seas', *The Weekend Australian,* 1 September 2001: 1.

9. A detailed account was provided by David Marr and Marian Wilkinson in a two-part article in the *Sydney Morning Herald,* 20–21 October 2001: 'They shall not land'.

10. Matt Price, 'Talkback callers turn off sympathy', *The Australian* 29 August 2001:2. The Australian media monitoring organization Rehame records that every week from August 20 till the end of October asylum seekers constituted one of the top three talkback issues. Most weeks it was the number one issue. At the beginning of the period it merged with the 'ethnic gangs' issue and of course after 11 September it was slightly overshadowed by the attacks on the US, although again it simply became merged with the latter in the views of many callers as asylum seekers were now depicted in the image of global terrorists and 'sleepers' rather than rapists.

11. The mixed and fluctuating messages from the US about who or what is the precise target of this war – the Bin Laden network, the Taliban, Iraq, Iran, other 'rogue states', any state that is not *for* 'the war on terror' (despite the inability to define this enemy with any precision or consistency) – are all revealing.

12. The Defence Minister's interviews on 13 September 2001 were on the *Sunrise* programme, Network Seven, a television interview on *Sky TV* and a radio interview with Derryn Hinch on 3AK. His party and parliamentary colleague, Peter Slipper's comments were reported by Mike Secombe, 'Politics of fear works well for PM', *Sydney Morning Herald* 19 September 2001:1.

13. On President Bill Clinton's Plan Columbia, involving $1.3 billion in military aid to suppress the Columbian cocaine cartels, see Julian Borger, 'US sidesteps its drug problem with $1.3bn military fix in Columbia', *Guardian Weekly,* 29 June–5 July 2000:4. A year later acknowledgement that Plan Columbia had had little impact on the flow of cocaine to the US led to proposals by President Bush to inject further funds and deploy private military personnel in Columbia and its neighbours: Peter Beaumont, 'Bush to raise "private army" in drugs war', *Guardian Weekly,* 26 July 26–1 August 2001: 5.

14. The statistical details in this section are drawn from Smith (1997) unless otherwise indicated.

15. See 'France confronts ghosts of Algeria', *Guardian Weekly,* 21–27 December, 2000, 20.

16. Robert Fisk, Middle East correspondent for the *Independent,* has relentlessly exposed both the efforts at censorship and the unsavoury realities they are designed to mask in the West's role in the Middle East and currently in Afghanistan.

References

Anderson, B. (1991) *Imagined Communities – Reflections on the Origin and Spread of Nationalism*, revised edition. London: Verso.

Brzezinski, Z. (1993) *Out of Control – Global Turmoil on the Eve of the 21st Century*. New York: Macmillan.

Carrington, K. (1998) *Who Killed Leigh Leigh? A Story of Shame and Mateship in an Australian Town*. Sydney: Random House.

Chomsky, N. (2001) *September 11*. Crows Nest: Allen & Unwin.

Cohen, S. (1996) 'Crime and politics: spot the difference', *British Journal of Sociology*, 47(1): 1–21.

Cohen, S. (2001) *States of Denial – Knowing about Atrocities and Suffering*. Cambridge: Polity Press.

Cooper, R. (1997) 'Is there a new world order?', in Mulgan, G. (ed.), *Life After Politics – New Thinking for the Twenty First Century*. London: Fontana.

Corradi, J., Fagen, P. and Garreton, M. (eds) (1992) *Fear at the Edge – State Terror and Resistance in Latin America*. Berkeley and Los Angeles: University of California Press.

Davidson, J. and Rees-Mogg, W. (1998) *The Sovereign Individual*. London: Pan Books.

Dorfman, A. (1998) *Heading South, Looking North*. London: Sceptre.

Elias, N. (1978) *The Civilizing Process, Volume 1 – The History of Manners*. New York: Pantheon Books.

Elias, N. (1982) *The Civilizing Process, Volume 2 – State Formation and Civilization*. Oxford: Basil Blackwell.

Elias, N. (1988) 'Violence and civilization', in Keane, J. (ed.), *Civil Society and the State – New European Perspectives*. London: Verso.

Elias, N. (1996) *The Germans*. Cambridge: Polity Press.

Enzensberger, H. (1994) *Civil War*. London: Granta.

Foucault, M. (1979) *Discipline and Punish – the Birth of the Prison*. London: Peregrine Books.

Foucault, M. (1997) 'What is Enlightenment?', in S. Lotringer and L. Hochroth (eds), *The Politics of Truth*. New York: Semiotexe.

Fraser, N. (2000) *The Voice of Modern Hatred – Encounters with Europe's New Right*. London: Picador.

Fukuyama, F. (1992) *The End of History and the Last Man*. London: Penguin.

Fukuyama, F. (2001) 'History beyond the end – even as we wage war against terrorism, market democracy will inevitably prevail', *The Australian*, 9 October 2001: 15.

Garland, D. (1994) 'Of crimes and criminals: the development of criminology in Britain', in M. Maguire, R. Morgan R. and Reiner (eds) *The Oxford Handbook of Criminology*. Oxford: Clarendon.

Garland, D. (1996) 'The limits of the sovereign state: strategies of crime control in contemporary society', *British Journal of Criminology*, 36(4): 445–71.

Glover, J. (2001) *Humanity – a Moral History of the Twentieth Century*. London: Pimlico.

Gourevitch, P. (2000) *We Wish to Inform You that Tomorrow We Will Be Killed with Our Families*. London: Picador.

Hall, J. and Paul, T. (1999) 'The State and the Future of World Politics', in T. Paul and J. Hall (eds), *International Order and the Future of World Politics*. Cambridge: Cambridge University Press.

Heisbourg, F. (1997) *The Future of Warfare*. London: Phoenix.

Hirst, P. and Thompson, G. (1996) *Globalisation in Question*. Cambridge: Polity Press.

Hirst, P. (undated) 'The International Origins of National Sovereignty'. Unpublished manuscript.

Hobbes, T. (1968) *Leviathan*. [1651] London: Penguin.

Hobsbawm, E. (1995) *Age of Extremes*. London: Abacus.

Hobsbawm, E. (1998) 'Barbarism: a user's guide', in *On History*. London: Abacus.

Hobsbawm, E. (2000) *The New Century*. London: Abacus.

Hogg, R. (1996) 'Criminological failure and governmental effect', *Current Issues in Criminal Justice*, 8(1): 43–58.

Hogg, R. (1998) 'Criminology, violence and the nation state', *Current Issues in Criminal Justice*, 9(3): 335–40.

Holsti, K. (1999) 'The coming chaos? Armed conflict in the world's periphery', in T. Paul and J. Hall (eds), *International Order and the Future of World Politics*. Cambridge: Cambridge University Press.

Huntington, S. (1998) *The Clash of Civilizations and the Remaking of World Order*. London: Touchstone Books.

Ignatieff, M. (1998) *The Warrior's Honour – Ethnic War and the Modern Conscience*. London: Chatto & Windus.

Jordan, B. (1996) *A Theory of Poverty and Social Exclusion*. Cambridge: Polity Press.

Juergensmeyer, M. (1993) *The New Cold War? Religious Nationalism Confronts the Secular State*. Berkeley, CA: University of California Press.

Kaplan, R. (1997) *The Ends of the Earth – a Journey at the Dawn of the 21st Century*. London: Papermac.

Keane, J. (1996) *Reflections on Violence*. London: Verso.

Landmine Monitor (2001) *Landmines in Afghanistan*. Landmine Monitor Fact Sheet, www.icbl.org/lm.

Lukes, S. and Scull, A. (eds) (1984) *Durkheim and the Law*. Oxford: Basil Blackwell.

Manne, R. (2001) 'Exclusionary nationalism', in P. Craven (ed.), *The Best Australian Essays 2001*. Melbourne: Black Inc.

Mares, P. (2001) *Borderline – Australia's Treatment of Refugees and Asylum Seekers*. Sydney: UNSW Press.

Markus, A. (2001) *Race – John Howard and the remaking of Australia*. Crows Nest: Allen & Unwin.

Mukherjee, S. and Graycar, A. (1997) *Crime and Justice in Australia 1997*, 2nd edn. Sydney: Hawkins Press.

O'Callaghan, M. (1999) *Enemies Within – Papua New Guinea, Australia, and the Sandline Crisis: the Inside Story*. Sydney: Doubleday.

Parsons, A. (1995) *From Cold War to Hot Peace – UN Interventions 1947–1995*. London: Penguin.

Paul, T. and Hall, J. (eds) (1999) *International Order and the Future of World Politics*. Cambridge: Cambridge University Press.

Peters, E. (1996) *Torture*, expanded edition. Philadelphia, PA: University of Pennsylvania Press.

Robertson, G. (2000) *Crimes Against Humanity – the Struggle for Global Justice*. Ringwood: Penguin.

Rorty, R. (1998) *Achieving our World*. Cambridge: Harvard University Press.

Rorty, R. (1999) *Philosophy and Social Hope*. London: Penguin.

Schwendinger, H. and Schwendinger, J. (1975) 'Defenders of order or guardians of human rights?', in J. Taylor, P. Walton, and J. Young (eds), *Critical Criminology*. London: Routledge & Kegan Paul.

Shawcross, W. (2000) *Deliver Us From Evil – Warlords and Peacekeepers in a World of Endless Conflict*. London: Bloomsbury.

Silber, L. and Little, A. (1995) *The Death of Yugoslavia*. London: Penguin and BBC Books.

Smith, D. (1997) *The State of War and Peace Atlas*, 3rd edn., London: Penguin.

Spierenburg, P. (1996) 'Long-term trends in homicide: theoretical reflections and dutch evidence, fifteenth to twentieth centuries', in E. Johnson and E. Monkkonen (eds), *The Civilization of Crime – Violence in Town and Country since the Middle Ages*. Urbana and Chicago, IL: University of Illinois Press.

Thompson, J. (1994) *Mercenaries, Pirates and Sovereigns*, Princeton, NJ: Princeton University Press.

van Creveld, M. (1999) *The Rise and Decline of the State*. Cambridge: Cambridge University Press.

van der Veer, P. (1999) 'Political religion in the twenty-first century', in T. Paul and J. Hall (eds) *International Order and the Future of World Politics*. Cambridge: Cambridge University Press.

Vidal-Naquet, P. (1963) *Torture: Cancer of Democracy*. London: Penguin.

Chapter 9

Left, right or straight ahead: contemporary prospects for progressive and critical criminology

Judith Bessant

Introduction

When I first began thinking about the theme of this book, the prospects for creating a politically committed and progressive criminology, I felt excited about the idea of writing a chapter. However, once I sat down and actually started thinking and writing, the task became increasingly complex. My initial reactions framed as questions were: Isn't conventional criminology beyond redemption? Where do we look now for working instances of a progressive politics? After all, what has changed in Australian criminology since O'Connor's survey of the discipline when he argued that:

> American and British developments [like] labelling, conflict theory and radical deviancy theory which occurred prior to and during the decade of publishing (1968–1977) were ignored [here]?
>
> (O'Connor, 1980: 16)

What has changed since O'Malley and Carson's survey at the end of the 1980s? They detected a few promising signs that Australian criminology was joining the '...modern mainstream of critical, radical and more theoretical criminology research' (O'Malley and Carson, 1989: 333). Yet they also noted that mainstream Australian criminology was still characterised by the fact that:

Conventional correctional and conservative criminology has enjoyed a very protracted period of intellectual and academic
hegemony in Australia, a longevity which can be highlighted by
using developments in the United Kingdom, where more radical
debate and theorisation have been fairly commonplace for some
time, as convenient benchmarks.

(O'Malley and Carson, 1989: 335)

And what of criminology in the United Kingdom with its 'critical, radical
and theoretical criminology research'? Rock's (1997) survey of British
criminology hardly justifies such a characterisation, a point compounded
by a reading of *The Oxford Handbook of Criminology* (Maguire, Morgan and
Reiner, 1997). Hasn't David Garland (1994: 18) indicted conventional
modern criminology seeing only a hegemonic and conventional
criminology based on an uneasy alliance between a 'governmental
project' and a 'science of causes'?[1] Garland's point is that in terms of
promoting a progressive political commitment, neither of these two
orientations, separately or together, are able to realise such an outcome.

Then I thought, what do we make of the prevailing claims that our
time is one characterised by the 'exhaustion of utopian possibilities'
(Habermas, 1989)? Moreover, hasn't the demise of 'actually existing
socialism' represented by the collapse of the USSR and the Eastern bloc of
states in 1991 confirmed that the long-standing 'crisis of Marxism'
(identified as such as early as the 1950s) was more than just a bad dose of
intellectual irritability? Doesn't the resurrection of 'economic liberalism',
talk about the 'end of history' and the convergence of the major political
parties evident in the rise of the 'Third Way' signify a real political and
intellectual crisis for the left?

This 'crisis of the left' is often connected to the rise of 'cultural studies',
postmodernism and Foucauldian tendencies in key social science
disciplines. These inclinations are generally seen as excessively theoretical, unintelligible, apolitical and ethically relativist and as such are
regarded by 'vintage radicals' like Stanley Cohen (2001) with suspicion –
if not total contempt.

Over the last two decades... a small but very articulate and elegant
section of the Western intelligentsia has been marketing – mostly
with good intentions, indeed usually in the name of 'radicalism' a
very different form of denial. Their leading product is brand name
'deconstructionist' and 'post-modernist' theory in which 'truth' and
'reality' are always placed in ironical inverted commas...

(Cohen, 2001: 280)[2]

Our time is said to be one of pessimism, splintered solidarities and 'self indulgent' postmodernists leaving many people wondering where to go from here. Given all this, can we begin talking about developing a contemporary progressive criminology and on what basis can we do so?

In this chapter I ask four related questions: How should contemporary criminology be characterised? Do the various critical traditions in criminology offer any prospect for developing a radical or progressive criminology? What role could 'postmodernist' social theory play in promoting a progressive project? Is there any potential in post-foundationalist frameworks for carving out new spaces for critique; can they generate new solidarities, and can they be tied to progressive social action? This also entails asking what is meant by progressive political theory and practice today.

To consider these questions I use a three-point heuristic in recognition of the fact that over the past few centuries critical scholars of various kinds have asked three questions: What is the nature of the reality we want to change? What kind of knowledge is likely to promote change in a liberatory direction? What role can/does power play in hindering or promoting liberatory change? Radical or progressive theorists have been preoccupied with reality, power and knowledge. They have been attentive to these areas because one of the obstacles to change is the way social power operates to maintain the status quo. So what is the state of play in contemporary conventional criminology?

The Problem of Contemporary Conventional Criminology

There are various ways contemporary criminology can be characterised, but whatever way it is portrayed it needs to acknowledge that mainstream or conventional criminology is almost exclusively empirical. It is a criminology whose proponents are suspicious of theory despite the numerous theoretical propositions inherent in their taken-for-granted formulations of research questions, themes and methods.

This criminology is practised by social scientists who take their primary categories ('crime', 'crime rates', 'violence', 'victims', etc.) for granted (Mukherjee, 1996).[3] They assume that the canons of 'proper social science' research are valid and useful for research. This involves assumptions about objectivity, value neutrality, the need for precise operationalisation of their concepts, the application of scientific method, and the best ways to collect and measure their data (see White and Haines, 1996). They argue that criminology is a respectable intellectual discipline, identifiable by activities like criminologists correcting each other's data and findings and by theoretical debate between advocates for the various paradigms like strain theory, subcultural theory, etc. (Hazlehurst, 1996). There is also an affirmation of the belief that governments, the media and the community value their practical and empirically credible reports on crime rates, patterns of offence, their measurements of risk and their recommendations on crime prevention.

The general self-identification of criminology as a practical discipline relies on assumptions (Sumner, 1994) that also underpin the work of apparently counter-traditions (see Wilson and Herrnstein, 1985; Braithwaite, 1989; Gottfredson and Hirschi, 1990). They include ontological assumptions that there is a single, unitary and consistent social order and/or moral consensus; that transgressions such as delinquency and crime can be accurately identified and measured against that social order; that transgressions like deviance and criminality are objective phenomena susceptible to scientific study; and that the characteristics that make behaviour deviant or criminal are inherent in behaviour. They also include the methodological assumption that crime and delinquency are coherent and discrete categories. Criminality is not seen as behaviour that is normative or relative to particular social contexts, nor is the observer seen as playing an important role in identifying the conduct as deviant. They also include the quest for a general theory of deviance or crime as a central objective for the discipline.

What are the prospects for retrieving or developing a critical progressive criminology from conventional criminology? If we examine the state of conventional criminology today the reply may not be good.[4] Anyone reading, for example, Garland's (1992) discussion of criminology as a government project and his observations about the limitations of empiricism informing the discipline would conclude that conventional criminology offers little to those wanting a vehicle for a liberatory project. This is also indicated by the fate of the critical criminologies of the 1960s and 1970s.

Many of the assumptions informing conventional criminology have been criticised from various opposing traditions. Sumner (1992), for example offers insights into critiques coming from the 'labelling theorists' (symbolic interactionists and social constructionists). Similarly critiques from the 'new criminology' (Taylor, Walton and Young, 1973) indicate why the above mentioned claims were untenable. However, despite those challenges, conventional criminology has more than survived – it has prospered.

The new criminologists' self-identification as left realists after critiquing the economic determinism of Marxist criminology may also have reassured mainstream criminologists that they were on the right track despite the assaults. Sumner's (1994) obituary of the 'sociology of deviance' showed why sociologists could no longer teach or research deviance in the old-fashioned way. Yet this denunciation too has had no apparent effect on conventional criminology.

This absence of reflexivity indicates no capacity on the part of proponents of conventional criminology to respond effectively to critique; it indicates a self-assurance about the virtues of their position which allows them to proceed regardless. If the critical traditions failed to rehabilitate criminology then, do they offer any prospects for a critical progressive criminology now?

The Critical Traditions and Prospects for a Critical Progressive Criminology

There was a succession of critical assaults on conventional criminology. The symbolic interactionists drew on a long-standing interpretive tradition as they undermined the positivist foundations of conventional criminology. The neo-Marxist critique of the orthodoxy, particularly with the 'new criminology' (Taylor, Walton and Young, 1973) paralleled feminist criminology in the 1970s. These developments raise questions about whether the critiques offered provide a basis for a contemporary progressive theory and practice. Among other things these critical traditions were intended as subversive of the prevailing orthodox claims about three issues:

- the nature of reality, particularly the relationship between 'crime' and 'social order';

- the nature of disciplinary or social scientific knowledge that involved a challenge to the prevailing 'realism' of the discipline;

- the problem of power.

Each of the critical traditions responded to these questions differently.

The symbolic interactionists

The symbolic interactionists[5] undermined the naturalist and objectivist underpinnings of the empirical positivist orthodoxy's account of social reality and social behaviour. Unlike the orthodox account of society as an objective reality, symbolic interactionists saw social reality as constructed in and through social interactions and social institutions. These interactions they argued are constructed symbolically, especially through language. For symbolic interactionists, social reality is what people describe as real through their interactions. Social action and social reality arise from meanings being given to events and objects, and on agreements about those meanings. Thus a criminal act is not an objective phenomenon, but is made into a criminal act because of the definitions and meanings given to it. For the symbolic interactionists crime was the result of people making choices and interpreting the world in various ways.

Theoretically, symbolic interactionists were opposed to macro-level analyses and rejected structural explanations and categories (i.e. alienation, class, structure, deviance). This entailed a critique of conventional criminology's preoccupation with identifying 'societal' and 'structural' factors said to force people into transgressing boundaries that marked social consensus. They rejected claims that the criminal resulted from ineffectual socialisation, family pathology and social disorganisation. For Garfinkel these categories were pointless, and he suggested that social scientists could spend their time more productively if they studied how people create realities through language categories (Garfinkel, 1967).

For symbolic interactionists, knowledge-making is an ethnographic and interpretative exercise. Methodologically symbolic interactionists rejected the analysis of social facts and preferred participant observation applied to micro-analyses of social interactions between 'social control agents' and 'deviants'.

Power was understood as operating at micro levels in the construction of 'deviant' or 'criminal' actions. Theorists like Becker (1963) and Goffman (1968) redefined concepts central to criminology (i.e. 'the criminal' and 'crime'), treating them not as objective givens but as the consequence of micro-political acts. Rather than being inherent in an act, crime resulted from certain people assuming a policing role and acting as agents of social control. It was they who labelled or observed others and subsequently defined them as criminal. Moral and legal concepts, conventionally known as natural, came to be seen as the product of definite social and political institutional processes (Sumner, 1994: 203).

In many ways the philosophical approach of the symbolic interactionists was close to that of contemporary post-foundationalists. Both, for example, discard the traditional preoccupation with epistemological foundations, emphasising instead how social practices embedded in language provide the discursive basis for knowledge claims.

Marxists and 'the New Criminology'

In the early 1970s when academic Marxism was at its peak, Ian Taylor, Paul Walton and Jock Young published *The New Criminology* (1973). They were self-declared radical members of England's New Left and the National Deviancy Conference (NDC). Muncie describes their work as an:

> ...attack on traditional positivist and correctionalist criminology, arguing that this tradition acted as little more than an academic justification for the existing discriminatory practices in the penal and criminal justice systems...[It] sought to illustrate how crime was politically and economically constructed through the capacity and ability of state institutions within the political economy of advanced capitalism, to define and confer criminality on others.
>
> (Muncie, 1998: 221)

Taylor, Walton and Young claimed their intervention was a left project intended to reveal the political processes underlying deviance and crime. They were critical of the correctionalist bias in conventional criminology and sought a more sociologically informed theoretical framework for criminology that was free from the psychological and biological assumptions of traditional social sciences and conventional criminology.

Taylor, Walton and Young sought to politicise criminology (Muncie, 1998: 279). Their critique of earlier criminology was cutting. Like the symbolic interactionists, the new criminologists rejected conventional criminology and the assumption that crime was objective (that it identified individual pathology caused by biological, psychosociological factors and constituted an offence against a normative consensus). They also rejected conventional Marxism's economic determinist, reductionist explanations of criminal conduct which argued that crime was the product of 'the dangerous classes', a 'lumpenproletariat' or what is now called the 'underclass' (Taylor, Walton and Young, 1973: 209–36).

They claimed to seek a complete overhaul of the social theory of deviance (1973: 279) which would involve constructing a 'political economy of criminal action', that moved 'criminology out of its own imprisonment'. However, what they offered in place of the orthodoxy was a brief plan of the elements of a 'new criminology'. In the final chapter of *The New Criminology* they outlined the elements of a 'fully social theory of deviance' which encompassed both the wider and the immediate origins of deviant action, social reaction and the dynamics and effects of the deviant process as a whole. This ambitious agenda combined political economy and social psychology, structure and agency and action and reaction (Taylor, Walton and Young, 1973: 270–8).

In developing their theory for a 'new criminology', Taylor, Walton and Young identified the following key specifications (Young, 1997: 24). People, they argued, are determined and determining in the context of a plural and diverse society. Society is class based and divided by inequalities of wealth and power. Any theory of crime will be a sequential process model that is also historical. There is a dialectic between structure and consciousness that relates to motives (consciousness and ideology) which are situated actions (in specific historical contexts). A holistic view of society and the individual is required. A theory must offer the same explanations of social reaction and action to both the theorist and her/his object of study. The theory should also be empirically based and able to explain various forms of deviancy.

The major problem with their approach was that, having rejected the older structuralist, objectivist and economic reductionist Marxism (Taylor, Walton and Young, 1973: 209–10), how would they present an alternative? It was not clear how (without restating old economic reductionist explanations) they would develop a different criminology that showed how '... historical periods, characterized by particular sets of social relationships and means of production, give rise to attempts by the economically and socially powerful to order society in particular ways' (Taylor, Walton and Young, 1973: 220).

The alternative sketched at the end of *The New Criminology* remained undeveloped. Instead, within a few years Jock Young, in particular, was signalling what would be his later move in the direction of 'left realism' and an acceptance that conventional criminology had two features worth holding on to: crime was real and it was amenable to causal explanation explicable in terms of a causal theory (Young, 1977, 1979). It is also a concern that they failed to acknowledge the role of women and the rise of the women's movement which by the 1970s had emerged as a formidable and popular social movement.

Feminist criminology

Unlike the 'new criminology' of the 1970s, feminist criminology as a radical tradition has not only survived, but also continues to be an important contributor to ongoing debates. This is partly due to the political diversity and dynamics of feminism itself. Contemporary feminist criminology includes a full range of contesting theoretical positions – liberal feminism, Marxist and socialist feminism, radical or separatist feminism and post-feminism. Unlike the new criminologists who were largely located in universities and who conceived their practice in traditional academic terms, many academic feminists have maintained effective links with the women's movement (Gelsthorpe and Morris, 1988). They have been active and effective in developing anti-sexist positions and alternative politics, policies, methodologies and discourses.

Accepting the heterogeneity of contemporary feminism and feminist criminology, most feminists do share a commitment to challenging the epistemological, ontological, moral and political assumptions that inform 'patriarchal' discourses. Indeed the variety of theoretical positions informing feminist engagements with criminology has dramatically increased the diversity of interventions – including the complete repudiation of criminology (Stanko, 1993; Smart, 1989). The first wave of feminist critiques of criminology (Smart, 1976) was succeeded by a heterogeneous array of feminist investigations covering victimology (McCarthy, 1997), women's imprisonment (Howe, 1994; Cook and Davies, 1999), violence against women (Smart and Smart, 1978; Carrington, 1998; Easteal, 1992) and judicial bias (Scutt, 1995), to mention just a few.

When feminists discuss social reality the focus tends to be on gender relations and sexual divisions of labour. When feminists engage in criminology more attention is paid to the way women as victims and criminals are disregarded and/or misrepresented (Smart, 1976; Carrington, 1993; Cain, 1989; Heidensohn, 1985; Cain, 1989; Gelsthorpe, 1989). For feminists these problems cannot be corrected just by 'inserting' the word 'woman' or 'girl' into existing criminological theories, but require entirely different approaches to knowledge that are sensitive to issues of gender.

Postmodernist feminists reject the idea that patriarchal structures force men and women into simple or clear gender roles, emphasising instead participation in the gendering practices of identity formation. Postmodernist feminists like Walby (1992) and Nicholson (1990) also reject the idea of a 'natural' or 'normal' female 'character' because such approaches disregard the diversity of women's experiences. They question too the notion that feminists can provide an all-encompassing explanation of women's oppression and prescribe overarching solutions to that persecution (Tong, 1989).

Feminist critiques of criminology have presented substantial epistemological challenges to conventional research methodologies (Kelly, 1992; Stanko, 1985). While most feminists are critical of mainstream – or what some call 'male-stream' – knowledge and research and see their job as providing critical analysis, many also engage in emancipatory practices that support women. (See Chapter 5 by Carrington in this volume for a fuller account of the history and dynamics of feminist criminology and its problematic engagement with critical criminology.)

What then of another critical tradition usually referred to as postmodernism?

Post-foundationalism

What is conventionally referred to as 'postmodernism' has since the 1970s acquired considerable space and authority in the university. Here I refer to 'post-foundationalism' rather than 'postmodernism' and poststructuralism. One reason for this is the heterogeneity of contemporary intellectual currents contributing to a post-foundationalist movement. It incorporates North American pragmatism, poststructuralism, deconstructionism and postmodernism as well as post-colonialism and post-feminism,[6] encompassing a diverse range of writers (e.g. Nietzsche, Saussure, William James, bell hooks, Bahktin and Wittgenstein).

It is also important to note that what is now commonly referred to as postmodernism is not that new. The full impact of these interventions may be relatively recent, but this movement draws on a long tradition of scepticism connected to democratic and anti-authoritarian projects. Indeed, although it is customary to see it as an anti-Enlightenment movement, it draws on the scepticism evident among Enlightenment philosophers like Diderot and Rousseau who were questioning relationships between knowledge claims and power. Kant too was an anti-foundationalist who investigated the constitutive character of knowledge.

It would be fair to say that criminology is one of the social sciences that has been influenced least by post-foundationalism. Most criminologists continue working as modernists. However, despite this general resistance a small number of criminologists have drawn on post-foundationalist ideas. Fattah (1997), for example, offers a critique of modernist criminology combining a post-foundationalist scepticism linked to a humanist ethic. Others have explored the implications of post-foundationalism criticising and renovating conventional criminology (see Henry and Milovanovic, 1991; Hunt, 1991; Young, 1997; Howe, 1994; Carrington, 1993, 1997). Post-foundationalist ideas are also apparent in related areas like socio-legal studies, feminist theory and the sociology of deviance.

Acknowledging the difficulties of general statements about this variegated group it is reasonable to say there are common themes (elaborated below) and reason for optimism in seeing post-foundationalist thought as an important resource for reworking democratic social theory and politics.

1. Although post-foundationalists are often accused of denying the existence of an external or material reality, what they share is a rejection of the idea that reality determines knowledge. They share scepticism about claims that knowledge is gained through direct correspondence with reality.

227

2. Those working from a post-foundationalist position can be recognised by their suspicion of common-sense or taken-for-granted knowledge. This means they dispute conventional knowledge claims of objectivity evident in their suggestions that the categories we operate with do not necessarily refer to actual material things, but are negotiated and constituted. They argue for example that categories like 'crime' and 'unemployment' are the outcome of constitutive epistemological practices in which the exercise of power is apparent.

3. There is a common claim by post-foundationalists that knowledge reflects various 'truth practices' (see Wittgenstein's language games), and that those truths and knowledge claims are embedded in discourses in which no foundational point of reference can be found to arbitrate between the contesting claims (Rorty, 1999: 23–46).

4. There is a shared suspicion of authoritative knowledge represented as such because it is objective and produced by scientific rational procedures. Such knowledge claims, it is argued, reflect the operation of social power.

5. They reject the idea that a set of knowledge claims can be produced that accurately reflect reality. This view leads to misgivings on the part of post-foundationalists about general social or political claims based on metanarratives including those relating to class structure or gender structure. Following from this is Foucault's rejection of the idea that there is a single flow or quantity of power unequally distributed; rather power is seen to be everywhere and is manifested in micro-situations.

6. Writers like Foucault (1980) and others also identified the ways modern states draw on the technologies of the social sciences in securing knowledge of the population and the resources available to them. The collection of economic and social statistics and the dependence of government on the social sciences reflects this necessity. This will-to-power by governments or *bio-power* is what Foucault refers to when demonstrating how governments, from the seventeenth century on, measured and regulated their populations. For poststructuralists the social sciences play a critical role in ensuring states secure their authority and political legitimacy. *Bio-power* as the product of research on the well-being of the population has been heavily drawn upon by modern governments, evident for example in the emergence of scientific criminology in the latter part of the nineteenth century.

7. As well as doubts about the objectivity of knowledge and categories, post-foundationalists query the claim central to mainstream criminology – namely that the social or moral order is a coherent, binding set of commonly shared values and beliefs. They argue that moral order is the outcome of power relations embedded in certain practices of governance and claims to truth. For criminology this acknowledgement means categories like 'criminal', 'deviance', 'the crime rate' are ways of knowing that are specific to our culture. For theorists like Foucault these knowledges are used to identify, define, categorise and regulate people as irrational, normal and abnormal elements in the population.

8. The emphasis on differences, the idea of multiple knowledges and a rejection of ideas about a single flow of power is what sustains a suspicion of Marxists, positivists and orthodox forms of social sciences, and indeed most Enlightenment beliefs in reason and progress (see Harvey, 1989). This is part of the critique about the ways powerful elites use empirical and rational technologies to support their own political-moral position, or simply to legitimate the way things already are.

Where To From Here?

The task remains to address the question: what options are there for those interested in left or progressive social action? With post-foundationalism in mind, there are two separate questions. What is the potential of post-foundationalist epistemologies in carving out new spaces for critique? This question raises the issue of its role in supporting a theoretical and critical project. Is the kind of critique post-foundationalists represent useful for developing a progressive political project? A second question relates to its capacity in terms of informing political action about issues like inequality, racism, injustice, sexism or ageism. This question is also concerned with whether post-foundationalism can help generate solidarities or links with groups engaged in progressive social action.

At this point it is worth noting that the post-foundationalist position has become the frequent target of attack for more conventional and conservative criminologists who see such challenges as not only irreverent, but apolitical, abstract and ephemeral. It is frequently asserted that a key weakness of post-foundationalists is their failure to accept the 'objectivity of reality' and that their writing and research is not embedded in the actual or 'material' world. This, it is argued, renders the post-foundationalist approaches ethically nihilist and thereby morally inferior to other metanarratives, which by implication have clear and practical political agendas. Cohen complains that the postmodernist and poststructuralist position is one where 'morality and values are relativistic, culturally specific, and lacking any universal force' (Cohen, 2001: 280).

To argue this is to miss the points made about the cultural and historical specificity of knowledge. I agree with Cohen that some writers working under the banner of postmodernism take their arguments to ridiculous extremes, claiming nothing is real and nothing can be empirically demonstrated. Thus all accounts of an event including complete denials of their existence have equal weight. Such claims are not only foolish, they are dangerous and ethically void. However, because some writers take aspects of post-foundationalist thinking to such absurd extremes should not mean ignoring the numerous features of post-foundationalist thinking that can be allied to progressive politics.

I argue that post-foundationalist thinking offers a range of valuable opportunities for critical theory and social action. I reiterate that this acknowledgement does not mean I advocate a wholesale acceptance of post-foundationalism. Rather it is a recognition that there are numerous features of post-foundationalism that are helpful for developing a theoretically committed criminology, not least of which is the constructive value of critique. I now briefly identify those features of post-foundationalism.

Power, Reality and Knowledge

If the task is to reveal the operations of power relations then one way of achieving this is by challenging the idea that reality objectively shapes our knowledge about 'the material world'. This can be achieved through a critical analysis of language and larger pattern of discourses. For a post-foundationalist, meanings given to an event, a group or individual are *always* contestable. Thus the way we use language opens a central and highly political area of critique, dispute and progressive change. Suspicion of common-sense knowledge involves contesting knowledge claims based on conventional models of objectivity.

The politics of discourse is a political struggle that can reveal exercises of power across a range of social practices and institutions. As Foucault argued:

discourse is not that which translates struggles ... but is the thing for which there is struggle, discourse is the power which is seized.

(Foucault, 1984: 110)

This approach involves more than simply subverting particular forms of power. It involves pointing to alternative realities, sets of practices and meanings. For example, the 'harsh material realities of poverty' can become 'outlawing factors' that constitute crime. Power to create and change reality can be contested; it can generate new ways of knowing that involve deciding what counts as real, as a crime, as a criminal, delinquent and as true.

The politics of discourse also involves engaging in the politics of inclusion and exclusion, and in challenging certain categories reliant on essentialist thinking. Post-foundationalists point out that essentialism is a type of inquiry where an entity or set of practices comes to be known in terms of an assumed essence or basic nature said to be shared by all who belong to the groups in question. Often this involves inventing or exaggerating a quality or trait, then applying it to all members of the group. Essentialist categories assume a level of sameness that usually does not exist. Why is this problematic in terms of a progressive or critical theory? Essentialism frequently involves careless thinking, and the application of perceived characteristics and expectations about a group that more often than not have little if any relationship to the complexity of their lives and how they see themselves (Butler, 1990). Essentialist categories fail to pass any normal tests of verifiability confirming that one or a set of identifiable features can be assigned to all members of the group. Typically essentialist categories that underwrite most conventional conservative and radical criminology involve the imposition of a collective identity on group/s, many of whom may share little if anything in common.[7]

Post-foundationalists are sceptical of essentialising categories that have traditionally been central to various forms of governance as well as to liberatory projects which presuppose that the liberators know what is best for those they are supposedly liberating. This raises awkward questions about, for example, the role of 'middle-class', 'white' and predominantly 'male reformers' who assume to know what others want and need as they work for the liberation of Aboriginal people, 'the working class', young people, women, etc. For post-foundationalists such categories rely on assumptions and particular metanarratives which can be as politically dangerous and counterproductive for those being emancipated. As feminists and many others have demonstrated, the constitution of particular categories can have an extremely disempowering effect. We need only look at the work of feminist criminologists like Carrington to appreciate the political value in the deconstruction of categories like youth in terms of young female offenders (Carrington, 1993). This critique and insight opens space for new interventions that are different from those identified in conventional Marxist and essentialist feminist paradigms.

The women's movement has shifted from its earlier 'structuralist' and singularist accounts of power which involved relinquishing or to some degree dissolving the traditional determinism which held that 'patri-archal power structures' oppressed all women uniformly. Among other things, this shift involved acknowledging differences between women that positions them very diversely in terms of gender politics. For many feminists this has meant identifying and involving women who are differently positioned (as indigenous, ethnic, disabled, lesbian, etc.) to produce numerous feminisms that identify people in relation to ethnicity, gender, sexuality and so on. Post-foundationalist feminism does not depend on an essentialist understanding of power or of identity. Rather it encourages a form of political contestation that is open to the diversity in women's lives that can matter as much as being a woman (Butler, 1990; Brooks, 1997; Hopkins, 1999).

Like essentialist categories, conventional understandings of power have been challenged by post-foundationalists. As O'Malley observed that the 'discovery of the social' left its stamp on social liberals, social democrats and Bolsheviks. The social entailed 'the constitution of [society as] a collective entity with properties that could not be reduced to its individual constituents' (O'Malley, 1996: 4). Such an account of the social informed conventional understandings of power represented as a social-systemic, hierarchical structure located in a few concentrated sites like the state or the structural arrangement of economic resources. Post-foundationalists do not conceive power as a quantifiable good that flows in a hierarchical top-down way. For many post-foundationalists power is everywhere, is exercised in micro-settings and through technical means in specific institutional sites, and is recognised for its negative as well as its enabling capacities. Compared to conventional accounts of power, post-foundationalists have a greater appreciation of the diverse forms it can take and greater awareness of the multiplicity of sites in which it is exercised and found. This recognition alone increases the possibilities for a more strategic kind of politics.

Post-foundationalists have a keen interest in addressing the role of modern government in the management of populations – or what Foucault called 'bio-politics'. As Durkheim observed in the 1890s, 'modern societies' were becoming more state-centric (see also Cerny,

1990). And as Yeatman (1990) points out, modern 'state-centric' modes of managing populations need to make the production of policies and interventions into our lives seem natural. The state's management projects involve problematising parts of the population which thereby highlights its jurisdictional reach. For Yeatman the contemporary proliferation of policies is the result of an increasing complexity of society.

> This complexity results from, [even] as it creates, a plurality and fragmentation of voices which seek to be heard within the policy process.
>
> (Yeatman, 1990: 154)

We now see a multiplication of interests indicating how different identities are created and framed by the increasingly complex management tasks facing any contemporary nation-state.

Post-foundationalists propose different accounts of policy-making to more conventional models associated with the liberal tradition of social administration. The liberal tradition saw policy-making as a rational process informed by the 'discovery' of social problems. Its proponents spoke of a funnel of causality where truth and knowledge flowed from the broadest possible level (i.e. socio-economic structures) mediated by patterns of power, culture and ideology and institutions where it was contested, slowly moving on and narrowing down to policy-making processes, producing specific policies.

Feminist theorists like Pateman (1987) along with poststructuralists such as Foucault and Yeatman (1990) have developed new ways of understanding the historical sociology of the state. Post-foundationalists suggest rather than tracking a 'rational' process of policy-making – involving the 'discovery' of social problems – that attention be paid to the character of language and particularly the use of metaphor when explaining policy as discursive activity (Schon, 1980: 255).

Out of these divergent strands has come the 'policy community model' of policy studies (Brooks, 1994). For Brooks this model offers a good way of studying political interest groups because it accepts that policy-making is a fragmented process and because it avoids grand macro-level theorisation (Brooks, 1994; Heclo and Masden, 1987). One of the important aspects of the policy community approach to policy is the way it theorises the role of the intellectually and professionally trained in constructing the problem.

If we appreciate the social and the historical processes that constitute policy processes, then there is value in analysing and contesting the discursive framing of policy problems and solutions. From this perspective, if we are serious about identifying power relations and contesting the way things are, then the necessity to challenge particular dominant discourses becomes an apparent, even urgent task. Thus part of a critical and progressive strategy involves the systematic deconstruction of many social categories thereby revealing power relations that constituted specific particular renderings of reality. The task in deconstructing discourse is to unravel the unseen and overt intentions of those claiming legitimacy or a particular expertise or knowledge over others.

In this way the policy community model helps reveal the exercise of power in the constitutive production of crime problems. Questioning the objectivity of the problem challenges its natural status as it is described and contests the power of those doing the reporting. Recognising the role of the intellectually trained in constituting social problems and responses within a policy-making community also helps open space for political engagement.

I have identified the value of a post-foundationalism that acknowledges a critical and sceptical role for those committed to progressive politics. But what of progressive politics? I now turn to a discussion of this question.

What Is Meant By Progressive Political Theory and Practice Today?

By progressive politics I mean a theory and practice that recognises experiences of injustice and oppression and that continues to refer to principles such as justice and fairness. It is a position that recognises how many people continue to face exploitation, how many continue to be subject to prejudices that injure and disempower them, and how many people are excluded economically, oppressed politically and suffer in major ways diminished life opportunities. A contemporary progressive politics recognises that these circumstances need to be transformed.

In considering the prospects for reconstituting a progressive politics, it is worth asking if there is value in attempting to revive the political theories and practices associated with Marx. The critiques of Marxist/ Bolshevik theories and sets of practice that came from poststructuralist and postmodernist critics were largely well founded. They questioned the idea that metanarratives about reason and class struggle as the key to history and modernity were credible. Too many progressive intellectual and political projects in the West after 1917 accepted the idea that socialism could and did actually exist. Too many progressives failed to question taken-for-granted claims that critique merely involved documenting the abuses and inequities within an unjust social order that was already on a path towards an inevitable revolutionary encounter with history.

Marx's theoretical work (1844–83) also had a basic problem – it had no politics in terms of strategies for action and had terrible gender politics. Lenin on the other hand after 1917 was excessively political in promoting an extreme form of political action where anything judged necessary for realising the proletarian revolution was deemed acceptable. The Bolsheviks' subsequent 'successful politics' depended on the mobilisation of widespread terror and state power to accomplish whatever the Bolshevik leadership defined as desirable and/or inevitable. Indeed the establishment of 'socialist' regimes in the wake of Marx's theories and Lenin's politics were uneven and in some cases unacceptable as a model of 'best progressive practice'. While it has become customary since the collapse of the USSR in October 1991 to declare that this brought an end to progressive socialist or left politics, some things are worth remembering.

Acknowledging some of the problems and criticisms associated with metanarratives about the history of liberty and democracy, I suggest that contemporary progressive politics needs to include a commitment to the continuing radicalisation of democratic politics. This may mean, for example, the promotion and extension of ideas about citizenship, ecological viability, etc., while seeking within these confines a broad and inclusive alliance between a diversity of groups who define themselves in terms of the above mentioned politics.

Notwithstanding the effects of the Comintern and the deformations of domestic politics wrought by defenders of Soviet, Sino and other 'socialist' regimes, it is worth remembering there always existed a much wider range of progressive political practices and ideas throughout the twentieth century than was encompassed by the Bolshevik et al. models of progressive politics. There is much to be gleaned from the continuing theories and practices represented in other expressions of progressive politics – such as the union movement, the women's movements, the social democratic and Labour parties. After all, wasn't the creation of the Australian Labour Party an extension of a social movement that evolved thanks to labour breakaways in the late 1800s from the liberals, free traders or protectionists who had represented them? There are also social movements, including the peace, environmental and civil rights movements, the anti-colonial campaigns, and church and community-based movements for international cooperation and development.

I also argue against the lament of those grieving for what they see as the loss of utopian activity – a golden past or future (Habermas, 1989), as well as the determinist accounts of globalisation (Watts, 2000). There is good reason for optimism rather than a lack of expectation and pessimism given the continuing viability and vitality of social movements (S11 and ongoing campaigns against Australia's refugee policies etc.) and increasing evidence of the political demise, intellectual debility and numerous dysfunctions emerging from the 'success' of 'economic liberal' policies and practices since the 1970s.

The prospects for social action can be identified in part by acknowledging the importance of such pre-existing organisations and the availability of recruitment and communication networks, and other resources such as information, money and expertise. This suggests a need to broaden our idea about the sphere of politics. I use the term 'politics' in ways that point beyond politics as just institutional politics, the formal political parties and policy processes sustained and managed by the state. This is not to deny the important role of such political activity in creating change, it is only to say that I am thinking of a broader notion of politics. More specifically, I include the 'pre-political' terrain of activities in everyday life, various cultural identities and forms of politics (e.g. youth culture) not traditionally recognised as political. This broader notion of what is understood as political has the advantage of recognising the complexity of issues, groups, interests and modes of interaction in which power is present and exercised to achieve certain effects.

There is also the role of the university and, more generally, the intellectually trained to consider. Despite recent assaults on most universities and their inherent conservatism, universities and academics have a major part to play in the development of progressive politics. This capacity was most evident in the 1960s when university staff and students aligned with social movements such as the peace movement and anti-Vietnam, anti-conscription, women's, gay and black rights movements (see Chapter 3 in this volume for one such detailed account). Without advocating a return to the past, I argue that academics working in today's universities have opportunities to generate progressive forms of political action. This can occur through teaching in undergraduate and postgraduate programmes, through writing and knowledge-making. Also, if we are to understand the constitutive role of the intellectually trained in policy-making and politics, then university academic staff have the potential to tie their scholarly activities to progressive social action. In other words, university teachers have considerable capacity to shape the public and political agenda. Finally, universities have the capacity to help generate progressive politics through what has generally come to be called 'community outreach', that is through alliances with other groups and organisations (unions, community groups and government).

Conclusion

To return to the question I set out to address in this chapter: where do we begin in talking about progressive politics? As indicated at the start of this chapter, if one of the biggest obstacles to change is the way things already are, then we could be in trouble. As my earlier characterisation of conventional and alternative radical-new criminology indicates, they are largely antithetical to any prospect of progressive politics. Feminism is, however, an exception. It holds out considerable hope partly because many feminists persistently engage with a major social movement as well as with the theoretical challenges posed by post-foundationalist ideas.

Post-foundationalist frameworks can help carve out new spaces for critique and can generate new solidarities tied to progressive social action. Post-foundationalists contest conventional criminological claims to know thereby revealing the exercise of certain forms of power. They question the idea that reality objectively shapes our knowledge about offenders, imprisonment, crime rates, delinquents and so on. This opens opportunities to construct alternative readings while undermining the authority of traditional knowledge-makers. And, given functionalist positivist criminology's allegiance to conservative political interests, this in itself is a progressive political act.

Post-foundationalists understand power in ways that appreciate both its negative and enabling effects. They recognise its technical means and offer an appreciation of the multiplicity of sites in which power is exercised as well as the diversity of forms it can take.

The Foucauldian preference not to separate theory from practice means theorising, research, teaching and indeed any activity related to the knowledge-making process is political; it means the theoretical is linked to, indeed is, political action. Theory informs ways of seeing and doing; it shapes policy, practice and political action in the broad cultural sense of the term. A political commitment to progressive social change also needs to be seen as part of scholarship and other academic practices. What is needed is the continuation of epistemological and methodological projects that challenge and deconstruct the meanings and truth claims of dominant criminological discourses.

Most urgently needed is an enhancement of humanism without accepting the paradigms traditionally allied to humanism. This requires an ability and will to think critically and act progressively. To say what a progressive criminology might look like involves talking about theories and practices concerned with injustices, oppression, exploitation and exclusion. It means continuing as part of our academic agenda the deconstruction and retheorisation of problematic relations between certain groups, crime, justice and equity. This entails continuing to deconstruct dominant knowledge forms about 'crime'. This involves a conscious effort not to be too self-referential, to actively involve the perspectives of those usually excluded from theorising, knowledge-making and practice. It involves a continued commitment to democratic politics, alliances with social movements and the politicisation of universities.

Notes

1. By the 'governmental project' Garland (1994) meant the empirical inquiries which sought to enhance the administration of justice by charting the patterns of crime and monitoring the practices of police and prisons (Garland, 1994: 18). The 'science of causes' aimed to develop an aetiological, explanatory science based on the assumption that criminals can be differentiated from non-criminals (Garland, 1994:18).
2. The likelihood that Cohen may have changed his mind about this is indicated in his statement in the early 1990s that: 'I do not believe that criminology is ready for the massive reordering of its intellectual history that Foucault's theory demands' (Cohen, 1992: 257), while simultaneously (1997) censuring post-modernists.
3. Mukherjee (1996) is an example of a critical empiricist who accepts there are technical or jurisdictional problems with the processes of data gathering but goes no further.
4. In Hazlehurst (1996) a conventional left-liberalism is evident, while in White and Haines (1996) are echoes of a traditional left sensibility. This, however, is compromised by an unwillingness in my view to question the framework of conventional criminology.
5. By 'symbolic interactionism' I refer to a diverse set of sociological themes and approaches found *inter alia* in the work of sociologist Howard Becker (1963) and David Matza (1969). Some emphasised the various aspects of the symbolic nature of social interaction and the idea that social reality is constructed by people, while others drew on phenomenologists (i.e., Schutz, 1972; Berger and Luckmann, 1969) concerned with how people experienced their social relation-ships and life. This paralleled Garfinkel's (1979) 'ethnomethodology', while others such as Howard Becker (1963) and Erving Goffman (1959) identified themselves as 'labelling theorists'. While acknowledging the important differences between them I refer to them collectively as 'symbolic interac-tionists'.
6. This movement or set of traditions included poststructuralists, postmodernists and deconstructionists like Roland Barthes, Jean-François Lyotard, Jean Baudrillard, Michel Foucault, Terry Eagleton and Frederic Jameson.
7. In response to some feminist interventions it has been suggested that the experiences of 'white, affluent, western' women are very different from those of women living in villages such as in Morocco or Rwanda. Similarly in discussions

about radical penal politics writers like Spivak (1988), Carlen (1985, 1990), Smart (1989) and Howe (1994) discuss the politics of letting women prisoners speak for themselves. This means we need to struggle with the problem of claims of 'the oppressed' to speak for themselves, a claim that renounces any representation from outsiders. This raises questions of conscience and ethics: how ought we act as observers of acts that cause significant harm to others.

References

Australian Bureau of Statistics (2000) *Australian Social Trends 2000*. ABS, Catalogue No. 4102.0.

Becker, H. (1963) *Outsiders – Studies in the Sociology of Deviance*. New York: Free Press.

Berger, P. and Luckmann. T. (1969) *The Social Construction of Reality*. London: Penguin.

Best, S. and Kellner, D. (1992) *Postmodern Theory: Critical Interrogations*. London: Macmillan.

Braithwaite, J. (1989) *Crime, Shame and Reintegration*. Melbourne: Cambridge University Press.

Brooks, A. (1997) *Post-feminism: Feminism, Cultural Theory and Cultural Forms*. London: Routledge.

Brooks, S. (1994) 'Policy communities and the social sciences', in S. Brooks and A. G. Gagnon (eds), *The Political Influence of Ideas*. Westport, CT: Prager.

Butler, J. (1990) *Gender Trouble: Feminism and the Subversion Identity*. New York: Routledge.

Cain, M. (1989) 'Realism, Femininsm, Methodology and Law', *International Journal of the Sociology of Law*, 18(1): 1–18.

Carcash, C. and Grant, A. (2000) *Australian Corrections; Main Demographic Characteristics of Prison Populations, Trends and Issues Paper No. 150*. Canberra: Australian Institute of Criminology.

Carlen, P. (1985) *Criminal Women*. Cambridge: Polity Press.

Carlen, P. (1990) *Alternatives to Women's Imprisonment*. Buckingham: Open University Press.

Carrington, K. (1993) *Offending Girls*. Sydney: Allen & Unwin.

Carrington, K. (1997) 'Postmodernism and feminist criminologies': fragmenting the criminological subject', in P. Walton and J. Young (eds), *The New Criminology Revisited*. London: Macmillan.

Carrington, K. (1998) *Who Killed Leigh Leigh?: A Story of Shame and Mateship in an Australian Town*. Sydney: Random House.

Cerny, P. (1990) *The Structure of Politics*. San Francisco, CA: Sage.

Cicourel, A. (1968) *The Social Organisation of Juvenile Justice*. London: Heinemann.

Clark, K. and Holquist, M. (1984) *Mikhail Bahktin*. Cambridge, MA: Belknap Press, Harvard University.

Cohen, S. (1992) *Against Criminology*. New Brunswick, NJ: Transaction.

Cohen, S. (1997) 'Intellectual scepticism and political commitment: the case of radical criminology', in P. Walton and J. Young (eds), *The New Criminology Revisited*. London: Macmillan.

Cohen, S. (2001) *States of Denial: Knowing about Atrocities and Suffering*. Cambridge: Polity Press.

Cook, S. and Davies, S. (1999) *Harsh Punishment: International Experiences of Women's Imprisonment*. Boston, MA: North University Press.

Easteal, P. (1992) 'Battered woman syndrome: What is reasonable?', *Alternative Law Journal*, 17: 220–4.

Fattah, E. (1997) *Criminology: Past Present and Future*. London: Macmillan.

Foucault, M. (1984) 'The order of discourse', in M. Shapiro (ed.), *Language and Politics*. New York: New York University Press.

Garfinkel, H. (1967) *Studies in Ethnomethodology*. Englewood Cliffs, NJ: Prentice Hall.

Garland, D. (1990) *Punishment and Modern Society: A Study in Social Theory*. Oxford: Oxford University Press.

Garland, D. (1992) 'Criminological knowledge and its relation to power', *British Journal of Criminology*, 32(4): 403–22.

Garland, D. (1994) 'Of Crimes and Criminals: the Development of Criminology in Britain' in M. McGuire, R. Morgan and R. Reiner (eds), *The Oxford Handbook of Criminology*, 2nd edn. Oxford: Clarendon Press.

Gelsthorpe, L. (1989) *Sexism and the Female Offender*. Aldershot: Gower.

Gelsthorpe, L. and Morris, A. (1988) 'Feminism and criminology in Britain', *British Journal of Criminology*, 28: 93–110.

Goffman, E. (1959) *The Presentation of Self in Everyday Life*. Garden City, NY: Doubleday.

Goffman, E. (1968) *Stigma – Notes on the Management of Spoiled Identity*. London: Penguin.

Gottfredson, M. and Hirschi, T. (1990) *A General Theory of Crime*. Stanford, CA: Stanford University Press.

Habermas, J. (1989) *The New Conservatism: Cultural Criticism and the Historians' Debate*. Cambridge: Polity Press.

Hacking, I. (1995) 'Three parables', in R. Goodman (ed.), *Pragmatism: A Contemporary Reader*. London: Routledge.

Hacking, I. (1999) *The Social Construction of What?* Cambridge, MA: Harvard University Press.

Harvey, D. (1989) *The Condition of Postmodernity: An Enquiry into the Origins of Cultural Change*. Oxford: Blackwell.

Hazlehurst, K. (ed.) (1996) *Crime and Justice: An Australian Textbook in Criminology*. Sydney: Law Book Company.

Heclo, H. and Masden, H. (1987) *Policy and Politics in Sweden: Principled Pragmatism*. Philadelphia, PA: Temple University Press.

Heidensohn, F. (1985) *Women and Crime*. London: Macmillan.

Henry, S. and Milovanovic, D. (1991) 'Constitutive criminology: the maturation of critical criminology, *Criminology*, 29: 293–315.

Henry, S. and Milovanovic, D. (1994) 'The constitution of constitutive criminology: a postmodern approach to criminological theory', in Nelken, D., (ed.) *The Futures of Criminology*. London: Sage.

Hopkins, S. (1999) 'Pop heroines and feminine icons: youthful femininity and popular culture'. Unpublished PhD, Queensland University of Technology.

Howe, A. (1994) *Punish and Critique: Towards a Feminist Analysis of Penality*. London: Routledge.

Hunt, A. (1991) 'Postmodernism and critical criminology', in B. MacLean and D. Milovanovic (eds), *New Directions in Critical Criminology*. Vancouver: Collective Press.

Kelly, L. (1992) 'Journeying into reverse: possibilities and problems in feminist research on sexual violence', in L. Gelsthorpe and A. Morris (eds), *Feminist Perspectives in Criminology*. Buckingham: Open University Press.

McCarthy, T. (1997) 'Rethinking theories of victimology: men's violence against women', in S. Cook and J. Bessant (eds), *Women's Encounters with Violence*. Thousand Oaks, CA: Sage.

Maguire, M., Morgan, R. and Reiner, R. (eds) (1997), *The Oxford Handbook of Criminology*, 2nd edn. Oxford: Oxford University Press.

Matza, D. (1969) *Becoming Deviant*. Englewood Cliffs, NJ: Prentice Hall.

Mukherjee, S. (1996) 'Measuring crime: the magnitude of the crime problem', in Hazlehurst, K. (ed), *Crime and Justice: An Australian Textbook in Criminology*. Sydney: Law Book Company.

Muncie, J. (1998) 'Reassessing Competing Paradigms in Criminological Theory', in P. Walton and J. Young (eds), *The New Criminology Revisited*. London: Macmillan.

O'Connor, M. (1980) 'A decade of the Australian and New Zealand Journal of Criminology 1968–1977', *Australian and New Zealand Journal of Criminology*, 13: 11–21.

O'Malley, P. (1996) 'Criminology and the new liberalism', 2nd *Annual Edwards Lecture*. Toronto: University of Toronto: 1–19.

O'Malley, P. and Carson, K. (1989) 'The Institutional foundations of contemporary Australian criminology', *Australian and New Zealand Journal of Sociology*, 25(3): 333–55.

Pateman, C. (1987) 'The patriarchal welfare state, women and democracy' in A Gutman, (ed.), *Democracy and the Welfare State*. Princeton, NJ: Princeton University Press.

Rock, P. (1997) 'The social organisation of British criminology', in Maguire, M., Morgan, R. and Reiner, R. (eds), *The Oxford Handbook of Criminology*. Oxford: Oxford University Press.

Rorty, R. (1999) *Philosophy and Social Hope*. London: Penguin.

Schon, D. (1980) 'Generative metaphor: a perspective on problem setting in social policy', in A. Ortony (ed.), *Metaphor and Thought*. Cambridge: Cambridge University Press.

Schutz, A. (1972) *The Phenomenology of the Social World*. London: Heinemann.

Schwartz, M. and Friedrichs, D. (1994) 'Postmodern thought and criminological discontent: new metaphors for understanding violence', *Criminology*, 32(2): 221–46.

Scutt, J. (1995) 'Judicial bias or legal bias? Battery, women, and the law', in J. Bessant, K. Carrington, K. and S. Cook, (eds), *Cultures of Crime and Violence: The Australian Experience*. Bundoora: LaTrobe University Press.

Smart, C. (1976) *Women, Crime and Criminology*. London: Routledge.

Smart, C. and Smart, B. (1978) 'Accounting for rape: reality and myth in press reporting', in C. Smart and B. Smart (eds), *Women, sexuality and social control*. London: Routledge.

Smart, C. (1989) 'Feminist approaches to criminology or postmodern woman meets atavistic man', in L. Gelsthorpe and A. Morris (eds), *Feminist Perspectives in Criminology*. Buckingham: Open University Press.

Spivak, G. (1988) 'Can the subaltern speak?', in C. Nelson and L. Grossberg (eds), *Marxism and the Interpretation of Culture*. Macmillan: London.

Stanko, E. (1985) *Intimate Intrusions: Women's Experience of Male Violence*. London: Virago.

Stanko, E. (1993) *Feminist Criminology: An Oxymoron?* Paper presented to the British Criminology Conference, Cardiff.

Sumner, C. (1994) *The Sociology of Deviance: An Obituary.* Buckingham: Open University Press.

Taylor, I. Walton, P. and Young, J. (1973) *The New Criminology.* London: Routledge & Kegan Paul.

Taylor, I. Walton, P. and Young, J. (1975) (eds) *Critical Criminology.* London: Routledge & Kegan Paul.

Tong, R. (1989) *Feminist Thought.* London: Unwin Hyman.

Watts, R. (2000) 'Politics in a time of globalisation', *Just Policy*, 18–19(19/20): 17–24.

White, R. and Haines, F. (1996) *Crime and Criminology: An Introduction.* Melbourne: Oxford University Press.

Wilson, J. and Hernstein, R. (1985) *Crime and Human Nature.* New York: Simon & Schuster.

Woodiwiss, A. (1990) *Social Theory after Postmodernism: Rethinking Production, Law and Class.* Winchester: Unwin Hyman.

Yeatman, A. (1990) *Bureaucrats, Femocrats, Democrats.* Sydney: Allen & Unwin.

Young, J. (1975) 'Working class criminology', in I. Taylor, P. Walton and J. Young (eds) *Critical Criminology.* London: Routledge & Kegal Paul.

Young, J. (1979) 'Left idealism, reformism and beyond: from new criminology to Marxism', in NDC/CSE (eds), *Capitalism and the Rule of Law.* London: Hutchinson.

Young, J. (1997) 'Breaking Windows: Situating the New Criminology', in P. Walton and J. Young (eds), *The New Criminology Revisited.* London: Macmillan.

Chapter 10

Critical criminology? In praise of an oxymoron and its enemies

Pat Carlen

Introduction

This chapter addresses two related questions:

- Is there a 'tradition' of critical criminology able to be sustained and worth sustaining under current conditions?
- If so, what are its defining elements?

My answer is yes to both parts, and, as I suggest in the chapter's title, although the term critical criminology can easily (and has repeatedly been) impugned as a contradiction in terms – most famously by Paul Hirst (1975), Carol Smart (1990) and Stan Cohen (1989) – it is never more worthy and capable of constant renewal than when it has as many enemies as it has today. But first, and briefly, what is to be understood by the term 'critical criminology'?

Critical Criminology

Until I set out to write this, I had never thought of 'critical criminology' as being remotely related to anything I myself might practise: first, because I have always been reluctant to use a label to justify a knowledge claim; second, because, for the same reason, I have been equally reluctant to engage in methodological exegeses; and, third, because I've never been sure what 'critical' criminology can mean in the academic context, where, as I understand it, all knowledge production is, ideally, supposed to be critical. However, as I wanted to take part in the conference wherein this book had its genesis, I had to overcome these scruples, and set myself to thinking about what critical criminology might mean. Because, however difficult it is to define 'critical criminology', there certainly is a lot of criminology around just now which is not critical (or anything else for that matter), while increasingly the 'criminological environment' in Britain is being organised around assumptions which are not only 'anti-critical' but also anti-intellectual and, in so far as they inhibit the production of new knowledge, anti-social.

Yet, alien as seem the concerns and assumptions of many whom I meet at 'criminology' conferences, and who, I therefore have to assume, are holding forth as 'criminologists', I myself don't hold with criminology's critics who claim that criminology must be, and indeed has always been, ideologically tainted by its empirical referent. For, in so far as the criticism about ideological contamination (as criminology's critics would see it) applies to criminology, it applies to all social science, indeed all science. So that leaves me not caring very much about subject or position labels, and certainly not wanting to engage in any master narrative about crime – Marxist, critical or what have you, and just with two defining characteristics of what for me is a 'critical criminology'.

First, for me there is only one substantive question for a critical criminology and that is: what are the relationships between social and criminal justice? And second, as far as method is concerned, for me a *critical criminology* has constantly to refuse to accept that the significance of any crime-related phenomenon is already known for all time and all places.

When I talk of the enemies of critical criminology, therefore, I am not referring to people but to texts, dimensions of texts, dominant or obscure epistemologies or ideologies and all the disciplinary practices relating to the production of criminological knowledge – whether it be found in the academy or the courts or the prisons. Of course, all knowledge-work, whether striving to be critical or not, is produced within ideological conditions that are inimical to the critical project. The point is that the *critical project*, in my opinion, should strive continuously both to cherish its inherent and inherently contradictory tendencies *and to work on them*... (what other people have called reflexivity, I suppose).

So what are these inherent and inherently contradictory tendencies which are inimical midwives of the critical project? Well (in no particular order), they are: theoreticism, politicism, populism, value-free and value-added, pseudo-scientism, trimming and clubbing. However, because this chapter is in part praise of those enemies precisely because they can only be known through recognition of their integral and critical opposites – though never in a dualistic configuration – I will frame the discussion around the difficulties of working and writing both within and without those contradictions.

The Enemies

1. Theoreticism

AGAINST Theoreticism: FOR Theory

For as long as I have been doing sociological analysis, I have had an ambivalence about the role of theorists in critical social research. On the one hand, I hold totally to the view that a coherent theoretical framework (either explanatory or interpretive) is an essential prerequisite to any type of analysis at all, but especially for a critical analysis which should produce new knowledge. On the other, it seems to me that within the practice of sociology and criminology there has perennially been a tendency toward an elitist theoreticism, the defining characteristics of which are themselves often contradictory: for, on the one hand, because the relationships (or not) between the empirical (or nominative) referent and theory are always open to question, there is often the implication that the less relevance the theory might have to the empirical referent the better; while on the other, there is, equally often, the implication that a theory has certain predictive qualities which have an all-time one-to-one relationship with the empirical phenomenon, and, therefore, that a politics can be read off from a theory. Any such stance – that is, any one which presupposes that a politics can be read off from a theory, and, which in so presupposing, confuses the empirical object with the theoretical object – fails to grasp two critical principles: that the ordering of things can always be otherwise; and that the conditions for change constantly change.

2. Politicism

AGAINST Politicism: FOR Politics

Politicism is the opposite of theoreticism – an assumption that a theory can be devised in the service of a politics. In the 1980s and 1990s left realists (see Matthews and Young 1986), fell into the trap of politicism when they argued that because a left realist theory was designed to incorporate all popular concerns about crime it would have more chance of being incorporated into criminal justice policy. This, in my opinion, was the main cause of the perspective's lack of coherence and inability to produce any new critical knowledge at all. Having said that, I did admire the left realists for taking an explicit political stance, for making their domain assumptions clear, and, at least on the political front, not engaging in trimming, a dubious practice which I discuss later.

3. Populism

AGAINST Populism: FOR interventionism

One of the dilemmas of a critical criminology – or a political party (as New Labour in England regularly informs its Old Labour relicts) is that unless its ideas are disseminated to politicians, they will have no effect on policy at all – they will be stillborn. Yet, in order to popularise a critical theory or analysis, it is often necessary to trim it till it loses its radical or political edge and is ripe for incorporation into prevailing ideologies. It has therefore seemed to me that critical criminologists should recognise a division of labour – they must retain their academic integrity when writing theoretically – that is, they must refuse to sweeten the theoretical pill – while at the same time working with campaigning groups and journalists to try to influence the types of radical and journalistic interventions that can be made. However, that is difficult in England at the present time when the government repressively promotes a particular conception of social science as a pseudo-scientific justification for its own policies. Which brings me to...

4. Pseudo-Scientism

AGAINST pseudo-scientism: FOR science

One of the more reprehensible foibles of England's present Labour government is that it has continued its predecessors' practice of quite explicitly conflating government interest with a particular scientific method – that is, empiricist quantitative method – and then elevating that method as the only one guaranteed to deliver truth. Thus it claims that all arguments for change, especially radical change, have to be 'evidence-based'. Such a reasonable and disarming edict! Until one remembers how it works out. For instance, during the 1990s – when I was conducting research on homelessness (Carlen, 1996) – it was constantly claimed by the Tory governments that nothing could be done about homelessness until the numbers of homeless people had been ascertained. As most homelessness is hidden, and official homelessness has a most eccentric definition, nothing was done about homelessness.

Likewise with any possibility of reducing the female prison population via sentencing reform: always the argument is that only figures count and that as there are so few female prisoners it is difficult to get any evidence-based research that can ever 'count'. On the other hand, at the present time there is much official trumpeting of the specious claim that appropriate prison programmes can reduce crime! And the 'figures' are even now being produced to 'prove' it (see Carlen, 2002).

You know the story. But where it took a new twist under the 1980s Tory administrations is that this pseudo-scientificity (pseudo because it elevates one conception of science into a truth – a procedure which leads to an ideological closure) was imposed not only on the academic community but also on the evaluation of all professional knowledge and practice, including that of criminal justice professionals. This emphasis on positivistic auditing has continued to this day, and has been effective not only in 'papering over' some of the worst cracks in the system but also in silencing critics from within the system who have nowadays become overburdened with the very paperwork upon which both the 'truth' of their own system and their promotion within it will depend (i.e. Power, 1997). Thus pseudo-scientific procedure has recently been strengthened in its perennial role of disciplining critics of the **status quo**.

5. Value-Free/Value-Added Injunctions

AGAINST value-free and value-added: FOR moral discourse

As we all know, issues as to whether or not social science can be 'value-free' have long dominated academic social science debate. Here I will not pose the question with regard to criminology because, first of all, I think that it's obvious that no social science can be value-free, and secondly, because I cannot imagine why anyone should ever want it to be. Unfortunately, the 'evidence-based' political rhetoric in England is not only inseminating debates about social policy, but also a whole range of other social assessments, for example – and poles apart – the evaluation of grant applications and the evaluation of prison regimes. In the former it leads to a refusal to recognise that all science has a moral dimension; in the latter, it leads to an erasure of moral discourse from debates about how prisoners should be treated.

First grant applications: there is such an emphasis on the importance of quantitative research in England now that even spelling out the domain assumptions that provoke one research question rather than another risks being labelled as 'bias'. Thus when I recently stated in a grant application that one reason why I was looking at alternatives to women's imprisonment was because I subscribed to the Tory Home

Secretary's expressed opinion that 'prisons make [bad] people worse', a member of the commissioning panel expressed concern that I admitted to holding 'biased' views on imprisonment. Yet I was putting forth this domain assumption as a necessary procedure for the kind of science that I practise. Even more ironically – given the objections to 'bias' – in every application to the Research Council the applicant has to say how the research will 'add value' and all research applications have to be assessed by 'users'. Two obvious questions arise: whose values? and which users? And how does one know how to answer these questions unless one always and already knows the answers to the research questions and whose interests they will serve?

Now, it is in this context that I presently feel very strongly that *critical criminologists* should both resist political attempts to impose only one type of research method on social science *and* engage in an unfashionable crusade to bring 'morals' back into public discourse about the relationships between social and criminal justice. And I have chosen the term morals deliberately.

When I was recently doing research in the United States I was asked how one could evaluate a programme for homeless drug users which was not having much success in terms of immediately turning young women away from drug usage, but which was improving their general health, increasing their education levels and, in some cases (though only in *some* cases) reducing the frequency of their being in trouble with the police and courts. When I asked the programme leaders whether they could make an argument that attendance at the programme was 'good in itself', or whether they could put forward arguments based on the morality of providing shelter for otherwise homeless and destitute women, they were quite troubled and slightly embarrassed. The immediate response was to inquire as to whether I was, as they put it, 'religious', and, when I replied that I was not, they went on to explain to me that to talk of either 'moral good' or morality would make their financial backers think that the project leaders themselves were employed by a religious organisation, and that that would not go down very well. Nor, they said, did they want to be seen as 'do gooders'. They wanted to be seen as realists. Yet they *were* doing good, and their answers to my interview questions suggested that 'doing good' had been one of their main objectives in setting up the programme. I am not criticising their strategy. What I am regretting is that what I saw just one instance of in the United States, mirrors the dominant situation in England nowadays, where professionals in the criminal justice system have to do good by stealth for fear of being seen as being unprofessional 'do gooders' whose non-quantifiable moral or qualitative inputs into their work are defined not only as being non-auditable but also, and, consequently as having 'no value', where, in fact, the moral dimension of both social policy and social science is suppressed (see Carlen, 2002).

6. Trimming and Clubbing

AGAINST trimming and clubbing: FOR scientific integrity

By now, many of you will have realised that what I am calling a 'critical' criminology would be no more and no less than one which adheres to the liberal, classical ideal of science – that it should be: open; constantly recognising, questioning and, if necessary, denying the conditions of its own existence; and neither 'trimming' its questions to make them politically correct or expedient, nor 'clubbing' – that is, pulling its punches – either to conform with contemporary academic fashions or political prejudices, or in response to downright bullying by either political or academic powers that be. For above all it seems to me that a critical criminology must try not only to think the unthinkable about crime, but also to speak the unspeakable about the conditions *in which* and *by which* it is known.

So, In Conclusion...

At this point I am beginning to think that the question posed for me by the editors has provoked a sermon rather than an academic paper, and that to be setting out the defining elements of a critical criminology is even more oxymoronic than the term 'critical criminology' itself. For a critical criminology, falling as it does between theory and politics, is primarily about strategy, and therefore its protocols have to be very loosely binding on its practitioners, who will inevitably shape their practice according to both their own talents and calculation of the balance of political needs and forces at specific times, and who, moreover, if they have any political nous whatsoever, will keep their tactics to themselves. At moments of critical struggle, one person's critical theory is likely to be seen as another person's theoreticism and so on and so forth. Who cares? In my opinion, all that is really critical is: first not to close-off debate; and, secondly, to refuse to collude in any criminology that occludes the relationships between social and criminal justice. (An injunction, of course, which is a contradiction in itself.)

Bibliography

Carlen, P. (1996) *Jigsaw: A Political Criminology of Youth Homelessness*. Buckingham: Open University Press.

Carlen, P. (ed.) (2002) *Women and Punishment: The Struggle for Justice*. Cullompton: Willan Publishers.

Cohen, S. (1989) *Against Criminology*. New Brunswick, NJ: Transaction.

Hirst, P. (1975) 'Marx and Engels on law, crime and morality', in I. Taylor, P. Walton, and J. Young (eds), *Critical Criminology*. London: Routledge & Kegan Paul.

Matthews, R. and Young, J. (1986) *Confronting Crime*. London: Macmillan.

Power, M. (1997) *Audit Society*. Oxford: Oxford University Press.

Smart, C. (1990) 'Feminist approaches to criminology – or postmodern woman meets atavistic man', in L. Gelsthorpe and A. Morris (eds), *Feminist Perspectives in Criminology*. Buckingham: Open University Press.

Chapter 11

Critical criminology in the twenty-first century: critique, irony and the always unfinished

Jock Young

I do not wish to end this account without mentioning a rather amusing episode. Right in the middle of the Third National [Criminology] Conference, taking place in Cambridge in July 1968, a group of seven young social scientists and criminologists, participants of the Conference, met secretly and decided to establish an independent 'National Deviancy Conference' and soon afterwards they duly met in York. At the time, it reminded me a little of naughty schoolboys playing a nasty game on their stern headmaster. It was not necessary to go 'underground' because we were not in any way opposed to discussing new approaches to the sociology of deviance ... Although not invited to their conference in York I asked one of my senior colleagues in the Institute to go there as an observer.

My attitude was by no means hostile or patronizing. As I stated at the time, movements in ideas, like life in general, often lead to seeming unexpected baffling results. Those were the years of dissent, protest and ferment in the United States with their unmistakable echoes in Britain. They affected not only the ways people acted, but also their thinking on many matters relating to social life and its reinterpretations. But it was also a reaction to some extent inevitable and to some extent misguided of the new generation of British criminologists against what appeared to be the

stolid establishment of Criminology as personified by the Cambridge Institute and probably also by its first Director.

(Sir Leon Radzinowicz, 1999: 229–30)

Critical criminology is the criminology of late modernity. Its inception
was in the late 1960s and early 1970s at the cusp of change, its inspiration
a world where oppressive relationships of class, age, gender and ethnicity
became highlighted and evident (in that historical order) and where the
pluralism, ambiguity and shift of values heralded a society where
migration and human creativity created a diversity of cultures in close
propinquity and interaction. In Britain the key academic organisation
which provided a theatre for such debates was the National Deviancy
Conference (NDC). Here, as Stan Cohen astutely noted, 'well before
Foucault and a long way from the Left Bank – our little corner of the
human sciences was seized by a deconstructionist impulse' (Cohen, 1998:
101). Indeed the NDC was pivoted around deconstruction and anti-
essentialism. It dwelt on the social construction of gender, sexual
proclivity, crime, suicide, drugs and mental states while fiercely criticising
the major discourses of modernity, positivism and classicism, and its
institutions, whether it was the prison or the clinic. The NDC was
anarchistic and antinomian, set deep in the counterculture of the time.
My own involvement in it was initially reluctant to say the least. It was a
time when we regarded people with 9 to 5 jobs as complete failures, lived
in communes and regarded the 'straight' world with complete disdain. I
was living in Notting Hill where Pink Floyd played weekly at the local
parish hall, Jimi Hendrix was at Middle Earth and there was poetry in the
streets. Academic conferences were not exactly where it was at. I was
persuaded to go to the first NDC in York in 1968. I remember Mike Brake
– later to be well known for his books on youth culture (Brake, 1980, 1985)
– saying to me the evening we arrived, 'What *are* we doing here, man?
Let's get out quick and get to Leeds where there's much better clubs.' We
stayed all the same and next day I gave my first academic paper, 'The
Role of Police as Amplifiers of Deviancy, Negotiators of Reality and
Translators of Fantasy' (1971a). A pretentious title but it still captures for
me a constant theme of the way in which powerful forces in society
create demons out of illusions which then, through stigma and
oppression, take on a reality of their own.

The NDC was hectic, irreverent, transgressive and, above all, fun. It
took no notice of disciplinary boundaries – it was as important an arena
for the emerging field of cultural studies (Stuart Hall, Mike Featherstone,
Paul Willis and Dick Hebdidge all gave papers), anti-psychiatry (Peter
Sedgwick, Jeff Coulter), critical legal theory (Boaventura de Sousa Santos

and Sol Picciotto) and the sociology of sexualities (Ken Plummer, Mary McIntosh), as it was for the sociology of deviance (see the account in Cohen, 1988; Young, 1998). Perhaps, however, it was the pluralism and social constructionism of deviancy theory that gave it such a pivotal role. There was a frenetic quality to the NDC: there were 14 conferences held between the end of 1968 and the end of 1973 and papers, articles and books seemed to emerge in an endless stream – exciting and excitable.

Within criminology and the sociology of deviance the adversary was clear. Variously named 'positivism' or 'correctionalism' or 'establishment criminology', it was individualistic in focus, technicist in outlook and minimalist in theory – its aim was the social engineering of the 'maladjusted' individual into the ranks of the consensual and contented society. It was summed up by the title of an emblematic text, Barbara Wootton's *Social Science and Pathology*, published in 1959, which, supported by the Nuffield Foundation, sought to review the contribution of the social sciences to 'the prevention and cure of the social problems associated with unacceptable forms of deviant behaviour' (Wootton, 1959: 9). The intellectual history of this assault on this rather piecemeal ensemble of ideas, which had its institutional centre at the Institute of Criminology at Cambridge, was to involve two stages (Downes, 1988). The first, immediately preceding the first NDC, was the decade of the 1960s during which sociology expanded rapidly within the academy and sociologists turned to the extraordinary flourishing American sociology of deviance, both in its subcultural and interactionist variants. In the US, unlike Britain, a long-standing sociological tradition concerned with crime had been extant throughout the century with Vold, Sutherland, The Chicago School and Merton – themselves inheritors of late and early twentieth century European sociology. The explanatory project which spurred on the sociological involvement in crime and deviance was the rise in crime for, as David Downes put it: 'The appeal of American theory was that it addressed the problem, and seemingly furnished a framework for its resolution, of the persistent rise in official crime rates despite the appearance of both greater affluence and diminishing inequality in the major industrial societies'. For, 'genetics and psychology were seen as offering little purchase on what were perceived as startling differences in crime rates between societies and within societies over relatively short periods of time' (Downes, 1988:177).

Criminology is, as John Lea (1998) points out, not so much a discipline as a field, its distinctiveness is not its knowledge base but the form of its focus: theories of crime, criminal law and the relation between the two – in this it is a sub-category of the sociology of deviance. It can, and never should be, conceived of as a separate discipline; its categories and processes are social constructs – they have no separate ontological reality. It cannot, therefore, exist separately from social theory as its concerns are inevitably with the nature of social order and disorder. Not only have all of the major social theorists concerned themselves with order, disorder and regulation, but there has been across the century clear links between the great theorists of modernity and the criminological canon. Witness Durkheim, Merton and the anomie theorists; Marx, Engels, Bonger and Marxist criminology; the influence of Simmel and Wirth on the Chicago School and the conflict theorisation of G. B. Vold; of Schutz and Mead on Becker and labelling theories. Despite this obvious intimacy of intellectual concern, there has been a constant tendency for criminology, particularly in its more practical and administrative manifestations, to cut itself off from grand theory. Such a situation was paramount in Britain in the postwar period and the turn, or should we say *reconnection*, of criminology to sociology was a major first step out of empiricism. The second phase which Downes traces was the foundation of the NDC in 1968 and in the ten years that followed it, this took on the new American sociology of deviance and considerably radicalised it. It is this phase which gave rise to the 'new' or 'critical' criminology. This presented itself as a series of 'ironies' which served to turn establishment criminology on its head.

- *Self-fulfilment* – that illusions and stereotypes of crime can be real in their consequences and self-fulfilling in reality.

- *Seriousness* – that crime occurred throughout the social structure and that the crimes of the powerful were more serious in their consequences than the crimes of the poor.

- *Ontology* – that crime has no ontological reality and that the 'same' behaviour can be constructed totally differently. Thus, for example, a serial killer could be either a psychopathic monster or a hero if dropping bombs daily in the Afghan War.

- *Decentring* – that the criminal justice system is not the front-line defence against crime but a minor part of the system of social control, itself crucially dependent on informal norms of civil society.

- *Selectivity* – that criminal law, although phrased in a language of formal equality, is targeted in a way that is selective and substantially unequal.

- *Counter-productivity* – that the prison and the criminal justice system produces criminals rather than defusing criminality.

- *Socialisation* – that the core values of competitiveness, acquisitiveness, individualism and hedonism are close to the motivations for crime, so that the well socialised person is more likely to offend than the undersocialised.

- *Contradiction* – that the ideals which legitimate and hold the system together are the very ones which society thwarts and the frustrations generated seem to break the system apart.

- *Function* – that 'the criminal', 'the outsider', 'the other', far from destroying the fabric of society, produce stereotypes which hold the fabric together.

- *Secondary harm* – that the primary harm of a social problem is frequently of a lesser order than the secondary harm accruing from the intervention to control it. The prime example of this being the regulation of drug use.

Critical criminology in the subsequent years

> Leaving aside the existence of interesting disputes and divisions, it is clear that the new perspective overall has now become established and institutionalised. In the same way initially outrageous art movements (such as Dado and surrealism) eventually became respectable, so too has the new deviance and criminology become part of the accepted order of things. Its practitioners are ensconced in orthodox academic departments, journals, examining boards and publishing companies. No booklist would be complete without one.
>
> (Cohen, 1981: 241)

Thus Stan Cohen talks of the institutionalisation of that which was once iconoclastic. Critical criminology has become a staple of textbooks, its concerns form the basis of secondary school sociology exams, it runs conferences, journals and research programmes. Indeed, in Britain, outside of course Cambridge, the majority of centres which teach criminology are within the rubric of critical criminology.

However, in recent years a drastically different version of the subsequent history of critical criminology, and of criminology in general, has gained currency. We have seen an inkling of this in the introductory quote from Sir Leon Radzinowicz's memoirs with his patronising comments (see Cottee, 2001), which present critical commentary as an amusing interlude before getting back to the business of serious criminology. But the most elaborated presentation of such a revisionist history is that of David Garland in a series of pieces from *Punishment and Welfare* (1985) to *The Culture of Control* (2001; see also 1988, 1997, 1999 and with R. Sparks, 2000).

The hegemony of the practical

Garland sees the history of criminology, proper, as a history of the criminology that emerged around the institutions of control. For the first two-thirds of the twentieth century this was correctionalism – with its stress on individual positivism, and then subsequently what he terms the 'crime control complex' with its emphasis on rational choice and situational control. That is a transition from a modern to a late modern criminology, the first sited in the penal-welfare institutions, the second sited in the institutions and practices of private sector crime prevention. It is the latter which is the predominant theory of today – 'the criminology of everyday life' – but there are two other currents – a residuum of correctionalism and a neo-conservative, anti-modernism. Whereas the criminology of everyday life sees the offenders as normal, rational consumers 'just like us', the criminology of the other sees the offender as 'the other'. It is the criminology of everyday which he sees as going with the grain of everyday life – as being more naturalistically true to reality.

The critical moment

> In retrospect, the decade of the 1970s appears as a watershed, in which the intellectual, institutional and political assumptions of modern criminology were challenged, often in the name of a more radical social politics. It was during this decade that there arose a more critical and reflexive style of criminology, and a more explicit questioning of criminology's relation to the state, to criminal justice, and to the disciplinary processes of welfare capitalism. Criminology became, at least for a while, concerned to link its ideas and analyses to the broader themes of social thought and less concerned to be an applied discipline. It became more enamoured of sociological theory and more critical of criminal justice practice. In these years, criminology's centre of gravity shifted a little, becoming more reflexive, more critical, and more theoretical. As it happens, this was a short-lived moment [which] did not last long. Before long, new post-correctional forms of crime control emerged and criminology became immersed in applied questions once again...
>
> (Garland and Sparks, 2000: 13-14).

Critical criminology is not then seen as a harbinger of the future but a phase which had its moment in the past. Garland does not deny its influence, but it is muted – indeed academic criminology as a whole is strangely marginalised in this account. Rather his focus is on the 'surfaces' concerned with crime control out of which criminology is seen to emerge as power/knowledge bases in a Foucauldian fashion. Thus the move from positivism to control theory, his major transition, is seen as reflecting the change in the *site* of crime control, from the penal-welfare system to private crime prevention – both commercial and among the population as a whole.

The critical midwife

> A movement that initially aimed to enhance prisoners' rights, minimize imprisonment, restrict state power, and end predictive restraint, ultimately ushered in policies that did quite the opposite. How is this strange turn of events to be explained?...
>
> (Garland, 2001:53)

> Somehow the anti-correctionalist movement opened the way for a set of changes it could not envisage and could not control...The processes that undermined the credibility of penal-welfarism were not the same as the ones that subsequently unravelled it. The original damage to the structure came about in the early 1970s as a result of radical and reactionary forces working in tandem, but with the former in the dominant position. The further assault on the system in the 1980s and 1990s occurred in the context of a more regressive public mood and temper...and as part of the creation of a new and less inclusive crime narrative.
>
> (Garland, 2001: 72-73).

Although the moment of radical criminology was, in Garland's analysis, short, it was momentous in its impact although this impact was scarcely in the direction intended! The NDC, together with their American counterparts, mounted a scathing criticism of the criminal justice system and the prison in particular, pointing to its counter-productiveness and the utter failure of the rehabilitative ideal as captured in the spirit of the ironies that I have outlined earlier. According to Garland the effect was together with other reformers to undermine the whole intellectual credibility of the penal-welfare basis of modern criminology. In doing this they played into the hands of the reactionary forces which followed them, thus from the 1980s onwards the political success of the New Right rejected the rehabilitative ideal, as they did the notion of social causes of crime, and replaced it with its successor, the 'crime-control complex' with its stress on retribution and incapacitation in prisons and situational crime prevention.

257

Wait a moment

My problem with Garland's revisionist history of critical criminology is
that it simply does not correspond to reality. The critical tradition both in
theory and research palpably flourishes. Textbooks in theory – whatever
their political persuasion – all contain chapters on critical criminology
and its present developments, while the radical textbooks (and there are
very many of them) have a standard progression through the canon of
criminological theory with critical criminology as the culmination. It is
true that varieties of neoliberal criminology (e.g. Felson, Clarke and
Wilson) have emerged in the last fifteen years, but they are still a minor
part of academic criminology, are likely to remain so and have a
correspondingly small (and much demeaned) role in the textbooks. To
this Garland would argue that:

> Not all criminology is consonant with, or relevant to, the character
> of contemporary social life. There is a huge inertia built into
> academic production which ensures the theoretical traditions
> continue long after they cease to connect to 'the real world'. I have
> focused upon the criminologies of everyday life because I believe
> they do connect to the present in an interesting and revealing way.
> (Garland, 1999: 362).

So much of the academic tradition does not connect. I cannot see how
this is true of critical criminology either politically or in terms of its
relationship to 'the grain' of everyday life. The ten ironies I have listed
would seem to me to be as important today as they ever were, in fact all
the more so with the growth of the American gulag, the penchant for the
scape-goating of the poor, the immigrant and the drug user, and the way
in which crime control has become a major currency of politics. As for
everyday life, Garland may believe that the rational choice and routine
activities theories go with the grain of everyday life in late modernity –
indeed his most recent book, *The Culture of Control*, uses such theories as
its explanatory basis – but such neoliberal discourses capture only a
limited part of that reality. Contrast this with a critical criminology which
insists that out there, in a world of broken narratives where economic
and ontological insecurity abounds, where crime, far from being
mundane and calculative, is transgressive and sensual, where punishment is frequently vituperative and vindictive and where society, rather
than being a one-dimensional scenario of rational contractual atoms, is
divisive, contested, contradictory and ironic (see Young, forthcoming).

Finally, as to the role of critical criminology as the midwife to reaction, the criticisms evolved in the 1970s were directed against the fact that prisons failed to rehabilitate and that a quasi-medical model of rehabilitation was growing with notions of 'treating' offenders and involving indeterminate sentences to be served until 'cure' was achieved. That is, it was directed against the failure of the prisons and fake notions of rehabilitation. These arguments were not an argument against rehabilitation *per se*, although, as was constantly indicated, if the conditions which led to crime were ameliorated there would be considerably less people in prison needing rehabilitation. That right-wing commentators seized upon the obvious inadequacies of the prison was scarcely the 'fault' of critical criminology. The spin they put on the facts of failure was a product of New Right thinking, not of criminological radicals. As it is, the extensive expansion in recent years of quasi-medical treatment programmes for drug abuse and various offences, the massive rise of cognitive behavioural programmes within prisons (see Carlen, 2002) and the concomitant emergence of individual positivism in the shape of psychological criminology in the academy not only invalidate Garland's claim of a transition away from penal-welfarism but underscores the need for a renewal of critique on precisely the same lines as before.

The flourishing of critical criminology

My argument so far is that critical criminology in this age of the gulag and the punitive turn is massively needed – it is the counter-voice to neoliberalism and conservatism. And what is more, critical criminology is flourishing. The most incisive recent textbooks are all in this genre: witness Mark Lanier and Stuart Henry's *Essential Criminology* (1998), René van Swaaningen's *Critical Criminology: Visions from Europe* (1997), John Lea's *Crime and Modernity* (2002), Rob White and Fiona Haines' *Crime and Criminology* (2000), Gregg Barak's *Integrating Criminologies* (1998), John Tierney's *Criminology: Theory and Context* (1996), Wayne Morrison's *Theoretical Criminology: From Modernity to Post-Modernism* (1995), Roger Matthews' *Doing Time* (1999), Russell Hogg and Dave Brown's *Rethinking Law and Order* (1998), Jayne Mooney's *Gender, Violence and the Social Order* (2000) and Ian Taylor's *Crime in Context* (1999). It has produced the most exciting ethnography and critique of the last ten years. Read Phillipe Bourgois' 'Just Another Night in the Shooting Gallery' (1998), Jeff Ferrell's 'Criminological Verstehen: Inside the Immediacy of Crime' (1997), Lois Wacquant's *Les Prisons de la Misère* (1999), Nils Christie's *Crime Control as Industry* (2000), Vincenzo Ruggiero's *Crime and Markets* (2000), Damian

Zaitch's (2001) wonderful study of Colombian cocaine dealing in Rotterdam, Pat Carlen's *Jigsaw* (1996), or look at Walter DeKeseredy and his associates' remarkable study of crime and poverty in a Canadian public housing estate with its acute awareness of gender and ethnicity (DeKeseredy *et al.*, forthcoming). Critical criminology has been at the cutting edge of the discipline and is international in its scope, think of the burgeoning literature on governmentality (e.g. Stenson, 1998; Rose, 2000; O'Malley, 1999), on masculinity (Jefferson, 2002; Hall, 2002; Messerschmidt, 2000), Phil Scraton's intrepid investigative criminology in the harrowing *Hillsborough: The Truth* (2000), the opening up of the crime prevention discourses to critical analysis by Adam Crawford (1998) and Gordon Hughes (1998), the development of work on youth and justice by John Muncie (1999), Shahid Alvi (2000) and John Pitts (2001), Ruth Jamieson's pioneering work on the criminology of war (1998, 1999), or the extraordinary flourishing of cultural criminology (Ferrell et al., 2001; Ferrell and Saunders, 1995; Presdee, 2000) and feminist criminology (see Carrington's Chapter this volume for a detailed analysis of the integral contribution of feminist criminologies to critical criminology).

What is of course true is that the vast expansion of the criminal justice system has resulted in a plethora of evaluative studies, research programmes and vocational courses (see Robinson, 2001) which have generated a substantial institutional base for administrative criminology. All of this further underscores the necessity of a critical voice to counter the minimalist, theoretical 'noise' constantly arising from out of the crime control complex.

The illegitimacy of critique

There are, however, writers who maintain that late modernity has brought with it a new predicament wherein the space for fundamental critique is rapidly shrinking. George Pavlich, for example, in an article entitled 'Criticism and Criminology: In Search of Legitimacy' (1999), maintains that criticism within critical criminology has been subject to a diluting pragmatism, interesting itself in matters of crime control and technical efficiency, on the one hand, or basing itself on emancipatory rhetoric with an untenable belief in universal 'progress' and the possibilities of a utopian future on the other. For the uncertainties of postmodern times do not allow us to securely appeal to such emancipatory strategies and when these are absent the danger is that recourse will be made to the technical and the administrative which merely aids the system to work and to continue the status quo. Pavlich, therefore, proposes that to make a critique which has legitimacy we must reject both of these strategies.

So here we are with Phillipe Rushton on the BBC this morning as I shave, telling us how crime and IQ will soon be located in a specific gene and the gene relates to race, while yesterday ex-Commissioner Kerik is claiming on national TV the crime drop in New York City as his own, and advising London in the spirit of zero tolerance to come down heavy on cannabis users, while Mayor Ken Livingstone is demanding that the city massively ups its police force to New York levels in order to 'win the fight against crime', while in the south of the city police are tearing up their rule books and specifically targeting black youth with or without suspicion. Meanwhile, across the Atlantic, a gulag of an immense size and historical significance has emerged, President Bush II has conflated the war against terror, the war against crime and the war against drugs, while vicious farce is being enacted in Camp X-Ray in Guantanamo Bay, Cuba (See Hogg's chapter this volume for arguments supporting the importance of trans-national criminologies in the twenty-first century).

Yet amid all of this we are advised that in order to maintain the legitimacy of our critique we should abstain from narratives which are either emancipatory or follow the 'performance logic of techno-adminis-trative reasoning' (Pavlich, 1999:42). Instead we are advised, via Lyotard, to use 'paralogic' – literally that which is against reason. For 'paralogy always gestures towards the unknown; it licenses attempts to find new ideas, to formulate new links within language that yield novel enunciations' (Pavlich, 1999: 43). If this is not too clear Pavlich further elaborates:

> Yet what critical genres might paralogy legitimate? No doubt this question would require more detailed elaboration in the context of 'crime-related' discourses than is possible here. However, the concept implies multiple critical practices bound neither to emancipation metanarratives nor to technical formulations of crime.

He clarifies this even further:

> the point of critique is not to discover the essential or necessary unity of given historical limits; rather, its role is to focus on contingent processes that render such limited 'realities' possible. Accordingly, criticism need not entail the practice of comparing, or judging local 'realities' with 'universal' principles – rather it could develop an ethos that continuously directs itself to absence, the otherness which makes possible the so-called 'realities' contained by given historical limits.
>
> (Pavlich, 1999: 43)

Thus the critical criminologist is advised to dig a deep and impenetrable moat around the ivory tower of the academy within which the 'exuberant' discourses of unreason reign – while outside a plethora of cruel and insistent practices occur which systematically limit human emancipation while being justified by false technical and administrative reasons.

In fact it is important, if we are to critique the practices of the present-day system, to demonstrate their technical and administrative incompetence – the exposure of the irony depends on this. It is true, however, that technical critique alone leads to the danger of an autopoetic theory which is internally self-referring and may function just to reduce tension in the system (see Lea, 1998). Hence the need for this critique to be conducted in the context of an emancipatory discourse. It is unclear how paralogic can conceivably provide a methodology by which we can tie the immediate and the technical to the long term and the transformative in a way which effectively expedites reform yet does not succumb to the perils of utopian blueprints. This reduces to two problems: the problem of transformation and the problem of a guiding narrative. The answer to the first question is aided by consideration of the work of Nancy Fraser, the second by reference to Zygmunt Bauman, the major theorist of late/post or, as he would have it, liquid modernity. To outline this it is necessary to situate the problems of transformation and change and their relationship to crime and punishment within the changed social terrain within which we now live.

The coordinates of order: class and identity in the late modernity

At this point before mapping the terrain of late modernity I wish to briefly establish coordinates. Nancy Fraser in her influential *Justice Interruptus: Critical Reflections on the Post-Socialist Condition* (1997) outlines two types of politics: those centring around distributive justice and those centring around the justice of recognition – that is class politics and identity politics. In *The Exclusive Society* (1999) I point out the two fundamental problems in a liberal democracy to be the need to distribute rewards fairly so as to encourage commitment to work within the division of labour and the need to encourage respect between individuals and groups so that the self-seeking individualism characteristic of a competitive society does not lead to a situation of war of all against all. Individuals must experience their rewards as fair and just and they must feel valued and respected.

Let us develop the distinction between the sphere of distribution and that of recognition. Central to distributive justice is the notion of fairness of reward and in developed societies this entails a meritocracy, that is where merit is matched to reward. Justice of recognition involves the notion of respect and status allocated to all but if we stretch the concept a little further it also involves the notion of the level of esteem or social status being related justly. Indeed both the discourses of distributive justice and recognition have the notion of a basic equality (all must receive a base level of reward as part of being citizens) but on top of this, rather than a general equality of outcome, a hierarchy of reward and recognition dependent on the individual's achievements.

How does this help inform us as to the genesis of crime and punishment? Firstly, that a major cause of crime lies in deprivation that is, very frequently, the combination of feeling relatively deprived economically (which causes discontent) and misrecognised socially and politically (which causes disaffection). The classic combination is to be marginalised economically and treated as a second-rate citizen on the street by the police. Secondly, a common argument is that widespread economic and ontological insecurity in the population engenders a punitive response to crime and deviancy (see, for example, Luttwak, 1995; Young, 2001).

As we shall see in the process of the transition from modernity to late modernity powerful currents shake the social structure transforming the nature of relative deprivation, causing new modes of misrecognition and exclusion, while at the same time being accompanied by widespread economic and ontological insecurity. The purchase of each of these currents impacts differentially throughout the social structure by each of the prime social axes of class, age, ethnicity and gender.

The journey into late modernity

The last third of the twentieth century has witnessed a remarkable transformation in the lives of citizens living in advanced industrial societies. The golden age of the postwar settlement with high employment, stable family structures and consensual values underpinned by the safety net of the welfare state has been replaced by a world of structural unemployment, economic precariousness, a systematic cutting of welfare provisions and the growing instability of family life and interpersonal relations. And where there once was a consensus of value, there is now burgeoning pluralism and individualism (see Hobsbawm, 1994). A world of material and ontological security from cradle to grave is replaced by precariousness and uncertainty and where social commentators of the 1950s and 1960s berated the complacency of a comfortable 'never had it so good' generation, those of today talk of a risk society where social change becomes the central dynamo of existence and where anything might happen. As Anthony Giddens put it: 'to live in the world produced by high modernity has the feeling of riding a juggernaut' (Giddens, 1991:28; see also Beck, 1992; Berman, 1983).

Such a change has been brought about by market forces which have systematically transformed both the sphere of production and consumption. This shift from Fordism to Post-Fordism involves the unravelling of the world of work where the primary labour market of secure employment and 'safe' careers shrinks, the secondary labour market of short-term contracts, flexibility and insecurity increases as does the growth of an underclass of the structurally unemployed.

Secondly, the world of leisure is transformed from one of mass basic consumption, to one where choice and preference is elevated to a major ideal and where the constant stress on immediacy, hedonism and self-actualisation has had a profound effect on late modern sensibilities (see Campbell, 1987; Featherstone, 1985). These changes both in work and leisure, characteristic of the late modern period, generate a situation of widespread relative deprivation and heightened individualism. Market forces generate a more unequal and less meritocratic society, market values encourage an ethos of every person for themselves, and together these create a combination which is severely criminogenic. Such a process is combined with a decline in the forces of informal social control, as communities are disintegrated by social mobility and left to decay as capital finds more profitable areas to invest and develop. At the same time, families are stressed and fragmented by the decline in communities systems of support, the reduction of state support and the more diverse pressures of work (see Currie, 1997; Wilson, 1996). Thus, as the pressures which lead to crime increase, the forces which attempt to control it decrease.

The journey into late modernity involves both a change in perceptions of the fairness of distributive justice and in the security of identity. There is a shift in relative deprivation from being a comparison between groups (what Runciman, 1966, calls 'fraternal' relative deprivation) to that which is between individuals (what Runciman terms 'egoistic' relative deprivation). The likely effect on crime is, I would suggest, to move from a pattern of committing crimes *outside* of one's neighbourhood on other richer people to committing crimes in an internecine way *within* one's neighbourhood. That is the frustrations generated by relative deprivation become focused inside the 'community' rather than, as formerly, projected out of it.

But it is also in the realm of identity that relative deprivation is increased and transformed. For here, on one side, you have raised expectations: the spin off of the consumer society is the market in *lifestyles*. On the other hand, both in work and in leisure, there has been a disembeddedness. That is identity is no longer secure; it is fragmentary and transitional – all of which is underscored by a culture of reflexivity which no longer takes the world for granted. The identity crisis permeates our society. As the security of the lifelong job, as the comfort of stability in marriage and relationships fade, as movement makes community a phantasmagoria where each unit of the structure stays in place but each individual occupant regularly moves, where the structure itself expands and transforms and where the habit of reflexivity itself makes choice part of everyday life and problematises the taken for granted – all of these things call into question the notion of a fixed, solid sense of self. Essentialism offers a panacea for this sense of disembeddedness.

The identity crisis and the attractions of essentialism

In *The Exclusive Society* I discuss the attractions of essentialism to the ontologically insecure and denigrated. To believe that one's culture, 'race', gender or community has a fixed essence which is valorised and unchanging is, of course, by its very nature the answer to a feeling that the human condition is one of shifting sands, and that the social order is feckless and arbitrary. To successfully essentialise oneself it is of great purchase to negatively essentialise others, that is to ascribe to the *other* either features which *lack* one's own values (and solidity) or which are an *inversion* of one's own cherished beliefs about one's self. To seek identity for oneself, in an essentialist fashion, inevitably involves denying or denigrating the identity of others.

Crime and its control is a prime site for essentialisation. Who, by definition, could be a better candidate for such a negative 'othering' than the criminal and the culture that he or she is seen to live in? Thus the criminal underclass replete with single mothers and living in slum estates or ghettos, drug addicts committing crime to maintain their habits and the immigrants who commit crime to deceitfully enter the country and continue their lives of crime, in order to maintain themselves become the three major foci of emerging discourses around law and order – that is the welfare 'scrounger', the 'junkie', and the 'immigrant'.

This triptych of deviancy, each picture reflecting the others in a late modern portrait of degeneracy and despair, comes to dominate public discussion of social problems. As the discourse develops their ontologies become distinct and different from 'normal' people, their social norms absent or aberrant, their natures frequently racialised and rendered inferior. Crime as a product of our society becomes separated from the social structure: it is viewed as a result of distinct aetiologies, it embodies differing values, it emanates from distinct and feared areas of the city, areas that are contrasted with the organic community where social trust and harmony are seen to reside.

Nancy Fraser: affirmative and transformative politics

The problem of crime is inevitably one of order, and the problem of order is that of justice. To tackle predatory crime and punitive responses we must, therefore, involve the politics of distribution and the politics of recognition. We must, in short, intervene both upon a material and a symbolic level. Discussion of reform is usually concerned with the former for without some form of redistribution any considerable reduction in crime is unlikely. The significance of the symbolic level is less explored and has changed remarkably with the transition to late modernity. First of all a more individualistic society generates greater and greater demands for self-actualisation and recognition, secondly, the increased sense of disembeddedness makes, at the same time, a sense of secure identity more and more precarious; thirdly, a potent solution to this ontological uncertainty is that of essentialism; fourthly such a fake sense of solidity is more easily achieved by regaling others; lastly such a dehumanisation of others can be a potent facilitation both of crime (particularly violence) and a punitive attitude towards the criminal. It is therefore crucial that we attend to the problems of identity, arguing for policies which ensure a sense of self-worth and actualisation yet which do not rest upon the fake premises of essentialism where others are systematically denigrated and then abused.

Nancy Fraser in *Justice Interruptus* develops an extremely useful typology of the politics of reform based on the two dimensions of redistribution and recognition. Reform, she argues, must recognise the necessity of changes in both these areas assuaging the failings of distributive justice, misrecognition and devaluation. But to this dichotomy she adds a further distinction: between the politics of affirmation and the politics of transformation. Affirmative politics merely involves the surface transfer of resources without changing the basic underlying divisions whereas transformative politics seek to eliminate the basic underlying structures of injustice (see Young, 1999; Mooney, 2000). Thus in the area of redistribution affirmative remedies involve, for example, coercing the underclass into the labour market at extremely low wages. Their underclass position is merely reproduced this time within the lower reaches of the market place (see Levitas, 1996). This dragooning of people from one category of exclusion to another ('getting the people to work', as the Social Exclusion Unit (1999) put it, with its cheerless *double entendre*) is experienced all too frequently not as inclusion but as exclusion, not as the 'free' sale of labour but as straightforward coercion. Relative deprivation would, of course, not be solved by such 'inclusionary' politics and the sources of discontent which are liable to generate high crime rates would be unabated. Transformative redistribution, on the other hand, would involve such measures as retraining so that jobs could be gained and then rewarded on a meritocratic basis – thus putting a genuine element of equality into equal opportunity policies, the recognition of non-paid work (e.g. child rearing, caring for ageing parents) as of vital importance for social reproduction, the creation of viable childcare infrastructures for women with children, and the enforcement of a minimum wage at a level which allows the individual an existence which is neither demeaning nor severely straitening in circumstance. Above all it would not fetishise paid work – it would not view such work as the vital prerequisite for full citizenship, for acceptance and inclusion in society.

An affirmative politics of recognition does not question the various essentialisms of difference. That is, in the case of conventional multi-culturalism, what is stressed is the need for the positive recognition of various groups on equal terms, for example Irish, African-Caribbeans, gays, women, etc. In contrast, transformative politics seek to break down and destabilise and deconstruct the categories by questioning the very notion of fixed identity and essence. Thus the invented notion of tradition is challenged, the overlapping, interwoven nature of what are supposedly separate cultures stressed, and the ambiguity and blurred nature of boundaries emphasised. Diversity is encouraged and, where non-oppressive, celebrated, but difference is seen as a phenomenon of cultures in flux not essences which are fixed.

In the case of crime and punishment, the critique of essences both in criminal victimisation and in punishment is a high priority. The category of hate crimes must be widened out in the realisation that a considerable proportion of acts of violence involve vocabularies of motive which debase and dehumanise the victim (see Young, 1990). Thus not only crimes against gays and blacks, but against women, the elderly, the poor, etc. In terms of our response to crime it is vital that the essentialism which runs through the discourses about crime and its causes is thoroughly debunked (See also chapters by Jefferson, Carrington this volume).

Important, here, is to confront and shatter the triptych which locates crime spatially and socially in three loci – the underclass, the drug user and the immigrant. Such a combination, portrayed as interdependent and very frequently racialised, is presented as the major source of crime and disorder in our society. Against this we must emphasise that crime occurs throughout the structure of society and that its origins lie not in a separate aetiology but in the structure of society and its core values. The identification of a distinct criminal class is an endeavour bound to failure.

Thus Fraser points us to the understanding that what may seem the most obvious of responses to a problem may result in the opposite and that what is seemingly progressive can be counterproductive. She indicates, if you want, ironies in social intervention. Let me conclude this section by briefly examining drug control. As is well documented, the Conservative, punitive, 'obvious' approach to illicit drug use raises drug prices, creates a base for organised crime, encourages dilution and adulteration of drugs, increases crime, violence and mortality. It generates, as critical criminology indicated, the irony in which the primary harm of drugs (the problem before intervention) is considerably less than the secondary harm of drugs (the problem after intervention). Let us turn now to medicalisation, a response which on the surface looks progressive and indeed is touted as the liberal alternative to the 'drug wars'. The irony here is that the provision of a sick role model with a social script attached which predicts a perpetual problem of relapse is self-fulfilling. And indeed drugs clinics are scandalous for their recidivism rates and individuals in desperate social and personal predicaments queue up to take on the addict role. For the sick role provides an essence which gives a fake solidity or identity and a series of 'excuses' which absolves and distances the individual from his or her predicament (see Auld et al., 1986; Young, 1971b).

From a critical perspective, the first task is to deconstruct the legal–illegal division between psychoactive drugs and situate the effects and harm of drugs within social situations and predicaments. You cannot read the essence of a drug from a pharmacopoeia. The very same drugs can be a grave risk, good fun or a blessing depending on social context. Secondly, we must expose the wrong of punitive sanctions and the war against drugs while combating the essentialism of the medical approach. Then finally we must turn to the social context focusing *only* on those drug users whose dire social predicament drives them to highly risky use. Here the task becomes to transform the social situation and involves the problematic that Fraser has developed, namely that we oppose reforms whether punitive or medical which serve to capture the drug user in his or her role and social predicament and we support those which genuinely change the social predicament and de-essentialise drug use.

The unfinishable: an endless narrative

I have pointed to the two major components of a transformative politics but this still leaves us the problem of the narrative which guides such a transformation. In the past emancipatory politics have set out endpoints, detailed utopias which are markers to where the programme seeks to arrive and sets itself at rest. The history of such social democratic and communist metanarratives has involved, invariably, the problem of what conceivably could be the endnote and what debatably is the compass of justice and, at worst, the enmeshment of such ideals in state bureaucracy and totalitarianism. Zygmunt Bauman has been centrally concerned with the concept of justice in contemporary times. He starts with his notion of postmodernity; for him it is not the end of modernity, but it is 'modernity without illusion'. Commentating on his change in position he writes:

> At the time that I wrote *Socialism: The Active Utopia* [1976], something had broken once for all: the vision of socialism (or, for that matter, of the 'good society') as a state to be achieved, a state bound to become at some point 'the final state' of humanity. Instead, there emerged the vision of socialism (and more generally of utopia) as a horizon, constantly on the move, perpetually receding, but guiding the travel; or like a spike prodding the conscience, a nagging rebuke that cast complacency and self-adoration out of bounds and out of question. It was now the utopia itself, not the state of affairs it was meant to bring about, that bore the mark of eternity. Its attraction was not in the promise of rest, but in keeping humans forever on the move, in calling them to fight ever new injustices and to take the side of the successive echelons of the left behind, injured, humiliated.
>
> (Bauman and Tester, 2001:49).

He envisages instead an endless narrative, a project which is a continuous unfinishable process and a utopian ideal which is constantly contested, yet nags and persists; it is in his phrase a 'knife pressed at the future':

> In our times, the concept of injustice is more hotly contested than at any other time in history. It prompts daily reconnaissance skirmishes and recognition wars on ever new fronts. No iniquity is likely to be accepted as 'part of life' for long and borne meekly and placidly. By proxy, also, the idea of justice has become hazier than ever before, and given the mind-boggling pace at which

seemingly uncontroversial patterns are rebranded as manifestations of injustice and iniquity, few people would risk committing themselves to blueprints of the 'just society' in the sense of a society thoroughly cleansed of old injustices and giving birth to no new ones.

This is one aspect of the emerging 'liquid modernity' which gives morality grounds for hope. Ever more forms of human misery are reclassified from 'necessary' into 'super-numerary' and excessive, and we all grow ever more impatient with everything so classified. Does this mean that we move closer to the state of 'ultimate justice'?... Today's justices tend to be tomorrow's injustices and this 'until-further-noticeness' is bound to mark them all. A just society is as I understand it...a society perpetually vigilant for injustice and never sure that its arrangements are just enough...justice is a horizon which a just society tries to reach, a horizon which moves further away with every step forward that society makes. Insisting on taking such steps and not relenting in this insistence, come what may, are what make a society just.

(Bauman and Tester, 2001:64–5).

The necessity of critique

David Matza in his pivotal book *Becoming Deviant*, published in 1969, which of all texts heralds the shift into late modernity, points to the need for 'naturalism', the necessity of replacing the 'correctionalist' approach to deviance with an 'appreciative one': to be faithful to the nature of the phenomenon under study. And if one does this, he notes, rather than the social world seeming clear cut and delineated, 'the distinction between deviant and conventional phenomena [is seen as] blurred, complicated and sometimes devious' (Matza, 1969:68). He uses two concepts to summarise the relationship between the conventional and the deviant: *overlap* and *irony*. Overlap stresses the ultimate convergence between the *normatively* good and the bad, between virtue and evil, the way that one often looks like the other, the way one runs into another in an unbroken narrative line, the way in which one conceals the other. Irony runs on from this – it is the inversion of the conventional view that over time good and evil run in separate sequences: whereas in fact vice can result from virtue and virtue from vice. 'The key element is...inherent qualities of phenomena that despite their hidden nature, culminate in outcomes that mock the expected result ' (Matza, 1969:70).

I believe that recognition of the blurred, devious and ironic nature of reality – although true of all time – presents itself all the more clearly in late modernity where the shift and pluralism of values encourage the double take, threatening daily what Alfred Schutz called the 'taken for granted world of everyday life' (see Young, 1999); further, that it is such a questioning of the solidity of the social world and the stated purposes of its institutions which comes close to what we mean by the word 'critical'. Zygmunt Bauman in recent interviews ponders on the nature of critical theory: 'What I understand by that term is the kind of theorising which accepts that, first, "things are not necessarily what they seem to be" and second that "the world may be different from what it is" ...' And Bauman is fiercely dismissive of those who would view human culture as a thing of inertia, the place of habit, routine, absence of reflection – a sort of stabilising 'preservative' of humanity. As we have seen, the taken for granted world described by Alfred Schutz begins to disintegrate in late modernity, reflex gives way to reflexivity. In contrast, he says: 'Once you accept culture with its endemic restlessness and its inborn inclination to transcendence as the fundamental characteristic of the human mode of being, the idea of "critical theory" appears pleonastic, like "buttery butter" or "metallic iron". Theory which wants to be faithful and adequate to its object cannot but be "critical"' (Bauman and Tester, 2001:33).

All good sociology is critical, as is all competent criminology. It is my belief that critical criminology is more relevant today than ever and that the critical attitude fits the experience of later modernity. If we return to the themes of the ten ironies it is striking how the problems faced in the 1970s are built larger today and how the concerns are more a harbinger of the present than a moment of the past. Every single one of the ironies, from the counterproductive nature of the prison to the role of stigmatisation and othering in law and order politics, are of immense relevance. We are privileged to work in an area which has its focus on the fundamental dislocations of justice that occur throughout our social order, a place of irony and contest, of vituperation and transgression. Those who would seek to marginalise critical criminology fail to comprehend its purchase on the grain of social reality; those in our own camp who would narrow their definition of the 'critical' to the sectarian or the esoteric, fail to understand the central position of critique as a counterbalance to neoliberalism and its administrative discourses. Let us set about our task keeping in mind the urgency of opposition, yet with an eye for irony imbued, as always, with a sense of fun.

References

Alvi, S. (2000) *Youth and the Canadian Criminal Justice System*. Cincinnati OH: Anderson Publishing.

Auld, J., Dorn, N. and South, N. (1986) 'Irregular Work, Irregular Pleasures', in R. Matthews and J. Young (eds) *Confronting Crime*. London: Sage.

Barak, G. (1998) *Integrating Criminologies*. Boston: Allyn & Bacon.

Bauman, Z. (1976) *Socialism: The Active Utopia*. London: Allen & Unwin.

Bauman, Z. (2000) *Liquid Modernity*. Cambridge: Polity Press.

Bauman, Z. and Tester, K. (2001) *Conversations with Zygmunt Bauman*. Cambridge: Polity Press.

Beck, U. (1992) *Risk Society*. London: Sage.

Berman, M. (1983) *All That's Solid Melts Into Air*. London: Verso.

Bourgois, P. (1998) 'Just Another Night in a Shooting Gallery', *Theory, Culture and Society*, 15 (2):37–66.

Brake, M. (1980) *The Sociology of Youth Culture and Youth Subcultures*. London: Routledge & Kegan Paul.

Brake, M. (1985) *Comparative Youth Culture*. London: Routledge & Kegan Paul.

Campbell, C. (1987) *The Romantic Ethic and the Spirit of Modern Consumerism*. Oxford: Blackwell.

Carlen, P. (1996) *Jigsaw: A Political Criminology of Youth Homelessness*. Buckingham: Open University Press.

Carlen, P. (2002) 'Carceral Clawback', *Punishment and Society*, 4(1):15-21.

Christie, N. (2000) *Crime Control as Industry*, 3rd edn. London: Routledge.

Cohen, S. (1981) 'Footprints in the Sand', in M Fitzgerald, G. McLennan and J. Pawson (eds), *Crime and Society*. London: Routledge & Kegan Paul.

Cohen, S. (1998) 'Intellectual Scepticism and Political Commitment: the Case of Radical Criminology' in P. Walton and J. Young (eds) *The New Criminology Revisited*. London: Macmillan.

Cottee, S. (2001) 'Adventures in Criminology: Radzinowicz, A Review Essay', *Theoretical Criminology* 5(2):253–64.

Crawford, A. (1998) *Crime Prevention and Community Safety*. London: Longman.

Currie, E. (1997) 'Market, Crime and Community', *Theoretical Criminology*, 1(2):147–172.

DeKeseredy, W., Alvi, S., Schwartz, M. and Tomaszewski, A. (forthcoming) *Under Siege: Poverty and Crime in a Canadian Public Housing Estate*. Toronto: University of Toronto Press.

Downes, D. (1988) 'The Sociology of Crime and Social Control in Britain 1960–1987', in P. Rock (ed.) *The History of British Criminology*. Oxford: Oxford University Press.

Featherstone, M. (1985) 'Lifestyle and Consumer Culture', *Theory, Culture and Society*, 4:57–70.

Ferrell, J. (1997) 'Criminological Verstehen: Inside the Immediacy of Crime', *Justice Quarterly*, 14(1):3–23.

Ferrell, J. and Saunders, C. (eds) (1995) *Cultural Criminology*. Boston: Northeastern University Press.

Ferrell, J., Milovanovic, D. and Lyng, S. (2001) 'Edgework, Media Practices and the Elongation of Meaning', *Theoretical Criminology*, 5(2):177–202.

Fraser, N. (1997) *Justice Interruptus: Critical Reflections on the Post-Socialist Condition*.

New York: Routledge.

Garland, D. (1985) *Punishment and Welfare*. Aldershot: Gower.

Garland, D. (1988) 'British Criminology before 1935', in P. Rock (ed.), *The History of British Criminology*. Oxford: Oxford University Press.

Garland, D. (1995) 'Penal Modernism and Postmodernism', in T. Bloomberg and S. Cohen (eds), *Punishment and Social Control*. New York: Aldine De Gruyer.

Garland, D. (1997) 'The Development of British Criminology' in M. Maguire, R. Morgan and R. Reiner (eds) *The Oxford Handbook of Criminology*, 2nd edn. Oxford: Clarendon Press.

Garland, D. (1999) 'The Commonplace and the Catastrophic', *Theoretical Criminology*, 3(3):353–64.

Garland, D. (2001) *The Culture of Control*. Oxford: Oxford University Press.

Garland, D. and Sparks, R. (2000) 'Criminology, Social Theory and the Challenge of Our Times' in D. Garland and R. Sparks (eds) *Criminology and Social Theory*. Oxford: Oxford University Press.

Giddens, A. (1991) *Modernity and Self-Identity*. Cambridge: Polity Press.

Gorz, A. (1999) *Reclaiming Work: Beyond the Wage-Based Society*. Cambridge: Polity Press.

Hall, S. (2002) 'Daubing the Drudges of Fury', *Theoretical Criminology*, 6(1):35–6.

Hobsbawm, E. (1994) *The Age of Extremes*. London: Michael Joseph.

Hogg, R. and Brown, D. (1998) *Rethinking Law and Order*. Annandale, NSW: Pluto Press.

Hughes, G. (1998) *Understanding Crime Prevention*. Buckingham: Open University Press.

Jamieson, R. (1998) 'Towards a Criminology of War in Europe', in V. Ruggiero, N. South and I. Taylor (eds) *The New European Criminology*. London: Routledge.

Jamieson, R. (1999) 'Genocide and the Social Production of Immorality', *Theoretical Criminology*, 3(2):131–46.

Jefferson, T. (2002) 'Subordinating Hegemonic Masculinity', *Theoretical Criminology*, 6(1):63–88.

Katz, J. (1988) *The Seductions of Crime*. New York: Basic Books.

Lanier, M. and Henry, S. (1998) *Essential Criminology*. Boulder, CO: Westview.

Lea, J. (1998) 'Criminology and Postmodernity', in P. Walton and J. Young (eds), *The New Criminology Revisited*. London: Macmillan.

Lea, J. (2002) *Crime and Modernity*. London: Sage.

Levitas, R. (1996) 'The Concept of Social Exclusion and the New Durkheimian Hegemony', *Critical Social Policy*, 16:5–20.

Luttwak, E. (1995) 'Turbo-Charged Capitalism and Its Consequences', *London Review of Books*, 17 (21), 2 November:6–7.

Matthews, R. (1999) *Doing Time*. London: Macmillan.

Matza, D. (1969) *Becoming Deviant*. Englewood Cliffs, NJ: Prentice Hall.

Messerschmidt, J. (2000) *Nine Lives; Adolescent Masculinities, the Body and Violence*. Boulder, CO: Westview.

Mooney, J. (2000) *Gender, Violence and The Social Order*. London: Macmillan.

Morrison, W. (1995) *Theoretical Criminology: From Modernity to Post-Modernism*.

Muncie, J. (1999) *Youth and Crime*. London: Sage.

O'Malley, P. (1999) 'Volatile Punishments: Contemporary Penality and Neo-Liberal Government', *Theoretical Criminology*, 3(2):175–96.

Pavlich, G. (1999), 'Criticism and Criminology', *Theoretical Criminology* 3(1):29–51.

Pitts, J. (2001) *The New Politics of Youth Crime*. London: Palgrave.

Presdee, M. (2000) *Cultural Criminology and the Carnival of Crime*. London: Routledge.

Radzinowicz, L. (1999) *Adventures in Criminology*, London: Routledge.

Robinson, M. (2001) 'Whither Criminal Justice: An Argument for a Reform of Discipline', *Critical Criminology*, 10(2):97–106.

Rose, N. (2000) 'Government and Control', in D. Garland and R. Sparks (eds) *Criminology and Social Theory*. Oxford: Oxford University Press.

Ruggiero, V. (2000) *Crime and Markets*. Oxford: Oxford University Press.

Runciman, W. (1966) *Relative Deprivation and Social Justice*. London: Routledge & Kegan Paul.

Scraton, P. (2000) *Hillsborough: The Truth*. Edinburgh: Mainstream Publishing.

Social Exclusion Unit (1999) *Bringing Britain Together: A National Strategy for Neighbourhood Renewal*. London: Stationery Office.

Stenson, K. (1998) 'Beyond Histories of the Present', *Economy and Society*, 27(4):333–52.

Stenson, K. and Edwards, A. (2001) 'Rethinking Crime Control in Advanced Liberal Government' in K. Stenson and R. Sullivan (eds) *Crime, Risk and Justice*. Cullompton: Willan Publishing.

Taylor, I. (1999) *Crime in Context*. Oxford: Polity Press.

Tierney, J. (1996) *Criminology: Theory and Context*. Hemel Hempstead: Prentice Hall.

van Swaaningen, R. (1997) *Critical Criminology: Visions from Europe*. London: Sage.

Wacquant, L. (1999) *Les Prisons de la Misère*. Paris: Éditions: Rasions d'agir.

White, R. and Haines, F. (2000), *Crime and Criminology*, 2nd edn. Melbourne: Oxford University Press.

Wilson, W. J. (1996) *When Work Disappears*. New York: Knopf.

Wootton, B. (1959) *Social Science and Pathology*. London: Allen & Unwin.

Young, I. M. (1990) *Justice and the Politics of Difference*. Princeton, NJ: Princeton University Press.

Young, J. (1971a) 'The Role of the Police as Amplifiers of Deviancy, Negotiators of Reality and Translators of Fantasy', in S. Cohen (ed.) *Images of Deviance*. Harmondsworth: Penguin.

Young, J. (1971b) *The Drugtakers*. London: Paladin.

Young, J. (1998) 'Breaking Windows: Situating the New Criminology', in P. Walton and J. Young (eds) *The New Criminology Revisited*. London: Macmillan.

Young, J. (1999) *The Exclusive Society*. London: Sage.

Young, J. (2001) 'Identity, Community and Social Exclusion' in R. Matthews and J. Pitts (eds) *Crime, Disorder and Community Safety*. London: Routledge.

Young, J. (forthcoming) 'Searching for a New Criminology of Everyday Life', Review Article, *The Culture of Control* D. Garland, in *British Journal of Criminology*.

Zaitch, D. (2001) *Traquetos*. Amsterdam School for Social Science Research.

General index

abolitionism, 80-1, 88, 97, 134
Aboriginal communities, sexual violence, 129-30
academic social sciences, 19, 20
academics, progressive political action, 236
acts, in public discourse, 25, 26-7
administrative criminology, 147
    boundary between critical criminology and, 2
    power, 34
    strengthening of, 33
affirmative politics, 266-7
Afghanistan, 191, 208
Age of Extremes, 204-5
Albion's Fatal Tree, 78
alliance building, 94-6
Alternative Criminology Journal, 75
Althusserianism, 77-8
anarchy, new, 197-200
anti-correctionalist movement, 257
anti-rape group, 47
antisocial behaviour, 31, 32
army, deployment of British, 22
asylum seekers, 188-9, 191, 201-2
Auburn, 186-7
Australia
    critical criminology, 73-104
    war in Afghanistan, 208
Australian and New Zealand Journal of Criminology, 86
Australian Prostitutes Collective, 133-4
authoritarian populism, 23, 24, 25, 82, 89
authoritarianism
    interpreting, 20-5
    moral renewal, 32

barbarisation, 198
barbarism, contemporary conflicts, 197, 199
Becoming Deviant, 270
behaviour
    product of reason and emotion, 152
    in public discourse, 26-7

social and cultural forces, 182
Berkeley School of Criminology
    assassination of, 48-55
    political subculture, 61-4
    rise of, 41-8
bifurcations, 34, 60
bio-politics, 232
bio-power, 228
biologism, 119
Birmingham Centre for Cultural Studies, 78
Black Panther party, 51
boat people, 188-9
Bolsheviks, 235
bombing, 52, 207
books
    influential, 79-83
    radical criminologists, 46-7
Brave New World, 171
burden of proof, 102
burglary, 157-8

Cambodian invasion, 41, 52
capitalism, 19-20, 147, 202-5
Capitalism and the Rule of Law, 78
capitalist states, physical violence, 22
categories, disempowerment, 231-2
chain gangs, 176
Changing the Subject, 145
chaos theory, 60
Charlie Company, 159, 160
child custody, 30
children
    New Labour policies, 30-2
    structural constraints, 29
churches, fight against mandatory sentencing, 96
civil injunctions, 31
civil policing, 22
civilians
    mass slaughter, 198, 199
    targets of war, 207
civilisational thesis, 200-2
civilising process, 193

class
  feminist criminology, 124, 125-6
  late modernity, 262-3
  offenders as victims of, 151
  and racial composition, 63
  radical criminology studies, 46, 78
  structural constraints, 29
Clockwork Orange, 171
clubbing, 249
cluster bombs, 200
Cold War, end of, 195, 200
collateral damage, 207
collective action, 205-9
Coming Crisis of Western Sociology, The, 18
community, as quasi-prison, 170
Community Service Orders, 88
complexity theory, 60
consensus, 23
constitutive criminology, 58
control theory, 148
convict history, 84
correctionalism, 2, 253, 256, 270
corruption, US government, 54
crime
  ascription of, 26
  in criminology, 192
  essentialist analysis, 132
  fear of, 160
  functionalism, 74
  getting tough on, 32
  issues, public ownership, 102
  organised, 196
  pleasurable dimension, 158
  presentation of information about, 175
  radical criminology studies, 45-6
  social and cultural centrality of, 79
  sociology, 1-2, 3
  transnational, 196
  tryptich of, 265-6, 268
Crime in Context, 79
crime control
  essentialism, 265
  government responses to, 96
crime control complex, 256
Crime and Disorder Act, 31-2
crime prevention
  funding, 33
  theory of, 147
Crime, Shame and Reintegration, 83, 98-9
Crime and Social Justice, 46
criminal justice
  alliance, critical criminologists, 94-6
  critical analysis, 34
  racism, 44
  salience of sex or class, 125

studies, 33, 43, 45
criminal law, 102
criminalisation, 26, 127
criminality, 19, 221
criminals, line between non-criminals and, 176
criminologies of catastrophe, 91-4
criminologists
  critical, 94-6
  left realist, 134
  postmodern, 58-9
  radical, 2, 41-8
criminology
  beyond the nation state, 185-213
  failure of, 101-2
  macro theories, 60
  offenders in contemporary, 146-51
  problem of contemporary conventional, 220-2
  radical break in, 21
  undergraduate courses, 33
  see also critical criminology; feminist criminology; new criminology; psychosocial criminology
Criminology and Social Control, 79
Criminology Students Association, 52
Criminology, violence and the Nation State, 185
crises
  of aetiology, 149
  in hegemony, 82, 89
  of the left, 219
critical analysis
  advancement of, 26
  power relations, 29
  as resistance, 30-7
  state power, 21
critical criminologists, alliance, criminal justice movements, 94-6
critical criminology
  Australia, 73-104
  contemporary prospects for, 218-38
  enemies, 245-9
  feminism, 123
  introduction, 1-12
  neglect of offenders, 145-6
  punitive society, 168-83
  in twenty-first century, 251-71
  under-representation of, 33-4
  United States, 41-64
critical research, 35
critical thinking, compromise of, 33
Criticism and Criminology: In Search of Legitimacy, 260
critique

bureaucratisation of, 193-4
in consensual sex, 156
in contemporary world, 197-8
line between predatory and
protective, 204
in new global order, 203
politically sanctioned, 202
see also male violence; physical
violence; sexual violence
Visions of Social Control, 82-3, 168, 169-71
voluntariness, 88, 89
vulnerability, 213

war
civilisational tensions, 200-2
concentrated in poorest regions, 202
crimes, US, 52-4
criminology of, 158-60
cultivated, 197-8
on drugs, US, 196
late twentieth century, 207
on terrorism, 92, 190-1, 199
warfare

chemical and biological, 203
technological, 194, 198
Whigs and Hunters, 78
Wolfgang Committee, 49
women
structural constraints, 29
see also feminism
Women, Crime and Criminology, 115-16
Women's Imprisonment, 83, 93
women's movement, 232
work, late modernity, 264
World Trade Center, 92, 160-2

xenophobia, 201

young people
structural constraints, 29
victimisation of, 127-8
see also children; juvenile delinquents
youth justice, 30-2

zero tolerance, 31

283

Name index

Agnew, Spiro, 54
Amis, Martin, 162
Angelou, Maya, 37
Arrigo, Bruce, 59

Balbus, I., 88
Barak, Gregg, 45
Barber, Bob, 44
Baudrillard, J., 57, 58
Bauman, Zygmunt, 262, 269, 271
Becker, Howard, 17-18, 19, 26, 223
Bentham, Jeremy, 45, 88
Bertrand, Marie, 43, 116
Bin Laden, Osama, 190, 201
Blair, Tony, 30
Boehringer, Gill, 55
Bohm, Robert, 62
Borges, Sandra S., 44
Brady, James, 43, 45
Braithwaite, John, 83, 97, 98-9
Brake, Mike, 252
Brooks, A., 233
Brown, D. and Hogg, R., 87, 88
Brown, David, 55
Buckley, Kevin, 53
Burgess, Anthony, 171
Buruma, Ian, 161

Cain, Maurine, 118
Calley, Lt., 159, 160
Carlen, Pat, 83, 93
Carlson, Susan, 63
Carrington, K., 232
Carson, K., 218
Chambliss, William, 55
Chesney-Lind, Meda, 44
Chomsky, Noam, 36, 212
Christie, Nils, 26, 32, 33, 178
Clements, Joyce, 44, 45
Cohen, Stanley, 3, 20, 26, 36, 75, 82-3, 88,
    91, 123, 128, 168, 169-71, 211, 219, 230,
    252, 255
Coles, Frances, 45
Cooper, Lynn B., 44, 46
Cooper, Robert, 197, 209

Currie, Elliot 43, 44, 62

Dahmer, Jeffrey, 150
Daly, Kathy, 122
Davidson, J. and Rees-Mogg, W., 203,
    204, 205
Davis, John, 43, 44
Del Olmo, Rosa, 55
Dod, Suzie, 47
Dodd, David, 45
Dorfman, Ariel, 92
Downes, David, 252
Drewe, Robert, 92
Dubois, David, 43
Durkheim, E., 191, 232

Elias, Norbert, 192-3
Emerson, Ralph Emerson, 54
Ericson, Richard, 78

Farrington, David, 148
Fattah, E., 227
Ferrell, Jeff, 59
Fong, Melanie, 44
Foucault, M., 28, 77, 78, 81, 87, 212-13,
    228, 232
Fraser, Nancy, 262, 266-8
Fujimoto, Tetsuya, 45

Gain, Charles R., 51
Garfinkel, H., 223
Garland, David, 79, 83, 96, 219, 256-7, 258
Gein, Ed, 150
Giddens, Anthony, 264
Gilmore, Gary, 158
Glick, Ronald, 46
Glover, Jonathan, 198, 211
Goffman, E., 223
Golding, William, 179
Goodrich, P., 121-2
Gorman, Paul, 50
Gouldner, Alvin, 18, 77
Gourevitch, Philip, 210-11
Grabiner, Gene, 44
Grabiner, Virginia Engquist, 44-5

284